The Theory and Practice of Environmental and Resource Economics

NEW HORIZONS IN ENVIRONMENTAL ECONOMICS

Series Editors: Wallace E. Oates, *Professor of Economics, University of Maryland, USA* and Henk Folmer, *Professor of General Economics, Wageningen University and Professor of Environmental Economics, Tilburg University, The Netherlands*

This important series is designed to make a significant contribution to the development of the principles and practices of environmental economics. It includes both theoretical and empirical work. International in scope, it addresses issues of current and future concern in both East and West and in developed and developing countries.

The main purpose of the series is to create a forum for the publication of high quality work and to show how economic analysis can make a contribution to understanding and resolving the environmental problems confronting the world in the twenty-first century.

Recent titles in the series include:

Amenities and Rural Development
Theory, Methods and Public Policy
Edited by Gary Paul Green, Steven C. Deller and David W. Marcouiller

The Evolution of Markets for Water
Theory and Practice in Australia
Edited by Jeff Bennett

Integrated Assessment and Management of Public Resources
Edited by Joseph C. Cooper, Federico Perali and Marcella Veronesi

Climate Change and the Economics of the World's Fisheries
Examples of Small Pelagic Stocks
Edited by Rögnvaldur Hannesson, Manuel Barange and Samuel F. Herrick Jr

The Theory and Practice of Environmental and Resource Economics
Essays in Honour of Karl-Gustaf Löfgren
Edited by Thomas Aronsson, Roger Axelsson and Runar Brännlund

The International Yearbook of Environmental and Resource Economics 2006/2007
A Survey of Current Issues
Edited by Tom Tietenberg and Henk Folmer

Choice Modelling and the Transfer of Environmental Values
Edited by John Rolfe and Jeff Bennett

The Impact of Climate Change on Regional Systems
A Comprehensive Analysis of California
Edited by Joel Smith and Robert Mendelsohn

Explorations in Environmental and Natural Resource Economics
Essays in Honor of Gardner M. Brown, Jr.
Edited by Robert Halvorsen and David Layton

Using Experimental Methods in Environmental and Resource Economics
Edited by John A. List

Economic Modelling of Climate Change and Energy Policies
Carlos de Miguel, Xavier Labandeira and Baltasar Manzano

The Theory and Practice of Environmental and Resource Economics

Essays in Honour of Karl-Gustaf Löfgren

Edited by

Thomas Aronsson
Professor of Economics

Roger Axelsson
Associate Professor of Economics

Runar Brännlund
Professor of Economics, Department of Economics, Umeå University, Sweden

NEW HORIZONS IN ENVIRONMENTAL ECONOMICS

Edward Elgar
Cheltenham, UK • Northampton, MA, USA

Published by
Edward Elgar Publishing Limited
Glensanda House
Montpellier Parade
Cheltenham
Glos GL50 1UA
UK

Edward Elgar Publishing, Inc.
136 West Street
Suite 202
Northampton
Massachusetts 01060
USA

A catalogue record for this book
is available from the British Library

ISBN-13: 978 1 84542 649 1
ISBN-10: 1 84542 649 5

Printed and bound in Great Britain by MPG Books Ltd, Bodmin, Cornwall

Contents

Contributors

Aronsson, Thomas: Department of Economics, Umeå University, Sweden

Backlund, Kenneth: Department of Economics, Umeå University, Sweden

Balk, Bert M.: Erasmus Research Institute of Management, Erasmus University of Rotterdam and Methods and Informatics Department, Statistics Netherlands, Voorburg, the Netherlands

Berck, Peter: Department of Agricultural and Resource Economics, University of California, Berkeley, USA

Bergland, Olvar: Department of Economics and Resource Management, Agricultural University of Norway, Ås, Norway

Brännlund, Runar: Department of Economics, University of Umeå and Department of Forest Economics, Swedish University of Agricultural Sciences, Umeå, Sweden

Färe, Rolf: Department of Economics and Department of Agricultural and Resource Economics, Oregon State University, Corvallis, USA

Favada, Ibrahim Moulifla: Department of Economics, University of Helsinki, Finland

Fisher, Anthony: Department of Agricultural and Resource Economics, University of California, Berkeley, USA

Folmer, Henk: Department of Economics and CentER, Tilburg University and Department of Social Sciences, Wageningen University, the Netherlands

Grosskopf, Shawna: Department of Agricultural and Resource Economics, Oregon State University, Corvallis, USA

Håkansson, Cecilia: Department of Forest Economics, Swedish University of Agricultural Sciences, Umeå, Sweden

Hanemann, W. Michael: Department of Agricultural and Resource Economics, University of California, Berkeley, USA

Heal, Geoffrey: Columbia Business School, New York, USA

Hess, H. Peter: Manager, Analysis Group, Inc., Menlo Park, CA, USA

Hultkrantz, Lars: Department of Economics, Statistics and Informatics, Örebro University, Sweden

Johansson, Per-Olov: Department of Economics, Stockholm School of Economics, Sweden and Department of Economics, University of Oslo, Norway

Kriström, Bengt: Department of Forest Economics, Swedish University of Agricultural Sciences, Umeå, Sweden

Kuuluvainen, Jari: Department of Economics, University of Helsinki, Finland

Li, Chuan-Zhong: Department of Economics, Uppsala University, Sweden

Lindmark, Magnus: Department of Economic History, University of Umeå, Sweden

Mäler, Karl-Göran: The Beijer International Institute of Ecological Economics, The Royal Swedish Academy of Sciences, Stockholm, Sweden

Narain, Urvashi: Resources for the Future, Washington DC, USA

Pham Do, Kim Hang: Department of Applied and International Economics, Massey University, Palmerston North, New Zealand

Puu, Tönu: Center for Regional Science CERUM, Umeå University, Sweden

Ready, Richard: Department of Agricultural Economics and Rural Sociology, Penn State University, University Park, USA

Romstad, Eirik: Department of Economics and Resource Management, Agricultural University of Norway, Ås, Norway

Shogren, Jason F.: Department of Economics and Finance, University of Wyoming, Laramie, USA

Sjögren, Tomas: Department of Economics, Umeå University, Sweden

Stamland, Tommy: Department of Finance, Norwegian School of Economics and Business, Bergen, Norway

Uusivuori, Jussi: Department of Economics, University of Helsinki, Finland

Weitzman, Martin L.: Department of Economics, Harvard University, Cambridge, USA

Wikström, Magnus: Department of Economics, Umeå University, Sweden

Introduction[1]

This book is dedicated to Professor Karl-Gustaf Löfgren and is a gift in connection with his 60th birthday on December 16, 2003. The celebrations started as early as in June 2003, when the 'Karl-Gustaf Löfgren' symposium was held at Ulvön in conjunction with the 10th Ulvön Conference on Environmental Economics. Several of the chapters in this volume were presented at the symposium.

A Festschrift is typically organized and compiled by former students and colleagues. This is also the case here. The compilation of the book has been easy and difficult at the same time. The easiness was, of course, due to the vast number of potential contributors, and those we contacted responded in a positive way. However, this was also the source of the difficulty. Karl-Gustaf has been active in many different areas of economics, he has many former students, and he has numerous friends and colleagues all over the world. The difficulty, then, was to decide on whether the Festschrift should contain contributions from all areas or just from one particular area. The decision, finally, was that the Festschrift should (at least in a weak sense) be focused on environmental and resource economics. This particular choice was made for several reasons; the main reason being that this is an area where Karl-Gustaf has been very active during the last 15 years, and it is also the area where he has made some of his most significant contributions to economics. Given this choice, the problem of choosing contributors became a little less difficult. However, since Karl-Gustaf has been a leading researcher in this area for more than two decades, the choice set was still substantial.

Karl-Gustaf has made significant contributions to both theoretical and empirical research. The reader of this volume will recognize that the contributions span a wide spectrum of topics, theoretical as well as empirical. This topic sprawl is deliberate and just reflects the nature of Karl-Gustaf's interests in, and contributions to, environmental and resource economics.

Karl-Gustaf has been a major capacity builder in terms of the research environment, both at the Department of Economics at Umeå University, and at the Department of Forest Economics at the Swedish University of Agricultural Sciences. With this book, we would like to honor him for his talent, hard work, enthusiasm and friendship.

A SHORT BIOGRAPHY

Karl-Gustaf began his academic career with studies in economics, mathematics, statistics and political science at the brand new Umeå University in the mid 1960s, which resulted in a BA degree in 1968. Since Umeå University was new at that time, the Department of Economics was, to some extent, still under 'construction'. This, in combination with his talent and interest in economics, gave him a position as assistant lecturer (1:e amanuens) already during his undergraduate studies.[2]

After his BA he continued to work as an assistant lecturer and became Fil. Lic. in 1972. It is worth mentioning that his Licentiate thesis dealt with price discrimination, a subject he returned to almost 15 years later as a professor in forest economics. His academic career continued in the same young department, and in 1977 he defended his PhD thesis. Karl-Gustaf's research was focused on macroeconomics and labor economics.

Despite this research focus, which was quite remote from environmental and resource economics, he became full professor in forest economics at the Department of Forest Economics, Swedish University of Agricultural Sciences, in 1979. He took the new job seriously and immediately spent one semester at the University of Wisconsin, Madison. During his visit, Karl-Gustaf laid out the foundation for one of his most significant contributions to forest economics, *The Economics of Forestry and Natural Resources*, which was coauthored by Per-Olov Johansson. The book was published in 1985, but preliminary versions were already used at the beginning of the 1980s in the graduate program at the Department of Forest Economics. The book was a success and became a classic used almost everywhere.[3] During his 10 years at the department of forest economics Karl-Gustaf created a leading and internationally recognized institution in forest economics. His enthusiasm and skill created a unique research environment, infectious to anyone who came close.

After almost 10 years, Karl-Gustaf returned to the Department of Economics at Umeå University in the fall of 1988. Although his new chair was oriented towards labor economics, his research effort covered other areas as well. Karl-Gustaf's contribution to economics after 1988 is substantial. Since the mid 1990s, one of his major research areas is welfare measurement in dynamic economies with imperfect markets; so-called 'social accounting'. Much of his research in this area is summarized in two of his more recent books, *Welfare Measurement, Sustainability and Green National Accounting*, coauthored by Thomas Aronsson and Per-Olov Johansson, and *Welfare Measurement in Imperfect Markets*, coauthored by Thomas Aronsson and Kenneth Backlund.

Karl-Gustaf's role in the scientific community is manifested by the fact that he has been a member of the Swedish Academy of Sciences since 1999 and member of The Prize Committee for the Alfred Nobel Memorial Prize in Economics since 1993. During the period 1987–1992 he was also a member of the Swedish Council of Economic Advisors (the government's advisory group on economics issues), showing recognition also outside academia.[4]

NOTES

1. We acknowledge the positive responses and patience from those who have been involved in the project. In particular, we would like to thank Linda Holmlund and Linda Thunström at the Department of Economics at Umeå University for their work during the process. We also acknowledge the Research Fund at the Umeå School of Business and Economics for their financial support to the symposium held at Ulvön.
2. It should be mentioned here that Karl-Gustaf was also a tough fighter in the boxing ring, and a bone-hard midfielder in Sandviks IK.
3. His scientific contribution to the forest science community in Sweden was manifested in 1996 when he became an elected member of The Royal Academy of Agriculture and Forestry.
4. He has also been a member of The Gastronomic Academy of Northern Sweden since 2000, even though his culinary competence has been questioned at several occasions (especially at the Ulvön meetings).

Umeå, June 2005

Thomas Aronsson   Roger Axelsson   Runar Brännlund

1. Sustainability: What Does It Tell Us?

Geoffrey Heal

1. BACKGROUND

In this chapter I review the concept of sustainability, looking at its intellectual pedigree, asking what value it has added to our understanding of environmental and resource-use issues, and what it implies for the way we should run the economy. The focus all the time is on the concept underlying sustainability, and not on the word itself, as the popularity of the word seems to be associated with the Bruntland Report, whereas the underlying concepts go back at least half a century further.

Two concerns lie at the heart of discussions of sustainability: a concern for the interests of those who will live in the distant future, and a concern for the constraints imposed on human activity by the ecological and biogeochemical foundations of our societies. These capture what is common to many definitions of sustainability, the best known of which is probably the Bruntland Report's comment that 'Sustainable development is development that meets the needs of the present without compromising the ability of future generations to meet their own needs'. Other definitions are more precise, requiring for example that utility levels be nondecreasing over time,[1] or that resource stocks be nondecreasing, or that capital stocks in total (including natural capital) be nondecreasing.[2] All of these formulations are attempting to ensure that our current impact on society's natural resource base does not undermine the welfare of future generations. They seek to do this either directly by bounding welfare below or indirectly by bounding below the capital stocks instrumental in providing future welfare.

Did we need new concepts and models to talk intelligently about these issues, or were they already captured by existing economics? I argue that few substantially novel intellectual issues have been raised by the discussions of sustainability. It is possible to model the concerns of sustainability within the pre-existing corpus of economics, and indeed many key ingredients of the debate about sustainability have appeared in the economics literature before under different key words.

Certainly a concern for the very long run and the welfare of future generations raises old questions, dating back to Ramsey (1928). Even if we have not answered these questions fully, we have discussed them at length. Likewise we may not yet have modeled well the constraints imposed by our society's biogeochemical infrastructure, but doing so probably raises no totally new theoretical issues. Focussing on these raises questions about how we specify the technological constraints under which society operates, whether these involve nonlinearities, nonconvexities, irreversibilities, etc. Both of the issues defining sustainability – long-run welfare and constraints on growth – are also at the heart of another area of economics, optimal growth theory. Ramsey's classic work initiated this field and placed the issue of balancing the welfares of present and future squarely on the agenda: indeed Ramsey's comment that 'Discounting future utilities is ethically indefensible and arises purely from a weakness of the imagination' states a position that most environmentalists would agree with, were they aware of it.

The literature on optimal growth with exhaustible and renewable resources covered many of the ingredients of sustainability back in the 1970s. The papers in the *Review of Economic Studies Symposium* of 1974 posed and answered some of the questions central to many contemporary discussions of sustainability. Papers in that symposium modeled the impact that the presence of exhaustible resources would have on an economy's long-run growth, and focussed on the issue of substitutability between natural resources and capital, still seen as one of the central issues here. Proposition 4 of Stiglitz (1974a) almost uses the word sustainability – 'a necessary and sufficient condition for sustaining a constant level of consumption per capita is that the ratio of the rate of technical change, γ, to the rate of population growth must be greater than or equal to the share of natural resources'. On a later page (p. 131), he goes on to say that 'The fact that there is a limited amount of natural resources and natural resources are necessary for production does not necessarily imply that the economy must eventually stagnate and then decline. Two offsetting forces have been identified: technical change and capital accumulation. Even with no technical change, capital accumulation can offset the effects of the declining inputs of natural resources, so long as capital is "more important" than natural resources'. Stiglitz derives these results from a model with a Cobb–Douglas production function, a special case that allows analytical solutions. In the same volume Dasgupta and Heal (1974) look at these issues with a more general production function and obtain similar characterizations. They talk about 'the implications that a finite earth has for intertemporal planning' and identify the elasticity of substitution in production (unity in the Cobb–Douglas case) as a key parameter determining whether consumption can continue to grow in the face of an exhaustible resource. Even with no technical progress, this is possible if the elasticity exceeds one. One of the facts to emerge from the literature of the 1970s is that paths that are optimal in a utilitarian sense need not satisfy the sustainability criterion even when sustainable growth is possible. The classic illustration is the case of a Cobb–Douglas production function using capital and a depletable resource: in this case sustainable growth is feasible if the elasticity of output with respect to manufactured capital exceeds that with respect to natural resources (see Solow 1974). Nevertheless Dasgupta and Heal (1979) showed that for a positive discount rate a utilitarian optimum will involve consumption approaching zero in the long run.

All of these discussions of technical progress and substitution possibilities sound quite contemporary, even though they are now 30 years old. The reality is that many of the concerns of the sustainability literature – real and valid concerns – were captured to some degree in the literature on optimal growth. This literature focused on the long run, and in some cases on the constraints on growth posed by exhaustible resources. Understanding sustainability is really a matter of getting the specifications of objectives and constraints correct in these models. I will illustrate this by looking at the simplest of these, the Hotelling model (Hotelling 1931). This was in 1931 the first to combine a focus on resource depletion with a concern for long-run economic development. And as we know, that model in its original form cannot say much about sustainability because economic activity is not sustainable. But it can be modified to capture some of the issues and illustrate one of my main points.

2. THE HOTELLING MODEL

Recall the simplest and most classical formulation of the problem of the optimal management of a natural resource. This is Hotelling's formulation, which assumes the resource to be exhaustible. The function $u(c_t)$ is a utility function which is assumed throughout to be increasing, strictly concave and twice continuously differentiable, so that the first derivative is positive and the second negative; u' and u'' denote the first and second derivatives of u respectively; c is consumption and s_t the stock of a resource remaining at time t. The problem can be stated formally as max $\int_0^\infty u(c_t)\,\mathrm{e}^{-\delta t}\,\mathrm{d}t$ s.t. $s_t \geq 0$ and $\dot{s}_t = -c_t$ where of course $s_t = s_0 - \int_0^t c_f\,\mathrm{d}f$. A dot over a variable is always used to denote its time derivative.

The first-order conditions for a solution require that $u' = \lambda$ and $\dot{\lambda}_t - \delta\lambda_t = 0$, i.e. $\lambda_t = \lambda_0\,\mathrm{e}^{\delta t}$. What are the implications of this for consumption paths? To start with, consider a simple case. Let $u(c_t) = \log c_t$. Then $c_t = c_0\,\mathrm{e}^{-\delta t}$ so consumption falls exponentially at the discount rate. Nothing is conserved or sustained for ever, and the present and future are treated very unequally. The ratio c_t/c_0 of initial consumption c_0 to consumption at date t, c_t, decreases exponentially with time: $c_t/c_0 = \mathrm{e}^{-\delta t}$. The inequality between generations increases exponentially over time. In the general case, we have $u''(c_t)\dot{c}_t = \delta u'(c_t)$ so that $\dot{c}/c = -\delta/\eta$, where $\eta = -c_t u''(c_t)/u'(c_t) > 0$ and is the elasticity of marginal utility of consumption: it is also a measure of risk aversion and of the curvature of the function $u(c)$.

In the next section we see that a relatively small change, acknowledging an explicit value for the resource stock, alters everything. It makes the problem qualitatively different. We still work with an exhaustible resource, so that the set of feasible paths is unaltered, but the valuation of the remaining stock alters optimal use patterns radically and introduces real substance into the discussion of sustainability. Making the resource renewable takes this process even further (see Heal 1998). Another strategy for making the model richer is to allow for the accumulation of capital, which can to some degree substitute for the resource. This is the approach that was taken initially by Dasgupta and Heal (1974, 1979), who showed that positive consumption levels may be sustained for ever even with an exhaustible resource, provided that there is considerable scope for substitution of produced capital for the resource.

3. VALUING A DEPLETABLE STOCK

It is important to recognize explicitly the mechanisms through which environmental assets contribute to economic well-being. In this vein we supplement the pure depletion problem by adding the remaining stock of the resource as an argument of the utility function, so that we now recognize explicitly that the stock of the resource, still exhaustible, may be a source of value. Examples of environmental resources for which this would be appropriate include biodiversity, which in the sense of the range of species or some measure of their variation is a depletable asset: once it is reduced through extinction, it can never be restored to its original value. And clearly the stock of biodiversity is a source of many services. Another example is a forest, which yields a flow of wood for consumption as well as recreational facilities and carbon sequestration services in removing CO_2 from the atmosphere. Forests are of course usually renewable rather than depletable, but a tropical hardwood forest may to a first approximation be thought of as depletable. Other examples are a landscape, which can be farmed to yield a flow of output or enjoyed as a stock, or the atmosphere which can be used to yield a flow of services as a sink for pollution or enjoyed as a stock of clean air.[3]

The basic problem is now

$$\max \int_0^\infty u(c_t, s_t)\, e^{-\delta t}\, dt \quad \text{s.t. } s_t \geq 0 \quad \text{and} \quad \dot{s}_t = -c_t,$$

where the only alteration from the previous section is in the inclusion of the stock as an argument of the utility function, leading to qualitatively different conclusions. Now, in contrast to the previous case, it may be optimal to preserve some of the resource stock indefinitely. How much is sensitive to the precise specification of the objective, and we investigate several alternatives.

3.1. Utilitarian Optimal Paths

The first-order conditions require that the derivative of utility with respect to consumption must be greater than or equal to the shadow price of the resource: $u_c(c_t, s_t) \leq \lambda_t, = \lambda_t$ if $c_t > 0$ where $u_c \equiv \partial u(c, s)/\partial c$, etc. The condition describing the movement of the shadow price over time is $\dot{\lambda}_t - \delta\lambda_t = -u_s(c_t, s_t)$.

For simplicity I consider the case when the utility function is additively separable: $u(c_t, s_t) = u_1(c_t) + u_2(s_t)$ where as always the u functions are increasing, strictly concave and twice continuously differentiable. Then, letting a prime denote the derivative of a function of one variable with respect to its argument, the conditions for optimality become:

$$u_1'(c_t) \leq \lambda_t, = \lambda_t \text{ if } c_t > 0, \dot{\lambda}_t - \delta\lambda_t = -u_2'(s_t). \tag{1}$$

In the previous case, the shadow price of the resource grew indefinitely: now in contrast there may be a solution at which c_t, s_t and λ_t are constant.

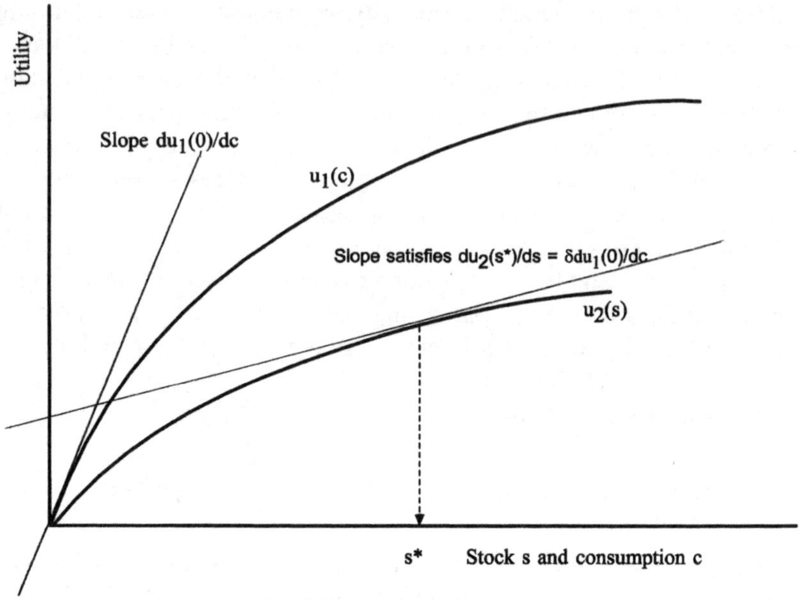

Figure 1.1. A stationary solution with the marginal utility of the stock equal to that of the flow divided by the discount rate

Note that if consumption is constant, it must of course be zero: this is the only feasible constant consumption. And note that if the shadow price is constant, then $\delta\lambda_t = u_2'(s_t)$. So at a stationary solution of the first-order conditions (1)

$$\delta \leq \frac{u_2'(s^*)}{u_1'(0)}, \text{ with equality if } c_t > 0, \tag{2}$$

where s^* is the constant value of the remaining resource stock. This equation has a simple interpretation: it requires that the slope of an indifference curve in the $s - c$ plane, the ratio of the marginal utilities of the stock and flow, equal (or exceed) the discount rate. The stationary configuration for this model is shown in Figure 1.1: the constant level of the stock is one at which the derivative of utility with respect to the stock (the slope of the curve u_2) equals the slope of u_1, the utility-of-consumption function, at the origin, times the discount rate δ.

Figure 1.2 shows the dynamics of an optimal policy, which involve depleting the resource stock by consuming it until it is run down to s^*, and then stopping consumption and preserving the stock for ever. There is an

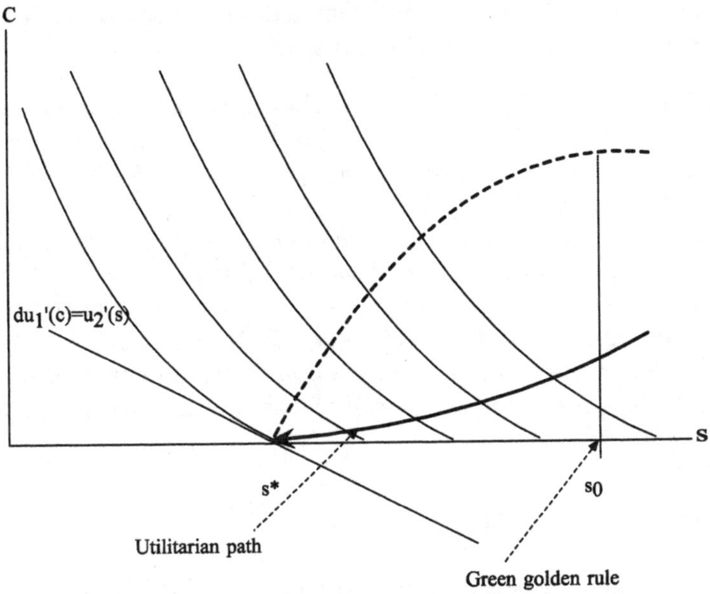

Figure 1.2. The dynamics of an optimal solution showing the maintenance of a positive stock for ever

important difference between the solution to the present problem, and that to the classic Hotelling problem. In the present framework a positive stock may be preserved for ever on an optimal path: exactly how much depends on the discount rate and on the utility functions, but this is a qualitative difference between the two problems. So the concept of 'sustainability' seems to have some relevance in the context of this solution.

When will it be optimal in this context to preserve a positive stock level for ever? This depends on the behavior of the utility function as the consumption level goes to zero. If the marginal utility of consumption goes to infinity as consumption goes to zero, as is often assumed, then Equation (2) has no solution and there is no stationary state. This is the case with a Cobb–Douglas function, or with a separable utility function in which $u_1(c)$ has a constant elasticity of marginal utility. In any of these cases, the indifference curves in the $c - s$ plane do not cross the horizontal axis, but asymptote towards it. These are cases in which the flow from the resources is in some sense 'essential'. There is no substitute for it and it cannot be allowed to fall to zero. It is natural that in these cases no stock will be preserved. Note that whether there is a substitute for the stock – i.e.

the behavior of $u_2'(0)$ – is not important in determining whether a positive stock remains. We can summarize this as follows:

PROPOSITION 1. *Consider an optimal solution when the utility function is additively separable, $u(c, s) = u_1(c) + u_2(s)$. A sufficient condition for this to involve the preservation of a positive stock for ever is that the marginal utility of consumption at zero is finite, $u_1'(0) < \infty$, and that there exists a finite stock level s^*, the optimal stationary stock, such that $u_1'(0)\delta = u_2'(s^*)$. In this case, if the initial stock $s_0 > s^*$, then total consumption over time will equal $s_0 - s^*$: if $s_0 \leq s*$, then consumption will always be zero and the entire stock will be conserved on an optimal path. If on the other hand the marginal utility of consumption at $c = 0$ is infinite, then it will not be optimal to conserve any positive stock level indefinitely.*

3.2. The Green Golden Rule

A second difference arising from the inclusion of the stock as a source of utility comes when we ask the question: 'Which configuration of the economy gives the maximum sustainable utility level?', a question motivated by the 'golden rule of economic growth' introduced in the 1960s by Phelps (1961), and by our present interest in sustainability. In the Hotelling formulation, there is no interesting answer to this question: the only utility level maintainable for ever is that associated with zero consumption. In the present model, however, the question is quite interesting, as there are many utility levels that can be maintained for ever. Clearly in the very long run no positive consumption level can be maintained and utility must be derived from the stock only. So the answer to the question 'Which configuration of the economy gives the maximum sustainable utility level?' must be 'the utility level associated with the initial stock (the biggest stock ever) and zero consumption'. Formally, in finding the maximum utility that can be sustained indefinitely we are maximizing $u(0, s)$ where $s \leq s_0$, and the solution is clearly to preserve the entire stock and never consume anything. This is the solution that has been called the green golden rule (Beltratti et al. 1995): it is the path which of all feasible paths gives the highest value of the long-run level of utility.[4] It can be formalized as the solution to $\max_{\text{feasible paths}} \lim_{t\to\infty} u(c_t, s_t)$. Formally,

PROPOSITION 2. *The maximum sustainable utility level is attained by conserving the entire initial stock.*

3.3. The Rawlsian Optimum

An alternative approach to sustainability is using the Rawlsian definition of justice between generations. In the case of the current model, the green golden rule happens to be the path which is optimal in the Rawlsian sense, i.e., which maximizes the welfare of the generation which is least well off. It is easy to see this point. On any path which involves positive consumption, the utility level is eventually nonincreasing over time. So the least-well-off generation is the 'last' generation: in fact there is no 'last' generation, so more accurately the lowest welfare level is the limiting welfare level. But this is maximized by the green golden rule, which maximizes the sustainable, and so the limiting, welfare level over all feasible paths.

3.4. Overtaking

In an attempt to avoid the problems of zero discount rates, and yet give equal weight to present and future, von Weizäcker (1967) introduced the overtaking criterion:

DEFINITION 1. A path c^1 is said to weakly overtake a path c^2 if there exists a time T^* such that for all $T > T^*$, we have $\int_0^T u(c_t^1)dt \geq \int_0^T u(c_t^2)dt$. The path c^1 is said to strictly overtake c^2 if the inequality is strict.

This is an ingenious approach: it replaces infinite integrals by finite ones, and says that one path is better than another if from some date on cumulative utility on that path is greater. This is a relationship that can be checked even if both cumulative utility totals go to infinity as $T \to \infty$, so this approach does to some degree extend the applicability of an approach based on a zero discount rate. The overtaking criterion ranks paths with different limiting utility values according to those limiting values (Heal 1998). Consequently the overtaking optimal path is the green golden rule, the path along which nothing is consumed and the entire initial stock is maintained intact. This is also the Rawlsian optimum. This is a remarkable coincidence of views. Note that with these three criteria complete conservation of the initial stock is optimal, whatever the size of the initial stock. Nothing in these arguments depends on the size of the initial stock. In some ways this is surprising: intuitively, one might feel that whether to conserve or not should depend on the size of the initial stock. This is true of the discounted utilitarian solution.

3.5. Implications of the Hotelling Model

What we have seen from the previous sections is that even a model as basic as the Hotelling model, which has been around for nearly three quarters of a century, can provide insights into sustainability: it is a matter of understanding how natural resources affect human welfare – whether only directly through consumption or additionally through the services of the stock – and then of specifying appropriately our concern for future generations. How we do this makes a lot of difference to the outcome but even in the case of discounted utilitarianism, that least favorable to the future, we can find sustainable outcomes when we have specified fully how the remaining stock affects our well-being. There are several ways of specifying concern for the future: via the green golden rule, Rawls' approach, utilitarianism with a zero discount rate, and these all imply that an optimal policy will leave the entire stock intact for ever, emphatically a sustainable outcome. Conceptually therefore it is not hard to specify an optimal growth model that gives insights into the possibility of efficient and sustainable paths, and allows us to characterize them.

4. FROM THEORY TO MEASUREMENT

I turn next from the conceptual to the practical aspects of the issues that go with sustainability. The empirical or policy-related counterpart of discussions of sustainability has been a concern with 'green accounting' or the revision of national income accounts to reflect better the impact of our current consumption and investment choices on the wellbeing of successor generations. The aim here is to devise accounting systems that indicate whether we are behaving in accordance with one of the concepts of sustainability.

In finite horizon general equilibrium models it is quite clear how to measure national income and how to judge whether a small change is a potential welfare improvement. Indeed both problems have the same solution. Under the standard assumptions about completeness of markets and absence of externalities, if $p^*$is a competitive equilibrium price vector and c^* is the equilibrium aggregate consumption level then national income is $p^*.c^*$, the total value of consumption at equilibrium prices, and a small change in the allocation of resources is a potential Pareto improvement if and only if it increases the value of this inner product. This measure of national income is a linear approximation to a true welfare measure, which is the source of the need to consider only small changes in resource allocation.[5] With infinite horizon models, in contrast, there is no general agreement on how to measure changes in welfare, or on what is the right measure of national income, or on how the two relate.

In fact the finite results extend to an infinite horizon representative agent model, and in the process resolve many issues in the debate about how to measure welfare in a dynamic model, how to measure 'green national income', and how to measure 'sustainability'.[6] The dynamic extension of the finite horizon case is a measure of wealth rather than income, and in this respect is in keeping with Samuelson's remark that in extending national income to a dynamic context, 'we find that the only valid approximation to a measure of welfare comes from computing *wealth-like* magnitudes ...' (Samuelson 1961, p. 57, line 4 on). Perhaps surprisingly, it also relates closely to an empirical measure of sustainability that is increasingly widely used, the World Bank's measure of 'genuine savings'. Because of this, this measure is observable and has been measured for a number of countries (see Arrow et al. 2004). The extension of the standard welfare measure to the infinite horizon case is not straightforward: the finite-dimensional version is proven by using separating hyperplane theorems, which are not easily used in the infinite-dimensional case. Our arguments circumvent these problems by drawing instead on results from dynamic programming and optimal control, and can be thought of as completing a research program set out in Samuelson's (1961) insightful early contribution, which has been neglected in subsequent literature. The following discussion is based closely on Heal and Kriström (2005).

4.1. Dynamic Accounting

Let the vector $c(t)$ be an m-vector of flows of goods consumed and giving utility at time t, and $s(t)$ be an n-vector of stocks at time t, also possibly sources of utility. Each stock $s_i(t)$ changes over time in a way which may depend on the values of all stocks and of all flows:

$$\dot{s}_i(t) = d_i(c(t), s(t)), \quad i = 1, \ldots, n. \tag{3}$$

The economy's objective is to maximize the discounted (at discount rate δ) integral of utilities (4):

$$\max \int_0^\infty u(c(t), s(t))\, \mathrm{e}^{-\delta t}\, \mathrm{d}t \tag{4}$$

subject to (3). Utility is a function of s as well as c because some stocks may affect welfare directly as well as through their impact on consumption, as for example is the case with human capital or with forests. The utility function u is assumed strictly concave and the reproduction functions $d_i(c(t), s(t))$ concave. This general formulation makes it possible to include human capital and other assets. Note that if $n = m = 1$ and $u = u(c)$ and $\dot{s} = f(s) - c$ we have the Ramsey–Solow model. When u does not depend on s and (3) takes the form $\dot{s}_i(t) = -c_i(t)$ we have the Hotelling model. The general formulation we have chosen captures the possible contributions of environmental stocks to consumer utility and to productive efficiency. This is a general representative agent or optimal growth model, a distinct framework from the general equilibrium model standard in welfare economics, but it nevertheless allows us to establish an analogous set of results.

To solve this problem we construct a Hamiltonian which takes the form

$$H(t) = u(c(t), s(t))e^{-\delta t} + \sum_{i=1}^{n} \lambda_i(t)\, e^{-\delta t} d_i(c(t), s(t)), \tag{5}$$

where the $\lambda_i(t)$ are the shadow prices of the stocks.

The first-order conditions for optimality can be summarized as

$$\frac{\partial u(c(t), s(t))}{\partial c_j} = -\sum_{i=1}^{n} \lambda_{i,t} \frac{\partial d_i(c(t), s(t))}{\partial c_j}, \tag{6}$$

$$\dot{\lambda}_i(t) - \delta\lambda_i(t) = -\frac{\partial u(c(t), s(t))}{\partial s_i} - \sum_{k=1}^{n} \lambda_k(t) \frac{\partial d_k(c(t), s(t))}{\partial s_i}. \tag{7}$$

4.2. Measuring Future Welfare

We make use of the state valuation function $V(s)$, which we define in the usual manner:

$$V(s_0) = \max_{\{c_t\}} \int_0^{\infty} u(c, s)\, e^{-\delta t}\, dt,$$

$$\dot{s}_{i,t} = d_i(c_t, s_t), \quad i = 1, \ldots, n, \quad s_0 \text{ given.}$$

The expression V is the true nonlinear welfare measure and we will show that an extension of the finite horizon national income to the infinite case is a linear approximation to V, just as $p^*.c^*$ is a linear approximation to the true welfare measure in the finite case. By standard results,

$$\frac{\partial V}{\partial s_i} = \lambda_i, \tag{8}$$

so that the shadow price of the i-th stock is the marginal social productivity of that stock. It immediately follows that

$$\frac{\mathrm{d}V}{\mathrm{d}t} = \sum_i \lambda_i \dot{s}_i. \tag{9}$$

We can obtain a second expression for the rate of change of the state valuation function by differentiating under the integral sign in the definition of V. Equating the two expressions for $\mathrm{d}V/\mathrm{d}t$ gives $\delta V = H$. Rearranging as $V = H/\delta$ gives a generalization of Weitzman's much-cited 1976 result that the Hamiltonian is a utility level which if maintained for ever gives welfare equal to that on an optimal path.

We define national wealth NW as the present value of all future consumption of goods and services,

DEFINITION 2. National wealth along the optimal path is

$$NW = \int_0^\infty \left\{ \langle p_c(t), c^*(t) \rangle + \langle p_s(t), s^*(t) \rangle \right\} \mathrm{e}^{-\delta t}\, \mathrm{d}t.$$

Here $\langle p_c(t), c^*(t) \rangle$ represents the inner product of the price vector $p_c(t)$ at time t with the consumption vector $c^*(t)$ at time t. NW is just the infinite horizon analog of the conventional finite horizon national income measure, and Fisher was the first to use the term wealth for such a magnitude.[7] Samuelson (1961) sets out the need for working with preferences over consumption paths that are functions of time if we are to measure national income correctly in a dynamic context but, not surprisingly given when he was writing, shies away from doing this. The prices to be used here are natural and intuitive ones: they are the derivatives of the utility function. It is then possible to establish that any small change which increases this measure is a welfare improvement. Any small change in a path which has a positive present value at these prices will increase welfare, and vice versa. An increase in NW is therefore a necessary and sufficient condition for a welfare increase:

THEOREM 1. *A variation* $\{\Delta c(t), \Delta s(t)\}_{t=0}^{\infty}$ *on optimal path* $\{c^*(t), s^*(t)\}_{t=0}^{\infty}$ *has positive present value and so is an increase in*

NW, if and only if the implementation of this variation leads to an increase in welfare.

This theorem is important: it tells us that any other linear index indicates a small increase in welfare if and only if it agrees locally with NW, which is therefore the benchmark for welfare indices. The alternative measure of wealth, used *inter alia* by Dasgupta and Mäler (2000), is the value of stocks at shadow prices, $W = \sum_i \lambda_i s_i$.

Note from Equation (9) that the rate of change of the state valuation function is the rate of change of W at constant prices. Building on this and the earlier definitions we can establish an important relationship between the rates of change of national wealth NW and the state valuation function V: they are equal up to a first-order approximation.

THEOREM 2 (Heal and Kriström 2005). *The rate of change of NW equals that of V up to a first-order approximation.*

4.3. Implications

Change in NW is a linear approximation to change in V, the true welfare measure in the discounted utilitarian case, and NW is a linear index. NW therefore plays a role exactly analogous to the standard general equilibrium measure in the finite horizon case. From (9) we have also that

$$\frac{\mathrm{d}NW}{\mathrm{d}t} = \sum_i \lambda_i \dot{s}_i + O(2) \tag{10}$$

where $O(2)$ contains terms of the second order and higher. What is interesting here is that $\sum_i \lambda_i \dot{s}_i$ is observable in principle, depending only on current values of variables, and indeed is what Hamilton and Clemens have termed 'genuine savings' (see Hamilton and Clemens 1999, and also Arrow et al. 2004). So the change in NW is observable and equals, to a first-order approximation, a measure that has been suggested as appropriate for measuring how an economy's long-term productive potential is changing, or how sustainable is its development. This is an insight that Samuelson (1961) missed – he states of the NW measure that 'I know of no way of even approximating from market valuations of factors what the values of consumption quantities Q at prices P would be'. Perhaps this is because he focussed on measuring wealth rather than the change in wealth.

There is a direct connection to the literature on sustainability, as V measures the economy's long-term welfare potential and that this be non-decreasing has been suggested as an interpretation of sustainability (for a review, see Heal 1998, Arrow et al. 2004). In this context sustainability is equivalent to nondecreasing national wealth (Dasgupta and Mäler 2000, amongst others).

5. MEASUREMENT

As remarked above, $\sum_i \lambda_i \dot{s}_i$ is in principle observable and is a good approximation to the change of NW over time and to the change in the total future present value of utility, V. It tells us whether the total value of a nation's capital stock, at current prices, is rising or falling. If it is rising then the implications of depletion of some stocks for the future are more than offset by the increases in others. Hamilton and Clemens have begun attempts to measure this, calling it 'genuine savings', and recently those attempts have been extended by an interdisciplinary cooperation between economists and ecologists (Arrow et al. 2004). In this final part of my overview I comment on these attempts, on what they tell us about the world, and what we learn from them about the theory. Attempts at measurement based on a new theory always tell us as much about the theory as they do about the quantities measured.

Table 1.1 shows the results that Arrow et al. (2004) find when we compute $\sum_i \lambda_i \dot{s}_i$ for a wide range of countries, including two rich industrial countries, the US and the UK, two rapidly growing developing countries, India and China, two very poor developing regions, Bangladesh and Sub-Saharan Africa, and one mineral-exporting region, the Middle East and North Africa. The data cover the period 1970–2001[8] and are taken from the World Bank (2003).

The first numerical column in Table 1.1 shows domestic net investment, which is the starting point of the calculations and an estimate of investment in physical capital. To this is added expenditure on education as an indicator of investment in human capital, and we then add investment (usually disinvestment) in various types of environmental capital. The third numerical column shows an estimate of the social cost of CO_2 emissions, the fourth the depletion of energy resources (particularly large for the Middle East and North Africa) and the next is forest depletion, large for Nepal and zero for the US where there has actually been regrowth of forests over the period of interest. The final column gives the sum, an estimate of genuine

Table 1.1.

	Domestic net I	Education	CO_2	Energy	Mineral	Forest	GI
Bangladesh	7.89	1.53	0.25	0.61	0.00	1.41	7.14
India	11.74	3.29	1.17	2.89	0.46	1.05	9.47
Nepal	14.82	2.65	0.20	0.00	0.30	3.67	13.31
Pakistan	10.92	2.02	0.75	2.60	0.00	0.84	8.75
China	30.06	1.96	2.48	6.11	0.50	0.22	22.72
Sub-Saharan Africa	3.49	4.78	0.81	7.31	1.71	0.52	-2.09
M East N Africa	14.72	4.70	0.80	25.54	0.12	0.06	-7.09
UK	3.70	5.21	0.32	1.20	0.00	0.00	7.38
US	5.73	5.62	0.42	1.95	0.05	0.00	8.94

investment as a percentage of national income. Full details of the data and the calculations are given in Arrow et al. (2004).

Clearly there are many shortcomings here, and I shall talk about correcting some of them shortly. Amongst the shortcomings that we do not correct are the inadequacy of educational expenditure as a measure of investment in human capital, and the incompleteness of the list of categories of environmental capital for whose depletion we allow. Both could be serious sources of error, but it has not been possible to obtain data to take this process further. Nonetheless the numbers that emerge make some intuitive sense. For example, for the Middle East and North Africa a domestic net investment of +14.72 per cent turns into a genuine savings of −7.09 per cent after allowing for the depletion of energy resources, drawing attention to the fact that this part of the world lives unsustainably by depleting an exhaustible resource, as in the Hotelling models reviewed earlier. Sub-Saharan Africa is also shown to be living unsustainably, a tragic and not surprising result. Allowance for the impact of HIV/AIDS on human capital would probably make their genuine investment number even worse. The remaining countries all appear from these numbers to have positive genuine investment and so to be meeting one of the criteria for sustainability, namely that the present value of future welfare obtainable from capital stocks be nondecreasing. However, all of these numbers omit two factors that could be important: one is population change, omitted from the earlier discussion but a real issue in several countries, and the other is technical change. A higher rate of population growth will presumably increase the

Table 1.2.

	GI	Growth GW	Pop G	Growth GW pc	TFP growth	Growth Gen W pc	Growth GDP pc
Bangladesh	7.14	1.07	2.16	–1.09	0.81	0.30	1.88
India	9.47	1.42	1.99	–0.57	0.64	0.54	2.96
Nepal	13.31	2.00	2.24	–0.24	0.51	0.63	1.86
Pakistan	8.75	1.31	2.66	2.06	1.13	0.59	2.21
China	22.72	3.41	1.35	–3.05	3.64	8.33	7.77
Sub-Saharan Africa	–2.09	–0.31	2.74	–3.05	0.28	–2.58	–0.01
M East N Africa	–7.09	–1.06	2.37	–3.43	–0.23	–3.82	0.74
UK	7.38	1.48	0.18	1.30	0.58	2.29	2.19
US	8.94	1.79	1.07	0.72	0.02	0.75	1.99

level of investment required to maintain living standards constant, so that the numbers in Table 1.1 will overstate the extent of sustainability with a growing population and *vice versa*. Technological progress will act in the opposite direction, allowing humans to extract more welfare from a given set of resources. So we make two more modifications to the data in Table 1.1, adjusting for population growth and for technological progress. Neither was a part of the theory developed in the earlier parts of this chapter, and indeed as far as I am aware there is little or no discussion of either of these issues in the literature on sustainability or on optimal growth with environmental resources. Yet intuition suggests that they are important, and the numbers in Arrow et al. confirm this, indicating a lacuna in the theory developed so far.

Table 1.2 shows the results of these modifications. The first column is the last column from Table 1.1, our preliminary estimates of genuine savings. The second column gives an estimate of the growth rate of genuine wealth derived from the previous column using an assumed GDP/wealth ratio,[9] and the fourth gives the growth rate of genuine wealth per capita, using the population growth rate given in the third numerical column. This is followed by an estimate of the growth rate of total factor productivity and then the growth rate of per capital genuine wealth adjusted for total factor productivity growth. For comparison purposes the last column gives the conventional figure for growth of GDP per capita.

Only two estimates of the growth of genuine wealth per capita are negative, the same two as before, but many others are probably not significantly positive. The high population growth rates of Bangladesh, Nepal and Sub-Saharan Africa all act to reduce their countries' rates of genuine savings.

6. CONCLUSIONS

An intellectual framework within which we can address issues related to sustainability, issues relating to the welfare of future generations and to the impact of natural resource constraints, has been available at least since the 1970s and at least in part since the 1930s. The original developments by Ramsey and Hotelling were the cutting edge theory of their times: had there been Nobel prizes in economics in the 1930s both would surely have been strong candidates. Interestingly, some of the contributions of the 1970s were also by the leading theorists of the times – Solow and Stiglitz in particular.

An intellectual framework for thinking about future welfare and resource constraints is satisfying but to be really useful it has to be accompanied by a measurable index that lets us judge our current performance against these criteria and ask whether we are in fact depleting society's natural resources to a degree that prejudices the welfare of future generations. To make this judgement we need a computable index that measures the trends in the constraints on future welfare and the natural measure of this is ΔNW, a first-order approximation to welfare change and an extension to the dynamic context of changes in national income. Although ΔNW involves variables at all future dates, it is approximated by observable data, namely $\sum_i \lambda_i \dot{s}_i$. This is a known quantity, already estimated by the World Bank and named genuine savings by Hamilton and Clemens. Measuring it accurately is not easy and Arrow et al. have attempted to refine and extend the Hamilton and Clemens calculations, allowing for population growth and technical progress. There are still some obvious shortcomings: in particular measures of environmental depletion and of investment in human capital are clearly inadequate. Nevertheless this work seems to indicate a way of measuring economic development that takes into account the factors at issue in the discussions of sustainability, and suggests that we may before too long be able to establish whether current rates of use of the natural environment, coupled with investment in other forms of capital and with technological progress, are consistent with the growth of future welfare.

NOTES

1. Pezzey (1989) and for a review, see Asheim et al. (2001).
2. For a review, see Smulders (2001).
3. This framework was introduced by Krautkraemer (1985), and developed further by him in 1986.
4. This is formalized as the maximum limiting utility value. However, other formalizations are in principle possible: for example, as the maximum of the lim sup of the utility values. The differences between alternatives become of significance only when positive limit sets of feasible trajectories may be limit cycles or other more complex attractors.
5. For an early contribution, see Samuelson (1950).
6. For contributions to that debate, see Asheim and Weitzman (2001), Dasgupta and Mäler (2000) and Heal (1998). For a survey of the field, see Heal and Kriström (2005).
7. This definition was used in Heal (1998). Note that Irving Fisher defines wealth at the present discounted value of all future consumption (see Samuelson 1961, p. 51). So this is in fact a Fisherian definition of wealth. He did not define wealth as the value of assets at market prices – an alternative definition that has tempted some.
8. To be precise, the coverage is as follows: Bangladesh 1973–2001, India 1970–2001, Nepal 1970–2001, China 1982–2001 (without 1994), Sub-Saharan Africa 1974–1982 and 1986–2001, ME and NA 1976–1989 and 1991–2001, UK 1971–2001 and US 1970–2001.
9. See Arrow et al. (2004) for details.

REFERENCES

Arrow K.J., P.S. Dasgupta, L. Goulder, G.C. Daily, P.R. Ehrlich, G.M. Heal, S. Levin, K.-G. Maler, S. Schneider, D. Starrett and B. Walker (2004), 'Are we consuming too much?', *Journal of Economic Perspectives*, 18(3), 147–172.

Asheim, G.B. and M.L. Weitzman (2001), 'Does NNP growth indicate welfare improvement?', *Economics Letters*, 73, 233–239.

Asheim, G., W. Buchholz and B. Tungodden (2001), 'Justifying sustainability', *Journal of Environmental Economics and Management*, 41(3), 252–268.

Beltratti, A., G. Chichilnisky and G.M. Heal (1995), 'The green golden rule', *Economics Letters*, 49, 175–179.

Dasgupta, P.S. and G.M. Heal (1974), 'The optimal depletion of exhaustible resources', *Review of Economic Studies*, Symposium, pp. 3–28.

Dasgupta, P.S. and G.M. Heal (1979), *Economic Theory and Exhaustible Resources*, Cambridge: Cambridge University Press.

Dasgupta P.S. and K.-G. Mäler (2000), 'Net national product, wealth and social well-being', *Environment and Development Economics*, 5, 69–93.

Hamilton, K. and M. Clemens (1999), 'Genuine savings rates in developing countries', *The World Bank Economic Review*, 13(2), 333–356.

Heal, G.M. (1998), *Valuing the Future: Economic Theory and Sustainability*, New York: Columbia University Press.

Heal, G.M. (2000), *Nature and the Marketplace*, Washington DC: Island Press.

Heal, G. and B. Kriström (2005), 'National income and the environment', K.-G. Mäler and J. Vincent (eds), *Handbook of Environmental Economics*, Vol. 3, Amsterdam: North-Holland, forthcoming.

Hotelling, H. (1931), 'The economics of exhaustible resources', *Journal of Political Economy*, 39, 137–175.

Krautkraemer, J.A. (1985), 'Optimal growth, resource amenities and the preservation of natural environments', *Review of Economic Studies*, 52, 153–170.

Krautkraemer, J.A. (1986), 'Optimal depletion with resource amenities and a backstop technology', *Resources and Energy*, 8, 133–149.

Pezzey, J. (1989), 'Economic analysis of sustainable growth and development', Environmental Department Working Paper No. 15, World Bank, Washington DC.

Phelps, E.S. (1961), 'The golden rule of accumulation: A fable for growthmen', *American Economic Review*, 638–643.

Ramsey, F. (1928), 'A mathematical theory of saving', *Economic Journal*, 38, 543–559.

Rawls, J. (1972), *A Theory of Justice*, Oxford: Clarendon Press.

Samuelson, P.A. (1950), 'Evaluation of real national income', *Oxford Economic Papers* (New Series), 1–29.

Samuelson, P.A. (1961), 'The evaluation of "social income", capital formation and wealth', in F.A. Lutz and D.C. Hague (eds), *The Theory of Capital*, New York: St. Martins Press, chapter 3, pp. 32–57.

Smulders, S. (2001), 'Economic growth and environmental quality', in H. Folmer and L. Gabel (eds), *Principles of Environmental Economics*, Cheltenham, UK and Northampton, MA, USA: Edward Elgar, chapter 21.

Solow, R.M. (1974), 'Intergenerational equity and exhaustible resources', *Review of Economic Studies*, Symposium, pp. 29–45.

Stiglitz, J.E. (1974a), 'Growth with exhaustible natural resources: Efficient and optimal paths', *Review of Economic Studies*, Symposium, pp. 123–138.

Stiglitz, J.E. (1974b), 'Growth with exhaustible natural resources: The competitive economy', *Review of Economic Studies*, Symposium, pp. 139–152.

von Weizäcker, C.C. (1967), 'Lemmas for a theory of approximately optimal growth', *Review of Economic Studies*, 143–151.

Weitzman, M.L. (1976), 'On the welfare significance of net national product in a dynamic economy', *Quarterly Journal of Economics*, 90, 156–162.

World Bank (2003), 'World development indicators', http://devdata.worldbank.org/dataonline, accessed September 2003.

2. Environment and Decision-Making under Risk and Uncertainty

Karl-Göran Mäler

1. INTRODUCTION

In the 1960s, Burton Weisbrod (1964) posed the fundamental question: If we are facing a decision on maintaining a (natural or man-made) structure or irreversably destroying it, would we not be willing to pay for keeping the option of using the structure in the future? Weisbrod called this the option value of the structure and argued that this option value should be added to the current demand for using the structure in order to have an efficient outcome. There have been two approaches to developing this idea within formal models. The first, with Krutilla et al. (1972) as the pioneering contribution, focused on the role of risk aversion. The main question was whether the Weisbrod option value would be positive or not. It was argued that if the decision maker is risk averse, the option value must be positive. However, further research showed that it could be of either sign. In the next section we will see that the sign of the option value (in this context) will depend on the covariance between preferences (defined as the marginal utility of the structure) and the marginal utility of income or wealth. As this covariance can be of either sign, it follows that the option value can be of either sign, but we will now consider the factors determining the sign.

The second approach, which is closer to what Weisbrod probably was interested in, was the discovery that the existence of forthcoming information in the future is of importance for determining the value of the structure today. The expected value of this forthcoming information, conditional on the continued existence of the structure, will be the option value. This approach was simultanously analysed by Arrow and Fisher (1974) and Henry (1974a, 1974b). With their assumptions, the option value would always be positive, implying a more conservative strategy in exploiting the structure irreversibly. In this chapter, I will not, however, discuss this interpretation of option value extensively. However, in the last section, I will present an elementary account of these ideas. For a more complete review of both notions of option values, see Fisher and Mäler (2005).

2. DECISION-MAKING AND RISK, A STATIC FRAMEWORK

2.1. The Basic Framework

As is traditional, we assume that uncertainty can be described by a set of events or states of the world. Each event contains all the information relevant for decision-making and the uncertainty consists of not knowing which event that will occur. The particular features characterizing an event we are interested in are income W, supply of environmental resources Q, and preferences as measured by utility functions $U(W, Q)$. Note that this means that the individual is not certain what his preferences will be, unless he knows the event that will occur. In this section we will mainly use the indirect utility function, and moreover, we will not, except in the last section, consider price uncertainty. One case in which price uncertainty may be quite important is the uncertainty about future interest rates. We will therefore come back to an analysis of that case later. Finally, we will assume that Q is one-dimensional. Generalizations to the case when Q has many but finite dimensions are straightforward.

Let us start by considering one arbitrary individual. For him each event i will describe his income W_i, the supply of environmental services Q_i, and utility function U_i. Let there be a probability measure λ_i over the set of events. The preferences of the individual can then be represented by a von Neumann–Morgenstern expected utility.

$$\int U^i(W_i, Q_i)d\lambda_i = EU^i(W_i, Q_i) \tag{1}$$

This means that we will study simultaneously both what has been called supply uncertainty, that is the uncertainty about Q, and demand uncertainty, i.e. uncertainty about the preferences. As usual, we will assume that the individual is risk averse. This is in the simplest case defined as the case when the individual refuses to accept a fair bet, i.e. a bet with expectation zero. It is then easy to prove that risk aversion is equivalent to concave utility functions. However, in our case the utility functions U_i vary from event to event and the situation is slightly more complicated. In view of the confusion about the appropriate definition of risk aversion in this situation, it may be worthwhile to give a brief analysis of the problem.

2.1.1. *Risk Aversion*

In discussing risk aversion, the focus is on the income or wealth variable, so we assume *for this discussion only*, that the environmental quality variable is constant over all possible events. Then we can also for simplicity suppress that variable. Assume now the individual has to choose between accepting a fair lottery Y with the price Y_i if event i occurs. The conventional definition of risk aversion is now that if $E(Y) \leq 0$, i.e. if the expected value of the lottery is not positive, then a risk averse individual would not accept a lottery ticket. Based on this definition, Schmalensee found that risk aversion means that the marginal utility of income must be constant over all events. However, in view of the fact that income W varies over events, a risk averter may very well accept a lottery with negative expected value if the lottery is negatively correlated with income. In this case will the lottery act as an insurance. Thus we should look at the total lottery $W + Y = Z$. Assume then that

$$E(Z) = \overline{Z} \tag{2}$$

If

$$E(U(Z)) \leq E(U(Z)), \tag{3}$$

then we may, for the moment, say that the individual is risk averse (note that the right-hand side is different from $U(\overline{Z})$, since U is dependent on which event will occur).

Obviously, if the utility functions are independent of states, then risk version would be equivalent to a concave utility function. However, with state dependent utility functions this is no longer so. The reason is that a positive or negative correlation between Z and the marginal utility of income now becomes an important factor. With positive correlation it may happen that

$$E(U(Z)) > EU(\overline{Z})).. \tag{4}$$

However, this possibility of correlation between marginal utility of income and income has hardly anything to do with common sense interpretation of risk aversion. Therefore, our definition of risk aversion is modified as follows.

DEFINITION 1. An individual is risk averse if

$$E(U(Z) - U(\overline{Z})) \leq 0$$

for all distributions of Z and U provided that they are independently distributed.

It is now easy to see that the state contingent utility function of a risk averse individual must be concave in income and conversely, concave state contingent utility functions imply risk aversion.

In fact, with U and Z independently distributed, the definition can be written as a repeated expectation

$$E_U E_Z(U(Z) - U(\overline{Z})) \leq 0$$

for all distributions of Z.

A necessary and sufficient condition for this is that for all states

$$E_Z(U(Z) - U(\overline{Z})) \leq Z$$

for all states. Thus we have the following theorem:

THEOREM 1. *An individual is risk averse if and only if his utility function is concave in all events.*

In what follows, we will generally assume that risk aversion characterizes the behavior of the individual and thus we will be using concave utility functions.[1]

In the next sections we will use the expected utility representation of preferences developed above in analysing some environmental quality decision situation.

2.2. The Value of Changes in Risk

Suppose that the different states are characterized by

(i) utility functions U^i,

(ii) wealth W_i,

(iii) environmental quality Q_i.

Moreover, there is a probability measure λ_i over the different states. Then, as we have seen, preferences can be represented by the expected utility

$$E_\lambda U^i(W_i, Q_i), \tag{5}$$

where E_λ indicates for which distribution the expectation is computed. Let us now consider the case when it is possible to change the probability distribution to λ' by, for example, environmental policy. Then expected utility is

$$E_{\lambda'} U^i(W_i, Q_i)$$

Different welfare measures for the change in probability distribution can now be defined. The compensating variation CV and the equivalent variation EV are defined by

$$E_{\lambda} U^i(W_i, Q_i) = E_{\lambda'} U^i(W_i - CV, Q_i), \tag{6}$$

$$E_{\lambda} U^i(W_i + EV, Q_i) = E_{\lambda'} U^i(W_i, Q_i).$$

These measures have the usual interpretations. CV is the amount that can be taken away from the individual when the probability distribution changes. If $CV > 0$, then the change in the distribution has increased the expected utility. EV is the amount that would increase expected utility with the same amount as would the change in the probability distribution. Both EV and CV are correct representations of the underlying preference structure and the choice between them is mainly a matter of convenience.

Another alternative representation of the environmental change is possible, which implies the one just given, but is more convenient in some applications. Instead of representing the environmental change as a change in the probability distribution, one can look at it as a change in the characterization of each state.

Assume then that each state is characterized by environmental quality Q_i so that expected utility is

$$\int U^i(W_i, Q_i)\, \mathrm{d}\lambda_i. \tag{7}$$

Assume now that the environmental quality changes in each state by ΔQ_i so that

$$Q_i' = Q_i + \Delta Q_i. \tag{8}$$

The expected utility is now

$$\int U^i(W_i, Q_i')\, \mathrm{d}\lambda_i. \tag{9}$$

It can be proved that provided certain conditions hold there is a probability distribution λ' so that

$$\int U^i(W_i, Q_i + \Delta Q_i) d\lambda_i = \int U^i(W_i, Q_i)\, \mathrm{d}\lambda_i.$$

With this new representation CV and EV are defined by

$$E_\lambda U^i(W_i, Q_i) = E_\lambda U^i(W_i - CV, Q_i') \tag{10}$$

and

$$E_\lambda U^i(W_i + EV, Q_i) = E_\lambda U(W, Q_i'). \tag{11}$$

The interpretation is exactly the same as the one given above. We will in the sequel only study CV. Define the compensating variation CV_i contingent upon the occurrence of state i as

$$U^i(W_i, Q_i) = U^i(W_i - C_i.Q_i'). \tag{12}$$

We will now try to relate CV to the expected value of CV_i. We have from the definitions

$$E_\lambda U^i(W_i - CV, Q_i') = E_\lambda U^i(W_i, Q_i) = E_\lambda U^i(W_i - CV_i, Q_i'). \tag{13}$$

By making a quadratic expansion around $\overline{W} - CV$, and Q', where $\overline{W} = E_\lambda W_i$ and subscripts denote partial derivatives, we have

$$\begin{aligned} &E_\lambda \left\{U^i + (W_i - \overline{W})U_W^i + \frac{1}{2}(W_i - \overline{W})^2 U_{WW}^i\right\} \\ &= E_\lambda \Big\{U^i + (W_i - \overline{W} - CV_i + CV)U_W^i + \\ &+ \frac{1}{2}(W_i - \overline{W} - CV_i + CV)^2 U_{WW}^i\Big\}. \end{aligned} \tag{14}$$

Define

- $\overline{CV} = E_\lambda CV_i$,
- $\mathrm{var}\,(CV_i) = E_\lambda (CV_i - \overline{CV})^2$,
- $\overline{U}_W = E_\lambda U_W^i(\overline{W} - CV, Q_i')$,
- $\mathrm{cov}\,(CV_i, U_W^i) = E_\lambda\{(CV_i - \overline{CV})(U_W^i - \overline{U_W})\}$,
- $\mathrm{cov}(CV_i, W_i) = E_\lambda\{(CV_i - \overline{CV})(W_i - \overline{W})\}$.

For simplicity, let us assume that $(CV_i - \overline{CV})$ is so small that $(CV_i - \overline{CV})^2$ can be neglected in expression containing $(CV_i - \overline{CV})$ (otherwise we have to solve the quadratic equation yielding complicated messy formulas but essentially the same qualitative conclusions). Then we obtain the desired relation between the expected state contingent compensated variations and the compensated variation CV:

$$CV = \overline{CV} + \frac{\operatorname{cov}(CV_i, U_W^i)}{\overline{U}_W} - $$

$$- \frac{1}{2} E_\lambda \left\{ \frac{U_{WW}^i}{\overline{U}_W} \left[(CV_i - \overline{CV})^2 + 2(CV_i - \overline{CV})(W_i - \overline{W}) \right] \right\}.$$

If we can assume that U_{WW} is state independent, the factor $-(U_{WW}^i/\overline{U}_W)$ can be identified as the Arrow–Pratt measure R of absolute risk aversion. Then

$$CV = \overline{CV} + \frac{\operatorname{cov}(CV_i, U_W^i)}{\overline{U}_W} + \frac{1}{2} R \left\{ \operatorname{var}(CV_i) + 2\operatorname{cov}(CV_i, W_i) \right\}. \quad (15)$$

This is our basic expression for the value of the change in environmental quality. It is based on a set of not too restrictive assumptions.

2.3. Aggregation over Individuals

In general, we are not interested, however, in the individual compensating variation but in the aggregate over the relevant population. Let the population be represented by the set H and denote variables for the individual with a superscript h.

It may happen that the individual state contingent values CV_i^h are dependent on the size of the population. If, for example, the total benefits are independent of the population size, then the individual benefits will in average decrease with increasing size. Even if the benefits are of a public goods nature, congestion may decrease the individual benefits if the number of users increases. Only when we have a pure public good without congestion will the individual compensating variations be independent of the size of population sharing the benefits.

Let therefore H be the measure of the set H (this double use of the letter H will not cause any confusion) and assume that CV_i^h is a function of $HCV_i^h(H)$. In general we would expect this to be a decreasing function, but with positive externalities it may in fact be increasing.

The total compensating variation is now (CV will now denote the total compensating variation over the whole population and similarly for $\overline{CV}$)

$$CV = \int_H CV^h \, dh \quad (16)$$

$$= \int_H \overline{CV}^h \,\mathrm{d}h + \int_H \frac{\operatorname{cov}(CV_i^h, U_W^{ih})}{\overline{U}_W^h}\,\mathrm{d}h + \tag{17}$$

$$+\frac{1}{2}\int_H R\left\{\operatorname{var}(CV_i^h) + 2\operatorname{cov}(CV_i^h, W_i^h)\right\}\mathrm{d}h. \tag{18}$$

Let us investigate the three terms in this expression. The first is

$$\int_H \overline{CV}^h \,\mathrm{d}h = \overline{CV},$$

which obviously is the aggregated expected state contingent benefits. The second term is

$$\int_H \frac{\operatorname{cov}(CV_i^h, U_W^{ih})}{\overline{U}_W^h}\,\mathrm{d}h.$$

The reason for this term is of course that the marginal utility of income is contingent on the state, and the utility value of the monetary benefits CV_i^h depends on the marginal utility of income. If CV_i^h and U_i^h are independently distributed for each individual h, then this term will vanish. We will in the next section see some examples where such an independence assumption may be reasonable.

Let

- $v^{ih} = \frac{U^{hi}}{\overline{U}_W^h}$,
- $\overline{CV}_i = \int_H CV_i^h \,\mathrm{d}$,
- $\overline{v}^i = \int_H v^{ih}\,\mathrm{d}h$,

and note that $\int v^{ih}\,\mathrm{d}\lambda_i = 1$.

Then the second term can be written as

$$\int_H \frac{\operatorname{cov}(CV_i^h, U_W^{ih})}{\overline{U}_W^h}\,\mathrm{d}h = \int_H \int (CV_i^h - \overline{CV}^h)(v^{ih} - 1)\,\mathrm{d}\lambda_i\,\mathrm{d}h$$

$$= \int\int CV_i^h v^{ih}\,\mathrm{d}\lambda_i\,\mathrm{d}h - H\overline{CV}$$

$$= \int\int (CV_i^h - \overline{CV}^h)(v^{ih} - \overline{v}^i)\,\mathrm{d}\lambda_i\,\mathrm{d}h + \int \overline{CV}_i(\overline{v}^i - 1)\,\mathrm{d}\lambda_i. \tag{19}$$

The mean value theorem gives an i' such that the last term becomes

$$\overline{CV}_i(\overline{v}^{i'} - 1).$$

If $\overline{CV}_i$ and $\overline{v}_i$ are distributed sufficiently symmetrically,

$$\overline{v}^{i'} \sim 1$$

and the expression in (19) becomes

$$H \operatorname{cov}(CV_i, v^i).$$

This covariance term characterizes for each state the variance between the benefits and the marginal utility of income over different individuals. If it can be assumed that different individuals are independent of each other in this respect, the covariance becomes zero and the term

$$\int \int \operatorname{cov}(CV_i^h v^{ih})\, d\lambda_i\, dh$$

vanishes although the covariance for each individual may be different from zero.

On the other hand, if there is a nonzero covariance over individuals, the term cannot be neglected. This may happen if the variations in benefits and marginal utility of income have a common cause, for example random changes in a certain price. We will look into this later.

There remains the third term,

$$\frac{1}{2} \int R^h (\operatorname{var}(CV_i^h) + 2\operatorname{cov}(CV_i^h, W_i^h))\, dh. \tag{20}$$

Obviously, this term represents the cost of bearing the risk of variations in CV_i^h. The following factors influence the size and sign of this term, the covariance between CV_i^h and W_i^h and the variance of CV_i^h, the degree of risk aversion and the joint distribution of these variables over states and individuals.

The next section will be devoted to a discussion of the cost of risk bearing and mechanisms for risk sharing.

2.4. The Cost of Risk Bearing

Assume that utility functions are identical in all states. As in the previous section, the cost for individual h of bearing the risk is

$$-\frac{1}{2} \frac{U_{WW}^h}{\overline{U}_W^h} \left\{\operatorname{var}(CV_i^h) + 2\operatorname{cov}(CV_i^h, W_i^h)\right\}. \tag{21}$$

When will this cost be positive, negative or zero?

(i) $R^h = -(U^h_{WW}/\overline{U}^h_W) = 0$, that if the individual is risk neutral, the cost of risk bearing is zero. However, we will assume this is not the case, that is $R > 0$.

(ii) If the bracket var $(CV^h_i) + 2\text{cov}\,(CV^h_i, W^h_i)$, then the cost is also zero. This can happen if the environmental change generates benefits that are essentially independent of income. If the bracket is negative, then the environmental mental change will act as an insurance and $CV^h < \overline{CV}^h$ and vice versa if the bracket is positive.

Let us now go back to the aggregate cost of risk bearing and consider different mechanisms for allocating the risk.

A. One mechanism would be to have no risk sharing at all. In that case the social cost of bearing the risk is

$$\frac{1}{2}\int_H R^h \left\{\text{var}\, CV^h_i + 2\text{cov}\,(CV^h_i, W^h_i)\right\} \mathrm{d}h. \tag{22}$$

If all individuals have the same absolute risk aversion and if the joint distribution of benefits and wealth is the product of distributions over individuals and states respective, i.e., if for all hCV^h_i and W^h_i are independent random variables, the aggregate cost is

$$\frac{1}{2}R\left\{\overline{CV}_i + 2\text{cov}\int_H \text{cov}\,(CV^h_i, W^h_i)\,\mathrm{d}h\right\}.$$

Depending on the distribution of covariance over the individuals, this aggregate cost may be positive, zero or negative.

B. If the risks are 'individual risks' in Malinvaud's meaning (Malinvaud 1972), the aggregate cost above will be approximately zero because the covariance term vanishes. Thus, society should behave in a risk neutral manner, and could achieve that by implementing an insurance scheme. An insurance scheme which is actuarially fair can be described as a measurable function x^h such that $E_\lambda x^h = 0$. If each consumer chooses the insurance that is best for her, we will have as a result that $\partial U_i/\partial W^h$ is equal across all states. The gain from the optimal insurance $x\overline{x}^h$ for individual h is given by

$$E_\lambda U^h(W^h + \overline{x}^h, Q') - E_\lambda U^h(W^h, Q') \approx \frac{1}{2}R^h \text{var}\,(x^h)\overline{U}^h_W. \tag{23}$$

Thus the variance term in the expression for CV in (22) corresponds to the premium an individual is willing to pay for an insurance that will eliminate the uncertainty. However, such a complete insurance system seems unrealistic in view of the serious problems of moral hazard due to the stochastic nature of preferences. Only if the uncertainty of the preferences is due to an objectively measurable variable can the moral hazard problem be overcome. We will in the next section find a case where such an insurance scheme exists, although not completely.

C. Let us now assume that individual benefits are highly correlated. Suppose for simplicity that the set H is finite $H = \{1, 2, \ldots, H\}$ and that individual benefits CV_i^h are constrained by

$$\sum_{h=1}^{H} CV_i^h = Y_i(H), \tag{24}$$

where $Y_i(H)$ is the total benefits in state i. We will see that the assumption that Y_i depends on H is crucial for the results we will derive.

Suppose total welfare can be written as[2]

$$\int \sum_{h=1}^{H} \beta^h U^h(W_i^h + CV_i^h, Q_i)\, \mathrm{d}\lambda_i. \tag{25}$$

Assuming that lump sum transfers are feasible in each state, the optimal allocation of the total benefits in each state among the individuals is given by

$$\max \sum_{h=1}^{H} \beta^h U^h(W_i^h + CV_i^h, Q_i) \tag{26}$$

s.t.

$$\sum_{h=1}^{H} CV_i^h = Y_i(H).$$

The necessary conditions are

$$\beta^h U_W^h - \mu = 0, \tag{27}$$

where μ is a Lagrange multiplier.

The maximum value of the objective function is denoted $V(Y_i(H))$.

The maximum of the objective functions in the original problem can now be written as

$$\max \int V(Y_i(H))\, \mathrm{d}\lambda_i. \tag{28}$$

Let the Arrow–Pratt measure of absolute risk aversion R_v be defined as

$$R_V = -\frac{V''}{V'}. \tag{29}$$

We know that $V' = \mu$ and thus

$$V'' = \frac{\mathrm{d}\mu}{\mathrm{d}Y}.$$

Differentiation of $\beta^h U_W^h = 0$ yields

$$V'' = \frac{U_W^h}{\sum_{h=1}^{H} \frac{1}{\beta^h}}. \tag{30}$$

Thus,

$$R_V = -\frac{U_{WW}^h}{\beta^h \sum_j \frac{1}{\beta^j} U_W^j}.$$

Let

$$\frac{1}{\beta^k} U_W^h = \min_j \frac{1}{\beta^j} U_W^k.$$

Then

$$R_V \leq -\frac{U_{WW}^h}{\beta^h H \frac{1}{\beta^k} U_W^k} = \frac{1}{H} \frac{\beta^k}{\beta^h} \left[-\frac{U_{WW}^h}{U_W^k} \right] \quad \text{for all } h. \tag{31}$$

Choose $h = k$ and note that the individual measure of absolute risk aversion is R_U

$$R_U = -\frac{U''}{U'}, \tag{32}$$

and so

$$R_V \leq \frac{1}{H} \frac{1}{R_k}. \tag{33}$$

With increasing size of the population the social risk aversion will therefore go to zero.

The social cost of risk bearing is now

$$\frac{1}{2} \frac{1}{H} R_U \left\{ \mathrm{var}\,(Y_i(H)) + 2\mathrm{cov}\,(Y_i(H), W_i(H)) \right\}, \tag{34}$$

where $W_i(H) = \sum_{h=1}^{H} W_i(h)$, i.e. national income.

(i) If the environmental asset is a pure public good[3] without congestion

$$Y_i(H) = HY_i \tag{35}$$

and the social cost of risk bearing is

$$R_U \{H \text{ var}(Y_i) + 2\text{cov}(Y_i, W_i)\} .$$

In this case, an increase in population will increase the total cost of risk bearing.

(ii) If the asset generates purely private benefits

$$Y_i(H) = Y_i \tag{36}$$

and the cost of risk bearing is

$$\frac{1}{H} R_U \{H \text{ var}(Y_i) + 2\text{cov}(Y_i, W_i)\} .$$

First, if Y_i and W_i are independent, it follows that the cost of risk tends to zero when the number of individuals sharing the risk increases.[4] If $W_i(H)$ is independent of H, then the cost of risk bearing also tends to zero with the number of individuals sharing the risk. If there is decreasing marginal returns with respect to H, so that $W_i(H)$ is decreasing, the same result obtains.

(iii) In the general case, if

$$\frac{Y_i(H)}{\sqrt{H}} \quad \text{and} \quad \frac{W_i(H)}{\sqrt{H}}$$

go to zero with increasing H, the cost of risk bearing will be smaller the larger the population is. The importance of this is obvious.

Even if insurance markets cannot work because of the correlation of the risks individuals are bearing, it is thus possible to reduce that cost in certain cases by letting more people bear the risk.

2.4.1. *Option Prices and Option Values*

Let us apply the theory developed in the last sections to the valuation of a natural assets. Consider the example provided by Schmalensee, i.e. the possible development of Yellowstone National Park which would irreversibly destroy its unique features. The environmental variable Q can in this case assume two values, Q' corresponding to preservation of the National Park and Q'' corresponding to irreversible destruction. Uncertainty comes partly from income uncertainty $\{W_i^h\}$ and partly from preference or utility uncertainty $\{U_i^h\}$.

CV^h is defined from

$$EU_i^h(W_i^h - CV^h, Q) = EU_i^h(W_i^h, Q''). \tag{37}$$

It is known as the option price, i.e. the price the individual is willing to pay for keeping the option of going to Yellowstone in the future. CV_i^h is defined from

$$U_i^h(W_i^h - CV_i^h, Q') = U_i^h(W_i^h, Q''). \tag{38}$$

From the previous sections, see Equation (15), we know that

$$CV^h = \overline{CV}^h + \frac{\operatorname{cov}(CV_i^h, U_{i,W}^h)}{\overline{U}_W^h} + \tag{39}$$

$$+ \frac{1}{2}R^h \left\{\operatorname{var}(CV_i^h) + 2\operatorname{cov}(CV_i^h, W_i^h)\right\}. \tag{40}$$

The difference between CV^h and $\overline{CV}^h$ is known as the option value OV^h

$$OV^h = CV^h - \overline{CV}^h \tag{41}$$

and a substantial discussion has taken place in the literature whether the option value is positive or negative (see Bohm 1975, Cicchetti and Freeman 1971, Schmalensee 1972, Krutilla et al. 1972, and Bishop 1982). It is clear from the formula above that the option value may be of either sign. However, it is at least possible to outline the factors influencing the size and sign of the option value.

The first term

$$\frac{\operatorname{cov}(CV_i^h, U_{i,W}^h)}{\overline{U}_W^h}$$

reflects the collinearity between CV_i^h and U_i^h. If the natural asset is not considered of high importance by the individual (i.e. it would occupy a big share of his budget if would have to pay for it), it is hard to see why random variations in the marginal utility of income should be of importance. Thus, this term should be small. Moreover, as we saw in the previous section, if we aggregate over individuals and if CV_i^h and $U_{i,W}^h$ are distributed independently for each state i over individuals, the aggregate will be close to zero. Thus, there seems to be reason to assume that this term is negligible.

The last term

$$\frac{1}{2}R^h \left\{\text{var}\,(CV_i^h) + 2\text{cov}\,(CV_i^h, W_i^h)\right\}$$

is on the other hand more interesting. Obviously, it is impossible to say anything in general about the sign and size of this term. However, for some particular cases, some conclusions may be drawn:

(i) If the uncertainty about future preferences is in a sense genuine, a knowledge about future income would not increase our ability to predict future benefits. Thus CV_i^h and W_i^h will not be correlated for any individual and the term simplifies to

$$\frac{1}{2}R^h\ \text{var}\,(CV_i^h),$$

which obviously is positive. In this case risk aversion will imply a positive option value. This is probably the case that corresponds most closely to the problem discussed by Weisbrod and Cicchetti and Freeman (Weisbrod 1964, Krutilla et al. 1972, Cicchetti and Freeman 1971).

(ii) The uncertainty about future preferences may be due to uncertainty about some economic variable not explicitly in the utility function. If the natural asset is a recreational facility and if high future oil prices shifts recreational demand from foreign facilities to the domestic asset and vice versa, it is reasonable to assume that CV_i^h and W_i^h are negatively correlated. Thus the risk premium term for the individual in that case

$$\frac{1}{2}R^h \left\{\text{var}\,(CV_i^h) + 2\text{cov}\,(CV_i^h, W_i^h)\right\}$$

may have either sign depending on whether the second term dominates the first or not. It may therefore happen that the individual has a positive option value. However, from the point of view of society, if the recreational asset is such that $\overline{CV}_i$ increases less than in proportion with the size of the population, the term $\frac{1}{H}\overline{CV}$ will be small and the covariance term will dominate.

Thus, even if the individual has a positive option value, society may, in spite of this, have a negative option value. The reason for this is that the risk component corresponding to the variance can be better shared through society and the remaining risk component is essentially an insurance against the future oil prices. In particular, this implies that investments in this facility should be discounted with a negative risk premium. Of course, if the facility is a pure public good with no congestion, then this result does not hold, and the risk term for society is simply the individual risk premium multiplied with the size of the population.

2.4.2. *Health Effects*

We will now consider the situation when Q_i represent health effects from pollution. Assume a pollution control policy has been proposed which would reduce the risk of getting pollution induced health effects. As we have seen previously this change in risk can be represented by a change in Q. We assume that preferences are state independent.

The willingness to pay of the individual for the proposed policy is then

$$CV^h = \overline{CV}^h + \frac{1}{2}R^h \left\{\text{var}(CV_i^h) + 2\text{cov}\,(CV_i^h, W_i^h)\right\}$$

if the state dependent benefits CV_i^h exist. Obviously, we are now analysing a problem so delicate that the expected utility representation may not be valid. Assume for example, that $Q = 0$ represents a state in which the individual contracts lung cancer and that $Q = 1$ represents a state in which the individual stays healthy. Our utility representation implies that there is a CV_i^h, so that

$$U^h(W_i^h + CV_i^h, 0) = U^h(W_i^h, 1)$$

However, there may not exist any compensation for contracting lung cancer and since state 0, has a positive probability, it follows that $\overline{CV^h} = \infty$! On the other hand, we know from everyday experience that people are willing to take risks involving contracting lung cancer (smokers, for example) which contradicts the hypothesis that $CV_i^h = \infty$. Thus, a linear utility may not be the best way of analysing the economic measurement of health effects. More important is that the quadratic approximation used to derive the formula above hardly is valid if the state contingent benefits vary substantially between different states. In spite of this we will, continue to use the framework developed in previous sections.

The health effects CV_i^h represent individual risks in the sense used previously. Thus, there is scope for an insurance system and if the population is large enough, the law of large numbers will guarantee each individual $\overline{CV^h}$ independent of state. Thus, in the aggregate, the risk premium will vanish and $CV = \int_H \overline{CV^h}\, dh$. This presumes, however, that there do exist complete insurance markets. In most western states well developed insurance companies are operating, offering customers protection for hospital expenses, medicine, doctors' fees, and income losses. Some of them also offer compensation for psychic suffering from the disease. However, hardly all the cost to the individual can be insured, so let us write

$$CV_i^h = X_i^h + Y_i^h,$$

where X_i^h is the insured part and Y_i^h the uninsurable part. Then

$$CV = \int_H \overline{CV}^h dh + \frac{1}{2}\int_H R^h\{\text{var}\,(Y_i^h) + \text{cov}\,(Y^h, W_i^h)\}\, dh. \qquad (42)$$

If the insurance covers income losses, one would not expect any correlation between Y_i^h and W_i^h and thus

$$\begin{aligned} CV &= \int_H \overline{CV}^h\, dh + \int_H R^h \text{var}\,(Y_i^h)\, dh \\ &= \int_H \overline{X}^h\, dh + \int_H \overline{Y}^h\, dh + \int_H R^h \text{var}(Y_i^h)\, dh. \end{aligned}$$

X_i^h corresponds to those benefits that are easily measured and therefore easily insured. In most cases X_i^h will stand for financial costs, i.e. expenditures on medical care and earning losses.

As we see from (43) $\int_H X_i^h\, dh$ is an underestimate of CV as the term $\int_H \overline{Y}^h\, dh + \int_H R^h \text{var}\,(Y_i^h)\, dh$, i.e. the expected cost from suffering and the associated risk premium is not included.

2.4.3. *Price Uncertainty*

Let us introduce the interest rate r as a variable in the indirect utility function and let us also assume that r is a stochastic variable. We will also neglect the many consumers case and instead assume that the utility represents social utility. The utility function is now

$$U_i(W_i, r, Q_i),$$

where i as previously represent the state of the world. We can now go through the same kind of exercise as we have done in previous sections in order to derive approximations to the true CV. The result is under essentially the same assumptions as before

$$CV = \overline{CV} + \frac{\text{cov}\,(CV_i, U_{i,W})}{\overline{U}_W} + \frac{1}{2}R\{\text{var}\,(CV_i) + 2\text{cov}\,(W_i, CV_i)\} - \quad (43)$$

$$- \frac{U_{r,W}}{\overline{U}_W}\text{cov}\,(r, CV_i), \quad (44)$$

where $U_{r,W} = \partial^2 U/\partial r \partial W$ has been assumed state independent. We will assume that $U_{r,W} < 0$, that is an increase in the price r will reduce the marginal utility of wealth. It is interesting to note that even if the individual is risk neutral so that the utility function is linear in wealth, the last term may be different from zero. In the simple case when preferences are state independent and represent risk neutral behavior we would have

$$CV = \overline{CV} - \frac{U_{r,W}}{\overline{U}_W}\text{cov}\,(r_i, CV_i). \quad (45)$$

Thus the possible correlation between on the one hand the state contingent benefits CV_i and the price (or the interest rate) will create a difference between the expected benefits $\overline{CV}$ and the true benefits CV. Is such a correlation to be expected? Should not the covariance between state contingent compensation variations and the interest rate be zero in general? The interest rate will either reflect the desired trade off between consumption in different time periods or the future marginal productivity of capital. In the latter case, the interpretation is that the interest rate gives an indication of the necessary capital investment today in order to increase consumption with one unit in a future time period. But the future marginal productivity of capital will in general be influenced of the availability of natural resources. An increase in the availability of resources will in general increase the expected future productivity and thereby the interest rate. If we are analysing a project with large environmental consequences, not only will the cost be large and state contingent benefits small because of that, but the interest rate will be small in the states that correspond to small benefits. Thus we should expect a negative covariance between CV_i and r_i. This means that, even in the absence of risk aversion and with state independent preferences, will the true benefit be smaller than the expected compensating variation. The covariance between interest rate and the benefits will thus act as if the decision maker is risk avert. Another way of seeing that is to look at the following formula for the present value of a current project with future environmental consequences.

$$NB_0 = C_0 - \frac{C_1}{1+r},$$

where C_0 is the present benefit, C_1 is the future cost from environmental degradation, r is the interest rate, and NB_0 is the present value of the net benefits. Assume that C_1 and r are stochastic variables and assume that the decision maker is risk neutral. The standard procedure is to calculate the number

$$C_0 - \frac{\overline{C}_1}{1+\overline{r}}, \tag{46}$$

where $\overline{C}_1$ and $\overline{r}$ are the expected values of C_1 and r. The expected value of NB_0 is, however,

$$\begin{aligned} E(NB_0) = C_0 - E\left\{\frac{C_1}{1+r}\right\} &\approx C_0 - E\{C_1(1-r)\} \\ &\approx C_0 + \frac{\overline{C}_1}{1+\overline{r}} - \operatorname{cov}(r, C_1). \end{aligned} \tag{47}$$

Once again, we see that the covariance between r and C_1 will affect the expected net benefits and with a positive correlation between r and C_1, the expected net benefit will be less that what would be calculated with the conventional practice.

3. INTERTEMPORAL RESOLUTION OF UNCERTAINTY

We will look at the following situation. Assume that a project is designed that will include the use of a particular environmental resource over several time periods. However, the value of this resource in the future time periods is not known with certainty. There is a possibility that information on these values may be generated over time. What is the appropriate decision-making framework? In most analyses of uncertainty of future environmental resource use, the information structure has been very simple. All information is contained in an a priori probability distribution and no more information will be available at a later stage. For some applications, this may be a realistic assumption. If the decision to use a natural asset in a special way can be completely reversed at a later stage (without any costs), the prospect of getting more information in the future does not have to be included in the analysis. In this case there are no essential intertemporal connections. In the other extreme when the decision is completely irreversible, the prospect of better information may be quite important and we will turn to a discussion of that situation.

The pioneering analysis of this problem was given by Arrow and Fisher (1974) and Henry (1974a), who showed that the prospect of being better informed at a later stage meant fewer irreversible decisions, given some assumptions on the nature of costs and benefits. We will illustrate their results but using a different approach. For a more complete discussion, see Fisher and Mäler (2005).

3.1. The Arrow–Fisher–Henry Analysis

The easiest way to present the Arrow–Fisher analysis is perhaps in terms of decision tree. Assume a decision maker has to decide whether to develop a piece of land or preserve it. This is represented by the two branches d_1 and p_1 in Figure 2.1. The development will be irreversible so if d_1 has been chosen in the first period, the decision maker has to continue with having the land developed in the second period, represented by the branch d_2. On the other hand, if she has chosen preservation in the first period, that is if she has followed the branch p_1, after the first period she has the choice of either developing the land – d_2 – or continue preserving it – p_2. However, although the benefits from developing the land are known at the initial node, the benefits from preservation is not. They can be high – B_{ph} – with probability q_1, or low – B_{pl} – with probability q_2. The benefits from developing the land in the first period is $B_d(1)$ and in the second period $B_d(2)$. We will assume that $B_{ph} > B_d(2) > B_{pl}$.

If she choses d_1 in the first period, the expected benefits are $B_d(1) + B_d(2)$. If on the other hand she choses preservation in the first period but development in the second period, the expected benefits are $B_d(2)$ which is less than the benefits from developing in the first period. Finally, if she choses preservation in both periods, the expected benefits are $q_1 B_{ph} + q_2 B_{pl}$. Thus she will, if she maximizes the expected value, chose p_1 if

$$B_d(1) + B_d(2) < q_1 B_{ph} + q_2 B_{pl} \tag{48}$$

and vice versa. Note that in this case, no information is forthcoming between period 1 and period 2 concerning the benefits from preservation. Let us now look at the case when information is forthcoming before a decision is being made for the second period.

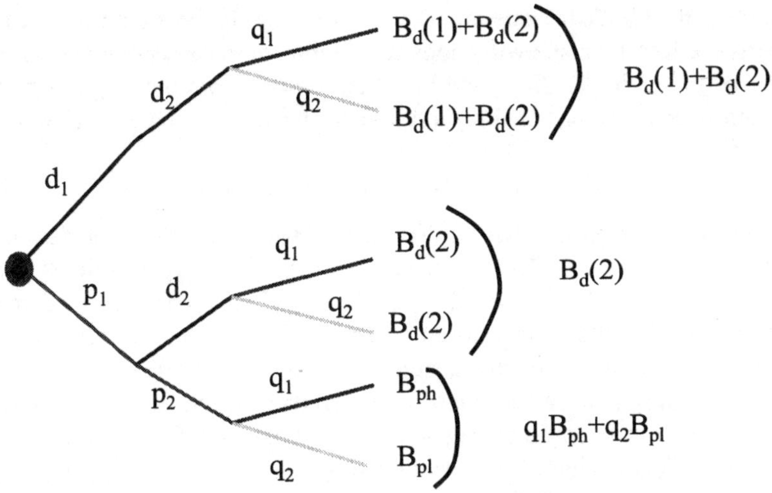

Figure 2.1. Decision tree when no information is forthcoming

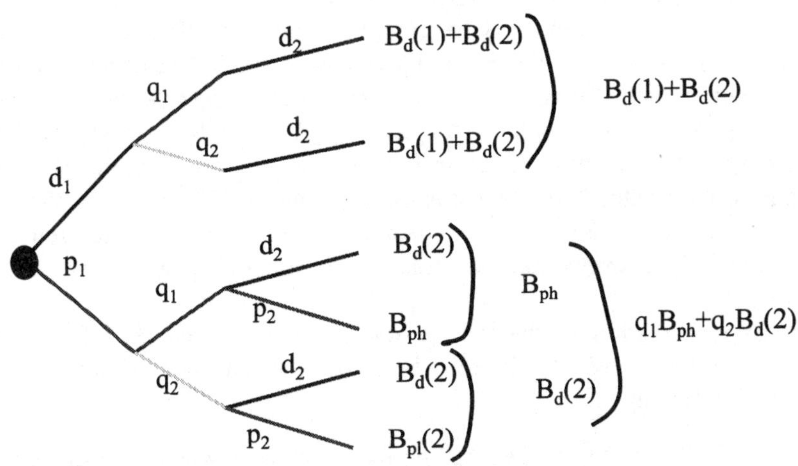

Figure 2.2. New information is forthcoming

As in the case above, if development is undertaken in the first period, then the expected benefits are $B_d(1) + B_d(2)$. However, if preservation is undertaken in the first period, the information on whether the preservation benefits are high or low will change the decision for the second period. Assume that the decision maker gets the signal in the beginning of the second period that the preservation benefits will be high, then she will choose continued preservation as $B_{ph} > B_d(2)$. Thus the benefits from preservation in both periods are B_{ph} in this case. If the signal is that the benefits are low, then she will choose development in the second period and the benefits are $B_d(2)$. Expected benefits, as seen from the original node, are then $q_1 B_{ph} + q_{2B_d}(2)$. Preservation in the first period will now take place if

$$B_d(1) + B_d(2) < q_1 B_{ph} + q_2 B_d(2). \tag{49}$$

If preservation in the first case is chosen when no new information is forthcoming, that is, if $B_d(1) + B_d(2) < q_1 B_{ph} + q_2 B_{pl}$, it follows from $B_d(2) > B_{pl}$, that $B_d(1) + B_d(2) < q_1 B_{ph} + q_2 B_d(2)$, and preservation in the first period will also be chosen when new information is forthcoming in the beginning of the second period.

Assume now that development is undertaken in the first period when new information is forthcoming, that is, assume that $B_d(1) + B_d(2) > q_1 B_{ph} + q_2 B_d(2)$. Then it follows that $B_d(1) + B_d(2) > q_1 B_{ph} + q_2 B_{pl}$, that is, development will also be undertaken.

Furthermore, as $q_1 B_{ph} + q_2 B_d(2) > q_1 B_{ph} + q_2 B_{pl}$, for some values of the benefits, preservation may be chosen when information is forthcoming but not when it is not forthcoming. Finally, the effective use of forthcoming information on the future benefits will, in the case of preservation, increase the value of the net benefits from $q_1 B_{ph} + q_2 B_{pl}$ to $q_1 B_{ph} + q_2 B_d(2)$. This increase in the objective function is known as the quasi option value, or simpy option value (note that this option value is different from the one discussed in the first part of this chapter), and it can also be interpreted as the value of the forthcoming information. Summarizing, we have

- if preservation in the first period is chosen when no information is forthcoming, it will also be chosen when such information is forthcoming;
- if development in the first period is chosen when information is forthcoming, it will also be chosen when no such information is forthcoming;
- there are cases when preservation will be chosen when information is forthcoming, but not when it is not forthcoming;
- the possibility of using forthcoming information creates a quasi option value.

3.2. Research Agenda

The general conclusion is that the combination of irreversibility and the possibility of new information will favour preservation. This is sometimes called the *irreversibility effect*. Moreover, any decision rule that is based on a mechanical use of expected benefits is bound to be erronous in a number of cases. Now it is easy to see that the concept of option value, discussed in a static framework in the previous sections, can be generalized to this situation with changing information over time and the option value will partly be the expected value of the forthcoming information (conditional that no irreversible changes have been made) and risk aversion. See Fisher and Mäler (2005) for a more complete analysis.

The simple Arrow–Fisher analysis is, because of its simplicity, quite revealing, but it also conceals many important issues, which need to be understood in order for the irreversibility effect to be useful. We will therefore discuss and make some attempts to analyse the following features.

- generalizations to general benefit functions;
- sharper definitions of the meaning of forthcoming information;
- active search for new information instead of passively waiting for it to occur;
- not complete irreversibility but a change that can be reversed at a cost;
- irreversibility is unknown.

Most of these issues are answered in the already mentioned chapter by Fisher and Mäler (2005).

NOTES

1. Note that is the same result as Bohm (1975) claimed, although the motivation is different.
2. This is not necessary for the analysis. Any assumption that keeps the individual small compared to the total income would give the same result, for example, if the total benefits are distributed so that $CV_i^h = \beta^h CV_i$ would yield the same result.
3. This case has been analysed within a different approach by Fisher (1973).
4. This result was derived by Arrow and Lind (1972).

REFERENCES

Arrow, K.J. and A.C. Fisher (1974), 'Environmental preservation, uncertainty, and irreversibility', *American Economic Review*, 88, 312–320.

Arrow, K. and R. Lind (1972), 'Uncertainty and the evaluation of public investment decisions', *American Economic Review*, 60.

Bishop, R. (1982), 'Option value: An exposition and extension', *Land Economics*, 58.

Bohm, P. (1975), 'Option demand and consumer's surplus: A comment', *American Economic Review*, 65.

Cicchetti, C. and A.M. Freeman III (1971), 'Option demand and consumer surplus: Further comment', *Quarterly Journal of Economics*, 85.

Fisher, A.C. (1973), 'Environmental externalities and the Arrow–Lind public investment theorem', *American Economic Review*, 63.

Fisher, A. and K.-G. Mäler (2005), 'Environment, uncertainty, and option values', in *Handbook of Environmental Economics*, Vol, 2, Amsterdam: North-Holland, forthcoming.

Henry, C. (1974a), 'Investment decisions under uncertainty: The irreversibility effect', *American Economic Review*, 64, 1006–1012.

Henry, C. (1974b), 'Option values in the economics of irreplaceable assets', *Review of Economic Studies: Symposium on the Economics of Exhaustible Resources*.

Krutilla, J.V., C.J. Cicchetti, A.M. Freeman III and C.S. Russel (1972), 'Observations on the economics of irreplaceable assets', in A. Kneese and B. Bower (eds), *Environmental Quality Analysis: Theory and Method in the Social Sciences*, Baltimore, MD: John Hopkins University Press.

Malinvaud, E. (1972), 'The allocation of individual risks in large markets', *Journal of Economic Theory*, 4.

Schmalensee, R. (1972), 'Option demand and consumer's surplus: Valuing price changes under uncertainty', *American Economic Review*, 62.

Weisbrod, B. (1964), 'Collective-consumption services of individual consumption goods', *Quarterly Journal of Economics*, 78, 471–477.

3. Fisher, Lindahl, and Hicks on Income: A Modern Analysis

Chuan-Zhong Li

1. INTRODUCTION

Economists have long been interested in the concept of income for conceptualization of business practices. While most classicists followed the Adam Smith definition of income as an increase in wealth, it was realized towards the end of the nineteenth century that income is more than cash as expressed by Von Bohm Bawerk's theory on capital and income. Since then, the concept of economic income began to be considered as an ex ante measure being the expectation of future values, which is in contrast to the accounting income being an ex post measure based on historical values. This includes the Fisher (1906) psychic income as the subjective utility yielded by goods and services consumed, the Lindahl (1933) income as a stream of interest on capital values (wealth), and the Hicks (1939) general theory of maximum sustainable consumption over time.

In the recent decades, there has been increasing concerns about natural resource depletion and environmental externalities, which was marked by the launching of the concept of sustainable development by the World Commission (1987). According to the Commission, sustainable development is defined as a development that can meet the need of the present without compromising the ability of the future generations to satisfy their needs. However, the exact content of the concept remains elusive in the literature. For example, how can human needs be measured? While researchers in different disciplines have been tackling the problem from different standpoints, economists have 'rediscovered' the economic concept of income studied by Fisher (1906), Lindahl (1933) and Hicks (1939) as a candidate measure of sustainability.

The renewed interest in the concept of economic income has spurred a widespread interest in comprehensive or green national accounting in recent years. As a result, how to define the income concept in a comprehensive national accounting framework and how to empirically measure it have become an important topic of economic research (Aronsson et al. 1997, Weitzman and Löfgren 1997, Hamilton and Clemens 1999, Dasgupta and Mäler 2000, Weitzman 2001, Arrow et al. 2003, Heal and Kriström 2005, Löfgren et al. 2005). A popular view in the literature is that a comprehensive net national product measure, which takes into account the value of natural and environmental resources and human capital, can be a suitable measure of national income and thus an indicator of sustainability. While Solow (1992, p. 17) claims that such comprehensive or green NNP, if properly defined, should correspond to the interest on a generalized capital (wealth), Dasgupta and Mäler (2001) argue that this is normally not the case.

In order to make the comprehensive (or green[1]) NNP measure consistent with sustainability, various attempts have been made to adjust the concept of green NNP. For example, Asheim (1997) modifies money NNP with a current growth of wealth plus the change in the infinitely long-run interest on wealth. However, this is hard to apply in national accounting practices since it would be difficult to assess the long-run interest rate over an infinite time horizon. In another attempt, Li and Löfgren (2002), drawn upon the ideas of Weitzman (2001), define a generalized comprehensive NNP (GCNNP) that involves an additional consumer surplus term. This is a theoretically correct welfare and sustainability measure, but it would require information on a complete, and presumably nonlinear, demand system in order to calculate the economy-wide consumer surplus. Most national-income statisticians would prefer to work with linear forms for practical convenience. In a recent paper, Dasgupta and Mäler (2001) have developed a linear index as a criterion for measuring sustainable development. The index defined is a comprehensive national wealth measure, i.e. the total value of all capital stocks relevant for human welfare evaluated at their accounting prices. However, it remains unclear how this linear wealth measure is related to the comprehensive (green) NNP.

In this chapter, we will re-examine the Fisher, Lindahl, and Hicks definitions of economic income in a modern theoretical framework of multi-sector optimal growth, drawn upon the ideas from Weitzman (1976), Aronsson et al. (1997), Dasgupta and Mäler (2000), and Löfgren et al. (2005). We will identify the conditions under which the different concepts can be reconciled to be consistent with each other, and explore their empirical relevance for developing indicators of economic sustainability.

In particular, we will show that the Wicksell (1936) definition of normal interest proves to be useful in defining an ideal net national income that would exactly correspond to the return on capital as anticipated by Solow (1992).

The remaining part of this chapter is structured as the following: Section 2 presents a multi-sector growth model and formalizes the concepts of utility and money NNP. Section 3 reviews the income definitions by Fisher, Lindahl and Hicks, and analyses their relationships in a modern theoretical framework. In Section 4, we show how the Hamiltonian function can be linearized with respect to the right variables so that it can be interpreted as the interest on capital, which is in line with Solow's conjecture. For this purpose, we have taken advantage of the normal rate of return as defined by Wicksell (1936). Section 5 sums up the chapter.

2. THE MULTI-SECTOR GROWTH MODEL

Let $\mathbf{C} = (C_1, C_2, \ldots, C_m)$ be an m-dimensional vector of consumption flows at a given time t, which is supposed to exhaust all the possible goods and services that are relevant to social welfare or the standard of living of a representative individual. In addition to the usual market commodities, environmental services such as forest amenities, biodiversity and ecosystem functions, in flow terms, are also considered to be a part of the consumption vector. This means that the prices of these services are rental prices. The utilitarian measure of intertemporal welfare at time $t = 0$ can be expressed as

$$W(0) = \int_0^\infty U(\mathbf{C}(t)) \exp(-\theta t)\,\mathrm{d}t, \tag{1}$$

where $U(\mathbf{C})$ is a given concave, nondecreasing, instantaneous utility function with continuous second-order derivative defined for $\mathbf{C} \geq 0$, and θ is the utility rate of discount.

Let $\mathbf{K} = (K_1, K_2, \ldots, K_n)$ be a vector of capital goods, which is assumed to contain all types of capital goods in the economy including natural resources such as minerals, forests, air, water, and even human capital in the form of technological knowledge. Net investments are, by definition, the change in capital stocks, i.e. $I_i = \dot{K}_i$, $i = 1, 2, \ldots, n$, which in a vector form can be expressed as

$$\mathbf{I} = \dot{\mathbf{K}}, \text{ given } \mathbf{K}(0) = \mathbf{K}_0 > 0. \tag{2}$$

At each point in time t, consumption $\mathbf{C}(t)$ and investment $\mathbf{I}(t)$ are allocated within the $m + 2n$-dimensional attainable possibility set $F(\alpha)$, conditional on a collection of parameters α (cf. Drèze and Stern 1987), such that

$$(\mathbf{C}(t), \mathbf{I}(t), \mathbf{K}(t)) \in F(\alpha) \tag{3}$$

which is presumed to be strictly convex. The parameters α may represent any premise that modifies the feasible set for consumption and investment allocations, such as legal, political, and behavioral constraints (Weitzman 2003). Conditional on such parameters, a social planner is assumed to maximize the current-value Hamiltonian at each point in time t

$$H(t) = U\left(\mathbf{C}(t)\right) + \mathbf{\Psi}(t)\mathbf{I}(t) \tag{4}$$

with respect to $\mathbf{C}(t)$ and $\mathbf{I}(t)$ subject to (3), where $\mathbf{\Psi}(t)$ is the n-dimensional vector of utility shadow prices of capital satisfying the following equation of motion

$$\dot{\mathbf{\Psi}} = \theta\mathbf{\Psi} - \nabla H_{\mathbf{K}}|_{*(t)}, \tag{5}$$

where the notion $|_{*(t)}$ means evaluation along the optimal trajectory over time. The maximized current-value Hamiltonian at time t is thus

$$H^*(t) \equiv U\left(\mathbf{C}^*(t)\right) + \mathbf{\Psi}(t)\mathbf{I}^*(t) \tag{6}$$

which can be interpreted as utility NNP, i.e. the sum of instantaneous utility derived from consumption and the value of investment. Weitzman (1976) and Kemp and van Long (1982) show that the utility NNP corresponds to a constancy equivalent of future utilities along the optimal path such that

$$\begin{aligned} W^*(t) &\equiv \int_t^\infty U(\mathbf{C}^*(s)) \exp(-\theta(s-t))\,\mathrm{d}s \\ &= \int_t^\infty H^*(t) \exp(-\theta(s-t))\,\mathrm{d}s. \end{aligned} \tag{7}$$

In the literature, the present discounted value of future utilities, $W^*(t)$, has also been interpreted as (utility) wealth, and the maximized current-value Hamiltonian (utility NNP) can be derived as the interest on wealth such that

$$H^*(t) = \theta W^*(t). \tag{8}$$

Since the utility rate of discount $\theta > 0$ is normally assumed to be a constant, utility NNP and wealth will go along the same direction. However, as utility is not directly measurable in practice, economists have been trying to find monetary surrogates for welfare measurement. If the utility function is linear in income, it can be shown that utility NNP would be exactly equal to money NNP (Weitzman 1976). Otherwise, when it comes to nonlinear utility functional forms, the linearized Hamiltonian with respect to consumption and investment, which is often termed as money NNP after a normalization, may not posses the same welfare significance as the utility NNP (Aronsson et al. 1997, Asheim 1997, Dasgupta and Mäler 2000, Li and Löfgren 2002).

In general, money NNP expressed as the linearized Hamiltonian does not correspond to the interest on wealth. To retain the welfare significance of money NNP, different adjustment attempts have been made in the recent years. In Asheim (1997), the attempt is to adjust the green (money) NNP by the 'growth of current wealth plus rate of change in the infinitely long-term consumption rate times current wealth'. The practical barrier seems to lie in the assessment of the infinitely long-term interest rate, i.e. a weighted average of the short-term interest rates over an infinite time horizon. In contrast, Weitzman (2001) and Li and Löfgren (2002) have made efforts to capture the economy-wide consumer surplus as an additional term to green money NNP for welfare measurement. Drawn upon the ideas from Weitzman (2001), Li and Löfgren (2002) have attempted to define a generalized comprehensive NNP concept being the sum of the ordinary comprehensive NNP and a consumer surplus term. They showed that such a generalized comprehensive NNP, although measured in monetary terms, conforms exactly to Weitzman foundation in (8). Compared to Asheim (1997), this measure can in principle be calculated on the basis of the current period information such as the short-run interest rate and a complete demand system without involving the infinitely long-term interest rate. The difficulty in applying this concept is that it would be very tedious for the National Accounting Authorities to estimate a complete and presumably nonlinear demand system for all goods and services in the economy.

It may be worth mentioning now that the aim of this chapter is not to render verdict on relative merits of these approaches. Instead, we will try to shed light on the issue by re-examining the Fisher–Lindahl–Hicks concepts of economic income and explore their interrelationships. Moreover, we will show that by a proper linearization, the resulting money measure of income is indeed the return on capital (capitalized value) as anticipated by Solow (1992). The trick is to choose the proper base for the linearization with respect to the right variables, by which we will also show that the puzzle with the spaceship model of exhaustible resources can also be resolved.

3. THE DIFFERENT CONCEPTS OF ECONOMIC INCOME

Fisher (1906) considered income as a series of personal psychic experiences in the form of enjoyments or perceived events of a more personal nature rather than of a business entity. In modern economics, such an income concept should correspond to the instantaneous utility derived from consuming goods and services. Since Fisher regarded consumption as so essential, he did not recognize savings as a part of income. The reason was that savings would generate a stream of consumption in the future, and thus an inclusion of savings as income would double count the current income. It is the later economists who have adapted this income concept to the business entity by taking savings into account. In the optimal growth model framework, Fisher's original definition of income may be expressed as $U(\mathbf{C})$ while the adapted version is $U(\mathbf{C}) + \mathbf{\Psi}(t)\mathbf{I}(t)$, i.e. the sum of 'consumption' value and the value of investment.

It can be said that Fisher was the very first economist to think about income in utility terms so as to have welfare interpretations. On the other hand, Fisher was also fully aware that utility was not observable so that he attempted to approximate his psychic income by the cost of living (the monetary value of final consumption of goods and services). This may now be expressed as $\mathbf{P}(t)\mathbf{C}(t)$, where $\mathbf{P}(t)$ is a vector of consumption prices. In the adapted version, the Fisher income becomes

$$\mathbf{Y}(t) = \mathbf{P}(t)\mathbf{C}(t) + \mathbf{Q}(t)\mathbf{I}(t), \tag{9}$$

where $\mathbf{Q}(t)$ is a vector of investment prices.

Lindahl (1933) was the first economist who considered income as the interest on wealth, i.e. the continuous appreciation of capital goods over time. The difference between the interest income and consumption for a given period was perceived as saving, which leads to the general concept of income as consumption plus saving. Unlike Fisher, however, Lindahl did not clarify whether or not the income concept would be defined in utility terms. If this would be the case, then the Lindahl concept of income may now be expressed as $H^*(t) = U(\mathbf{C}^*(t)) + \mathbf{\Psi}(t)\mathbf{I}^*(t)$, the nowadays well-known maximized current-value Hamiltonian. Obviously this can be expressed as the interest on wealth in the form of (8), which has been proved by Weitzman (1976) and Kemp and van Long (1982). However, when it comes to the money measure of income $\mathbf{Y}(t) = \mathbf{P}(t)\mathbf{C}(t) + \mathbf{Q}(t)\mathbf{I}(t)$, it is known nowadays that it is not the case. The reason for this is that the money rate of interest following the Euler equation is in general a function of time although the utility rate of discount is constant. Only in the case of a linear utility function with a constant positive rate of discount (the interest rate), can the money measure of income be expressed as the interest on wealth or the capitalized value of all capital goods.

Along the same line as Fisher and Lindahl, Hicks (1939) developed a general theory of economic income by defining a person's income as 'the maximum amount he can consume during a week and still expect to be as well-off at the end of the week as he was at the beginning of the week' (income no. 3). For national income accounting one may simply aggregate the personal incomes over all the citizens. Under the assumption of a constant discount rate, Hicks also proposed a 'capital intact' theory in that capital stocks (values) have to be kept intact before any income can be realized (income no. 1). In other words, income is the maximum amount people can consume without impoverishing themselves. As shown in Aronsson et al. (1997) and Nordhaus (1994), the two income concepts would coincide with each other in the absence of exogenous technical progress. When exogenous technical progress is present, then income no. 1 will underestimate the maximal sustainable consumption. There is a trick to go around the problem of exogenous technical progress by introducing an artificial capital stock variable being the technical knowledge (Aronsson et al. 1997). With a complete list of capital goods, the two income definitions by Hicks become consistent to each other.

In sum, when thinking in terms of utility measures, the adapted Fisher income taking into account the value of investment would be exactly equal to the interest on capital (Lindahl 1933), which in turn corresponds to the Hicks' (1939) maximum utility that can be derived from consumption while keeping the capital value intact. However, when it comes to monetary measures, things may get more complicated. One of the reasons is that the money interest rate is in general time-dependent. In spite of the theoretical complexities, money measures are the ones used in practice. In particular, national income is often measured by national product, which may either be measured as the sum of consumption and investment values, or equivalently as the sum of factor incomes when all relevant factors are accounted for.

In his keynote speech at the Resources for the Future (RFF), Solow (1992) claimed that when properly defined and properly calculated, NNP should be the return on capital, but Dasgupta and Mäler (2000) showed that generally this is not the case. In the next section, we will deal with this problem. We show, among other things, that the comprehensive NNP derived by linearizing the Hamiltonian with respect to the right variables gives a result that does support the Solow conjecture.

4. TOWARDS AN IDEAL MEASURE OF COMPREHENSIVE NNP

As discussed above, the net national product (NNP) when measured in monetary terms may not be a satisfactory welfare indicator no matter how comprehensive it is. It is possible that a positive growth in comprehensive NNP leads to a decrease in welfare. Only under rather restrictive assumptions of a linear utility function or constant investment prices in a steady state (Dasgupta and Mäler 2000), can NNP growth indicate welfare improvement.[2] To make NNP a satisfactory welfare measure, different efforts have been made in the literature. In Asheim (1997), for example, NNP is adjusted by among other things the product of the rate of change in the long-term interest rate (a weighted average over an infinite future) and the current wealth. Another attempt is made by Li and Löfgren (2002) drawn on the ideas of Weitzman (2001), i.e. to complete the comprehensive NNP with a consumer surplus term to restore the Weitzman foundation (8) in money metrics.

An intriguing question now is this: while the maximized current-value Hamiltonian or utility NNP can be expressed as a return on wealth and thereby works as a satisfactory welfare indicator, why can a linearized version of it being the money NNP lose its welfare significance? A close examination reveals that the culprit lies in that the maximized current-value Hamiltonian was linearized with respect to the 'wrong' variables. While wealth is defined in terms of the capitalized value of stocks $\mathbf{K}$, the Hamiltonian function has almost always been linearized with respect to consumption $\mathbf{C}$ and investment $\mathbf{I}$ with the investment prices $\mathbf{Q}$ treated as constant. In what follows, we will show that when the maximized current-value Hamiltonian is linearized with respect to the 'right' variables, the resulting expression of comprehensive money NNP has all the welfare properties as the utility NNP, which supports the Solow conjecture that 'properly defined and properly calculated, this year's net national product can always be regarded as this year's interest on society's total stock of capital'.

Following Arrow and Kurz (1970), we can express the optimal control $\mathbf{C}(t)$ in a feedback form such that $\mathbf{C}(t) = \mathbf{C}[\mathbf{K}(t)]$ and the net investment[3] as $\mathbf{I}(t) = \mathbf{I}[\mathbf{C}(t), \mathbf{K}(t)]$, provided that certain regularity conditions are satisfied. The co-state variable is by definition

$$\boldsymbol{\Psi}(t) = \boldsymbol{\Psi}[\mathbf{K}(t)] = \frac{\partial W(\mathbf{K}(t))}{\partial \mathbf{K}(t)}.$$

By inserting these expressions back to the maximized current-value Hamiltonian in (6), we obtain a concentrated maximized current Hamiltonian with respect to capital stocks $\mathbf{K}(t)$

$$\hat{H}(\mathbf{K}) \equiv U(\mathbf{C}(\mathbf{K})) + \boldsymbol{\Psi}(\mathbf{K})\mathbf{I}(\mathbf{C}, \mathbf{K}), \tag{10}$$

where the time argument is suppressed for notational ease.

Now, let us consider a small perturbation in the capital stocks by $\mathrm{d}\mathbf{K}$. The variation in the Hamiltonian value can then be expressed as

$$\begin{aligned} \mathrm{d}\hat{H} &\equiv \left\{ \frac{\partial U}{\partial \mathbf{C}} \frac{\partial \mathbf{C}}{\partial \mathbf{K}} + \boldsymbol{\Psi}(\mathbf{K}) \left[\frac{\partial \mathbf{I}}{\partial \mathbf{K}} + \frac{\partial \mathbf{I}}{\partial \mathbf{C}} \frac{\partial \mathbf{C}}{\partial \mathbf{K}} \right] + \frac{\partial \boldsymbol{\Psi}}{\partial \mathbf{K}} \mathbf{I}(\mathbf{C}, \mathbf{K}) \right\} \mathrm{d}\mathbf{K} \\ &= \left\{ \boldsymbol{\Psi}(\mathbf{K}) \frac{\partial \mathbf{I}}{\partial \mathbf{K}} + \frac{\partial \boldsymbol{\Psi}}{\partial \mathbf{K}} \dot{\mathbf{K}} \right\} \mathrm{d}\mathbf{K} \\ &= \left\{ \frac{\partial H^*}{\partial \mathbf{K}} + \dot{\boldsymbol{\Psi}} \right\} \mathrm{d}\mathbf{K}, \end{aligned} \tag{11}$$

where the second equality follows from the maximum principle

$$\frac{\partial U}{\partial \mathbf{C}} + \boldsymbol{\Psi}(\mathbf{K}) \frac{\partial \mathbf{I}}{\partial \mathbf{C}} = 0$$

and the definition $\dot{\mathbf{K}} = \mathbf{I}(\mathbf{C}, \mathbf{K})$, and the third one is due to the relationships

$$\frac{\partial H^*}{\partial \mathbf{K}} = \boldsymbol{\Psi}(\mathbf{K}) \frac{\partial \mathbf{I}}{\partial \mathbf{K}} \quad \text{and} \quad \frac{\partial \boldsymbol{\Psi}}{\partial \mathbf{K}} \dot{\mathbf{K}} = \frac{\partial \boldsymbol{\Psi}}{\partial \mathbf{K}} \frac{\partial \mathbf{K}}{\partial t} = \dot{\boldsymbol{\Psi}}.$$

Note that while the first term in parenthesis on the third line of (11), $\partial H^*/\partial \mathbf{K}$, corresponds to the marginal own rate of return on capital, the second term $\dot{\boldsymbol{\Psi}}$ captures the capital gain. The sum of them represents the total return on a marginal unit of capital. The partial derivative $\partial H^*/\partial \mathbf{K}$ may be interpreted as the rental price of capital in the sense that the owner would receive that amount if he rents out a unit of his capital during a short time period from t to $t + dt$. However, capital rental is not the only source of income for the owner. If there is a capital appreciation with $\dot{\mathbf{\Psi}} \geq 0$, then the owner would be able to consume more than the rental income without improvising himself, whereas the result will be the opposite in case of capital depreciation.

As such, the sum $(\partial H^*/\partial \mathbf{K}) + \dot{\mathbf{\Psi}}$ in (11) seems to be strongly related to Wicksell's (1936) normal rate of return characterized by the following three properties: (1) it corresponds to the natural rate of interest, (2) it establishes (dynamic competitive) equilibrium between demand and supply of saving, and (3) it is neutral to the price level. To see that the first property holds, one may think of $\partial H^*/\partial \mathbf{K}$ as the dividend from a security and $\dot{\mathbf{\Psi}}$ the capital gain over a short time period. For example, if the dividend to a stock is 2 per cent of the price at the beginning of the period, and the price itself increases by 3 per cent over the period, then the natural rate of return will be 5 per cent. The second property is a natural consequence of the dynamic competitive equilibrium solution (Weitzman 2003). To show that the rate of return is independent of the price level, let us recall the no-arbitrage condition

$$\frac{\partial H^*}{\partial \mathbf{K}} = \theta \mathbf{\Psi} - \dot{\mathbf{\Psi}}$$

along the optimal path, which can be rearranged to be

$$\frac{\partial H^*}{\partial \mathbf{K}} + \dot{\mathbf{\Psi}} = \theta \mathbf{\Psi}.$$

The normal rate of return (or the stationary rate of return) is thus

$$\left(\frac{\partial H^*}{\partial K_i} + \dot{\Psi}_i\right) \bigg/ \Psi_i = \theta \quad \text{for all } i = 1, 2, \ldots, n.$$

The logic here is that when calculating the capital rental $\partial H^*/\partial \mathbf{K}$, one deducts from any capital appreciation or depreciation, but when calculating the normal rate of return, one adds the capital appreciation or depreciation part back. Thus, the normal rate of return is simply θ, which is also equal to Weitzman's (2003) stationary rate of return!

Now, the expression on the third line of (11) may be written as $d\hat{H} = \theta \mathbf{\Psi}\, d\mathbf{K}$ or $d\hat{H} = \theta \lambda \mathbf{Q}\, d\mathbf{K}$, with λ as the marginal utility of income. With no loss of generality, we may normalize λ to unity, and thus obtain $d\hat{H} = \mathbf{R}\, d\mathbf{K} = \theta \mathbf{Q}\, d\mathbf{K}$, where $\mathbf{R} = \theta \mathbf{Q}$ is a vector of normal returns on the various types of capital goods, measured in monetary units. The underlying background total welfare measure can now be expressed as

$$\hat{Y}(t) = \mathbf{R}(t)\mathbf{K}(t), \tag{12}$$

i.e. the total return on capital services over a short time period, partly from capital rental and partly from capital gain. Let $\mathbf{R} = \mathbf{R}_1 + \mathbf{R}_2$, with $\mathbf{R}_1 = \partial H^*/\partial \mathbf{K}$ as the return on capital rental and $\mathbf{R}_2 = \dot{\mathbf{\Psi}}$ as the capital gain part. Then we can decompose $\hat{Y}(t)$ into two parts, i.e. $\hat{Y}(t) = \mathbf{R}_1\mathbf{K} + \mathbf{R}_2\mathbf{K}$. Note that the list of capital goods are considered as comprehensive including human capital, natural resources and environmental externalities in addition to manufactured capital. This means that within the first term $\mathbf{R}_1\mathbf{K}$, there are components such as wages, profits, rental income, and environmental services, the sum of which is the total factor income. What is new here is that in our adjusted comprehensive NNP in (12), we have a second component as the capital gain.

What about the welfare significance of this adjusted comprehensive NNP with capital gains taken into account? Well, it should be exactly the return on comprehensive wealth as defined by Dasgupta and Mäler (2000), i.e.

$$M(t) = \mathbf{Q}(t)\mathbf{K}(\mathbf{t}), \tag{13}$$

where $\mathbf{Q}(t)$ are the accounting prices of capital goods being the present discounted value of future marginal product from an extra unit of capital at time t. Comparing the expressions (12) and (13), we can see that

$$\hat{Y}(t) = \theta M(t) \tag{14}$$

such that the 'properly defined and properly calculated NNP' as expressed by Solow (1992) is exactly equal to the interest on (money) wealth. With such a relationship, NNP growth evaluated at constant prices $\mathbf{R}(t)$ at a given time t also becomes a correct welfare measure for welfare improvement since

$$\left.\frac{\mathrm{d}\hat{Y}(t)}{\mathrm{d}t}\right|_{R(t)=\text{constant}} = \mathbf{R}(t)\dot{\mathbf{K}}(t) \tag{15}$$

corresponds to the interest on genuine investments with $\theta > 0$ (Hamilton and Clemens 1999). For a hypothetical perturbation in the capital stocks $\mathbf{K}(t)$, the welfare effect should also be captured by $\mathrm{d}\hat{Y}(t)|_{R(t)=\text{constant}} = \mathbf{R}(t)\,\mathrm{d}\mathbf{K}(t)$. Why should the price vector $\mathbf{R}(t)$ be held as constant when taking the derivatives? The reason is that this price vector is a *period* rather than a *point* matter in that $\mathbf{R}(t)$ represents the normal rate of return on a unit of capital held *during* the period from the beginning to the end of the period. Thus, for a change in capital stocks or investment *within* the period, the price vector is held constant. Note that we have not deflated our new comprehensive NNP defined in (12) with any price indices, but the result can be readily adapted by replacing the utility rate of discount with the corresponding interest rate if the NNP measure is deflated. As long as such an interest rate has the same sign as the stationary rate θ, the welfare properties will remain the same.

5. AN ILLUSTRATION WITH THE SPACESHIP MODEL

We have chosen to illustrate the idea by working through a simple example used in Weitzman (2000). Consider a spaceship economy with a fixed initial capital stock $k(0) = k_0$. Let the instantaneous utility function be $\ln(c(t))$ and the resource stock dynamics be described by $\dot{k} = -c$, then the dynamic optimization problem can be formulated as

$$\max W(0) = \int_0^\infty \ln(c(t))\, \mathrm{e}^{-\theta t}\, \mathrm{d}t$$

$$\text{s.t. } \dot{k} = -c \quad \text{and} \quad k(0) = k_0. \tag{16}$$

The current-value Hamiltonian is

$$H(t) = \ln(c(t)) + \lambda(t)\dot{k} = \ln(c(t)) - \lambda(t)c(t). \tag{17}$$

The first-order optimality condition tells us that $\lambda(t) = 1/c(t)$, and the co-state equation reads $\dot{\lambda} = \theta\lambda$ or equivalently $\dot{c} = -\theta c$ which can be solved as $c(t) = c_0\, \mathrm{e}^{-\theta t} = \theta k_0\, \mathrm{e}^{-\theta t}$, where $c_0 = \theta k_0$ is the initial level of consumption determined by the total available initial stock. The resource dynamics can now be expressed as $\dot{k}(t) = -c(t) = -\theta k_0\, \mathrm{e}^{-\theta t}$. With the optimal solutions, the maximized current-value Hamiltonian at any time t can be written as

$$\hat{H}(k(t)) = \ln(\theta k(t)) - 1 \tag{18}$$

which is obviously the interest on utility wealth given by

$$\hat{W}(k(t)) = \frac{1}{\theta}\{\ln(\theta k(t)) - 1\}, \tag{19}$$

where $k(t) = k_0 \exp(-\theta t)$.

When linearizing the Hamiltonian (17) with respect to consumption and investment, the resulting NNP would be identically zero such that

$$Y(t) = p(t)c(t) - \lambda(t)c(t) = 0, \tag{20}$$

where the consumption price $p(t) = 1/c(t)$ equals the 'investment' price $\lambda(t)$ in this simple model. Obviously, such a zero NNP value has no welfare significance.

Now, let us linearize the maximized current-value Hamiltonian with respect to $k(t)$, then we have

$$\begin{aligned} \mathrm{d}\hat{H}(t) &= \frac{1}{k(t)}\,\mathrm{d}k(t) \\ &= \theta p(t)\,\mathrm{d}k(t) \end{aligned} \tag{21}$$

which supports the underlying ideal NNP measure

$$\hat{Y}(t) = R(t)k(t) = \theta p(t)k(t) \tag{22}$$

being the interest on wealth as defined by Dasgupta and Mäler (2000) and Arrow et al. (2003) as

$$W(k(t)) = p(t)k(t). \tag{23}$$

Note that the ideal NNP measure in (22) is sensitive to the capital stock. Each unit of capital is valued with the interest on the Hotelling rent. Compared to (20) that corresponds to a zero rental income, the ideal NNP captures the components of both the capital rental and capital gain.

6. CONCLUDING REMARKS

In this chapter, we have attempted to study the classical concepts of economic income in a modern theoretical framework. It has been shown that when adapted to include savings, the Fisher concept of psychic income becomes consistent with the Lindahl definition that income is the sum of 'consumption value' and the value of investment, which also corresponds to the interest on wealth when expressed in utility terms. Under certain assumptions such as constant utility rate of discount and no exogenous technical progress, the Fisher and Lindahl results can also be interpreted as Hicksian income being the maximal consumption that can be consumed now and still expect to consume that much in each enduring week. With exogenous technical progress, then, the Fisher and Lindahl results will be lower than the Hicksian income. To reconcile the concepts, Aronsson et al. (1997) defined an artificial variable as the stock of knowledge, with which the exogenous technical progress becomes an endogenous variable. With certain adaptations, the three classical concepts become consistent to each other as long as they are measured in psychic, i.e. utility, terms.

When it comes to money measures of income, then things have been more complicated. In most cases, economists derive the money measure of income through linearizing the maximized Hamiltonian (utility NNP) and rescaling the resulting expression by the marginal utility of income. With a complete list of the capital goods and services, the expression turns out to be comprehensive (or green) net national product. However, NNP defined as such is in general not the return on capital (Asheim 1997, Dasgupta and Mäler 2001). In this chapter we have shown that while wealth is normally defined in terms of capital stocks, NNP is often defined with respect to consumption and investment. This is the reason that the linearized Hamiltonian as NNP has lost its welfare significance. When all decision variables are expressed in terms of capital stocks, we have shown that the resulting ideal NNP is indeed the return on capital. For such an ideal NNP, we can express it as a Wicksell's 'normal rate of return' on wealth, where both capital rental and capital gain or loss are taken into account.

Turning back to Solow's conjecture, we can conclude that Solow is correct! By the help of the Weitzman spaceship model, we have shown that the ideal NNP, which is the 'normal rate' of return on wealth, is sensitive to the capital stocks, where the total wealth is defined by the product of accounting prices and the capital stocks (Dasgupta and Mäler 2000, Arrow et al. 2003).

ACKNOWLEDGEMENTS

This paper was presented at the 10th Ulvön Anniversary Conference on Environmental Economics and the Karl-Gustaf Löfgren Symposium, Ulvön, Sweden, 16–19 June 2003. The author would like to thank the conference and symposium participants for valuable comments and suggestions. The usual disclaimer applies.

NOTES

1. Throughout this chapter, the expressions 'comprehensive NNP' and 'green NNP' will be used interchangeably.
2. In a recent paper, Asheim and Weitzman (2001) showed that money NNP when deflated with a special Divisia price index can have welfare significance if the corresponding real income is constant.

3. A simple example for the investment variable is $\dot{k} = f(k) - c$ in the single-sector Ramsey growth model.

REFERENCES

Aronsson, T., P.O. Johansson and K.G. Löfgren (1997), *Welfare Measurement, Green NNP and Sustainability: A Growth Theoretical Approach*, Cheltenham, UK and Lyme, USA: Edward Elgar.

Aronsson, T., K.G. Löfgren and K. Backlund (2004), *Welfare Measurement in Imperfect Markets*, Cheltenham, UK and Northampton MA, USA: Edward Elgar.

Arrow, K., P. Dasgupta and K.G. Mäler (2003), 'Evaluating projects and assessing sustainable development in imperfect economies', *Environmental and Resource Economics*, 26, 647–685.

Arrow, K.J. and M. Kurz (1970), *Public Investment, the Rate of Return, and the Optimal Fiscal Policy*, Baltimore, MD: John Hopkin Press.

Asheim, G.B. (1997), 'Adjusting green NNP to measure sustainability', *Scandinavian Journal of Economics*, 99, 355–370.

Asheim, G.B. and M.L. Weitzman (2001), 'Does NNP growth indicate welfare improvement?', *Economic Letters*, 73, 233–239.

Dasgupta, P. and K.G. Mäler (2000), 'Net national product, wealth and social well-being', *Environment and Development Economics*, 5, 69–93.

Dasgupta, P. and K.G. Mäler (2001), 'Wealth as a criterion for sustainable development', *World Economics*, 2, 19–44.

Drèze, J. and N.H. Stern (1987), 'The theory of cost–benefit analysis', in Auerbach and Felstein (eds), *Handbook of Public Economics* (Chapter 14).

Fisher, I. (1906), *The Nature of Capital and Income*, New York: Macmillan.

Hamilton, K. and M. Clemens (1999), 'Genuine saving rates in developing countries', *The World Bank Economic Review*, 13, 333–356.

Heal, G. and B. Kriström (2005), *National Income and the Environment*, in K.G. Mäler and J. Vincent (eds), *Handbook of Environmental Economics*, forthcoming.

Hicks, J.R. (1939), *Value and Capital*, 2nd edn, New York: Oxford University Press.

Kemp, M.C. and N. van Long (1982), 'On the evolution of social income in a dynamic economy: Variations on a Samuelsonian theme', in G.R. Feiwell (ed.), *Samuelson and Neoclassical Economics*, Boston, MA: Kluwer-Nijhoff.

Li, C.Z. and K.G. Löfgren (2002), 'On the choice of metrics in dynamic welfare analysis: Utility versus money measures', Umeå Economic Studies No. 590.

Lindahl, E. (1933), *The Concept of Income. Essay in honor of Gösta Begge*, London: Allan and Unwin.

Löfgren, K.G., T. Aronsson and K. Backlund (2005), 'Resource scarcity, national accounting and growth', in K. Smith (ed.), Washington, DC: Resources for the Future, forthcoming.

Nordhaus, D.N. (1994), 'Reflections on the concept of sustainable economic growth', in L.L. Pasinetti and R.M. Solow (eds), *Economic Growth and the Structure of Long-Term Development*, Oxford: Oxford University Press.

Solow, R. (1992), *An Almost Practical Step Towards Sustainability*, 40th Anniversary Lecture, Washington, DC: Resource for the Future.

Weitzman, M.L. (1976), 'On the welfare significance of national product in a dynamic economy', *Quarterly Journal of Economics*, 90, 156–162.

Weitzman, M.L. (2000), 'The linearized Hamiltonian as comprehensive NDP', *Environment and Development Economics*, 5, 55–68.

Weitzman, M.L. (2001), 'A contribution to the theory of welfare accounting', *Scandinavian Journal of Economics*, 103, 1–24.

Weitzman, M.L. (2003), *Income, Capital, and the Maximum Principle*, Cambridge, MA: Harvard University Press.

Weitzman, M.L. and K.G. Löfgren (1997), 'On the welfare significance of green accounting as taught by parable', *Journal of Environmental Economics and Management*, 32, 139–153.

Wicksell, K. (1936), *Interest and Prices*, London: Macmillan [original edition in German *Geldzins und Güterpreise*, 1898].

World Commission (1987), *Our Common Future*, Oxford University Press.

4. Consumer Demand with Several Linear Constraints: A Global Analysis

W. Michael Hanemann

1. INTRODUCTION

Economists sometimes find themselves in the position of having to extend the neoclassical model of consumer demand to settings where, in addition to the conventional budget constraint, there are one or more additional linear constraints that restrict the consumer's utility maximization problem. Examples include point rationing (Tobin and Houthakker 1950–1951, Tobin 1952); models of time allocation where the time constraint cannot be collapsed into the budget constraint (de Serpa 1971, de Donnea 1972, McConnell 1975, Lyon 1978, Larson and Shaikh 2001); and multi-period portfolio allocation problems (Diamond and Yaari 1972). Without exception, the existing literature has focused on differential properties of the resulting demand functions, i.e. issues such as the effect of rationing on demand elasticities, the Le Chatelier–Samuelson Theorem, the generalization of the Hick–Slutsky decomposition, and other comparative static results (see Kusumoto 1976, Chichilnisky and Kalman 1978, Hatta 1980, Wan 1981, and the references cited above). By employing some 'tricks with utility functions' in the spirit of Gorman (1976), I am able to obtain a *global* characterization of these demand functions.[1] Specifically, I develop an algorithm for deriving the demand functions that apply when there are *M* linear constraints from those that apply when there is only a single constraint. The algorithm permits one to derive all of the existing comparative static results in a simple and compact manner. It also has some value for empirical demand analysis, because it shows how to compute the demand functions associated with maximization problems involving multiple linear constraint based on direct or indirect utility functions associated with known conventional demand functions.

The chapter is organized as follows. Section 2 presents some preliminary results which are needed for the main analysis, but are also of interest as 'tricks' in their own right. Section 3 considers the utility maximization problem with two linear constraints, summarizes the existing comparative static results, develops the new Global Representation Theorem, and shows how this can be used to derive and sharpen the existing comparative static results. Section 4 considers a utility maximization problem with three linear constraints and develops the analogous Global Representation Theorem for the solution to this problem in terms of known demand functions associated with a conventional single-constraint problem; the results developed here provide the basis for extension to problems involving more than three linear constraints. Section 5 offers some concluding observations.

2. PRELIMINARIES

Consider the conventional utility maximization problem

$$\underset{x_1,\ldots,x_N}{\text{maximize}}\ u(x) \qquad \text{s.t.} \sum_1^N p_i x_i = y, \tag{1}$$

where $u(x)$ is a conventional neoclassical utility function, i.e. twice continuously differentiable, increasing and strictly quasi-concave. Let $x_i = h^i(p, y), i = 1, \ldots, N$, be the ordinary demand functions associated with (1) and let $v(p, y)$ be the corresponding indirect utility function. Next consider a utility maximization problem like (1) but involving a different utility function, denoted $\tilde{u}(x)$, which however is related to $u(x)$ as specified in (2b). This utility maximization is:

$$\underset{x_1,\ldots,x_N}{\text{maximize}}\ \tilde{u}(x) \qquad \text{s.t.} \sum_1^N p_i x_i = y, \tag{2a}$$

where

$$\tilde{u}(x) = u\left(x_1, \ldots, x_{N-1}, x_N - \sum_1^{N-1} \psi_j x_j\right) \tag{2b}$$

for an arbitrary set of constants $\psi_1, \ldots, \psi_{N-1}$. Let $x_i = \tilde{h}^i(p, y), i = 1, \ldots, N$, be the ordinary demand functions corresponding to (2a, b) and let $\tilde{v}(p, y)$ be the corresponding indirect utility function. The relationship between the demand functions and indirect utility function associated with (1) and those associated with (2a, b) is given in the following lemma, which is proved in the Appendix:

LEMMA 1. *The two sets of demand and indirect utility functions satisfy*

$$\tilde{v}(p_1, \dots, p_N, y) = v[p_1 + p_N\psi_1, \dots, p_{N-1} + p_N\psi_{N-1}, p_N, y], \quad (3a)$$

$$\tilde{h}^i(p_1, \dots, p_N, y)$$
$$= h^i[p_1 + p_N\psi_1, \dots, p_{N-1} + p_N\psi_{N-1}, p_N, y],$$
$$i = 1, \dots, N_1, \quad (3b)$$

$$\tilde{h}^N(p_1, \dots, p_N, y)$$
$$= h^N[p_1 + p_N\psi_1, \dots, p_{N-1} + p_N\psi_{N-1}, p_N, y]$$
$$+ \sum_1^{N-1} \psi_j h^j[p_1 + p_N\psi_1, \dots, p_{N-1} + p_N\psi_{N-1}, p_N, y]. \quad (3c)$$

Now consider the utility maximization problem

$$\underset{x_1,\dots,x_N}{\text{maximize}}\ u(x, z) \quad \text{s.t.} \sum_1^N p_i x_i = y, \quad z \text{ fixed}, \quad (4a)$$

where in general z is a vector and $u(\cdot)$ has the conventional properties with respect to (x, z). Let $x_i = \hat{h}^i(p, z, y)$, $i = 1, \dots, N$ be the ordinary demand functions associated with (4a) and $\hat{v}(p, z, y)$ the corresponding indirect utility function. A different but related utility maximization is

$$\underset{x_1,\dots,x_N}{\text{maximize}}\ u(x, z) \quad \text{s.t.} \sum_1^N p_i x_i + \sum_i^M q_j z_j = y, \quad (4b)$$

where the q_j's are the prices of the z_j's. The solution to (4b) involves two sets of ordinary demand functions, $x_i = h_i^x(p, q, y)$, $i = 1, \dots, N$ and $z_j = h_j^z(p, q, y)$, $j = 1, \dots, M$, and an indirect utility function $v(p, q, y)$. The relation between the demand functions and indirect utility functions associated with (4a) and (4b) is as follows:

LEMMA 2. *Given* (p, z, y), *define the functions* $\hat{q}_j(p, z, y)$, $j = 1, \dots, M$ *to be the solution to*

$$z_j = h_j^z\left(p, \hat{q}, y + \sum \hat{q}_j z_j\right), \quad j = 1, \dots, M. \quad (5)$$

Then,

$$\hat{v}(p, z, y) = v\left(p, \hat{q}, y + \sum \hat{q}_j z_j\right), \quad (6a)$$

$$\hat{h}^i(p, z, y) = h_i^x\left(p, \hat{q}, y + \sum \hat{q}_j z_j\right), \quad i = 1, \ldots, N. \tag{6b}$$

The proof is contained in the Appendix. Given these preliminary results, I now turn to the main analysis.

3. TWO LINEAR CONSTRAINTS

The maximization in (1) is a conventional problem with a single linear constraint. I now consider what happens when there are two linear constraints:

$$\underset{x}{\text{maximize}}\ u(x) \quad \text{s.t.} \sum_1^N p_i x_i = y \quad \text{and} \sum_1^N w_i x_i = t, \tag{7}$$

where $u(x)$ is the same utility function as in (1), and $N > 2$. Let $x_i = \bar{h}^i(p, w, y, t)$, $i = 1, \ldots, N$, be the ordinary demand functions associated with (7) and $\bar{v}(p, w, y, t)$ the corresponding indirect utility function. The question to be addressed here is: what is the relationship between the demand functions and the indirect utility function associated with (7) and those associated with (1)? Specifically, if we know the formulas for $v(p, y)$ and $h^i(p, y)$ that solve (1), can we directly write down the formulas for $\bar{v}(p, w, y, t)$ and $\bar{h}^i(p, w, y, t)$ in (7)?

Before giving the answer, it is useful to set down what *is* known about the functions associated with (7). The following results are derived in Diamond and Yaari (1972) and Lyon (1978), and parallel the conventional properties associated with the solution to (1):

PROPOSITION 1.

(a) $\bar{v}(\cdot)$ *is quasiconvex and homogenous of degree zero in* (p, y).

(b) $\bar{v}(\cdot)$ *is quasiconvex and homogenous of degree zero in* (w, t).

(c) $\bar{v}(\cdot)$ *is decreasing in* (p, w) *and increasing in* (y, t).

(d) $\bar{h}^i(\cdot)$ *is homogenous of degree zero in* (p, y) *and also in* (w, t).

(e) *Roy's Identity*

$$\frac{\partial \bar{v}/\partial p_i}{\partial \bar{v}/\partial y} = \frac{\partial \bar{v}/\partial w_i}{\partial \bar{v}/\partial t} = -\bar{h}^i(p, w, y, t), \quad i = 1, \ldots, N. \tag{8}$$

Note that the last result may be rearranged into the form

$$\frac{\partial\bar{v}/\partial p_i}{\partial\bar{v}/\partial w_i} = \frac{\partial\bar{v}/\partial y}{\partial\bar{v}/\partial t}, \quad i = 1, \dots N, \tag{9}$$

which can be regarded as a set of restrictions on functional forms eligible to serve as indirect utility functions. The differential properties of the ordinary demand functions are as follows:

PROPOSITION 2.

(a) $\dfrac{\partial\bar{h}^i}{\partial p_j} = \dfrac{\partial x_i}{\partial p_j}\bigg|_{\text{compensated}} - x_j\dfrac{\partial\bar{h}^i}{\partial y}, \quad i, j = 1, \dots, N.$

(b) $\dfrac{\partial\bar{h}^i}{\partial w_j} = \dfrac{\partial x_i}{\partial w_j}\bigg|_{\text{compensated}} - x_j\dfrac{\partial\bar{h}^i}{\partial t}, \quad i, j = 1, \dots, N.$

Define the $(N \times N)$ *matrices* $\bar{S}^p$ *and* $\bar{S}^w$ *with typical elements*

$$\bar{S}^p_{ij} \equiv \frac{\partial\bar{h}^i}{\partial p_j} + x_j\frac{\partial\bar{h}^i}{\partial y} \quad \text{and} \quad \bar{S}^w_{ij} \equiv \frac{\partial\bar{h}^i}{\partial w_j} + x_j\frac{\partial\bar{h}^i}{\partial t}. \tag{10}$$

(c) $\bar{S}^p$ *and* $\bar{S}^w$ *are each symmetric, so that* $\bar{S}^p_{ij} = \bar{S}^p_{ji}$ *and* $\bar{S}^w_{ij} = \bar{S}^w_{ji}$.

(d) $\bar{S}^p$ *and* $\bar{S}^w$ *are each negative semi-definite, so that* $\bar{S}^p_{ii} \leq 0$ *and* $\bar{S}^w_{ii} \leq 0$.

(e) $\dfrac{\partial\bar{v}}{\partial t}\bar{S}^p_{ij} = \dfrac{\partial\bar{v}}{\partial y}\bar{S}^w_{ji}, \quad i, j = 1, \dots, N.$

Parts (a) and (b) follow from Theorem 2 in Chichilnisky and Kalman (1978). In part (a) the compensation is performed by adjusting y so as to maintain $u(x)$ constant, while in part (b) the compensation is performed by adjusting t. Parts (c), (d), and (e) can be obtained by manipulating Roy's Identity (8) or, alternatively, by specializing the comparative static results in Theorems 6 and 7 of Hatta (1980) and Theorem 1 of Wan (1981).

In order to obtain the global characterization of the functions $\bar{h}^i(\cdot)$ and $\bar{v}(\cdot)$, I first solve the second constraint in (7) for one of the x's – say, x_N – as a function of all the others

$$x_N = \frac{t}{w_N} - \sum_{1}^{N-1}\frac{w_i}{w_N}x_i \tag{11}$$

and substitute this into the first constraint in (7) to obtain

$$\sum_{1}^{N-1}\left(p_i - p_N\frac{w_i}{w_N}\right)x_i = y - p_N\frac{t}{w_N}. \tag{12}$$

Now consider the following utility maximization problem with a *single* constraint

$$\begin{aligned} &\underset{x_1,\ldots,x_{N-1}}{\text{maximize}}\; u\left[x_1,\ldots,x_{N-1},\frac{t}{w_N}-\sum_{1}^{N-1}\frac{w_i}{w_N}x_i\right] \\ &\text{s.t.} \sum_{1}^{N-1}\left(p_i - p_N\frac{w_i}{w_N}\right)x_i = y - p_N\frac{t}{w_N} \end{aligned} \tag{P}$$

and denote the resulting ordinary demand functions $x_i = h_i^*(p, w, y, t)$, $i = 1, \ldots, N-1$ and the corresponding indirect utility function $u = v^*(p, w, y, t)$. If one defines the function $h_N^*(\cdot)$ by

$$h_N^*(p, w, y, t) = \frac{t}{w_N} - \sum_{1}^{N-1}\frac{w_i}{w_N}h_i^*(p, w, t, y) \tag{13}$$

and compares (7) with (P), it is clear that the two problems are equivalent, i.e.,

$$\begin{aligned} \bar{v}(p, w, y, t) &\equiv v^*(p, w, y, t), \\ \bar{h}^i(p, w, y, t) &\equiv h_i^*(p, w, y, t), \quad i = 1, \ldots, N. \end{aligned} \tag{14}$$

It is necessary, therefore, to establish a relationship between the solutions to (P) and to (1). For this purpose, I introduce a fourth utility maximization problem

$$\begin{aligned} &\underset{x_1,\ldots,x_{N-1},z}{\text{maximize}}\; u\left[x_1,\ldots,x_{N-1},z-\sum_{1}^{N-1}\frac{w_i}{w_N}x_i\right] \\ &\text{s.t.} \sum_{1}^{N-1}\left(p_i - p_N\frac{w_i}{w_N}\right)x_i + qz = y - p_N\frac{t}{w_N} \end{aligned} \tag{D}$$

with solutions $x_i = \tilde{h}^i(p, w, q, y, t)$, $i = 1, \ldots, N-1$ and $z = \tilde{h}^N(p, w, q, y, t)$ and associated indirect utility function $\tilde{v}(p, w, q, y, t)$. One can now use Lemma 1 to compare problem (D) with (1) and obtain a relationship between $[\tilde{h}(\cdot), \tilde{v}(\cdot)]$ and $[h(\cdot), v(\cdot)]$. Then, one can use

Lemma 2 to compare problem (P) with (D) and obtain a relationship between $[h^*(\cdot), v^*(\cdot)]$ and $[\tilde{h}(\cdot), \tilde{v}(\cdot)]$. In this way, one can compare (P) with (1) and obtain the desired relationship between $[\bar{h}(\cdot), \bar{v}(\cdot)]$ and $[h(\cdot), v(\cdot)]$.

Applying Lemma 1 to (D) and setting $\psi_i = w_i/w_N$ yields the following solutions for the indirect utility and ordinary demand functions:

$$\begin{aligned}\tilde{v}(p, w, q, y, t) = v\Bigg[&\left(p_1 + (q - p_N)\frac{w_1}{w_N}\right), \ldots, \\ &\left(p_{N-1} + (q - p_N)\frac{w_{N-1}}{w_N}\right), q, y - p_N\frac{t}{w_N}\Bigg],\end{aligned} \tag{15a}$$

$$\begin{aligned}\tilde{h}^i(p, w, q, y, t) = h^i\Bigg[&\left(p_1 + (q - p_N)\frac{w_1}{w_N}\right), \ldots, \\ &\left(p_{N-1} + (q - p_N)\frac{w_{N-1}}{w_N}\right), q, y - p_N\frac{t}{w_N}\Bigg], \\ &i = 1, \ldots, N-1,\end{aligned} \tag{15b}$$

$$\begin{aligned}\tilde{h}^N(p, w, q, y, t) = h^N\Bigg[&\left(p_1 + (q - p_N)\frac{w_1}{w_N}\right), \ldots, \\ &\left(p_{N-1} + (q - p_N)\frac{w_{N-1}}{w_N}\right), q, y - p_N\frac{t}{w_N}\Bigg] \\ &+ \sum_1^{N-1}\frac{w_i}{w_N}h^i\Bigg[\left(p_1 + (q - p_N)\frac{w_1}{w_N}\right), \ldots, \\ &\left(p_{N-1} + (q - p_N)\frac{w_{N-1}}{w_N}\right), q, y - p_N\frac{t}{w_N}\Bigg].\end{aligned} \tag{15c}$$

Next, applying Lemma 2, one observes that, if the quantity $\bar{q}$ satisfies

$$\frac{t}{w_N} = \tilde{h}^N\left(p, w, \bar{q}, y + \bar{q}\frac{t}{w_N}, t\right), \tag{16}$$

then

$$h_i^*(p, w, y, t) = \tilde{h}^i\left(p, w, \bar{q}, y + \bar{q}\frac{t}{w_N}, t\right), \quad i = 1, \ldots, N-1 \tag{17a}$$

and

$$v^*(p, w, y, t) = \tilde{v}\left(p, w, \bar{q}, y + \bar{q}\frac{t}{w_N}, t\right). \tag{17b}$$

Substituting (15c) into (16) and multiplying through by w_N yields an equivalent expression which implicitly defines the function $\bar{q} = \bar{q}(p, w, y, t)$:

$$t = \sum_{1}^{N} w_i h^i \left[\left(p_1 + (\bar{q} - p_N)\frac{w_1}{w_N} \right), \ldots, \left(p_{N-1} + (\bar{q} - p_N)\frac{w_{N-1}}{w_N} \right), \bar{q}, y + (\bar{q} - p_N)\frac{t}{w_N} \right]. \tag{18}$$

Combining (13), (14), (15) and (17) completes the proof of the following theorem:

GLOBAL REPRESENTATION THEOREM. *Let $\bar{q}(p, w, y, t)$ satisfy (18). Then,*

$$\bar{h}^i(p, w, y, t) = h^i \left[\left(p_1 + (\bar{q} - p_N)\frac{w_1}{w_N} \right), \ldots, \left(p_{N-1} + (\bar{q} - p_N)\frac{w_{N-1}}{w_N} \right), \bar{q}, y + (\bar{q} - p_N)\frac{t}{w_N} \right], \quad i = 1, \ldots, N, \tag{19a}$$

$$\bar{v}(p, w, y, t) = v \left[\left(p_1 + (\bar{q} - p_N)\frac{w_1}{w_N} \right), \ldots, \left(p_{N-1} + (p - p_N)\frac{w_{N-1}}{w_N} \right), \bar{q}, y + (\bar{q} - p_N)\frac{t}{w_N} \right]. \tag{19b}$$

This is the desired global representation of the solution to (7).[2] A convenient simplification of this representation is obtained by introducing

$$\theta(p, w, y, t) \equiv \frac{[\bar{q}(p, w, y, t) - p_N]}{w_N}. \tag{20}$$

Making the corresponding substitution in (18), $\theta(\cdot)$ is defined implicitly by

$$t = \sum_{1}^{N} w_i h^i (p_1 + \theta w_1, \ldots, p_N + \theta w_N, y + \theta t). \tag{18'}$$

Using $\theta(p, w, y, t)$, the representation in (19a, b) becomes

$$\begin{aligned} x_i &= \bar{h}^i(p, w, y, t) \\ &= h^i(p_1 + \theta w_1, \ldots, p_N + \theta w_N, y + \theta t), \quad i = 1, \ldots, N, \end{aligned} \tag{19'a}$$

$$u = \bar{v}(p, w, y, t) = v(p_1 + \theta w_1, \ldots, p_N + \theta w_N, y + \theta t). \tag{19'b}$$

The theorem leads to the following algorithm for constructing the solution to the dual linear constraint problem (7) using known solutions to (1):

ALGORITHM.

Step 1: Take a system of demand functions $h^i(p, y)$ that is known to solve (1), and solve (18′) for $\theta = \theta(p, w, y, t)$.

Step 2: Combine $\theta(p, w, y, t)$ with $h^i(p, y)$ and $v(p, y)$ as indicated in (19′a, b) to obtain the demand system and indirect utility function associated with the solution to (7).

Note that an explicit representation of the direct utility function involved in (1) and (7) is *not* required. One can start out with an indirect utility function $v(p, y)$ at:

Step 0: Apply Roy's Identity to $v(p, y)$ to obtain the demand system $h^i(p, y)$.

Several observations about this result should be noted. First, if for some (p', w', y', t') the second constraint in (7) is not separately binding – i.e., $\sum w_i' h^i(p', y')$ – then it follows from (18) that

$$\bar{q}(p', w', y', t') = p_N' \tag{21a}$$

and

$$\theta(p', w', y', t') = 0. \tag{21b}$$

Moreover, by differentiating (18), it can be shown that, in the vicinity of this point,

$$\frac{\partial \bar{q}(p', w', y', t')}{\partial t} < 0. \tag{21c}$$

Otherwise, however, $\bar{q} \neq p_N$, $\theta > 0$, and the result in (21c) does not necessarily apply. The interpretation of $\theta(p, w, y, t)$ will become evident below.

Second, the global representation in (19a, b) or (19′a, b) can be used to derive all of the results in Propositions 1 and 2. For example, it is trivial to verify the adding up conditions, $\sum p_i \bar{h}^i(\cdot) = y$ and $\sum w_i \bar{h}^i(\cdot) = t$. Given the homogeneity properties of $v(\cdot)$ and $h^i(\cdot)$, (18) implies that $\bar{q}(p, w, y, t)$ is homogenous of degree 1 in (p, y) and degree 0 in (w, t); it follows from (21) that $\theta(p, w, y, t)$ is homogenous of degree 1 in (p, y) and degree -1 in (w, t). From (19a, b) or (19′a, b), this ensures the homogeneity of $\bar{v}(\cdot)$ and $\bar{h}^i(\cdot)$. Similarly, the quasiconvexity of $v(\cdot)$ implies that $\bar{v}(\cdot)$ is quasiconvex in (p, y) and (w, t). Straightforward differentiation of (18) and (19) yields Roy's Identity, from which the negative semi-definiteness and symmetry conditions in parts (c)–(e) of Proposition 2 may be deduced.

It is instructive to derive parts (c)–(e) of Proposition 2 directly from the Global Representation Theorem. Denote the Slutsky terms associated with the demand functions $h^i(\cdot)$ by

$$S_{ij}(p, y) \equiv \frac{\partial h^i(p, y)}{\partial p_j} + h^j(p, y)\frac{\partial h^i(p, y)}{\partial y}, \tag{22}$$

whereas, as noted in (10), those associated with the demand functions $\bar{h}^i(\cdot)$ are given by

$$\bar{S}^p_{ij}(p, w, y, t) \equiv \frac{\partial \bar{h}^i(p, w, y, t)}{\partial p_j} + \bar{h}^i(p, w, y, t)\frac{\partial \bar{h}^i(p, w, y, t)}{\partial y}. \tag{23}$$

Differentiation of (19′a) yields the following relationships linking the derivatives of $\bar{h}^i(\cdot)$ with respect to p_j and y to those of $h^i(\cdot)$:

$$\begin{aligned}\frac{\partial \bar{h}^i(p, w, y, t)}{\partial p_j} &= \frac{\partial h^i(\pi, \eta)}{\partial p_j} + \\ &+ \left[\sum w_k \frac{\partial h^i(\pi, \eta)}{\partial p_k} + t\frac{\partial h^i(\pi, \eta)}{\partial y}\right]\frac{\partial \theta}{\partial p_j},\end{aligned} \tag{24a}$$

$$\begin{aligned}\frac{\partial \bar{h}^i(p, w, y, t)}{\partial y} &= \frac{\partial h^i(\pi, \eta)}{\partial y} + \\ &+ \left[\sum w_k \frac{\partial h^i(\pi, \eta)}{\partial p_k} + t\frac{\partial h^i(\pi, \eta)}{\partial y}\right]\frac{\partial \theta}{\partial y},\end{aligned} \tag{24b}$$

where $\pi_i \equiv p_i + \theta w_i$, $i = 1, \ldots, N$, and $\eta \equiv y + \theta t$. Hence,

$$\bar{S}^p_{ij}(p, w, y, t) = S_{ij}(\pi, \eta) + \tag{25}$$

$$+\left[\sum w_k \frac{\partial h^i(\pi,\eta)}{\partial p_k} + t\frac{\partial h^i(\pi,\eta)}{\partial y}\right]\left[\frac{\partial \theta}{\partial p_j} + x_j \frac{\partial \theta}{\partial y}\right].$$

By using (18′), one obtains:

$$\begin{aligned}
&\left[\sum w_k \frac{\partial h^i(\pi,\eta)}{\partial p_k} + t\frac{\partial h^i(\pi,\eta)}{\partial y}\right] \\
&\quad = \left[\sum w_k \frac{\partial h^i(\pi,\eta)}{\partial p_k} + \sum w_k x_k \frac{\partial h^i(\pi,\eta)}{\partial y}\right] \\
&\quad = \sum w_j \left(\frac{\partial h^i(\pi,\eta)}{\partial p_j} + x_j \frac{\partial h^i(\pi,\eta)}{\partial y}\right) \\
&\quad = \sum w_j S_{ij}(\pi,\eta).
\end{aligned} \tag{26}$$

Implicit differentiation of (18′) yields:

$$\left[\frac{\partial \theta}{\partial p_j} + x_j \frac{\partial \theta}{\partial y}\right] = -\frac{1}{\Delta}\left[\sum w_i \frac{\partial h^i(\pi,\eta)}{\partial p_j} + x_j \sum w_i \frac{\partial h^i(\pi,\eta)}{\partial y}\right]$$

$$= -\frac{1}{\Delta}\sum w_i S_{ij}(\pi,\eta), \tag{27}$$

where

$$\Delta \equiv \sum\sum w_i w_j S_{ij}(\pi,\eta) \leq 0. \tag{28}$$

Substituting (26) and (27) into (25) yields the formula for one set of Slutsky terms associated with (7):

$$\bar{S}^p_{ij}(p,w,y,t) = S_{ij}(\pi,\eta) - \frac{\left[\sum w_j S_{ij}(\pi,\eta)\right]\left[\sum w_i S_{ij}(\pi,\eta)\right]}{\Delta}, \tag{29}$$

with $i, j = 1, \ldots, N$. From (29), it follows that $\bar{S}^p$ is symmetric and negative semi-definite. Similarly, from (19′a)

$$\frac{\partial \bar{h}^i(p,w,y,t)}{\partial w_j} = \theta \frac{\partial h^i(\pi,\eta)}{\partial p_j} + \tag{30a}$$

$$+\left[\sum w_k \frac{\partial h^i(\pi,\eta)}{\partial p_k} + t\frac{\partial h^i(\pi,\eta)}{\partial y}\right]\frac{\partial \theta}{\partial w_j},$$

$$\frac{\partial \bar{h}^i(p, w, y, t)}{\partial t} = \theta \frac{\partial h^i(\pi, \eta)}{\partial y} + \left[\sum w_k \frac{\partial h^i(\pi, \eta)}{\partial p_k} + t \frac{\partial h^i(\pi, \eta)}{\partial y}\right] \frac{\partial \theta}{\partial t}, \tag{30b}$$

and, from implicit differentiation of (18′),

$$\left[\frac{\partial \theta}{\partial w_j} + x_j \frac{\partial \theta}{\partial t}\right] = -\frac{1}{\Delta}\left[x_j + \sum w_i \frac{\partial h^i(\pi, \eta)}{\partial p_j}\theta - x_j + x_j \sum w_i \frac{\partial h^i(\pi, \eta)}{\partial y}\theta\right] = -\frac{\theta}{\Delta}\sum w_i S_{ij}(\pi, \eta). \tag{31}$$

Hence,

$$\bar{S}^w_{ij}(p, w, y, t) = \theta \bar{S}^p_{ij}(p, w, y, t), \quad i, j = 1, \ldots, N. \tag{32}$$

From this it follows that $\bar{S}^w$ is symmetric and negative semi-definite, which completes the derivation of parts (c) and (d) of Proposition 2.

With regard to part (e) of Proposition 2, differentiation of (19′b) yields

$$\frac{\partial \bar{v}(p, w, y, t)}{\partial t} = \theta \frac{\partial v(\pi, \eta)}{\partial y} + \left[\sum w_j \frac{\partial v(\pi, \eta)}{\partial p_j} + t \frac{\partial v(\pi, \eta)}{\partial y}\right] \frac{\partial \theta}{\partial t}, \tag{33a}$$

$$\frac{\partial \bar{v}(p, w, y, t)}{\partial y} = \frac{\partial v(\pi, \eta)}{\partial y} + \left[\sum w_j \frac{\partial v(\pi, \eta)}{\partial p_j} + t \frac{\partial v(\pi, \eta)}{\partial y}\right] \frac{\partial \theta}{\partial y}, \tag{33b}$$

However, using Roy's Identity

$$\left[\sum w_j \frac{\partial v(\pi, \eta)}{\partial p_j} + t \frac{\partial v(\pi, \eta)}{\partial y}\right] = \left[\sum w_j \frac{\partial v(\pi, \eta)}{\partial p_j} + \sum w_j x_j \frac{\partial v(\pi, \eta)}{\partial y}\right]$$

$$= \left[\sum w_j \frac{\partial v(\pi, \eta)}{\partial p_j} - \sum w_j \left(\frac{\partial v(\pi, \eta)/\partial p_j}{\partial v(\pi, \eta)/\partial y}\right) \frac{\partial v(\pi, \eta)}{\partial y}\right]$$

$$= 0.$$

Hence,

$$\theta(p, w, y, t) = \frac{\partial \bar{v}(p, w, y, t)}{\partial t} \Big/ \frac{\partial \bar{v}(p, w, y, t)}{\partial y}, \tag{34}$$

which provides an interpretation of θ and a proof that $\theta \geq 0$. Combining (34) with (32) yields part (e) of Proposition 2.

Third, it is important to recognize that, while θ is a function of (p, w, y, t), it is not an arbitrary function of these variables since it is required to satisfy the homogeneity properties noted above.[3] In addition, (27) and (31) imply restrictions on the derivatives of $\theta(p, w, y, t)$.

Fourth, setting $i = j$ in (29) yields a version of the Strong Le Chatelier–Samuelson Principle:

PROPOSITION 3. *For every* $i = 1, \ldots, N$,

$$\bar{S}^p_{ij}(p, w, y, t) = S_{ij}(\pi, \eta) - \frac{\left[\sum w_1 S_{i1}(\pi, \eta)\right]^2}{\Delta} \geq S_{ij}(\pi, \eta).$$

Thus, including the second set of constraints in (7) makes the own price derivative of the compensated demand function for x_i smaller in absolute value than when it is omitted. This result is stronger than Hatta's Theorem 8 for general, nonlinear constraints because that yields a Le Chatelier–Samuelson inequality holding only at the vector (p', w', y', t') which satisfies (21a). Proposition 3 shows that, in the case of linear constraints, this inequality holds generally – the own price derivative of the compensated demand function for x_i is smaller in absolute value when the second constraint is added to (7) than when it is omitted.

4. THREE LINEAR CONSTRAINTS

I now consider what happens when the maximization problem involves three linear constraints:

$$\underset{x}{\text{maximize}}\ u(x) \quad \text{s.t.} \sum p_i x_i = y, \quad \sum w_i x_i = t \quad \text{and} \quad \sum c_i x_i = k, \tag{35}$$

where $u(x)$ is the same utility function as in (1) and $N > 3$. Let $x_i = \bar{h}^i(p, w, c, y, t, k)$, $i = 1, \ldots, N$, denote the ordinary demand functions associated with (35), and let $\bar{v}(p, w, c, y, t, k)$ be the corresponding indirect utility function; as before the demand functions and indirect utility function associated with the single-constraint problem, (1), are denoted by $x_i = h^i(p, y)$ and $v(p, y)$.

To simplify (35), one uses the second and third constraints to solve for two of the x's – say, x_{N-1} and x_N – as functions of the others, yielding:

$$x_{N-1} = \frac{\alpha_{kt}}{\alpha_{N-1}} - \sum_{1}^{N-2} \frac{\alpha_i}{\alpha_{N-1}} x_i,$$

$$x_N = \frac{\beta_{kt}}{\beta_N} - \sum_{1}^{N-2} \frac{\beta_i}{\beta_N} x_i, \tag{36}$$

where

$$\alpha_i \equiv w_i c_N - w_N c_i, \quad \alpha_{kt} \equiv t c_N - w_N k,$$

$$\beta_i \equiv w_{N-1} c_i - w_i c_{N-1}, \quad \beta_{kt} \equiv w_{N-1} k - t c_{N-1}. \tag{37}$$

For future reference, note that

$$\alpha_{N-1} = \beta_N \quad \text{and} \quad \alpha_N = \beta_{N-1} = 0. \tag{37'}$$

Substituting these expressions for x_{N-1} and x_N into the utility function and the first budget constraint in (35) yields the following maximization problem with respect to the remaining variables $x_1, \ldots, x_{N-2}$

$$\underset{x_1,\ldots,x_{N-2}}{\text{maximize}}\ u\left[x_1, \ldots, x_{N-2}, \frac{\alpha_{kt}}{\alpha_{N-1}} - \sum_{1}^{N-2} \frac{\alpha_i}{\alpha_{N-1}} x_i, \frac{\beta_{kt}}{\beta_N} - \sum_{1}^{N-2} \frac{\beta_i}{\partial \beta_N} x_i\right]$$

$$\text{s.t.} \sum_{1}^{N-2} \pi_i x_i = y - \Gamma, \tag{38}$$

where

$$\pi_i \equiv p_i - \frac{p_{N-1}\alpha_i}{\alpha_{N-1}} - \frac{p_N \beta_i}{\beta_N} \quad \text{and} \quad \Gamma \equiv \frac{p_{N-1}\alpha_{kt}}{\alpha_{N-1}} + \frac{p_N \beta_{kt}}{\beta_N}.$$

Solving the maximization in (35) is equivalent to first solving the maximization in (38) and then substituting the resulting demand functions for

$x_1, \ldots, x_{N-2}$ into (36) to obtain the corresponding demand functions for x_{N-1} and x_N.

Next, I consider a utility maximization similar to (38), but with two extra choice variables and two extra prices

$$\underset{x_1,\ldots,x_{N-2},z_1,z_2}{\text{maximize}} \; u\left[x_1, \ldots, x_{N-2}, z_1 - \sum_1^{N-2} \frac{\alpha_i}{\alpha_{N-1}} x_i, z_2 - \sum_1^{N-2} \frac{\beta_i}{\beta_N} x_i\right]$$

$$\text{s.t.} \sum_1^{N-2} \pi_i x_i + q_1 z_1 + q_2 z_2 = y - \Gamma, \tag{39}$$

where π_i and Γ are the same as in (38). The solution to this maximization will be denoted $x_i = \tilde{h}^i(\cdot)$, $i = 1, \ldots, N-2$, $z_1 = \tilde{h}^{N-1}(\cdot)$, $z_2 = \tilde{h}^N(\cdot)$, and $u = \tilde{v}(\cdot)$. In order to compare the solution to (39) with that of (1), the following extension of Lemma 1 is required:[4]

LEMMA 3. *Let $x_i = \tilde{h}^i(p, y)$, $i = 1, \ldots, N$, and $\tilde{v}(p, y)$ be the ordinary demand functions and indirect utility function corresponding to the following utility maximization:*

$$\underset{x}{\text{maximize}} \; \tilde{u}(x) \equiv u\left(x_1, \ldots, x_{N-2}, x_{N-1} - \sum_1^{N-2} \varphi_j x_j, x_N - \sum_1^{N-2} \mu_j x_j\right)$$

$$\text{s.t.} \sum_1^{N} p_i x_i = y, \tag{40}$$

where $u(\cdot)$ is the same utility function as in (1). These functions are related to the ordinary demand functions and indirect utility functions associated with (1), $x_i = h^i(p, y)$ and $v(p, y)$, as follows:

$$\tilde{v}(p_1, \ldots, p_N, y) = v(\tau_1, \ldots, \tau_{N-2}, p_{N-1}, p_N, y), \tag{41a}$$

$$\tilde{h}^i(p_1, \ldots, p_N, y) = h^i(\tau_1, \ldots, \tau_{N-2}, p_{N-1}, p_N, y), \quad i = 1, \ldots, N-2, \tag{41b}$$

$$\tilde{h}^{N-1}(p_1, \ldots, p_N, y) = h^{N-1}(\tau_1, \ldots, \tau_{N-2}, p_{N-1}, p_N, y) + \\ + \sum_1^{N-2} \varphi_j h^j(\tau_1, \ldots, \tau_{N-2}, p_{N-1}, p_N, y), \tag{41c}$$

$$\tilde{h}^N(p_1, \ldots, p_N, y) = h^N(\tau_1, \ldots, \tau_{N-2}, p_{N-1}, p_N, y) + \\ + \sum_1^{N-2} \mu_j h^j(\tau_1, \ldots, \tau_{N-2}, p_{N-1}, p_N, y), \tag{41d}$$

where $\tau_i \equiv p_i + p_{N-1}\varphi_i + p_N\mu_i$.

Applying Lemma 3 to (39) yields the following formula for the solution to (39) expressed in terms of the demand functions and indirect utility function associated with (1):[5]

$$\begin{aligned} u &= \tilde{v}(\cdot) = v(\tau_1, \ldots, \tau_{N-2}, q_1, q_2, y - \Gamma), \\ x_i &= \tilde{h}^i(\cdot) = h^i(\tau_1, \ldots, \tau_{N-2}, q_1, q_2, y - \Gamma), \quad i = 1, \ldots, N-2, \\ z_1 &= \tilde{h}^{N-1}(\cdot) = \sum_1^N \frac{\alpha_i}{\alpha_{N-1}} h^i(\tau_1, \ldots, \tau_{N-2}, q_1, q_2, y - \Gamma), \\ z_2 &= \tilde{h}^N(\cdot) = \sum_1^N \frac{\beta_i}{\beta_N} h^i(\tau_1, \ldots, \tau_{N-2}, q_1, q_2, y - \Gamma), \end{aligned} \tag{42}$$

where

$$\tau_i \equiv p_i + \frac{\alpha_i}{\alpha_{N-1}}(q_1 - p_{N-1}) + \frac{\beta_i}{\beta_N}(q_2 - p_N)$$

and

$$\Gamma \equiv \frac{p_{N-1}\alpha_{kt}}{\alpha_{N-1}} + \frac{p_N\beta_{kt}}{\beta_N}.$$

Next, applying Lemma 2 to (42), one observes that if q_1 and q_2 satisfy

$$\alpha_{kt} = \sum_1^N \alpha_i h^i\left(\tau_1, \ldots, \tau_{N-2}, q_1, q_2, y - \Gamma + q_1\frac{\alpha_{kt}}{\alpha_{N-1}} + q_2\frac{\beta_{kt}}{\beta_N}\right), \tag{43a}$$

$$\beta_{kt} = \sum_1^N \beta_i h^i\left(\tau_1, \ldots, \tau_{N-2}, q_1, q_2, y - \Gamma + q_1\frac{\alpha_{kt}}{\alpha_{N-1}} + q_2\frac{\beta_{kt}}{\beta_N}\right), \tag{43b}$$

then the demand functions and indirect utility function associated with (38), expressed in terms of those associated with (1), are given by

$$x_i = h^i\left(\tau_1, \ldots, \tau_{N-2}, q_1, q_2, y - \Gamma + \right. \\ \left. + q_1\frac{\alpha_{kt}}{\alpha_{N-1}} + q_2\frac{\beta_{kt}}{\beta_N}\right), \quad i = 1, \ldots, N. \tag{43c}$$

$$u = v\left(\tau_1, \ldots, \tau_{N-2}, q_1, q_2, y - \Gamma + q_1 \frac{\alpha_{kt}}{\alpha_{N-1}} + q_2 \frac{\beta_{kt}}{\beta_N}\right). \tag{43d}$$

This may be further simplified by defining

$$\theta_1 \equiv (q_1 - p_{N-1})/\alpha_{N-1} \quad \text{and} \quad \theta_2 \equiv (q_2 - p_N)/\beta_N. \tag{44}$$

The representation theorem for the three constraint problem becomes:

SECOND GLOBAL REPRESENTATION THEOREM. *Given the maximization problem (1) with known solution $x_i = h^i(p, y)$ and $v(p, y)$, the solution to the maximization problem (35) is obtained as follows. Solve*

$$\begin{aligned}\alpha_{kt} &= \sum_1^N \alpha_i h^i(p_1 + \theta_1\alpha_1 + \theta_2\beta_1, \ldots, p_N + \\ &\quad + \theta_1\alpha_N + \theta_2\beta_N, y + \theta_1\alpha_{kt} + \theta_2\beta_{kt}),\end{aligned} \tag{45a}$$

$$\begin{aligned}\beta_{kt} &= \sum_1^N \beta_i h^i(p_1 + \theta_1\alpha_1 + \theta_2\beta_1, \ldots, p_N + \\ &\quad + \theta_1\alpha_N + \theta_2\beta_N, y + \theta_1\alpha_{kt} + \theta_2\beta_{kt}),\end{aligned} \tag{45b}$$

for $\theta_j = \theta_j(p, w, c, y, t, k)$, $j = 1, 2$, where (α_i, β_i) are given by (37). The solution to (35) can then be expressed as

$$\begin{aligned}x_i &= \bar{h}^i(p, w, c, y, t, k) \\ &= h^i(p_1 + \theta_1\alpha_1 + \theta_2\beta_1, \ldots, \\ &\quad p_N + \theta_1\alpha_N + \theta_2\beta_N, y + \theta_1\alpha_{kt} + \theta_2\beta_{kt}), \quad i = 1, \ldots, N.\end{aligned} \tag{45c}$$

$$\begin{aligned}u &= \bar{v}(p, w, c, y, t, k) \\ &= v(p_1 + \theta_1\alpha_1 + \theta_2\beta_1, \ldots, \\ &\quad p_N + \theta_1\alpha_N + \theta_2\beta_N, y + \theta_1\alpha_{kt} + \theta_2\beta_{kt}).\end{aligned} \tag{45d}$$

As in the case of two linear constraints, the properties of the demand functions $\bar{h}^i(p, w, c, y, t, k)$ can all be derived from (45a–d). For example, given the homogeneity properties of $v(\cdot)$ and $h^i(\cdot)$, (45a, b) imply that $\theta_1(p, w, c, y, t, k)$ and $\theta_2(p, w, c, y, t, k)$ are each homogenous of degree 1 in (p, y), and of degree -1 in (w, t) and also in (c, k).

Maximization problems with $M \geq 4$ linear constraints can be handled by a straightforward extension of the method shown here for dealing with the three-constraint problem (35). One first takes $(M-1)$ of the constraints, solves them for $(M-1)$ of the x's as linear functions of the remaining $(N-M)$ x's, as in (36), and then uses substitution to reduce the original maximization problem to an equivalent problem involving only a single linear constraint and $(N-M+1)$ choice variables, as in (38). One also sets up a parallel maximization problem with a single linear constraint but $(M-1)$ extra choice variables, as in (39). One applies the appropriate analog of Lemma 3 to solve the latter problem, as in (42), and then one applies Lemma 2 to obtain the desired representation of the solution to the original maximization problem in terms of the demand functions and indirect utility function associated with (1), as in (43a–d) or (45a–d). The structure of the representation will be similar to that in (45), with the demand functions taking the form

$$\begin{aligned} x_i &= \bar{h}^i(\cdot) \\ &= h^i(p_1 + \theta_1\alpha_1 + \theta_2\beta_1 + \theta_3\gamma_1 + \cdots, \ldots, \\ &\quad p_N + \theta_1\alpha_N + \theta_2\beta_N + \theta_3\gamma_N + \cdots, \\ &\quad y + \theta_1\bar{\alpha} + \theta_2\bar{\beta} + \theta_3\bar{\gamma} + \cdots), \end{aligned} \tag{46}$$

where $(\alpha_i, \beta_i, \gamma_i, \ldots)$ are functions of the coefficients in the $(M-1)$ linear constraints, $(\bar{\alpha}, \bar{\beta}, \bar{\gamma}, \ldots)$ are functions of both the coefficients and the right-hand sides of these constraints, and the θ_j are functions of the full set of variables appearing in the M constraints and are defined implicitly through a system of $(M-1)$ equations analogous to (45a, b).

5. CONCLUSIONS

The main results of this chapter, the Global Representation Theorems for utility maximization problems with two or three linear constraints, show how to derive the ordinary demand functions for these problems using known demand functions that solve the maximization problem with the same utility function but only a single, linear (budget) constraint. The structure of the demand functions – (19′a) in the case of two linear constraints, and (45c) in the case of three linear constraints – somewhat resembles that of Becker's (1965) model in which the time constraint can be combined with the budget constraint leading to a single constraint involving a 'full price' for each commodity consisting of the money price

(p_i) plus the monetized value of the time cost, and a 'full budget' consisting of exogenous money income plus the monetized value of total available time. The difference is that, here, the several constraints are separately binding, and the parameters which play the role of shadow prices – θ in the case of (19′a) and (θ_1, θ_2) in the case of (45c) – are endogenous, being themselves functions of the full set of variables that characterize the maximization problem. The demand function structure in (19′a) has already been identified by Larson and Shaikh (2001) as sufficient to satisfy the restrictions on the derivatives of the demand functions which are listed in Proposition 2. The contribution of this chapter is to show that this structure is necessary as well as sufficient.

In terms of computation, while the Global Representation Theorems presented here provide an algorithm for constructing demand functions that correspond to multi-constraint problems involving particular known direct or indirect utility functions, there is no guarantee of obtaining a *closed-form* representation of these demand functions. In fact, it is likely that it will be difficult if not impossible to obtain a closed-form representation of these demand functions. Consider, for example, the Cobb–Douglas utility function

$$u(x) = \prod_{1}^{N} x_i^{\gamma_i}, \quad \sum \gamma_i = 1, \tag{47a}$$

for which the standard demand functions take the simple form $x_i = h^i(p, y) = \gamma_i y / p_i$, $i = 1, \ldots, N$. When there is a second linear constraint, as in (7), the ordinary demand functions are now given by

$$x_i = \bar{h}^i(p, w, y, t) = \gamma_i (y + \theta t)/(p_i + \theta w_i), \tag{47b}$$

for $i = 1, \ldots, N$. However, as indicated in (18′), θ itself is a function of the parameters of the maximization problem, $\theta = \theta(p, w, y, t)$, since it has to satisfy

$$t = (y + \theta t) \sum_{1}^{N} \gamma_i \Big/ (p_i + \theta w_i). \tag{47c}$$

There is no closed form solution to (47c) for θ. Therefore, in this case there is no closed form solution for the demand functions $x_i = \bar{h}^i(p, w, y, t)$.[6] Nevertheless, one can always use numerical techniques to solve (47c) for θ, and then compute the value of the demand functions in (47b) when (47c) is satisfied. Thus, even when a closed form representation of the demand functions is not available for multi-constraint problems, the Global

Representation Theorems should be useful for the numerical calculation of the demands generated by these maximization problems.

APPENDIX

Proof of Lemma 1

The maximization in (2) corresponds to the following problem:

$$\underset{x_1,\ldots,x_{N-1}}{\text{maximize}}\ \tilde{u}(x_1,\ldots,x_N) = u\left(x_1,\ldots,x_{N-1},x_N - \sum_1^{N-1}\psi_j x_j\right)$$

$$\text{s.t.}\ \sum_1^N p_j x_j = y. \tag{A}$$

The budget constraint in (A) can be rewritten equivalently as

$$\begin{aligned} y = \sum_1^N p_j x_j &= \sum_1^{N-1}(p_j + p_N\psi_j)x_j + p_N\left(x_N - \sum_1^{N-1}\psi_j x_j\right) \\ &= \sum_1^{N-1}\pi_j x_j + p_N z, \end{aligned}$$

where

$$z \equiv x_N - \sum_1^{N-1}\psi_j x_j \quad \text{and} \quad \pi_j \equiv p_j + p_N\psi_j.$$

Next consider the following maximization problem, where $u(\cdot)$ denotes the same utility function as that in (A):

$$\underset{x_1,\ldots,x_{N-1},z}{\text{maximize}}\ u(x_1,\ldots,x_{N-1},z) \quad \text{s.t.}\ \sum_1^{N-1}\pi_j x_j + p_N z = y. \tag{B}$$

Let the solution to this be $(x^*_{(N)}, z^*)$, with the following corresponding ordinary demand functions and indirect utility function:

$$\begin{aligned} x_i^* &= h^i(\pi_1,\ldots,\pi_{N-1},p_N,y), \quad i = 1,\ldots,N-1, \\ z^* &= h^N(\pi_1,\ldots,\pi_{N-1},p_N,y), \\ u^* &= v(\pi_1,\ldots,\pi_{N-1},p_N,y). \end{aligned}$$

Problem (B) is essentially the same as the maximization in (1), except that (i) the last argument is here denoted z instead of x_N, and (ii) the prices of the first $N-1$ items are here denoted π_i instead of p_i. Take the solution to (B) and form $x_N^* \equiv z^* + \sum_1^{N-1} \psi_j x_j^*$. Then I claim that the vector $x^* \equiv (x_{(N)}^*, x_N^*)$ solves (A); this is equivalent to the statement made in Lemma 1.

Suppose this claim is not true; I now show that this leads to a contradiction.

If the claim is not true, there exists some $x' \neq x^*$ that solves (A). Note that x^* lies within the budget set of (A), since from (B):

$$\begin{aligned} y &= \sum_1^{N-1} \pi_j x_j^* + p_N z^* \\ &= \sum_1^{N-1} (p_j + p_N \psi_j) x_j^* + p_N z^* \\ &= \sum_1^{N-1} p_j x_j^* + p_N \left(z^* + \sum_1^{N-1} \psi_j x_j^* \right) \\ &= \sum_1^{N-1} p_j x_j^* + p_N x^*. \end{aligned}$$

Assume that (A) has a unique maximum. Since x^* lies within the budget set of (A) but does not solve (A), it follows that

$$u(x^*) < u(x').$$

However, it is also true that x' lies within the budget set of (B), since

$$y = \sum_1^N p_j x_j' = \sum_1^{N-1} \pi_j x_j' + p_N \left(x_N' - \sum_1^{N-1} \psi_j x_j' \right).$$

Assume that (B) has a unique maximum. Since x' lies within the budget set of (B) but is different from the vector x^* that *does* solve (B), it follows that

$$u(x') < u(x^*).$$

Hence, there is a contradiction. □

Proof of Lemma 2

Suppose that, in (4a), z is fixed at $\bar{z}$, and let x^* denote the corresponding solution to (4a). Let (x', z') denote the solution to

$$\underset{x,z}{\text{maximize}}\ u(x, z) \quad \text{s.t.} \sum px + \sum qz = y + \sum q\bar{z}. \tag{C}$$

Observe that if q on the right-hand side of (C) takes the value $\bar{q} \equiv \hat{q}(p, \bar{z}, y)$, then $z' = \bar{z}$; let $\bar{x}$ be the corresponding value of x'. Lemma 2 states that $x^* = \bar{x}$.

Suppose this is not true, so that $x^* \neq \bar{x}$. I now show that this leads to a contradiction.

Observe that $(\bar{x}, \bar{z})$ lies within the budget set of (4a) since

$$\sum p\bar{x} + \sum \bar{q}\,\bar{z} = y + \sum \bar{q}\,\bar{z} \rightarrow \sum p\bar{x} = y.$$

Assuming that (4a) has a unique solution, this implies that $u(\bar{x}, \bar{z}) < u(x^*, \bar{z})$. However, $(x^*, \bar{z})$ lies within the budget set of (C), since

$$\sum px^* = y \rightarrow \sum px^* + \sum \bar{q}\,\bar{z} = y + \sum \bar{q}\,\bar{z}.$$

Assume that (C) has a unique maximum; this implies that $u(x^*, \bar{z}) < u(\bar{x}, \bar{z})$, which yields a contradiction. □

Proof of Lemma 3

Observe that the budget constraint in (40) can be written as

$$\begin{aligned}
y &= \sum_1^N p_i x_i \\
&= \sum_1^{N-2} (p_i + p_{N-1}\varphi_i + p_N \mu_i) x_i + \\
&\quad + p_{N-1}\left(x_{N-1} - \sum_1^{N-2} \varphi_i x_i\right) + p_N\left(x_N - \sum_1^{N-2} \mu_i x_i\right) \\
&\equiv \sum_1^{N-2} \pi_i x_i + p_{N-1}\left(x_{N-1} - \sum_1^{N-2} \varphi_i x_i\right) + p_N\left(x_N - \sum_1^{N-2} \mu_i x_i\right).
\end{aligned}$$

Compare (40) with the following maximization problem:

$$\underset{x_1,\ldots,x_{N-2},z_1,z_2}{\text{maximize}} \quad u(x_1, \ldots, x_{N-2}, z_1, z_2)$$

$$\text{s.t.} \sum_1^{N-2} \pi_j x_j + p_{N-1} z_1 + p_N z_2 = y. \tag{D}$$

The claim is that, when

$$z_1 \equiv x_{N-1} - \sum_1^{N-2} \varphi_i x_i \quad \text{and} \quad z_2 \equiv x_N - \sum_1^{N-2} \mu_i x_i,$$

the maximization problems in (40) and in (D) are equivalent. If one were to suppose that the claim is not true, this would lead to a contradiction along the lines shown above in the proof of Lemma 1. □

NOTES

1. The literature cited above derives local results for the solution to maximization problems with multiple *nonlinear* constraints, while the global results developed here apply only for *linear* constraints. The simpler structure of the constraints makes it possible to obtain the stronger results.
2. It should be emphasized that the choice of good N in this context is entirely arbitrary, and any of the x_i's can be used for this purpose provided the corresponding w_i is nonzero. Moreover, the two constraints can be interchanged: the w_i's and t can be substituted for the p_i's and y in (18) or (18′) and in (19a, b) or (19′a, b).
3. These homogeneity properties can also be derived from (34).
4. The proof is given in the Appendix. Note that if $\varphi_j = 0$ for all $j = 1, \ldots, N-2$, then Lemma 3 generates Lemma 1.
5. Note that I have taken advantage of the fact that $\alpha_N = \beta_{N-1} = 0$ to simplify the summation so that it runs from 1 to N.
6. The source of the difficulty is the need for the shadow price function $\theta(p, w, y, t)$ to satisfy (18′). This does not appear to be satisfied by the empirical formula for the shadow value function used recently by Larson and Shaikh (2004), who model θ as a function of a single element of the vector w, say w_N, corresponding to the price of leisure (the wage rate), rather than the full set of variables (p, w, y, t). Their formula, $\theta = \lambda w_N$, does not appear to satisfy (18′) or to possess the homogeneity properties required of $\theta(p, w, y, t)$.

REFERENCES

Becker, G. (1965), 'A theory of the allocation of time', *Economic Journal*, 75(3), 493–517.

Chichilnisky, G. and P.J. Kalman (1978), 'Comparative statics of less neoclassical agents', *International Economic Review*, 19(1) (February), 141–148.

de Donnea, F.X. (1972), 'Consumer behavior, transport mode choice and value of time: Some micro-economics models', *Regional and Urban Economics*, 1(4), 355–382.

de Serpa, A.C. (1971), 'A theory of the economics of time', *Economic Journal*, 81 (December), 828–846.

Diamond, P.A. and M. Yaari (1972), 'Implications of the theory of rationing for consumers choice under uncertainty', *American Economic Review*, 62(3) (June), 333–343.

Gorman, W.M. (1976), 'Tricks with utility functions', in M. Artis and R. Nobay (eds), *Essays in Economic Analysis*, Cambridge: Cambridge University Press, pp. 211–243.

Hatta, T. (1980), 'Structure of the correspondence principle at an extremum point', *Review of Economic Studies*, 47, 987–997.

Kusumoto, S. (1976), 'Extensions of the Le Chatelier–Samuelson principle and their application to analytical economics – Constraints and economic analysis', *Econometrica*, 44(3) (May), 509–535.

Larson, D.M. and S.L. Shaikh (2001), 'Empirical specification requirements for two-constraint models of recreation demand', *American Journal of Agricultural Economics*, 83(2), 428–440.

Larson, D.M. and S.L. Shaikh (2004), 'Recreation demand choices and revealed values of leisure time', *Economic Inquiry*, 42(2) (April), 264–278.

Lyon, K.S. (1978), 'Consumer's surplus when consumers are subject to a time and an income constraint', *Review of Economic Studies*, 45(2), 377–380.

McConnell, K.E. (1975), 'Some problems in estimating the demand for outdoor recreation', *American Journal of Agricultural Economics*, (May), 330–339.

Tobin, J. (1952), 'A survey of the theory of rationing', *Econometrica*, 20(4) (October), 521–553.

Tobin, J. and H.S. Houthakker (1950–51), 'The effects of rationing on demand elasticities', *Review of Economic Studies*, 18, 140–153.

Wan, Y.-H. (1981), 'A generalized Slutsky matrix of the second kind', *Journal of Mathematical Analysis and Applications*, 81, 422–436.

5. Local Public Goods and Income Heterogeneity

Thomas Aronsson, Magnus Wikström, Kenneth Backlund and Tomas Sjögren

1. INTRODUCTION

A much debated issue is how the likelihood of collective action and the provision of public goods is affected by heterogeneity among individuals in a community. From a theoretical perspective Warr (1983) pointed out that if individuals, acting as players in a Nash game, voluntarily contribute towards a public good, the resulting allocation is not sensitive to the distribution of income. This result, known as the 'neutrality property' or 'Warr-neutrality', serves as a useful benchmark for discussing the effects of inequality on public goods provision. However, the result depends upon a number of assumptions. One such assumption is that all individuals choose to contribute towards the public good. Bergstrom et al. (1986) show that greater income inequality, that leads poorer individuals to free-ride by not contributing towards the public good, may imply that the provision of the public good increases.[1]

From a normative perspective, less effort has been devoted to the question of how the optimal provision of public goods should be affected by increasing income heterogeneity. Would we expect that the optimal provision of public goods is independent of the distribution of income as the neutrality property suggests? This chapter serves the purpose of discussing some of the factors that may render the optimal provision of a public good to be sensitive to changes in the income distribution. We choose to place our discussion within the context of a local public good.

Local governments fulfil distributional policy objectives without being able to redistribute incomes perfectly. Most often, such redistribution is conducted by supplying services which are (at least in part) private, such as social care, part of the educational program and health care services.

Therefore, if the local public policies are designed both to meet equality objectives and to provide local public goods, one may expect that changes in the distribution of income affect the allocation of public goods even if the mean income (e.g. the average tax base) remains unchanged.

There are a number of goods that may be characterized as local public goods. Environmental goods, such as public parks, urban forests and water fluoridation are key examples.[2] Admittedly, a large number of the goods provided locally have substantial private benefits to the residents. The factors discussed here would, however, be relevant also for goods with significant private characteristics, although the specific results would change.

In this chapter we study how a mean preserving increase in the spread of income in the locality influences the optimal provision of a local public good. The analysis is based on a two-type model, where the local residents can be either high income earners or low income earners.[3] We assume that the local government acts in accordance with a 'benthamite planner' by giving equal weight to the utilities of all local residents. Given this particular form of the social welfare function, three factors important for how the allocation of local public goods depends on the distribution of income are identified; (i) the local means of redistribution, (ii) the local residents' preferences and (iii) migration across localities.

The outline of the chapter is as follows. In Section 2, we begin by formulating a 'benchmark' model, which disregards the possibility of migration into or out of the locality, and where the decision maker has the means to reach a 'perfect' redistribution of private consumption. In this setting, we are able to derive a result which is analogous to the 'neutrality property' referred to above: a mean preserving increase in the spread of income does not affect the allocation of the public good. However, by relaxing the assumption that the local public sector is able to achieve a perfect redistribution of private consumption among the local residents, the 'neutrality property' will no longer apply. We provide two examples, which imply that the possibility to redistribute private consumption is restricted: one in which the only revenue source is a uniform lump sum tax, and the other where a proportional income tax is the only source of funds for the local government. In each of these cases, a mean preserving increase in the spread of income changes the optimal provision of the public good, and the direction of this change depends on the degree of risk aversion with respect to private consumption. In Section 3, we extend the model to allow for migration in the sense that the high income earners are (imperfectly) mobile across localities, and the general conclusion here will be that migration offsets the 'neutrality property'. If the population is mobile, a mean preserving increase in the spread of income will affect the optimal provision of the public good, even if the local government has the technical means of achieving a desired redistribution of private consumption. Section 4 concludes the chapter.

2. THE BENCHMARK MODEL: PERFECT REDISTRIBUTION

We shall begin by formulating a benchmark model, which is based on the assumptions that (i) the local public sector can redistribute private consumption perfectly and (ii) there is no migration across localities. These assumptions will be relaxed later. There are two types of individuals in the locality, l and h, with exogenously given (gross) incomes w^l and w^h such that $w^l < w^h$. The utility function of individual i is given by

$$u^i = u(w^i + z^i) + v(g), \quad i = l, h,$$

where $u(\cdot)$ and $v(\cdot)$ are strictly concave functions of private consumption, $w^i + z^i$, and a locally provided pure public good, g, respectively. The term z^i is a net transfer payment (positive or negative) from the locality to individual i. Local welfare is given by the utility sum, i.e.

$$W = n^l u^l + n^h u^h,$$

where n^l and n^h are, respectively, the number of low income earners and high income earners. The local public budget constraint is written as

$$-n^l z^l - n^h z^h - pg = 0$$

and p denotes the unit price of the public good.

Let us assume that the resource allocation is decided upon by a benthamite planner. The benthamite planner chooses z^l, z^h and g to maximize the welfare function subject to the budget constraint. If we denote by λ the Lagrange multiplier associated with the public budget constraint, the optimization problem becomes

$$\max_{\lambda, z^l, z^h, g} \; \Omega = n^l u^l + n^h u^h - \lambda[n^l z^l + n^h z^h + pg]. \qquad (1)$$

The first-order conditions are given by

$$\lambda; \quad -n^l z^l - n^h z^h - pg = 0, \tag{2}$$

$$z^l; \ n^l u_y^l - \lambda n^l = 0, \tag{3}$$

$$z^h; \ n^h u_y^h - \lambda n^h = 0, \tag{4}$$

$$g; \ n^l u_g^l + n^h u_g^h - \lambda p = 0, \tag{5}$$

where a subindex denotes a partial derivative, e.g. $u_y^h = \partial u^h / \partial y^h$, unless we mention otherwise. By using the short notations $y^l = w^l + z^l$ and $y^h = w^h + z^h$, we see that Equations (3) and (4) together imply $y^l = y^h$, which means that the optimal solution to problem (1) is characterized by perfect redistribution of private consumption. We will return to the implications of perfect redistribution below.

We begin by analysing how w^l and w^h affect the endogenous variables. The comparative statics with respect to w^l and w^h are given by

$$\partial g/\partial w^i > 0, \ \partial z^i/\partial w^i < 0 \text{ and } \partial z^i/\partial w^k > 0, \quad \text{for } i, k = l, h \text{ and } i \neq k.$$

The intuition is that the higher the income of a type i, the more he/she is willing to pay for public goods, and the less transfers to type i is needed to meet the equality objectives. Similarly, the higher the income of type i, the higher will be the net transfer to type k in order to reach perfect redistribution.

Let us now turn to the main issue in this section: how changes in the distribution of gross income will affect the allocation of the public good. To do this, we analyse the implications of a *mean preserving increase in the spread* of income. The effect on the provision of the public good, following from a mean preserving increase in the spread of income, can be written in general terms as

$$\frac{\partial g}{\partial w^h}_{\bar{I}=\text{const}} = \frac{\partial g}{\partial w^h} + \frac{\partial g}{\partial w^l} \cdot \frac{\partial w^l}{\partial w^h}_{\bar{I}=\text{const}},$$

where $\bar{I} = (n^l w^l + n^h w^h)/(n^l + n^h)$. We summarize the main result of the benchmark model as follows:

PROPOSITION 1. *The optimal solution to problem (1) implies that a mean preserving increase in the spread of income in the locality does not affect the provision of the local public good.*

The proof of Proposition 1 follows directly from a more general result in Section 3 and is, therefore, omitted. Proposition 1 gives a result analogous to the 'neutrality property' derived when the local residents act as players in a Nash game and contributes to a public good, which we referred to in the introduction. The intuition here is that, since the tax system contains a sufficient amount of instruments to obtain an equal distribution of private consumption *and* to achieve an efficient allocation of the public good, a mean preserving increase in the spread of income only causes the benthamite planner to change z^h and z^l to maintain the desired redistribution. The initial allocation of the public good will then remain optimal.

What if the tax system does not redistribute income perfectly? With imperfect means of redistribution, the distribution of private consumption will be affected by a mean preserving increase in the spread of income, and one would generally expect the local government to respond by changing the provision of the public good. To see this more clearly, let us analyse two special cases of imperfect redistribution, where the only source of funds for the public good is: (i) a uniform lump sum tax, $z^h = z^l = z$, in which case the possibility to redistribute income is absent and (ii) a proportional income tax,[4] where the net income (or private consumption) is given by $y^i = w^i(1-t)$ for $i = l, h$, and t is the local income tax rate. Let us begin with imperfect redistribution caused by lump sum taxation:

PROPOSITION 2. *Under a lump sum tax scheme with imperfect redistribution in the sense $y^l < y^h$, a mean preserving increase in the spread of income increases (decreases) the optimal provision of the public good if $u^l_{yy} - u^h_{yy}$ is positive (negative). It follows that, if the degree of absolute risk aversion is nonincreasing in private consumption, a mean preserving increase in the spread of income decreases the optimal provision of the public good.*

Proof. See the Appendix. □

Proposition 2 emphasizes the role of redistribution of income: since a uniform lump sum tax by definition is such that $y^l < y^h$, a mean preserving increase in the spread of income will, in general, affect the provision of local public goods. Note that the change of g may go in either direction. However, by imposing the assumption of nonincreasing absolute risk aversion, it follows that $|u^l_{yy}| > |u^h_{yy}|$, in which case it becomes optimal to decrease the provision of the public good. The reason is that, if we reduce the lump sum tax as a response to additional spread of income, then nonincreasing absolute risk aversion will imply that the increase in the marginal utility of private consumption facing the low income earners is greater than that facing the high income earners, which is desirable given the form of the local social welfare function set out above. Note, finally, that Proposition 2 applies to any tax/transfer system of a lump sum type as long as $y^l < y^h$.

Imperfect redistribution in the context of other tax/transfer schemes may have other implications for public spending than those corresponding to the lump sum tax. Consider the other special case of imperfect redistribution discussed above with $z^i = tw^i$, where t is a proportional income tax rate set by the locality. We have found:

PROPOSITION 3. *Suppose the public good is financed by a proportional income tax at rate t, which means $y^l < y^h$. It follows that a mean preserving increase in the spread of income increases (decreases) the optimal provision of the public good if*

$$[u^l_{yy}(\cdot)y^l - u^h_{yy}(\cdot)y^h] + [u^l_y(\cdot) - u^h_y(\cdot)]$$

is positive (negative).

Proof. See the Appendix. □

The first term in the formula of Proposition 3 is negative, if the degree of relative risk aversion is nonincreasing in private consumption. This is analogous to the condition imposed in Proposition 2 although based on relative, instead of absolute, risk aversion. The second term is positive and provides an unambiguous incentive to increase the provision. The reason is that a high income tax rate makes the distribution of private consumption across agents less sensitive to the distribution of gross income than what would be the case with a low income tax rate. The following result is a direct consequence of Proposition 3:

COROLLARY 1. *If the public good is financed by a proportional income tax, and if the degree of relative risk aversion is constant or increasing in private consumption, it follows that a mean preserving increase in the spread of income increases the provision of the public good.*

To see this, let us define $\delta^i = -[u^i_{yy}y^i]/u^i_y > 0$ for $i = l, h$. It follows from Proposition 3 that

$$\text{sign}\left.\frac{\partial g}{\partial w^h}\right|_{\bar{l}=\text{const}} = \text{sign}\,[(1-\delta^l)u^l_y - (1-\delta^h)u^h_y],$$

which is unambiguously positive if $\delta^h \geq \delta^l$.

3. MIGRATION

The main conclusion from the previous section is that, by relaxing the assumption about perfect redistribution in the benchmark model, the optimal provision of local public goods will be sensitive to the distribution of income in the locality. This section extends the benchmark model by allowing for migration across localities, which is important in the sense that migration affects the local tax base.

To simplify the notations, the initial (or pre-migration) population is normalized to equal one for both agent types, i.e. $n^l = n^h = 1$. Low income earners are immobile, and their preferences follow from the benchmark model in the previous section. High income earners are assumed to be (imperfectly) mobile across localities.[5] If a high income earner in locality i decides to stay, he/she will receive the utility

$$u_i^h = u(y_i^h) + v(g_i) + \theta_i,$$

where the subindex is used as an indicator of locality. The parameter $\theta_i \in [\underline{\theta}, \overline{\theta}]$ is interpreted as a 'taste for the home locality' among the high income earners, and is uniformly distributed with distribution function $F(\theta_i)$. If, on the other hand, the high income earner decides to migrate to another locality (here called j), he/she will receive

$$\overline{u}_j^h = u(y_j^h) + v(g_j).$$

Define by $\widetilde{\theta}_i$ the value of θ_i at which a high income earner is indifferent between staying in locality i and moving to locality j, i.e.

$$u(y_i^h) + v(g_i) + \widetilde{\theta}_i = \overline{u}_j^h.$$

It follows that the high income earner stays in locality i if $\theta_i \geq \widetilde{\theta}_i$, and the 'number of stayers' in locality i is $1 - F(\widetilde{\theta}_i)$.

There is also migration into locality i. High income earners in locality j receive the utility

$$u_j^h = u(y_j^h) + v(g_j) + \theta_j$$

if staying in locality j, where $\theta_j \in [\underline{\theta}, \overline{\theta}]$ is a uniformly distributed 'taste for home parameter'. The high income earner will migrate to locality i if $\theta_j < \widetilde{\theta}_j$, where

$$u(y_j^h) + v(g_j) + \widetilde{\theta}_j = \overline{u}_i^h$$

determines $\widetilde{\theta}_j$ (the value of θ_j at which the individual is indifferent between staying in j and moving to i), and $\overline{u}_i^h = u(y_i^h) + v(g_i)$ is the utility received if the resident chooses to migrate to locality i.

Let us now turn to the optimization problem facing the benthamite planner in locality i. The local welfare function can be written as

$$W_i = u_i^l + \int_{\widetilde{\theta}_i}^{\overline{\theta}} [\overline{u}_i^h + \theta_i] \, \mathrm{d}F(\theta_i) + F(\widetilde{\theta}_j)\overline{u}_i^h,$$

where $\overline{u}_i^h$ is defined as suggested above. The welfare function can be rewritten in a more convenient form if we collect the terms involving $\overline{u}_i^h$, i.e.

$$W_i = u_i^l + \widehat{n}^h \overline{u}_i^h + \int_{\widetilde{\theta}_i}^{\overline{\theta}} \theta_i \, \mathrm{d}F(\theta_i) \tag{6}$$

where $\widehat{n}_i^h = 1 - F(\widetilde{\theta}_i) + F(\widetilde{\theta}_j)$ can be interpreted as the 'relative number of high income earners' in locality i. In order to be able to focus the analysis on the role of migration, we shall provide the benthamite planner with the same policy instruments as in the benchmark model, which makes perfect redistribution a feasible option from a budget-technical point of view. The budget constraint is written as

$$-z_i^l - \widehat{n}_i^h z_i^h - p_i g_i = 0. \tag{7}$$

The optimization problem of the benthamite planner is to maximize the local welfare function given by Equation (6) subject to Equation (7). Since the analysis only concerns the behavior of locality i, we can suppress the locality indicator and write the benthamite planner's problem as follows:

$$\underset{\lambda, z^l, z^h, g}{\text{Max}} \; u^l + \widehat{n}^h \overline{u}^h + \int_{\widetilde{\theta}}^{\overline{\theta}} \theta \, \mathrm{d}F(\theta) - \lambda[z^l + \widehat{n}^h z^h + pg]. \tag{8}$$

3.1. A Myopic Local Government

It is instructive to begin by analysing a myopic local government, which does not recognize that its policy will affect the migratory behavior. As we are about to show, even if this assumption will imply perfect redistribution of private consumption, the distribution of private pre-tax income is, nevertheless, important for the provision of public goods.

A myopic local government means that the planner treats $\widehat{n}^h$ as exogenous in the optimization, in which case the necessary conditions for problem (8) are equivalent to those of the benchmark model in Section 2, i.e.

$$\lambda;\ -z^l-\widehat{n}^h z^h-pg=0, \tag{9}$$

$$z^l;\ u_y^l-\lambda=0, \tag{10}$$

$$z^h;\ \widehat{n}^h[\overline{u}_y^h-\lambda]=0, \tag{11}$$

$$g;\ (1+\widehat{n}^h)v_g-\lambda p=0, \tag{12}$$

where $u_y^l=\partial u^l/\partial y^l$, $\overline{u}_y^h=\partial\overline{u}^h/\partial y^h$ and $v_g=\partial v/\partial g$. It follows from Equations (10) and (11) that the optimal solution is characterized by perfect redistribution; $y^l=y^h$.

There is one important difference, though, between this model and the benchmark model set out in Section 2: even if the local government is myopic, the redistributive policy will affect the local tax base and, therefore, the ability to finance the local public good. Many of the qualitative properties of the benchmark model will, nevertheless, continue to apply here as well. The comparative statics are

$$\frac{\partial g}{\partial w^i}>0,\quad \frac{\partial z^i}{\partial w^k}>0,\quad \frac{\partial z^l}{\partial w^l}<0\quad\text{and}\quad \frac{\partial z^h}{\partial w^h}\gtrless 0$$

for $i,k=l,h$ and $i\neq k$, meaning that the responsiveness of the tax base to migration is not strong enough to fully offset the implications of perfect redistribution. In particular, a decrease of w^l reduces z^h despite the loss of tax base following from lower benefits to the high income earners. However, contrary to what was found in the benchmark model, we cannot show that an increase in w^h necessarily decreases z^h.

How will the optimal allocation of the public good respond to a mean preserving change in the spread of income? The mean income in the locality is given by $\overline{I}=(w^l+\widehat{n}^h w^h)/(1+\widehat{n}^h)$. Note first that

$$\left.\frac{dw^l}{dw^h}\right|_{\overline{I}=\text{const}}=\widehat{n}_y^h(\overline{I}-w^h)-\widehat{n}^h,$$

where $\widehat{n}_y^h>0$ is the effect on net in-migration of high income earners following from an increase in private consumption by high income earners. From this formula, it can be seen that the relationship between w^h and w^l given a constant $\overline{I}$ does not only depend on the relative number of high income earners as in the benchmark model; it also depends on the change in (net) migration following additional spread of income. Since $\widehat{n}_y^h>0$, the first term on the right-hand side is negative, which means that the negative relationship between w^h and w^l, with the mean income held constant, is stronger here than in the benchmark model. In other words, to preserve the mean income of the locality, w^l must decrease more for a given increase in w^h than in the benchmark model because of the migration effect. We are now in the position to explain the main result of this subsection:

PROPOSITION 4. *With a myopic local government, the solution to problem (8) implies that a mean preserving increase in the spread of income decreases the optimal provision of the public good.*

Proof. See the Appendix. □

To see the intuition behind the proposition, it is useful to analyse the formula for the response in g:

$$\frac{\partial g}{\partial w^h}_{\overline{I}=\text{const}} = \widehat{n}^h_y(\overline{I} - w^h)\frac{\partial g}{\partial w^h} \tag{13}$$

which follows because $\partial g/\partial w^h = \widehat{n}^h \partial g/\partial w^l$ in the myopic equilibrium (see the Appendix). Since a mean preserving increase in the spread of income causes net in-migration, perfect redistribution will imply that the change of $\widehat{n}^h z^h$ is smaller in absolute value than the change of z^l. Therefore, since migration makes perfect redistribution more costly, there are less resources left over for public good allocation. Equation (13) also explains why the public good remains unaffected in the benchmark model, where $\widehat{n}^h_y = 0$.

3.2. The Complete Model

Let us now relax the assumption of a myopic local government. The planner is, instead, assumed to recognize that the policies undertaken by the locality affect migration and use this information when solving the optimization problem. To simplify the notations as much as possible, note first that $\widetilde{\theta}_i = -\widetilde{\theta}_j$. The assumption that θ_i and θ_j are uniformly distributed on $[\underline{\theta}, \overline{\theta}]$ will then imply

$$\widehat{n}^h_y = \frac{\partial \widehat{n}^h}{\partial y^h} = -2C\frac{\partial \widetilde{\theta}}{\partial y^h} > 0,$$

$$\frac{\partial[\int_{\widetilde{\theta}}^{\overline{\theta}} \theta \, \mathrm{d}F(\theta)]}{\partial y^h} = \frac{1}{2}\widehat{n}^h_y \widetilde{\theta},$$

where $C = \mathrm{d}F(\widetilde{\theta})/\mathrm{d}\theta = [\overline{\theta} - \underline{\theta}]^{-1}$ is a constant, and $\partial\widetilde{\theta}/\partial y^h = -u_y^h < 0$. It follows that, when $\widehat{n}^h$ is treated as endogenous during optimization, the necessary conditions for problem (8) can be written as

$$\lambda; \quad -z^l - \widehat{n}^h z^h - pg = 0, \tag{14}$$

$$z^l; \; u_y^l - \lambda = 0, \tag{15}$$

$$z^h; \; \widehat{n}^h[u_y^h - \lambda] + \widehat{n}_y^h \left[\frac{u^h + \overline{u}_j^h}{2} - \lambda z^h \right] = 0, \tag{16}$$

$$g; \; (1 + \widehat{n}^h)v_g - \lambda p + \widehat{n}_g^h \left[\frac{u^h + \overline{u}_j^h}{2} - \lambda z^h \right] = 0, \tag{17}$$

where $\widehat{n}_g^h = -2C[\partial\widetilde{\theta}/\partial g] > 0$. Equations (14) and (15) are identical to their counterparts in the previous subsection, whereas the first-order conditions for z^h and g now contain the 'extra' term $(u^h + \overline{u}_j^h)/2 - \lambda z^h$, which is positive since $z^h < 0$. In Equation (16), we can interpret $\widehat{n}_y^h(u^h + \overline{u}_j^h)/2$ as the utility flow from in-migration when z^h increases marginally, while $\widehat{n}_y^h \lambda z^h$ measures the utility value of the flow of tax revenues. The third term on the right-hand side of Equation (17) can be given a similar interpretation in terms of g. By comparing the complete model set out here with the myopic local government of the previous subsection, we find:

LEMMA 1. *The solution to problem (8), when $\widehat{n}^h$ is treated as endogenous during optimization, implies; (i) imperfect redistribution, $y^l < y^h$ and (ii) the optimal provision of the local public good may either exceed, be equal to or fall short of that corresponding to the myopic solution.*

The first part of the lemma follows directly from Equations (15) and (16). To see the second part, note that the responsiveness of $\widehat{n}^h$ to changes in z^h and g determine the differences between the solution to the complete model and the solution corresponding to the myopic local government. If increases in z^h and g give rise to substantial net in-migration, then the complete model is likely to imply higher z^h and higher g than the myopic model. If, on the other hand, $\widehat{n}^h$ is only weakly responsive to changes in z^h and g, it follows that the solution to the complete model may imply less provision of local public goods than the solution to the myopic version of the model. However, the reader should note that it is not possible to have both z^h and g lower here than in the myopic equilibrium.

Turning to the comparative statics properties with respect to w^h and w^l, the only unambiguous result is $\partial z^l/\partial w^l < 0$, which has the same interpretation as in the benchmark model. If, in addition, the difference in private consumption (or net income) between the two groups is 'sufficiently small',[6] we will find $\partial g/\partial w^l > 0$ and $\partial z^h/\partial w^l > 0$. The intuition is that, if the equilibrium is sufficiently close to perfect redistribution, then the optimal responses to a change of w^l are close to those of the myopic model. However, the comparative statics with respect to w^h remain ambiguous (even if the economy operates close to the myopic equilibrium). The reason is that changes in w^h will not only influence migration indirectly via the public budget constraint (in a way similar to w^l), it will also have a direct effect on the net migration to the locality.

As expected from the comparative statics analysis, a mean preserving increase in the spread of income can change the provision of the local public good in either direction. Formally,

$$\frac{\partial g}{\partial w^h}_{\bar{I}=\text{const}} = \frac{\partial g}{w^h} + [\widehat{n}_y^h(\bar{I} - w^h) - \widehat{n}^h]\frac{\partial g}{\partial w^l}. \tag{18}$$

There are, at least, two important differences between the equilibrium in the complete model and the myopic equilibrium discussed in the previous subsection: the complete model neither requires $\partial g/\partial w^l > 0$, unless the difference between y^h and y^l is 'sufficiently small', nor does it require $\partial g/\partial w^h = \widehat{n}^h \partial g/\partial w^l$. With these two observations at our disposal, it is easy to derive the following result:

PROPOSITION 5. *If the private consumption levels of the two groups are sufficiently close in the sense that $u_y^h \geq (2/3)u_y^l$, a mean preserving increase in the spread of income can increase the provision of the public good only if $\partial g/\partial w^h > \widehat{n}^h \partial g/\partial w^l$.*

The first requirement in the proposition means that y^h and y^l are 'sufficiently close' in the sense of assuring that $\partial g/\partial w^l > 0$. As a consequence, we find that $\widehat{n}_y^h(\bar{I} - w^h)\partial g/\partial w^l < 0$ (like in the myopic equilibrium). It will then follow that a mean preserving increase in the spread of income decreases the provision of the public good, unless the allocation of the public good is very sensitive to changes in w^h. If it is not, the economy operates close enough to the myopic equilibrium to assure that Proposition 4 still applies.

To get some further intuition, note that the distribution of 'tastes for home' plays an important role in determining the effects of a mean preserving increase in the spread of income. If the taste distribution is heterogenous (in the sense that $\overline{\theta} - \underline{\theta}$ is large), the responsiveness of migration to policy is relatively small. Therefore, for a given initial distribution of income, a more heterogenous taste distribution makes redistribution less costly, implying that the decision maker will prefer more redistribution. As a consequence, it is more likely that the private consumption levels of the two groups meet the requirement given in the proposition above. On the other hand, if tastes are homogenous (i.e. $\overline{\theta} - \underline{\theta}$ is small), redistribution is relatively costly. In this case, the decision maker may not find it worthwhile to redistribute income to meet the requirement of the proposition. Therefore, the derivative $\partial g/\partial w^l$ may be negative, while $\partial g/\partial w^h$ may still be positive, implying that a mean preserving spread of income is more likely to increase the public good provision.

4. SUMMARY AND CONCLUSIONS

This chapter extends the analysis of local public spending by focusing attention on the importance of the distribution of income among local residents for the optimal provision of local public goods. The analysis is based on a two-type model, where the local residents can be either high income earners or low income earners, and the local government is assumed to act in accordance with a benthamite planner giving equal weight to the utilities of all local residents. The main purpose is to study how a mean preserving increase in the spread of income among the local residents affects the provision of the local public good. We would like to summarize the main results as follows:

- In a 'benchmark' version of the model, which does not allow for migration across localities and where the local decision maker has the means to accomplish perfect redistribution of private consumption, are we able to derive what resembles Warr's (1983) neutrality result concerning the provision of public goods in a noncooperative framework. This means that a change in the distribution of income, holding the average income constant, does not affect the optimal provision of local public goods.
- If, in the absence of migration, the local decision maker is unable to achieve perfect redistribution of private consumption, the results are sensitive to the degree of risk aversion with respect to private con-

sumption. We show that when taxes are lump sum, meaning that the local decision maker cannot obtain perfect redistribution, the optimal provision of the public good decreases as a response to increasing income heterogeneity if the degree of absolute risk aversion is a nonincreasing function of private consumption.

- By allowing high income earners to migrate between localities, the 'neutrality result' will no longer hold even if perfect redistribution is a feasible option from the viewpoint of the decision maker. This is most clearly seen in the case where the decision maker is myopic in the sense of not considering the migratory responses following from changes in the provision of the public good or the tax/transfer scheme. In this case, we show that a mean preserving spread of income unambigously decreases the optimal provision of the local public good. If the decision maker takes migratory responses into consideration when determinaing the optimal policy, we can no longer sign the effect on public good provision following from a mean preserving spread of income. The reason is that the results become dependent upon how sensitive net migration is to local public policies as well as the difference in gross income between high and low income earners.

There are a number of ways by which the present model can be extended. As mentioned in the introduction, many of the goods provided locally have public as well as private characteristics. Although the general conclusion of this chapter would not change, the specific results derived are obviously dependent on the assumptions made. Another extension would be to consider private contributions in order to 'top up' the publically determined expenditure levels. If the preservation of an urban forest is handled by the local government, some individuals might find it worthwhile to contribute in excess of the public budget because of environmental concern or because of income heterogeneity. Finally, there is an empirically relevant side of the discussion here. Local public expenditure determination generally considers income levels to explain expenditure levels. We have shown that income inequality may have important implications for expenditure levels. Thus, it remains for future research to study whether the spread of income is an empirically important determinant of the expenditures on local public goods.

APPENDIX

Proof of Proposition 2

When $z = z^l = z^h$, the first-order conditions are given by

$$-nz - pg = 0,$$
$$n^l(u^l_y - \lambda) + n^h(u^h_y - \lambda) = 0,$$
$$nv_g - \lambda p = 0,$$

where $n = n^h + n^l$. Differentiating the first-order conditions with respect to w^l and w^h, comparative statics can be found by solving the system

$$\begin{bmatrix} 0 & -n & -p \\ -n & n^l u^l_{yy} + n^h u^h_{yy} & 0 \\ -p & 0 & nv_{gg} \end{bmatrix} \begin{bmatrix} \partial\lambda/\partial w^i \\ \partial z/\partial w^i \\ \partial g/\partial w^i \end{bmatrix} = \begin{bmatrix} 0 \\ -n^i u^i_{yy} \\ 0 \end{bmatrix}, \quad i = l, h.$$

Note that $\partial g/\partial w^i = -pnn^i u^i_{yy}/|\overline{H}|$, where $|\overline{H}| > 0$ is the determinant of the bordered Hessian matrix given above. Substituting the derivatives into

$$\frac{\partial g}{\partial w^h}_{\overline{I}=\text{const}} = \frac{\partial g}{\partial w^h} + \frac{\partial g}{\partial w^l} \cdot \frac{\partial w^l}{\partial w^h}_{\overline{I}=\text{const}}, \tag{A1}$$

and noting that $(\partial w^l/\partial w^h)_{\overline{I}=\text{const}} = -n^h/n^l$, we obtain $(\partial g/\partial w^h)_{\overline{I}=\text{const}} = (u^l_{yy} - u^h_{yy})pnn^h/|\overline{H}|$. It follows that sign $[(\partial g/\partial w^h)_{\overline{I}=\text{const}}] =$ sign $[u^l_{yy} - u^h_{yy}]$. To relate this result to the degree of absolute risk aversion, rewrite the derivative as $(\partial g/\partial w^h)_{\overline{I}=\text{const}} = u^l_y a[(u^h_y/u^l_y)r^h - r^l]$, where $r^i = -u^i_{yy}/u^i_y$, $i = l, h$ is the degree of absolute risk aversion, and $a = pnn^h/|\overline{H}|$ is positive. Since, by imperfect redistribution, $u^h_y/u^l_y < 1$, it follows that $r^h \leqslant r^l$ is sufficient for the public good provision to decrease. □

Proof of Proposition 3

Under a linear income tax, $t > 0$, the budget constraint of the locality is given by

$$t(n^l w^l + n^h w^h) - pg = 0.$$

Forming the Lagrangian for this problem, the first-order conditions with respect to λ, t, and g are given by

$$t(n^l w^l + n^h w^h) - pg = 0,$$

$$-n^l w^l (u_y^l - \lambda) - n^h w^h (u_y^h - \lambda) = 0,$$

$$n v_g - \lambda p = 0,$$

where $n = n^h + n^l$. Differentiating the first-order conditions, gives the system

$$\begin{bmatrix} 0 & I & -p \\ I & \Omega_{tt} & 0 \\ -p & 0 & n v_{gg} \end{bmatrix} \begin{bmatrix} \partial\lambda/\partial w^i \\ \partial t/\partial w^i \\ \partial g/\partial w^i \end{bmatrix} = \begin{bmatrix} -tn^i \\ \omega_t^i n^i \\ 0 \end{bmatrix}, \quad i = l, h,$$

where $I = n^l w^l + n^h w^h$, $\Omega_{tt} = n^l (w^l)^2 u_{yy}^l + n^h (w^h)^2 u_{yy}^h$, and $\omega_t^i = u_y^i - \lambda + u_{yy}^i y^i$. Solving for $\partial g/\partial w^i$ gives $\partial g/\partial w^i = -pn^i (I\omega_t^i + t\Omega_{tt})/|\overline{H}|$. Finally, applying Equation (A1), it is found that $(\partial g/\partial w^h)_{\overline{I}=\text{const}} = pIn^h[(u_y^l - u_y^h) + (u_{yy}^l y^l - u_{yy}^h y^h)]$. □

Proof of Proposition 4

Differentiating conditions (9), (10), (11), and (12), results in the system

$$\begin{bmatrix} 0 & -1 & -\Omega_{\lambda z^h} & -\Omega_{\lambda g} \\ -1 & u_{yy}^l & 0 & 0 \\ -\widehat{n}^h & 0 & \widehat{n}^h u_{yy}^h & 0 \\ -p & 0 & \widehat{n}_y^h v_g & \Omega_{gg} \end{bmatrix} \begin{bmatrix} \partial\lambda/\partial w^l & \partial\lambda/\partial w^h \\ \partial z^l/\partial w^l & \partial z^l/\partial w^h \\ \partial z^h/\partial w^l & \partial z^h/\partial w^h \\ \partial g/\partial w^l & \partial g/\partial w^h \end{bmatrix}$$

$$= \begin{bmatrix} 0 & \widehat{n}_y^h z^h \\ -u_{yy}^l & 0 \\ 0 & -\widehat{n}^h u_{yy}^h \\ 0 & -\widehat{n}_y^h v_g \end{bmatrix},$$

where we naturally assume that $\Omega_{\lambda z^h} = \widehat{n}^h + \widehat{n}_y^h z^h$, the marginal cost of transfers to the high income earners, and $\Omega_{\lambda g} = p + \widehat{n}_g^h z^h$, the marginal cost of the public good, are positive. Finally, $\Omega_{gg} = (1 + \widehat{n}^h) v_{gg} + \widehat{n}_g^h v_g < 0$, where the sign requirement follows from fulfillment of the second-order conditions. The public good responses to w^l and w^h are $\partial g/\partial w^l = \widehat{n}^h u_{yy}^l A/|\overline{H}| > 0$, and $\partial g/\partial w^h = (\widehat{n}^h)^2 u_{yy}^l A/|\overline{H}| > 0$, where $A = \widehat{n}_y^h v_g - p u_{yy}^h > 0$, and $|\overline{H}| < 0$. Note that, in this case, $\partial g/\partial w^h = \widehat{n}^h \partial g/\partial w^l$. Applying Equation (A1), noting that, in this case, $(dw^l/dw^h)_{\overline{I}=\text{const}} = \widehat{n}_y^h(\overline{I} - w^h) - \widehat{n}^h$, results in $(\partial g/\partial w^h)_{\overline{I}=\text{const}} = \widehat{n}^h \partial g/\partial w^l + (\widehat{n}_y^h(\overline{I} - w^h) - \widehat{n}^h)\partial g/\partial w^l = \widehat{n}_y^h(\overline{I} - w^h)\partial g/\partial w^l$. □

NOTES

1. Sandler (1992) discusses some of the assumptions necessary to obtain the neutrality property.
2. A few empirical studies have addressed the role of heterogeneity for the allocation of environmental goods, see for example Varughese and Ostrom (2001) and Cardenas et al. (2002).
3. Similar models have been used, for example, by Wildasin (1991) and Boadway et al. (1998) to analyse fiscal externalities among localities in a federation.
4. Proportional income taxes are the main sources of funds for the local governments in the Nordic countries.
5. The assumption that high income earners are mobile while low income earners are not, is made to reflect the relative mobility of educational groups, which appears to be the common empirical observation. See Eliasson et al. (1998) for an empirical illustration.
6. The formal requirement is $u_y^h > (2/3)u_y^l$.

REFERENCES

Bergstrom, T., L. Blume and H. Varian (1986), 'On the private provision of public goods', *Journal of Public Economics*, 29, 25–49.

Boadway, R., M. Marchand and M. Vigneault (1998), 'The consequences of overlapping tax bases for redistribution and public spending in a federation', *Journal of Public Economics*, 68, 453–478.

Borchering, T.E. and R.T. Deacon (1972), 'The demand for services of non-federal government', *American Economic Review*, 62, 891–901.

Cardenas, J.C., J. Stranlund and C. Willis (2002), 'Economic inequality and burden-sharing in the provision of local environmental quality', *Ecological Economics*, 40, 379–395.

Deacon, R.T. (1978), 'A demand model for the local public sector', *Review of Economics and Statistics*, 60, 184–192.

Eliasson, K., U. Lindgren and O. Westerlund (1998), 'Geographical labour mobility: Migration or commuting?', Mimeo, Department of Economics, Umeå University.

Sandler, T. (1992), *Collective Action: Theory and Applications*, Ann Arbor, MI: University of Michigan Press.

Varughese, G. and E. Ostrom (2001), 'The contested role of heterogeneity in collective action: Some evidence from community forestry in Nepal', *World Development*, 29(5), 747–765.

Warr, P. (1983), 'The private provision of the public good is independent of the distribution of income', *Economics Letters*, 13, 207–211.

Wildasin, D.E. (1986), *Urban Public Finance*, Chur, Switzerland: Harwood Academic Publishers.

Wildasin, D.E. (1991), 'Income redistribution in a common labour market', *American Economic Review*, 81, 757–774.

6. Public Goods, Optimal Distortionary Taxation and Union Wage Setting

Thomas Aronsson, Kenneth Backlund, Tomas Sjögren and Magnus Wikström

1. INTRODUCTION

All developed societies use distortionary taxes, at least partially, to finance the provision of public goods such as police, national defense and the quality of the environment. It is therefore important to know how to use tax instruments in order to minimize the excess burden as well as how much of the public good to supply. Previous studies in this area are, to a large extent, based on the assumption that the private sector of the economy is competitive. For instance, the classical Samuelson (1954) condition – as well as the modifications of this condition resulting from the use of distortionary taxation – require that the private goods are bought and sold in competitive markets. Similarly, the Ramsey rule – and its special case of the 'inverse' elasticity rule – for optimal commodity and/or factor income taxation are normally associated with models where the markets are competitive. In practice, however, this assumption does not always seem to be a realistic description of the incentive structure underlying policy. The latter is particularly the case in Europe, where many countries have experienced high unemployment for a long time. It has also become a conventional wisdom that the presence of what appears to be 'equilibrium unemployment' may, at least in part, be due to the influence of trade unions over wage formation and employment. This leads to an interesting question: to what extent does imperfect competition in the labor market, resulting from union wage setting, affect the incentive structure underlying factor income taxation and public good provision?

This chapter concerns optimal factor income taxation and provision of public goods in a small open economy, which is characterized by union wage setting. To do this, we shall employ a general equilibrium model, where the tax instruments are linear taxes on labor income and capital income. The purpose here is to simultaneously address the conditions for optimal taxation and provision of public goods under excess supply of labor, and then compare the results with those arising when the labor market is competitive.

This chapter relates to earlier literature in primarily two fields: (i) the optimal provision of public goods under distortionary taxation and (ii) the optimal mixture of factor income taxation in unionized economies. Since the 1970s, several authors have addressed the question of how to choose a public good in an optimal way, when the tax revenues are raised by means of distortionary taxation. Atkinson and Stern (1974) analyse the optimality condition for a public good, which is financed by optimally chosen commodity taxes. Their results suggest that two mechanisms are at work in addition to those characterizing the Samuelson condition; first, the welfare cost of financing the public good may exceed the revenues collected from the private sector (the marginal cost of public funds is greater than one), and, second, changes in the public good affect the tax revenues via commodity demands and factor supplies.[1] Since the net effect of these two additional components remains ambiguous in general, it is not clear whether the distortionary tax contributes to increase or decrease the optimal public good. Gaube (2000) reexamines the problem of providing a public good under optimal commodity taxation, and derives a set of conditions (related to normality of private and public goods as well as substitutability among private goods) under which distortionary taxation reduces the optimal provision of the public good.

Another part of the literature has focused on the situation, where the government collects tax revenues by means of a nonlinear income tax. In this case, by using a variant of Stiglitz's (1982) two type model, Boadway and Keen (1993) show that it is optimal to under (over) provide the public good relative to the Samuelson condition if, and only if, the marginal rate of substitution between the public good and private consumption increases (decreases) with leisure, which also generalizes a result derived by Christiansen (1981). The optimality condition for the public good derived by Boadway and Keen (1993) is slightly extended by Edwards et al. (1994), who assume that the government is able to supplement the nonlinear income tax with linear commodity taxes.

The literature on factor income taxation in open economies is commonly based on the assumption that capital is mobile across countries, whereas labor is not. It has also become customary to assume that the hours of work per employed individual are fixed. Therefore, if the factor markets are competitive, the optimal tax structure is likely to imply a zero capital tax rate, or that capital is taxed at a lower rate than (the immobile) labor.[2] Koskela and Schöb (2000) introduce a labor market distortion into this framework by assuming that the wage rate is determined by bargaining between trade unions and firms. Since the labor market distortion gives rise to a welfare loss in addition to that caused by distortionary taxes, the optimal mixture of factor income taxation will differ from that corresponding to a competitive economy. If the government can use lump sum (or profit) taxes to collect the tax revenues, the optimal mixture of factor income taxation means a zero capital income tax rate and a subsidy towards labor, where the latter is used to offset the welfare effect of the labor market distortion. Similar results have been derived by Boeters and Schneider (1999) in the context of monopoly union wage setting. If, on the other hand, the government is not able to use lump sum taxation, Koskela and Schöb (2000) show that the optimal tax structure also depends on the elasticity of substitution between labor and capital. An interesting result is that if the capital income tax rate tends to decrease the wage rate (which it does in their CES framework when the elasticity of substitution exceeds one), the capital income tax rate will, in part, serve as a mechanism to reduce the welfare cost of the labor market distortion.

To our knowledge, only a few previous studies have been concerned with optimal taxation and public good provision simultaneously under labor market imperfections. Andersen et al. (1996) consider the situation where a public good is financed by labor income taxation, and the wage rate is determined by a monopoly union. The hours of work per individual are assumed to be fixed. One of their main results is that even if the public good is pure waste, it is optimal to provide a positive amount of the public good if a tax financed public expansion reduces unemployment. Bovenberg and van der Ploeg (1996) address the optimal mixture of labor income taxation, environmental taxation and public good provision in an economy, which is characterized by environmental damage of production and excess supply of labor. This framework is then used to study how the optimal tax mix, public good provision and unemployment are affected by a change in the preferences for environmental concern.

Our contribution differs from previous studies in several important ways. First, contrary to the papers by Boeters and Schneider (1999) and Koskela and Schöb (2000), employment is measured both in terms of hours of work per individual and the number of employed persons. This means that individuals can either be employed or unemployed and, if employed, that they can be rationed in terms of their hours of work. We shall develop a model that nests both the traditional expected utility approach to union wage setting (where the hours of work are fixed) and a competitive labor market as special cases. Second, this contribution aims at combining the study of optimal labor and capital income taxation in a unionized economy with the optimal provision of a public good. As we mentioned above, only a few previous studies have addressed optimal taxation, provision of public goods and labor market imperfections simultaneously, and the focuses of these studies are very different from ours.

The outline of the chapter is as follows. The model and the equilibrium in the private sector are described in Section 2. We will consider a small open economy, where the private sector and the government treat the world interest rate as exogenously given. In Section 3, we analyse the optimal provision of a public good, which is financed by optimal lump sum taxation. This provides a natural starting point, since the use of lump sum taxes makes it possible to show how the assumption about imperfect competition in the labor market may offset the Samuelson condition. Section 4 relaxes the assumption that the government can use lump sum taxes; instead, the government collects tax revenues by means of labor income taxation and capital income taxation. This is the main part of the analysis, where the optimal mixture of factor income taxation and public good provision are addressed simultaneously. We shall also compare the results with those arising when the labor market is competitive. Section 5 concludes the chapter.

2. A SMALL OPEN ECONOMY

Consider a small open economy where output, y, is produced by identical, competitive firms. Let n be the number of employed individuals and L total employment, where the latter is defined as the number of employed individuals times the hours of work per individual, l. In the production process, labor, L, and capital, K, are production factors, and the production function is given by $y = f(L, K)$, which is increasing and strictly concave in each argument. The production factors are technical complements, $f_{LK} > 0$, and the production function exhibits strictly decreasing returns to scale.

Profits are given by

$$\pi = f(L, K) - wL - rK, \tag{1}$$

where w denotes the real wage rate and r the domestic interest rate. Profits are evenly distributed among the population of m identical consumers in the economy. Optimal hiring policy of the firms satisfies the standard marginal productivity conditions $f_L = w$ and $f_K = r$, which implicitly define the labor demand function $L(w, r)$ with $L_w < 0$. For the subsequent analysis, it is convenient to define the wage elasticity of the labor demand as follows:

$$\varepsilon = \frac{wL_w}{L} = \frac{wf_{KK}}{nl[f_{LL}f_{KK} - f_{LK}^2]}, \tag{2}$$

where the second-order condition for profit maximization implies $f_{LL}f_{KK} - f_{LK}^2 > 0$.

Since we will concentrate on the efficiency aspects of public policy, we assume that the consumers have identical preferences. The consumers derive utility from the consumption of a private good, c, leisure, h, and a public good, g. The utility function is written $u = u(c, h, g)$, which is increasing in each argument and strictly quasiconcave. Total time available (H) can be divided between work and leisure such that $h = H - l$.

A consumer is either employed or unemployed. If employed, the budget constraint is written

$$c^e = [1 - \tau]wl + [1 - \theta]r[\bar{k} - z] + \bar{r}z + \frac{\pi}{m} - T^e, \tag{3}$$

where

c^e = the consumption of private goods by an employed individual,
τ = the labor income tax rate,
θ = the capital income tax rate,
$\bar{k}$ = a fixed capital endowment which cannot be used for consumption,
$\bar{r}$ = the fixed world interest rate,
z = the part of the capital endowment used for foreign investment,
T^e = a lump sum tax paid by each employed individual.

All consumers are endowed with a capital stock, $\bar{k}$, and have the option of renting this endowment (or part thereof) to domestic firms in return for the net of tax interest rate, $[1 - \theta]r$, or to rent it on the international capital market where they obtain the fixed world interest rate $\bar{r}$ in return.

The budget constraint of an unemployed individual ($l = 0$) is given by

$$c^u = [1-\theta]r[\bar{k}-z] + \bar{r}z + \frac{\pi}{m} - T^u, \tag{4}$$

in which c^u denotes the private consumption of an unemployed individual, and T^u is a lump sum tax paid by each unemployed individual. Since the lump sum tax is dependent upon the employment situation, we can interpret T^u as partly reflecting any desire to compensate the unemployed.

The only source of revenues for the government is taxation. We assume that the government cannot tax foreign investments; it can only tax the income from domestic capital and labor (or impose lump sum taxes). Therefore, the government's budget constraint can be written as

$$n\tau wl + m\theta r[\bar{k}-z] + nT^e + [m-n]T^u - g = 0. \tag{5}$$

Finally, note that the equilibrium in the capital market must imply that the net return on domestic assets is equal to the net return on foreign assets. The equilibrium condition in the capital market can be written as

$$[1-\theta]r = \bar{r}. \tag{6}$$

Equation (6) also implies that the budget constraints reduce to read $c^e = [1-\tau]wl + \varpi - T^e$ and $c^u = \varpi - T^u$, respectively, where $\varpi = \bar{r}\bar{k} + \pi/m$ is nonlabor income which consumers treat as exogenously given.

2.1. The Labor Market

To describe the labor market, we will apply a general model which comprises both the traditional expected utility model of trade union behavior (where the hours of work per individual are fixed) and the competitive labor market as special cases. This enables us to compare the effects of policy between regimes and relate our results to those of previous studies. To keep the analysis simple, we assume that the unions have monopoly power on the labor market.[3]

Consider a situation with many firm-specific identical unions, where each such union is small relative to the economy as a whole. Each union treats the nonlabor income of its members as exogenous.[4] Since the firm-specific unions are identical, we will simplify the analysis by aggregating the unions into a single union, which organizes all m consumers in the economy. The union's objective is to maximize the expected utility, U, of the representative member. If we assume that employment is determined by a random draw among the m union members, expected utility is given by

$$U = \frac{n}{m}u\left([1-\tau]wl + \varpi - T^e, H - l, g\right) + \left[1 - \frac{n}{m}\right]v(\varpi - T^u, H, g). \tag{7}$$

Note that $v(\varpi - T^u, H, g) = u(\varpi - T^u, H, g)$; the purpose of using $v(\cdot)$ as a notation for the utility of the unemployed is to simplify the notations in later parts of the chapter.

It will be convenient to describe the behavior of the union as if it chooses both the real wage rate and the hours of work per employed union member. The decision process can be viewed as a two stage procedure, where the union in the first stage unilaterally chooses l and w, while the firms in the second stage choose n along the labor demand function. The latter is observed by the union, which maximizes (7) subject to $n = L(w, r)/l$ and $m \geqslant n$. The first-order conditions become

$$\frac{\partial U}{\partial w} = L_w \frac{[u - v]}{lm} + \frac{L}{m}[1-\tau]u_c - \mu \frac{L_w}{l} = 0, \tag{8}$$

$$\frac{\partial U}{\partial l} = -\frac{L[u - v]}{l^2 m} + \frac{L}{lm}[[1-\tau]wu_c - u_h] + \mu \frac{L}{l^2} = 0, \tag{9}$$

$$\mu \left[m - \frac{L(w, r)}{l}\right] = 0, \tag{10}$$

where μ is the Lagrange multiplier associated with the inequality constraint $m \geqslant n$. Proposition 1 summarizes the most important implications of union policy:

PROPOSITION 1. *If $m > n$, the labor market equilibrium described by Equations (8)–(10) is characterized by involuntarily unemployed individuals, and employed individuals who are rationed in terms of of work. If $m = n$, there will only be rationing in terms of work hours. In addition, the following labor market models are nested special cases:*

(i) the traditional expected utility model of union behavior corresponds to the special case where $m > n$ and l is fixed, and

(ii) perfect competition in the labor market corresponds to the special case where $m = n$, while the union at the same time behaves as if $|\varepsilon| \to \infty$.

To provide an intuitive understanding of Proposition 1, let us begin with the case where $m > n$. Since $\mu = 0$ in this case, the optimal choices of w and l do not depend on m.[5] We can then use $L = nl$ and write Equation (8) as

$$\frac{L_w}{l}[u - v] + n[1 - \tau]lu_c = 0. \tag{11}$$

Equation (11) means that the marginal cost of increasing the real wage rate equals the marginal benefit of doing so. The marginal cost is the number of members who lose their jobs multiplied by the utility a member loses when he or she is transferred into the pool of unemployed members. The marginal benefit is the increase in utility gained by each member, $[1 - \tau]lu_c$, multiplied by the total number of employed members. This is the traditional optimality condition obtained in the standard union models (see for example McDonald and Solow 1981).

In a similar way, Equation (9) is the optimality condition for the choice of hours of work. The marginal benefit of an increase in l is represented by the positive effect an increase in the labor income has upon the utility of the employed. The marginal cost works via two channels: for a given real wage rate, an increase in l simultaneously reduces the number of employed individuals and increases the disutility of work for those employed. These two marginal cost terms imply that it is not rational to choose work hours to satisfy the efficiency condition in standard labor supply models, $[1 - \tau]\, wu_c - u_h = 0$. This can be seen if we combine first-order conditions (8) and (9) to obtain

$$[1 - \tau]\left[1 + \frac{1}{\varepsilon}\right] wu_c - u_h = 0. \tag{12}$$

Equation (12) implies that employed individuals are rationed in their supply of labor. This means that, in addition to causing some individuals to become involuntarily unemployed, union behavior also creates a second type of distortion via rationing of work hours. Note that condition (12) also implies $\varepsilon < -1$ which means that aggregate labor cost, $wL(w, r)$, is decreasing in w at the optimum.

Turning to the case where $m = n$, first-order conditions (8)–(10) reduce to (12). Even if all individuals are employed, the distortion via the rationing of work hours per individual still remains. Note also that in case the wage setter perceives that $|\varepsilon| \to \infty$, Equation (12) reduces to the efficiency condition corresponding to a competitive labor market.

Finally, to shorten the notations, we will rewrite Equation (11) as

$$[1 + \varepsilon][u - v] = -lu_h \tag{13}$$

which is derived by combining first-order conditions (8) and (9) to substitute for $[1-\tau]u_c$.

3. NONDISTORTIONARY TAXATION

In this section, τ and θ are set equal to zero in Equations (3)–(6), and the objective of the government is to choose T^e, T^u and g to maximize the consumers' welfare. We assume that the government has a utilitarian objective function in the sense of treating all consumers equally.[6] The objective function is written as

$$W = nu(c^e, H-l, g) + [m-n]v(c^u, H, g). \tag{14}$$

By following the convention in the literature on optimal taxation, we assume that the government chooses taxes and public expenditures before the private agents make their decisions. Since the government is acting leader, and the private sector follower, the government will recognize that the private decision variables – the real wage rate, work hours, employment, net foreign investment and consumption of employed and unemployed individuals – are affected by taxation and provision of public goods. The equilibrium conditions of the private sector, which implicitly define the private decision variables, are as follows:

$$f_L\left(nl, m[\bar{k}-z]\right) - w = 0, \tag{15}$$

$$f_K\left(nl, m[\bar{k}-z]\right) - \bar{r} = 0, \tag{16}$$

$$\left[1+\frac{1}{\varepsilon}\right] wu_c(c^e, H-l, g) - u_h(c^e, H-l, g) = 0, \tag{17}$$

$$[1+\varepsilon]\left[u(c^e, H-l, g) - v(c^u, H, g)\right] + lu_h(c^e, H-l, g) = 0, \tag{18}$$

$$f\left(nl, m[\bar{k}-z]\right) + m\bar{r}z + [m-n]wl - mc^e - mT^e = 0, \tag{19}$$

$$f\left(nl, m[\bar{k}-z]\right) + m\bar{r}z - wln - mc^u - mT^u = 0. \tag{20}$$

To derive resource constraints (19) and (20) we have used $c^e = wl + \varpi - T^e$ and $c^u = \varpi - T^u$ in combination with $L = nl$ and Equation (1).

Equations (15)–(20) implicitly define w, l, n, z, c^e and c^u as functions of T^e, T^u and g, respectively. The optimal fiscal policy is to choose taxes and provision of the public good to maximize the welfare subject to the government budget constraint and Equations (15)–(20). The Lagrangean corresponding to this problem is written as

$$\mathcal{L} = nu(c^e, H-l, g) + [m-n]v(c^u, H, g) + \lambda\left\{nT^e + [m-n]T^u - g\right\}, \tag{21}$$

where λ is the shadow price in terms of utility of raising an additional unit of revenue. The first-order conditions become

$$\begin{aligned} 0 = {} & \frac{\partial n}{\partial T^e}[u-v] + n\left[u_c\frac{\partial c^e}{\partial T^e} - u_h\frac{\partial l}{\partial T^e}\right] + [m-n]v_c\frac{\partial c^u}{\partial T^e} + \\ & + \lambda\left[n + \frac{\partial n}{\partial T^e}(T^e - T^u)\right], \end{aligned} \tag{22}$$

$$\begin{aligned} 0 = {} & \frac{\partial n}{\partial T^u}[u-v] + n\left[u_c\frac{\partial c^e}{\partial T^u} - u_h\frac{\partial l}{\partial T^u}\right] + [m-n]v_c\frac{\partial c^u}{\partial T^u} + \\ & + \lambda\left[(m-n) + \frac{\partial n}{\partial T^u}(T^e - T^u)\right], \end{aligned} \tag{23}$$

$$\begin{aligned} 0 = {} & \frac{\partial n}{\partial g}[u-v] + n\left[u_c\frac{\partial c^e}{\partial g} - u_h\frac{\partial l}{\partial g} + u_g\right] + \\ & + [m-n]\left[v_c\frac{\partial c^u}{\partial g} + v_g\right] + \lambda\left[\frac{\partial n}{\partial g}(T^e - T^u) - 1\right]. \end{aligned} \tag{24}$$

By following the convention in the literature, we define the marginal costs of public funds in real terms by dividing the optimally chosen Lagrange multiplier with the marginal utility of private consumption at the optimum. Since the employed and unemployed individuals do not necessarily pay the same lump sum tax, and the consumption possibilities depend on the employment situation, we will use two measures of the marginal cost of public funds in real terms, i.e. $MCPF^{T^e} = \lambda/u_c$ and $MCPF^{T^u} = \lambda/v_c$, respectively. We can derive the following result with respect to the optimal taxes:

PROPOSITION 2. *If the private sector obeys Equations (15)–(20), the optimal lump sum taxes are characterized by*

$$MCPF^{T^e} \times \left\{1 + \eta_{nT^e}\left[1 - \frac{T^u}{T^e}\right]\right\} = 1 - \eta_{LT^e}\delta_1, \tag{25}$$

$$MCPF^{T^u} \times \left\{1 + \eta_{[m-n]T^u}\left[1 - \frac{T^e}{T^u}\right]\right\} = 1 - \eta_{LT^u}\delta_2, \tag{26}$$

where $\delta_1, \delta_2 > 0$[7] *and*

$$\eta_{[m-n]T^u} = \frac{\partial\,[m-n]}{\partial T^u}\frac{T^u}{[m-n]},$$

$$\eta_{nT^e} = \frac{\partial n}{\partial T^e}\frac{T^e}{n}, \qquad \eta_{LT^j} = \frac{\partial L}{\partial T^j}\frac{T^j}{L}, \qquad j = e, u.$$

Proof. See the Appendix. □

An immediate implication of Proposition 2 is that the marginal cost of public funds in real terms will, in general, differ from unity because of the welfare cost resulting from imperfect competition in the labor market. To fully understand the consequences of the labor market imperfection, let us begin by briefly discussing the outcome in a competitive economy, which coincides with the special case of the model where $n = m$, while the union at the same time behaves as if $|\varepsilon| \to \infty$. Equation (18) will then become redundant, while Equation (17) reduces to read

$$wu_c(c^e, H-l, g) - u_h(c^e, H-l, g) = 0, \tag{17a}$$

meaning that Equations (15), (16), (17a), (19) and (20), together, constitute the conditions obeyed by the private sector. In this case, it is possible to show that $T^e = T^u = T$, $u_c = v_c$ and $\delta_1 = 0$. Equation (25) then reduces to read $MCPF^T = 1$, whereas Equation (26) will be redundant since there are no unemployed individuals in the competitive economy.

With the competitive economy as a reference case, we can identify two additional effects, which are caused by the labor market imperfection: (i) a tax base effect which arises when $T^e \neq T^u$ and (ii) a welfare effect of changes in total employment. To illustrate the tax base effect, captured by the terms within the bracket on the left-hand sides of Equations (25) and (26), consider the case where $T^e > T^u$, $\eta_{nT^e} > 0$ and $\eta_{[m-n]T^u} < 0$. Equations (25) and (26) will then imply that an increase of T^e/T^u works to decrease $MCPF^{T^e}$ and $MCPF^{T^u}$. The reason is that the higher level of employment increases the number of agents who pay a high tax ($T^e > T^u$).

Note also that changes in T^e and T^u affect the total employment via income effects, which are represented by $\eta_{LT^e}\delta_1$ and $\eta_{LT^u}\delta_2$, respectively. A welfare effect will then arise, because the employment is not optimally chosen at the equilibrium. To understand these terms, note that if $\eta_{LT^e} > 0$ ($\eta_{LT^u} > 0$), higher employment works in the direction of reducing $MCPF^{T^e}$ ($MCPF^{T^u}$). An interesting implication is that if the lump sum tax increases l and decreases n in such a way that the net effect on employment is positive, higher lump sum taxation will increase the welfare level even though the number of unemployed individuals increases.

The following result characterizes the optimal provision of the public good:

PROPOSITION 3. *If the government can finance the public good by optimal lump sum taxation, and the private sector obeys Equations (15)–(20), the optimal provision of the public good is characterized by*

$$\frac{nMRS^e}{MCPF^{T^e}} + \frac{[m-n]\,MRS^u}{MCPF^{T^u}} - MRT = -\frac{n\,[T^e - T^u]}{g}\eta_{ng} - \eta_{Lg}\delta_3, \quad (27)$$

where $\delta_3 > 0$[8] *and*

$$MRS^e = \frac{u_g}{u_c}, \quad MRS^u = \frac{v_g}{v_c}, \quad MRT = 1,$$

$$\eta_{ng} = \frac{\partial n}{\partial g}\frac{g}{n}, \quad \eta_{Lg} = \frac{\partial L}{\partial g}\frac{g}{L}.$$

Proof. See the Appendix. □

Equation (27) suggests that the deviations from the Samuelson condition are caused by three separate effects: (i) the marginal costs of public funds may differ from unity, (ii) a tax base effect arising when $T^e \neq T^u$ and (iii) an effect of the public good on total employment.

The importance of the marginal cost of public funds is due to the fact that the government recognizes the cost of raising public revenues. If an increase in T^j, $j = e, u$, induces a positive (negative) cost on top of the marginal cost of producing the public good, there is an additional incentive to decrease (increase) the provision of the public good. To illustrate, consider the simplified situation where $\eta_{Lg} = \eta_{ng} = 0$ meaning that the right-hand side of Equation (27) equals zero. Then, if $MCPF^{T^j} < (>)\ 1$, g is chosen such that $nMRS^e + [m-n]MRS^u - MRT < (>)\ 0$.

The tax base effect is part of the first term on the right-hand side of Equation (27). If employed individuals pay a higher lump sum tax than unemployed individuals, and if the employment increases (decreases), it follows that the tax revenues increase (decrease). This provides an incentive to increase (decrease) the provision of the public good. Finally, the employment effect arises because the total employment is not optimally chosen from society's point of view. If $\eta_{Lg} > 0$ ($\eta_{Lg} < 0$), there is an incentive for the government to overprovide (underprovide) the public good relative to the Samuelson condition, even if we were to assume that the marginal cost of public funds is equal to one and the tax base effect is absent.

In the special case discussed above, where Equations (15), (16), (17a), (19) and (20), together, constitute the conditions characterizing the equilibrium in the private sector, and if $n = m$, the outcome of the model coincides with that of a competitive economy. It is then possible to show that $MCPF^{T^e} = MCPF^T = 1$, $T^e = T^u$, $\delta_3 = 0$ and the second term on the left-hand side of Equation (24) is equal to zero. This means that Equation (27) reduces to the Samuelson condition $mMRS - MRT = 0$.

4. DISTORTIONARY TAXATION

This section is based on the assumptions that the government is not able to use lump sum taxes, and that the public revenues are raised by the labor income tax and the capital income tax. If $m > n$, equilibrium in the private sector is determined by the following set of equations:

$$f_L\left(nl, m[\bar{k} - z]\right) - w = 0, \tag{28}$$

$$[1 - \theta]f_K\left(nl, m[\bar{k} - z]\right) - \bar{r} = 0, \tag{29}$$

$$\left[1 + \frac{1}{\varepsilon}\right][1 - \tau]wu_c(c^e, H - l, g) - u_h(c^u, H - l, g) = 0, \tag{30}$$

$$[1 + \varepsilon]\left[u(c^e, H - l, g) - v(c^u, H, g)\right] + lu_h(c^u, H - l, g) = 0, \tag{31}$$

$$f\left(nl, m[\bar{k} - z]\right) + m\bar{r}z + [1 - \tau][m - n]wl - mc^e - R(\tau, \theta, g) = 0, \tag{32}$$

$$f\left(nl, m[\bar{k} - z]\right) + m\bar{r}z - [1 - \tau]wln - mc^u - R(\tau, \theta, g) = 0, \tag{33}$$

In Equations (32) and (33),

$$R(\tau, \theta, g) = n\tau wl + m\theta r[\bar{k} - z] \tag{34}$$

represents a short notation for the tax revenues. To simplify the analysis, we have chosen to disregard the possibility of redistribution via unemployment benefits. The reason in that, even if this assumption may have important implications for the levels of the tax rates and the public good, it does not affect the qualitative nature of the policy rules to be discussed below. The optimization problem facing the government is to choose τ, θ and g to maximize the welfare function subject to the budget constraint as well as to the restrictions that w, l, n, z, c^e and c^u are determined by (28)–(33). The Lagrangean corresponding to the government's problem can be written as

$$\mathcal{L} = nu\left(c^e, H - l, g\right) + [m - n]\, v\left(c^u, H, g\right) + \lambda\left[R(\tau, \theta, g) - g\right]. \quad (35)$$

The first-order conditions become

$$0 = \frac{\partial n}{\partial \tau}[u - v] + n\left[u_c \frac{\partial c^e}{\partial \tau} - u_h \frac{\partial l}{\partial \tau}\right] + + [m - n] v_c \frac{\partial c^u}{\partial \tau} + \lambda \frac{\partial R}{\partial \tau}, \quad (36)$$

$$0 = \frac{\partial n}{\partial \theta}[u - v] + n\left[u_c \frac{\partial c^e}{\partial \theta} - u_h \frac{\partial l}{\partial \theta}\right] + + [m - n] v_c \frac{\partial c^u}{\partial \theta} + \lambda \frac{\partial R}{\partial \theta}, \quad (37)$$

$$0 = \frac{\partial n}{\partial g}[u - v] + n\left[u_c \frac{\partial c^e}{\partial g} - u_h \frac{\partial l}{\partial g} + u_g\right] + + [m - n]\left[v_c \frac{\partial c^u}{\partial g} + v_g\right] + \lambda\left[\frac{\partial R}{\partial g} - 1\right]. \quad (38)$$

As in the previous section, it is convenient to relate the first-order conditions for the optimal taxation to the marginal cost of public funds in real terms. It is then important to recognize that the marginal utility of consumption is likely to differ between the employed and unemployed individuals. Since labor income taxes are only paid by employed individuals, we normalize by u_c when defining $MCPF_\tau = \lambda/u_c$. On the other hand, the capital income tax affects all individuals, which suggests to us that we should normalize by the marginal utility of consumption of the 'representative individual',

$$\bar{u}_c = \frac{n}{m} u_c + \left[1 - \frac{n}{m}\right] v_c,$$

when defining $MCPF_\theta = \lambda/\bar{u}_c$. The optimal tax structure can then be characterized as follows;

PROPOSITION 4. *If the private sector obeys Equations (28)–(33), the optimal taxation of labor income and capital income is characterized by*

$$MCPF_\tau \times \left[1+\beta_\tau\right] = 1 + \left[\tau\frac{1}{w}(f_{LL} - \frac{f_{LK}^2}{f_{KK}}) - \frac{\varphi_1}{wlnu_c}\right]L_\tau, \quad (39)$$

$$MCPF_\theta \times \left[1+\beta_\theta\right]$$
$$= 1 + \frac{1}{1-\theta}\left[\theta + \frac{n}{m}\tau\frac{l}{[\bar{k}-z]}\frac{f_{LK}}{f_{KK}}\right] - \frac{\varphi_2}{m\bar{u}_c r\left[\bar{k}-z\right]} +$$
$$+ \left[\frac{n}{m}\tau\frac{l}{r[\bar{k}-z]}(f_{LL} - \frac{f_{LK}^2}{f_{KK}}) - \frac{\varphi_1}{m\bar{u}_c r\left[\bar{k}-z\right]}\right]L_\theta, \quad (40)$$

where $MCPF_\tau = \lambda/u_c$, $MCPF_\theta = \lambda/\bar{u}_c$ *and*

$$\varphi_1 = [u_c - \bar{u}_c][1-\tau]L\left[f_{LL} - \frac{f_{LK}^2}{f_{KK}}\right] - \frac{[1-\tau]wu_c}{\varepsilon},$$

$$\varphi_2 = [u_c - \bar{u}_c][1-\tau]L\left\{\frac{f_{LK}}{f_{KK}}\frac{r}{[1-\theta]}\right\}.$$

The parameters β_τ and β_θ capture the tax base effects of increases in τ and θ, respectively, and are defined in the Appendix. Since the proof of Proposition 4 is analogous to the proof of Proposition 2, it has been omitted. Before interpreting Proposition 4, it will be convenient to write the condition for the public good in terms of the sum of marginal rates of substitution and the marginal rate of transformation. We will characterize the optimal provision of the public good by Proposition 5:

PROPOSITION 5. *If the public good is financed by the optimal taxes on labor income and capital income, and the private sector obeys Equations (28)–(33), the optimal provision of the public good is characterized by*

$$nMRS^e\frac{u_c}{\lambda} + [m-n]MRS^u\frac{v_c}{\lambda} - MRT = \frac{\left[\tau\gamma - \varphi_1\right]}{\lambda}L_g - R_g, \quad (41)$$

where

$$\gamma = \bar{u}_c L\left[f_{LL} - \frac{f_{LK}^2}{f_{KK}}\right] < 0.$$

The proof of Proposition 5 is analogous to the proof of Proposition 3 and is, therefore, omitted. In the remaining part of this chapter, we shall be concerned with the interpretation of Propositions 4 and 5.

4.1. Optimal Policy in a Competitive Economy

Let us begin by analysing the special case of the model where $n = m$, while the union at the same time behaves as if $|\varepsilon| \to \infty$, in which the outcome of the private decisions will be equivalent to that of a competitive economy. Equation (31) will then become redundant, whereas Equation (30) reduces to read

$$[1-\tau]wu_c(c^e, H-l, g) - u_h(c^e, H-l, g) = 0, \qquad \text{(30a)}$$

meaning that Equations (28), (29), (30a), (32) and (33), together, constitute the conditions obeyed by the private sector. In this case, $\overline{u}_c = u_c$, $\varphi_1 = \varphi_2 = 0$ and $MCPF_\tau = MCPF_\theta = MCPF$, meaning that Equations (39)–(41) reduce to their counterparts in a competitive economy. Furthermore, since n is fixed in the competitive economy, it follows that $L_\tau = ml_\tau$ and $L_\theta = ml_\theta$, so the influence of taxation on the total employment is solely determined by the effect on the hours of work.

Consider first the condition for optimal labor income taxation in Equation (39). Note that $f_{LL} - f_{LK}^2/f_{KK} < 0$ according to the second-order conditions for profit maximization. Therefore, if $l_\tau < 0$, and if the tax revenues are increasing in τ, in which case $1 + \beta_\tau > 0$, then $MCPF > 1$. This reflects the excess burden associated with distortionary taxation.

To interpret condition (40), which governs the optimal choice of θ, note that the first term on the right-hand side, $\theta/[1-\theta]$, captures the negative welfare effect associated with the tax distortion in the capital market. Furthermore, by the assumption of a competitive labor market, implying that $\varphi_1 = \varphi_2 = 0$ and $m = n$, only two additional terms remain on the right-hand side of Equation (40),

$$\frac{\tau}{[1-\theta]}\frac{l}{[\overline{k}-z]}\frac{f_{LK}}{f_{KK}} \quad \text{and} \quad \frac{\tau l}{r[\overline{k}-z]}\left(f_{LL} - \frac{f_{LK}^2}{f_{KK}}\right)L_\theta,$$

both of which are proportional to the labor income tax rate. One can use Equations (28) and (29) to show that the sum of these two terms can be written as $[\tau l/[r(\overline{k}-z)]]w_\theta$, where

$$w_\theta = \left[f_{LL} - \frac{f_{LK}^2}{f_{KK}}\right]L_\theta + \frac{f_{LK}}{f_{KK}}\frac{f_K}{(1-\theta)} \qquad (42)$$

measures how the real wage rate responds to higher capital income taxation. The first term on the right-hand side of Equation (42) can affect the real wage rate in either direction, since $L_\theta = ml_\theta$ can be either positive or negative. If $L_\theta > (<) \, 0$, this term is negative (positive) and contributes to decrease (increase) *MCPF*. The intuition is that, when the labor market is characterized by a tax distortion, there is a positive welfare effect associated with a decrease in the real wage rate. Turning to the second term on the right-hand side of Equation (42), and by recalling the assumption that the production factors are technical complements, we have $[f_{LK}/f_{KK}][f_K/(1-\theta)] < 0$. This term arises because an increase in the capital income tax rate reduces the domestic capital stock which, in turn, tends to reduce the marginal product of labor when the production factors are technical complements.

In the context of a competitive economy, Equation (41) simplifies to

$$mMRS\frac{u_c}{\lambda} - MRT = \frac{\tau\gamma}{\lambda}L_g - R_g \tag{43}$$

since $n = m$ and $\varphi_1 = 0$. To interpret Equation (43), consider the situation where $l_\tau < 0$ and $1 + \beta_\tau > 0$, which are standard assumptions implying $MCPF > 1$ and $u_c/\lambda < 1$. Then, if $L_g \leq 0$ and $R_g \leq 0$, we have $MRT < mMRS$. This is consistent with Pigou's claim that '(public) expenditure ought not to be carried so far as to make the real yield of the last unit of resources expended by the government equal to the real yield of the last unit left in the hands of the representative citizen' (Pigou 1947). If, on the other hand, $R_g > 0$ or $L_g > 0$, the sum of marginal rates of substitution may either exceed, or fall short of, the marginal rate of transformation.

4.2. Optimal Policy in a Unionized Economy

Since employed individuals have higher income than unemployed individuals, it follows that $c^e > c^u$. In addition, to be able to interpret Equations (39)–(41) in a simple way, we shall add some structure by assuming that the utility functions are such that $u_c < v_c$ at the optimum, which also means that $u_c < \bar{u}_c$ where $\bar{u}_c$ is interpreted as the marginal utility of consumption of the representative individual in the economy. Note also that $u_c < \bar{u}_c$ implies $\varphi_1 > 0$ and $\varphi_2 > 0$.

Let us begin by analysing the condition for optimal taxation of labor income, which is given by Equation (39). In comparison with the simplified formula corresponding to the competitive market economy, which we examined in the previous subsection, there is an extra term, $-\varphi_1/wlnu_c < 0$, within the bracket on the right-hand side. This term reflects the welfare cost of imperfect competition, which adds to the welfare cost arising from distortionary taxation. In other words, there is an extra welfare cost (gain) associated with distortionary labor income taxation in the unionized economy, if the total employment is decreasing (increasing) in τ.

However, despite this obvious implication of imperfect competition in the labor market, it is not straightforward to compare $MCPF_\tau$ between the unionized and competitive economies. This is so because the change in total employment arising from higher labor income taxation in the unionized economy is likely to differ from that in the competitive economy. In the competitive economy, $L_\tau = ml_\tau$ since $n = m$, while the corresponding effect in the unionized economy is given by $L_\tau = nl_\tau + ln_\tau$, where n_τ can be either positive or negative.

Turning to the condition for the capital income tax rate, Equation (40) suggests that there are three additional effects to consider, which are not present in the competitive economy. The first effect operates via the 'pre-existing' labor income tax. Since the labor income tax is only paid by employed individuals, the terms that are proportional to the labor income tax rate are scaled down by n/m, which means that the influence of the tax distortion in the labor market is weaker than in the competitive economy. The second effect works via the term $-\varphi_2/[mr[\bar{k} - z]] < 0$, the sign of which is due to the assumption that the production factors are technical complements. When the domestic capital stock is being reduced via higher capital income taxation, the real wage rate tends to decrease which, in turn, tends to increase the welfare in an economy, where union wage setting causes excess supply of labor. To interpret the third effect, the reader should observe that the influence of the capital income tax rate on the real wage rate also depends on how the capital income tax rate affects the employment. Therefore, the second effect mentioned above is either reinforced or offset by the term $-\varphi_1/[m\bar{u}_c r[\bar{k} - z]] < 0$, which is proportional to L_θ. This suggests that capital income taxation tends to offset the welfare cost associated with union setting if $L_\theta \geq 0$, and may either reinforce or offset this welfare cost if $L_\theta < 0$. In summary:

PROPOSITION 6. *If the private sector obeys Equations (28)–(33), the incentive structure underlying the choice of capital income tax rate will differ between the unionized and competitive economies because:*

(i) the higher the unemployment, the less important will be the tax distortion in the labor market for the optimal capital income tax rate, and

(ii) capital income taxation tends to offset the welfare cost of imperfect competition in the labor market if $L_\theta \geq 0$, and may either reinforce or offset this welfare cost if $L_\theta < 0$.

The second part of Proposition 6 appears to be in accordance with previous research. Koskela and Schöb (2000) recognize that capital income taxation will offset the welfare cost, which is due to the influence of trade unions over wage formation, if the capital income tax rate tends to reduce the real wage rate. However, the first result has not been recognized by previous research on the optimal mixture of factor income taxation in unionized economies, since the previous studies have treated the hours of work per employed as fixed. To interpret Proposition 6, consider the situation where $L_\theta \geq 0$, in which case an increase in the capital income tax rate decreases the real wage rate. Equation (40) then suggests that there is an additional incentive to tax capital income in the unionized economy in comparison with the competitive economy, since union wage setting is associated with a welfare cost. At the same time, the incentive to use the capital income tax rate to reduce the welfare cost of labor income taxation is likely to be weaker in the unionized economy than in the competitive economy. Therefore, even if it is desirable for the government to use the capital income tax to reduce the real wage rate, the incentive to do so is not necessarily stronger in the unionized economy than in the competitive economy.

Turning finally to the condition for the public good, a comparison between Equations (41) and (43) suggest that there are three incentive effects relevant for public good provision in the unionized economy in addition to those arising in the competitive economy: (i) the marginal cost of public funds in a unionized economy is, in general, different from that of a competitive economy, (ii) the marginal utility of the public good may depend on the employment situation, and (iii) there is an additional welfare effect of the public good via employment in the unionized economy.

Note first that the marginal cost of public funds in the unionized economy may either exceed, or fall short of, the marginal cost of public funds in the competitive economy. If $L_\tau < 0$ and of roughly the same magnitude in the unionized and competitive economies, then $MCPF_\tau$ is likely to be larger in the unionized economy than in the competitive economy because of the welfare cost associated with imperfect competition in the labor market. If, on the other hand, $L_\tau > 0$, the argument goes the other way around. However, since the employment response to labor income taxation is also likely to differ between the unionized and competitive economies, this comparison with respect to the marginal cost of public funds will remain inconclusive in general. To interpret the second effect, note that if the public good is complementary with leisure and/or substitutable to private consumption, it is not unreasonable to expect that $v_g > u_g$, which works in the direction of increasing the public good in the unionized economy relative to that of the competitive economy. On the other hand, if neither of these two conditions are fulfilled, this effect may work the other way around. Finally, the additional welfare effect of the public good via employment arises because $\varphi_1 > 0$ in the unionized economy. This effect reflects an incentive to provide more (less) of the public good in the unionized economy than in the competitive economy, if $L_g > (<) 0$.

4.3. Briefly on the Case where *g* is Pure Waste

As a brief digression, let us follow Andersen et al. (1996) by analysing whether it is welfare improving to introduce taxation, when the public good is pure waste, so $u_g = v_g = 0$. In the context of the model set out above, and by evaluating Equations (39) and (40) at the point where $\tau = \theta = 0$, we have

$$MCPF_\tau|_{\tau=\theta=0} = 1 - \frac{\varphi_1}{wlnu_c} L_\tau, \tag{44}$$

$$MCPF_\theta|_{\tau=\theta=0} = 1 - \frac{\varphi_2}{m\bar{u}_c r[\bar{k} - z]} - \frac{\varphi_1}{m\bar{u}_c r[\bar{k} - z]} L_\theta. \tag{45}$$

Clearly, in the special case where the economy is competitive, $\varphi_1 = \varphi_2 = 0$, and there will be no welfare effect associated with the introduction of infinitesimal taxes on labor income and capital income. Under union wage setting, on the other hand, the introduction of infinitesimal taxes on labor income and capital income will give rise to welfare effects, since the real wage rate and the employment were not optimally chosen to begin with. If $L_\tau < (>) 0$, there is a welfare cost (gain) associated with the introduction of a small tax on the labor income. Similarly, if $L_\theta < (>) 0$, the welfare effect of introducing a small capital income tax is ambiguous (positive). It may also be optimal to subsidize one of the production factors. For example, if $L_\tau < 0$ and $L_\theta > 0$, it is welfare improving to introduce a small tax on capital income and use the revenues to subsidize employment, if the prereform situation means that these taxes are set equal to zero.

5. SUMMARY AND DISCUSSION

In this chapter, we analyse optimal taxation and provision of a public good in a small open economy, which is characterized by union wage setting. Contrary to previous studies on the optimal taxation of factor income in unionized economies, employment is measured both in terms of the hours of work and the number of employed persons. This means that individuals can be either employed or unemployed and, if employed, that they can be rationed in terms of their hours of work. The main purpose here is to characterize the conditions for the optimal taxation of labor income and capital income and the condition for optimal provision of the public good under union wage setting, and then compare the results with those that would arise in a competitive economy. Our model is particularly convenient from that point of view, since the outcome of a special case of the model is equivalent to the outcome in a competitive economy.

Given the capital income tax rate, there is an extra welfare cost (gain) associated with labor income taxation in the unionized economy, in comparison with the competitive economy, if employment decreases (increases) with the labor income tax rate. This suggests that, if employment decreases with the labor income tax rate, and if the response in employment to labor income taxation is of roughly the same magnitude in the unionized and competitive economies, labor income taxation is more costly at the margin in the unionized economy than in the competitive economy. Despite this obvious implication of imperfect competition in the labor market, it is important to point out that the employment response to labor income taxation needs not be the same in the unionized and competitive economies. Therefore, if the employment response to labor income taxation is weaker in the unionized economy than in the competitive economy, the result might very well be the opposite to what was indicated above.

The condition for the optimal choice of capital income tax rate contains a very interesting result. It is well known from previous studies that if the capital income tax rate decreases the real wage rate, the capital income tax rate can be used to partly offset the welfare cost arising from union wage setting. In a similar way, since the hours of work are endogenous, there is a preexisting distortion from labor income taxation, which can also be offset by the capital income tax, if the capital income tax decreases the real wage rate. Interestingly, the latter effect is weaker in the unionized economy than in the competitive economy, since fewer individuals are employed in the unionized economy. This suggests to us that even if it were possible to use the capital income tax to decrease the real wage rate, the incentive to do so is not necessarily stronger in the unionized economy than in the competitive economy.

Since the consumers' valuation of the public good may depend on the employment situation, and the welfare cost arising from union wage setting may be either reinforced or offset by an increase in the public good, the incentives to provide the public good differ between the unionized and competitive economies. Let us just mention that part of the welfare effect of an increase in the public good is due to imperfect competition in the labor market: this effect will remain also in the simplified version of the model where the government finances the public good by optimal lump sum taxation. In other words, if an increase in the public good gives rise to a sufficiently large increase (decrease) in the employment, the optimal provision of the public good will be larger (smaller) in the unionized economy than in the competitive economy.

APPENDIX

Proof of Proposition 2

Without loss of generality, we shall focus on the derivation of Equation (25). Consider first Equations (15)–(20), which constitute the equilibrium conditions for the private sector. Since $\bar{r}$ is constant, Equation (16) implies

$$\frac{\partial z}{\partial T^e} = \frac{f_{LK}}{m f_{KK}}\left[n\frac{\partial l}{\partial T^e} + l\frac{\partial n}{\partial T^e}\right]. \tag{A1}$$

Then, by differentiating Equation (15) with respect to T^e and using the expression for $\partial z/\partial T^e$ in Equation (A1), we have

$$\frac{\partial w}{\partial T^e} = \left[f_{LL} - \frac{f_{LK}^2}{f_{KK}}\right]\left[n\frac{\partial l}{\partial T^e} + l\frac{\partial n}{\partial T^e}\right], \tag{A2}$$

where $f_{LL} - f_{LK}^2/f_{KK} < 0$.

The next step is to differentiate Equations (19) and (20) with respect to T^e. By using Equation (A2), these derivatives can be written as

$$\frac{\partial c^e}{\partial T^e} = w\frac{\partial l}{\partial T^e} + \left[1 - \frac{n}{m}\right]l\left[f_{LL} - \frac{f_{LK}^2}{f_{KK}}\right]\left[n\frac{\partial l}{\partial T^e} + l\frac{\partial n}{\partial T^e}\right] - 1, \tag{A3}$$

$$\frac{\partial c^u}{\partial T^e} = -\frac{n}{m}l\left[f_{LL} - \frac{f_{LK}^2}{f_{KK}}\right]\left[n\frac{\partial l}{\partial T^e} + l\frac{\partial n}{\partial T^e}\right]. \quad \text{(A4)}$$

Consider the first-order condition for T^e in Equation (21). By substituting Equations (A3) and (A4) into Equation (21) and then using Equations (17) and (18), we can write the first-order condition for T^e as

$$\begin{aligned}\frac{\partial \mathcal{L}}{\partial T^e} &= \left[\frac{\partial n}{\partial T^e}l + \frac{\partial l}{\partial T^e}n\right] \\ &\times \left\{-\frac{wu_c}{\varepsilon} + n\left[1 - \frac{n}{m}\right]l\left[f_{LL} - \frac{f_{LK}^2}{f_{KK}}\right][u_c - v_c]\right\} - \\ &- nu_c + \lambda\left\{n + \frac{\partial n}{\partial T^e}\left[T^e - T^u\right]\right\} = 0. \end{aligned} \quad \text{(A5)}$$

Since $L = nl$ implies

$$\frac{\partial L}{\partial T^e} = \frac{\partial n}{\partial T^e}l + \frac{\partial l}{\partial T^e}n$$

and by using the definition of ε in Equation (2), Equation (A5) can be rewritten to read

$$\begin{aligned}\frac{\partial \mathcal{L}}{\partial T^e} &= \frac{\partial L}{\partial T^e}\frac{wu_c}{\varepsilon}\left\{\left[1 - \frac{n}{m}\right]\left[1 - \frac{v_c}{u_c}\right] - 1\right\} - \\ &- nu_c + \lambda\left\{n + \frac{\partial n}{\partial T^e}[T^e - T^u]\right\} = 0. \end{aligned} \quad \text{(A6)}$$

By defining $MCPF^{T^e} = \lambda/u_c$, Equation (A6) can be written in terms of Equation (25). Equation (26) can be derived by applying an analogous procedure. □

5.1. Proof of Proposition 3

By applying the same procedure as in the proof of Proposition 2, we can derive

$$\frac{\partial w}{\partial g} = \left[f_{LL} - \frac{f_{LK}^2}{f_{KK}}\right]\left[n\frac{\partial l}{\partial g} + l\frac{\partial n}{\partial g}\right], \quad \text{(A7)}$$

$$\frac{\partial c^e}{\partial g} = w\frac{\partial l}{\partial g} + \left[1 - \frac{n}{m}\right]l\left[f_{LL} - \frac{f_{LK}^2}{f_{KK}}\right]\left[n\frac{\partial l}{\partial g} + l\frac{\partial n}{\partial g}\right], \quad \text{(A8)}$$

$$\frac{\partial c^u}{\partial g} = -\frac{n}{m}l\left[f_{LL} - \frac{f_{LK}^2}{f_{KK}}\right]\left[n\frac{\partial l}{\partial g} + l\frac{\partial n}{\partial g}\right]. \quad \text{(A9)}$$

Consider the first-order condition for g, which is given by Equation (23). By substituting Equations (A8) and (A9) into Equation (23) and using Equations (17) and (18), we have

$$\begin{aligned}\frac{\partial \mathcal{L}}{\partial g} &= \frac{\partial L}{\partial g}\left\{-\frac{wu_c}{\varepsilon} + n\left[1-\frac{n}{m}\right]l\left[f_{LL}-\frac{f_{LK}^2}{f_{KK}}\right][u_c - v_c]\right\} + \\ &+ nu_g + [m-n]\,v_g + \lambda\left\{\frac{\partial n}{\partial g}\left[T^e - T^u\right] - 1\right\} = 0, \qquad \text{(A10)}\end{aligned}$$

in which we have used $\partial L/\partial g = (\partial l/\partial g)n + (\partial n/\partial g)l$. If we simplify Equation (A10) by observing that $w/\varepsilon = L[f_{LL} - f_{LK}^2/f_{KK}]$ according to Equation (2), it is straightforward to write Equation (A10) in terms of Equation (27). □

Definitions of the Tax Base Effects

The tax base effects, β_τ and β_θ, in Equations (25) and (26) are given by

$$\beta_\tau = \frac{1}{wL}\left[\tau w + \tau L\left(f_{LL} - \frac{f_{LK}^2}{f_{KK}}\right) - \theta r\frac{f_{LK}}{f_{KK}}\right]\frac{\partial L}{\partial \tau},$$

$$\begin{aligned}\beta_\theta &= \frac{1}{mr(\bar{k}-z)}\left[\tau w + \tau L\left(f_{LL} - \frac{f_{LK}^2}{f_{KK}}\right) - \theta r\frac{f_{LK}}{f_{KK}}\right]\frac{\partial L}{\partial \theta} + \\ &+ \frac{1}{mr(\bar{k}-z)}\left[\frac{\tau Lr}{1-\theta}\frac{f_{LK}}{f_{KK}} + \frac{m\theta r(\bar{k}-z)}{1-\theta} + \frac{\theta r^2}{(1-\theta)f_{KK}}\right].\end{aligned}$$

ACKNOWLEDGEMENT

A research grant from the Jan Wallander and Tom Hedelius Foundation is gratefully acknowledged.

NOTES

1. See also the related work by Wildasin (1979, 1984), King (1986) and Wilson (1991).
2. See, for example, Bucovetsky and Wilson (1991) and Razin and Sadka (1991).

3. As long as the wage rates exceed the market clearing wage rates, the qualitative results to be derived below are not particularly sensitive to the choice between the monopoly union model and a more general bargaining model. This made us choose the monopoly union model over a more computationally burdensome alternative.
4. Recall that the nonlabor income is defined as $\overline{\omega} = \overline{rk} + \pi/m$, where π is the aggregate profit in the economy. This means that the profit income from the sector where the individual is employed makes up a very small proportion of π.
5. The feature that the bargained real wage rate at an interior solution is independent of the size of union membership is a result obtained in traditional union models (see for example Oswald 1985).
6. The reader should note that union wage setting causes a difference between individuals, which suggests that the assumption about a utilitarian objective function is not as harmless here as it might be under perfect competition. An alternative specification is
$$W = n\rho u(c^e, H - l, g) + (m - n)(1 - \rho)v(c^u, H, g),$$
where ρ is the weight given to employed individuals. This formulation nests both the utilitarian objective and the Rawlsian objective as special cases. We use the utilitarian objective function to simplify the comparison between the unionized economy and the competitive economy. At the same time, the conditions for optimal taxation and provision of public goods to be derived below as easily rewritten to reflect this more general objective function.
7. The terms δ_1 and δ_2 are given by
$$\delta_1 = \frac{wl}{\varepsilon T^e}\left\{\left[1 - \frac{n}{m}\right]\left[1 - \frac{v_c}{u_c}\right] - 1\right\} > 0,$$
$$\delta_2 = \frac{wL}{\varepsilon T^u\,[m - n]}\left\{\left[1 - \frac{n}{m}\right]\left[1 - \frac{v_c}{u_c}\right] - 1\right\}\frac{u_c}{v_c} > 0.$$
8. The term δ_3 is given by
$$\delta_3 = \frac{wL}{\varepsilon g}\left\{\left[1 - \frac{n}{m}\right]\left[1 - \frac{v_c}{u_c}\right] - 1\right\}\frac{u_c}{\lambda} > 0.$$

REFERENCES

Andersen, T.M., B. Sandemann Rasmussen and J. Rose Sörensen (1996), 'Optimal fiscal policy in open economies with labor market distortions', *Journal of Public Economics*, 63, 103–117.

Atkinson, A.B. and N.H. Stern (1974), 'Pigou, taxation and public goods', *Review of Economic Studies*, 41, 119–128.

Boadway, R. and M. Keen (1993), 'Public goods, self-selection and optimal taxation', *International Economic Review*, 34, 463–478.

Boeters, S. and K. Schneider (1999), 'Government versus union: The structure of optimal taxation in a unionized labor market', *Finanzarchiv*, 56, 174–187.

Bovenberg, A.L. and F. van der Ploeg (1996), 'Optimal taxation, public goods and environmental policy with involuntary unemployment', *Journal of Public Economics*, 62, 69–83.

Bucovetsky, S. and J.D. Wilson (1991), 'Tax competition with two tax instruments', *Regional Science and Urban Economics*, 21, 333–350.

Christiansen, V. (1981), 'Evaluation of public projects under optimal taxation', *Review of Economic Studies*, 47, 447–457.

Edwards, J., M. Keen and M. Tuomala (1994), 'Income tax, commodity tax and public good provision', *Finanzarchiv*, 51, 472–497.

Gaube, T. (2000), 'When do distortionary taxes reduce the optimal supply of public goods?', *Journal of Public Economics*, 76, 151–180.

King, M.A. (1986), 'A Pigouvian rule for the optimal provision of public goods', *Journal of Public Economics*, 30, 273–291.

Koskela, E. and R. Schöb (2000), 'Optimal factor income taxation in the presence of unemployment', Working Paper No. 279, Center for Economic Studies.

McDonald, I. and R. Solow (1981), 'Wage bargaining and employment', *American Economic Review*, 71(5), 896–908.

Oswald, A.J. (1985), 'The economic theory of trade unions: An introductory survey', *The Scandinavian Journal of Economics*, 87, 160–193.

Pigou, A.C. (1947), *A Study in Public Finance*, London: MacMillan.

Razin, A. and E. Sadka (1991), 'International tax competition and gains from tax harmonization', *Economics Letters*, 37, 69–76.

Samuelson, P.A. (1954), 'The pure theory of public expenditure', *Review of Economics and Statistics*, 36, 387–389.

Stiglitz, J.E. (1982), 'Self-selection and pareto efficient taxation', *Journal of Public Economics*, 17, 213–240.

Wildasin, D.E. (1979), 'Public good provision with optimal and nonoptimal commodity taxation', *Economics Letters*, 4, 59–64.

Wildasin, D.E. (1984), 'Optimal public good provision with distortionary taxation', *Economic Inquiry*, 22, 227–243.

Wilson, J.D. (1991), 'Optimal public good provision with limited lump-sum taxation', *American Economic Review*, 81, 153–166.

Wilson, J.D. (1999), 'Theories of tax competition', *National Tax Journal*, 52, 269–304.

7. Self-Selection and the Value of Lives Saved

Jason F. Shogren and Tommy Stamland

1. INTRODUCTION

The value of lives saved, or statistical life (VSL), can be inferred through real world wage–risk trade-offs made across different occupations (see Schelling 1968, Thaler and Rosen 1976, Viscusi 1992). Based on Adam Smith's idea of compensating wages, one can infer the VSL through the wage–risk trade-offs that arise across industries and occupations that offer higher wages for more risky jobs (Viscusi 1993, Freeman 1993, Hammitt 2000). Market data is used to draw out preferences for risk that are otherwise private information. Reviews of the wage–risk and hypothetical valuation survey literatures suggest that the VSL falls between \$2 to \$8 million (see Viscusi 1993). The VSL currently used by the Environmental Protection Agency (EPA) is about \$6 million per life saved (1999 dollars), based on the mean of a distribution fitted to the estimates from 26 VSL studies (see USEPA 2000).

But could this wage–risk-inferred value of lives saved be potentially misleading? Twenty-five years ago, Lipsey (1976) imagined that the Thaler–Rosen-style wage–risk method might be biased due to self-selection. He pointed out that the estimated value of risk reduction for a randomly selected member of the population will likely *underestimate* the population VSL since workers with low risk aversion tend to self-select into riskier occupations.[1] More recently, Shogren and Stamland (2002) also argue that the wage–risk is likely to be biased – but in the opposite direction. They argue that the wage–risk VSL is likely to be biased *upward* once one accounts for worker heterogeneity in both unobserved risk preferences and their personal skill to cope with risk (Ehrlich and Becker 1972, Shogren and Crocker 1999).[2] In equilibrium, an employer needs to pay the lowest skilled worker a wage to hire him; which implies that the other workers of higher skill and lower value for reduced risk who enter the job earn a rent. Since these higher skilled workers also enter into the job, the average risk is lower than the marginal worker's risk. The wage differential does not reflect this, however, because it is the marginal low skilled worker who sets the wage rate. Thus, the highest required wage differential among the workers is divided by their average risk so that the value of lives saved is inflated.

These disparate viewpoints differ in two key respects – the Lipsey view assumes a mobile self-selecting labor force with homogenous skill to reduce risk; Shogren and Stamland presume an immobile labor force with heterogeneous skill. The open question we address herein is whether the downward self-selection bias dominates or is dominated by the upward skill bias in the estimated wage–risk VSL. Since workers select for themselves whether to work in a relatively safe or risky job, we consider whether there remains a degree of heterogeneity across occupations sufficient to create a significant bias in the estimated values. If high- and low-skill workers self-select such that they separate into jobs by risk preference and skill, the bias is less important. But if workers pool together into the same occupation, the bias is likely to be significant. We run simulations to consider the impact on the bias from varying the distribution of risk, and the value of reduced risk, in the population.

Overall, for the given set of parameters we consider, the results support the idea that an upward bias persists even when people self-select into their job. We distinguish between and estimate both the degree of *Job Overestimation* – the percentage that the VSL exceeds the average value of risk reduction of the workers in the risky job, and the *Population Overestimation* – the percentage that the VSL exceeds the population average value of reduced mortality risk. This distinction matters because the relevant VSL for any project depends on which population the reduction in mortality risk would affect.

Two valuable results emerge in this chapter. First, three factors significantly impact the VSL's overestimation of the population average value of reduced mortality risk. Population overestimation is affected by (1) the percentage of workers who choose the dangerous job, (2) the relative uncertainty – the variation of skill between workers relative to the variation of the value of risk reduction, and (3) the population correlation between the level of risk and the value of risk reduction. The interaction between these three factors implies that no simple constant correction for VSL is likely to exist, and that attempts to correct the VSL bias requires the researcher to account for all factors concurrently. Second, although we find job *underestimation* of VSL arises if the population correlation is negative, few workers are in the dangerous job, and the relative uncertainty is low, job *overestimation* is the most common outcome for the parameters we considered. We find the population correlation and its interaction with the number of workers in the dangerous job is crucial to determining the magnitude of VSL bias. An increase in either correlation or workers tends to increase the bias in the VSL, and this increase is higher when both these variables are large.

2. THE MODEL

We first briefly review the Shogren and Stamland (2002) model of skill and the value of statistical life. Consider workers who differ in two *unobservable* respects: different skills to reduce risk and different values for reduced mortality risk. Different skill levels imply workers do not face the same probability of a fatal accident in the same job; different risk preferences means that they have different trade-offs between job wages and the on-the-job risk of a fatal accident. In the safe job, both worker types face no risk of a fatal accident. In the dangerous job, the likelihood of an accident decreases in the worker's skill. The safe job pays a compensation w_s, and the dangerous job pays w_d. The difference in the wages, $w_d - w_s$, is endogenously given so that the dangerous job is able to attract a given number of workers. The wage differential is set so it is just sufficient to compensate the worker in the dangerous job who requires the highest compensation for the additional risk.

There are T workers who each has his own value of reduced mortality risk, VOL_t, and his own risk associated with the dangerous job, $q_t \geq 0$ for all $t \in \{1, 2, \ldots, T\}$. Assume the workers' utility function takes the form $u(t, P, W) = W - P \cdot VOL_t$, where t denotes the worker's type, $P \in \{0, q_t\}$ is the worker's fatality risk in a job, and $W \in \{w_s, w_d\}$ is the worker's wage. This means, $w_d(t) \equiv w_s + q_t VOL_t$ is the wage that induces worker t to take the dangerous job. The probability a randomly selected worker has a fatal accident in the dangerous job is $\bar{q} \equiv 1/N \sum_{t=1}^{N} q_t$ when workers 1 through N work in the dangerous job.

We examine the VSL estimator, wherein the wages and the statistical probabilities of an accident are used to infer the value of a statistical life by taking the ratio of the wage differential to the risk differential, $VSL = (w_d - w_s)/\bar{q} = q_\tau VOL_\tau / \bar{q}$, where τ is the marginal worker in the dangerous job. Shogren and Stamland (2002) show that the diversity among workers in the dangerous job with respect to skill and value of reduced risk causes an upward bias in the VSL, *taking the distribution of these workers as given*. This presumption is not unreasonable if one accounts for friction in the labor market, e.g., socio-economics, the geographic distribution of jobs and workers, workers' willingness and ability to move between jobs, relocation and reeducation costs, and so on.

To explore whether market friction is necessary to cause a bias in the VSL, we now allow for *self-selection*. Suppose workers can self-select their job based on their skill and value of reduced risk. Self-selection decreases worker diversity because only those with low risk or low value of risk reduction, or both, will select the dangerous job. This low-diversity environment provides a best-case scenario to reduce or remove the VSL bias. We rank the workers according to their wage demands, $w_d(t)$, such that worker 1 has the lowest demanded wage and worker number T (of a total of T workers) demands the highest wage to take the dangerous job. This means that if there are N workers in the dangerous job in equilibrium, these are workers 1 through N and the equilibrium wage is $w_d = w_d(N)$. Let us look at an illustration.

In this example, assume the workers' risk is either 1.0, 2.5, or 4.0 ten thousands, the value of reduced risk of premature death is either 1, 2, or 3 million dollars, and these characteristics are independently and uniformly distributed in a population of 9 workers.[3] Table 7.1 ranks the workers according to their wage demand $w_d(t)$ when the safe wage is $w_s = \$20\,000$. The first column gives the worker's numerical rank, the second gives the worker's risk, q_t, in ten thousands, the third shows the worker's value of risk reduction in million dollars, and the fourth reveals how the worker was ranked based on the worker's demanded wage in dollars. The fifth and sixth columns give the cumulative average risk and value of reduced risk, in which the element in row N (for worker N) is a cumulative average over workers 1 through N. These two columns give the average risk and value of life in the dangerous job if there are N workers in this job, for $N = 1, 2, \ldots, 9$.

The seventh column gives the VSL estimate, which is the wage differential $w_d(t) - w_s$ divided by $\bar{q}$ as found in the cumulative average risk column. The *Job Overestimation* column reports the percentage with which the VSL exceeds the average value of risk reduction of the workers in the dangerous job, and the *Population Overestimation* reports the percentage with which the VSL exceeds the population average value of reduced mortality risk, \$2 million. As one can see, the job overestimation is positive when there is more than one worker in the dangerous job.

Table 7.1. The effect of self-selection on estimated VSL

Worker	Risk[1]	*VOL*[2]	$w_d(t)$[3]	Cumulative Avg. risk[1]	Cumulative Avg. *VOL*[2]	*VSL*[2]	Job over-estimation	Population over-estimation	Corr. q_t and VOL_t
1	1	1	20 100	1	1	1	0	–50%	NA
2	1	2	20 200	1	1.5	2	33%	0	NA
3	2.5	1	20 250	1.5	1.33	1.67	25%	–17%	–0.500
4	1	3	20 300	1.38	1.75	2.18	25%	9%	–0.522
5	4	1	20 400	1.9	1.6	2.11	32%	5%	–0.563
6	2.5	2	20 500	2	1.67	2.5	50%	25%	–0.500
7	2.5	3	20 750	2.07	1.86	3.62	95%	81%	–0.315
8	4	2	20 800	2.31	1.88	3.46	85%	73%	–0.231
9	4	3	21 200	2.5	2	4.8	140%	140%	0

(1) In ten thousands.
(2) In million dollars.
(3) In dollars.

Shogren and Stamland (2002) showed that if only one of the characteristics of the worker varies across the workers, the VSL is always a biased estimate of the value of reduced mortality risk for the workers in the dangerous job. We see this result again in Table 7.1. If workers #1 and #2 – who have identical risk – work in the dangerous job, the job overestimation is 33 per cent.

Note as the number of workers in the dangerous job is increased from two to three, four or five, the job overestimation is actually reduced. This occurs even though more workers cause more diversity in risk between the workers, and also more variation in the value of reduced risk when there are exactly four workers in the dangerous job. The reason for this reduced overestimation can be observed in the last column of the table. Although risk and the value of risk reduction are uncorrelated in the population of workers, self-selection induces a negative correlation between these characteristics among the workers in the dangerous job. This negative correlation means that if the marginal worker has a high risk relative to the intra-marginal workers, he is likely to have low value of risk reduction relative to the intra-marginal workers, and *vice versa*. The bias caused by the marginal worker having a high realization of either risk or the value of reduced mortality risk tends to be partially offset by a low realization of the other characteristic. This offset is only partial, though. Otherwise the marginal worker would not be marginal.[4] We observe that workers 3, 4, and 5 actually have the lowest possible realization of one characteristic, whereas their realization of the other characteristic is higher than for the workers that are intra-marginal to them. The self-selection into the dangerous job helps to mitigate the bias in the VSL, but unfortunately some bias remains.

When we have six or more workers in the dangerous job, the additional variation in the characteristics between the workers has grown sufficiently to offset the effect of this induced correlation. Now the induced negative correlation begins to dissipate as more workers are included in the dangerous job, forcing the job correlation towards the population correlation, which is zero. When the entire population works in the dangerous job, the two correlations are calculated for the same set of workers and must therefore be identical.

The VSL uses the data from the workers that choose the dangerous job to estimate the valuation of life revealed by their choice. But we see that the VSL does a poor job of estimating the value of risk reduction for these workers. If we were instead trying to infer the average value of risk

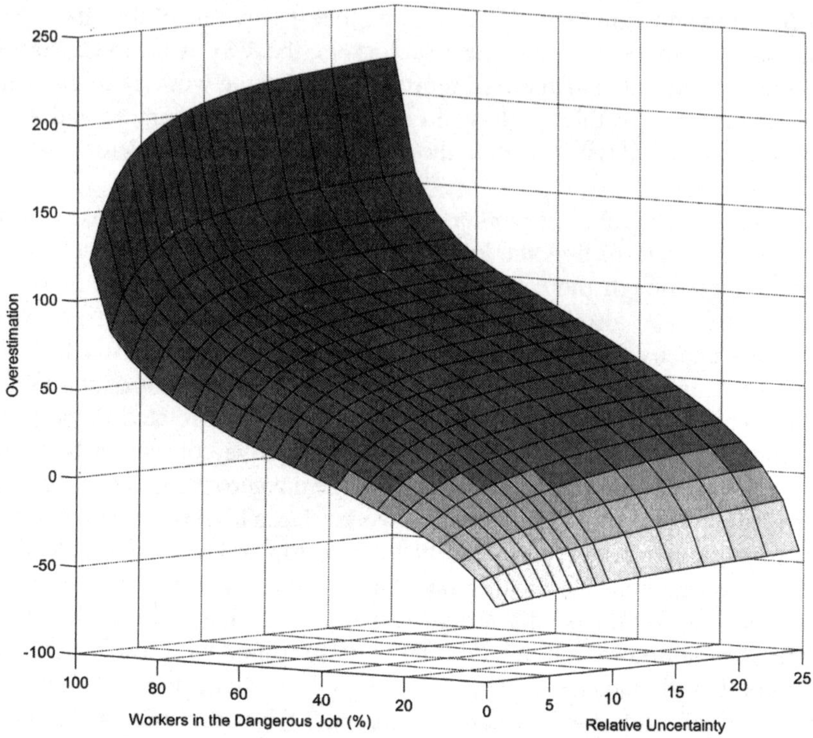

Figure 7.1. Overestimation of the population mean value of life population correlation = 0.5

reduction in the population, the VSL performs somewhat better. Observe that the population overestimation numbers, in column nine in Table 7.1, are lower than the job overestimation numbers.[5] The VSL underestimates the *population* average value of reduced mortality risk ($2 million) when there are one or three workers in the dangerous job. When there are two workers in the dangerous job, the VSL equals population average value, but this is accidental rather than planned. The VSL overestimates the population average value of reduced risk if there are four or more workers in the dangerous job, and this overestimation tends to increase with more workers in the dangerous job.

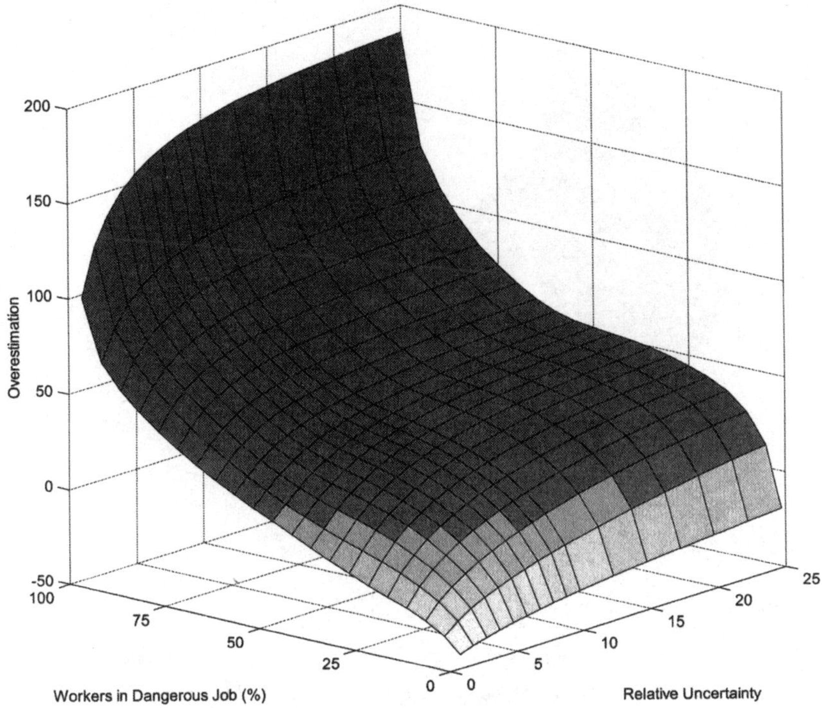

Figure 7.2. Overestimation of the population mean value of life population correlation = 0

3. SIMULATIONS

We now run simulations to examine in greater detail the issues exposed by our example about self-selection and the potential for a VSL bias.[6] Our simulations explore the impact on the VSL bias as the correlation between the risk and the value of reduced risk in the population ('the population correlation') is varied from -1 to 1. In the uncorrelated case,[7] the workers' value of reduced mortality risk are uniformly distributed over [\$1 million, \$3 million] and the risk is uniformly distributed over $[1/10\ 000, (RU + 1)/10\ 000]$ for $RU = 1, 2, \ldots, 10, 12.5, 15, \ldots, 25$. RU, short for *relative uncertainty*, measures the variation of skill between workers relative to the variation of the value of risk reduction because we keep the variance of the value of risk reduction constant.[8] For each population correlation,

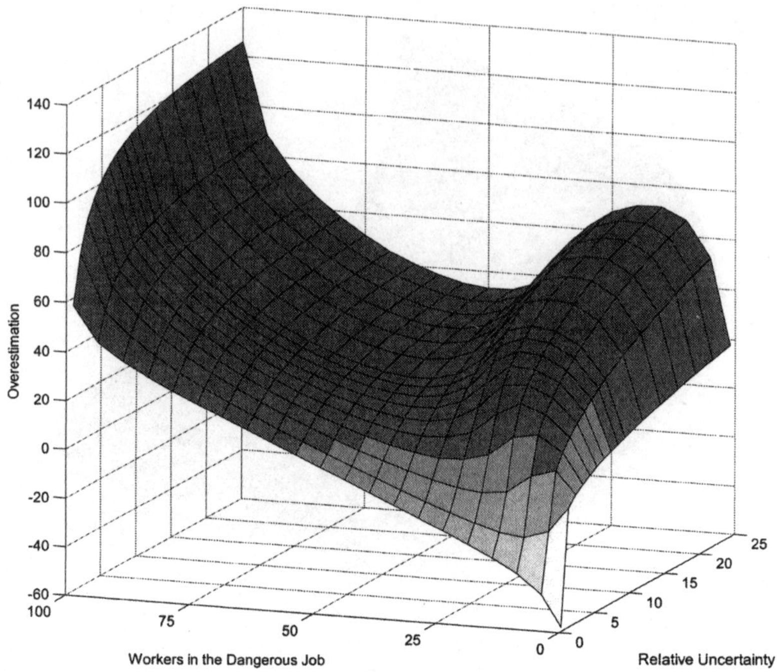

Figure 7.3. Overestimation of the population mean value of life population correlation $= -0.5$

1000 simulations are run, each with 10 000 workers. We look at the VSL obtained if 1 per cent, 5 per cent, 10 per cent, ..., 100 per cent of the workers choose the dangerous job.

Figures 7.1–7.3 compare the average VSL to the population average value of risk reduction to obtain the 'population overestimation'. The gray-shading of the 3D surfaces changes discontinuously when the overestimation changes sign. Light shades indicate that the VSL underestimates the value of risk reduction, darker shades indicate overestimation. The relative uncertainty, RU, is plotted along the X-axis, the percentage of workers in the dangerous job is plotted along the Y-axis, and the population overestimation is plotted along the Z-axis. As we increase the percentage of workers in the dangerous job (i.e. as we move along the Y-axis), we increase the diversity of the workers in that job in the sense that the variation of their risks and values of life increase. Therefore, we interpret the percentage of workers in the dangerous job as a measure of

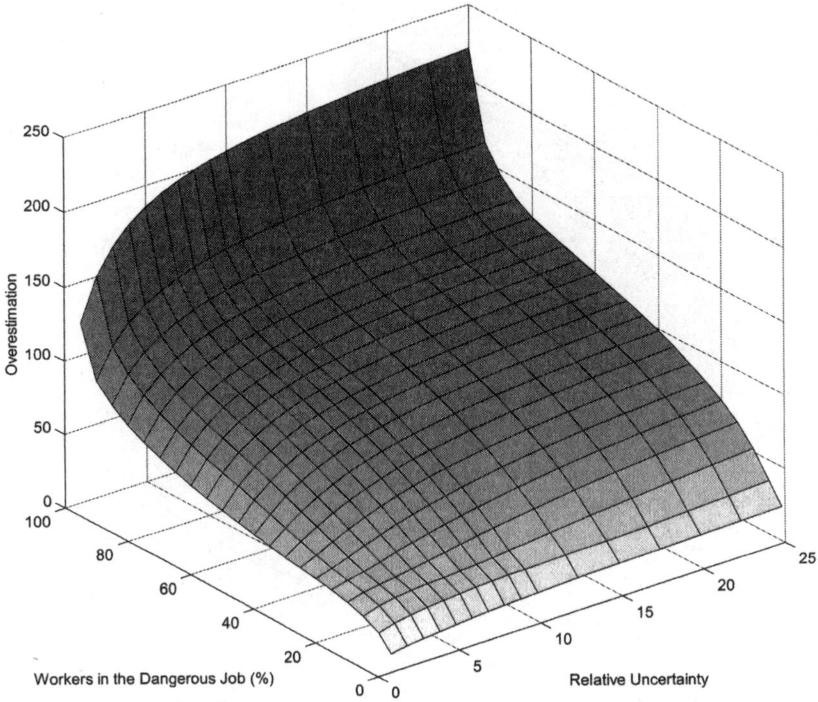

Figure 7.4. Overestimation of the job mean value of life population correlation = 0.5

worker diversity. Figures 7.1–7.3 show the population overestimation for population correlations of 0.5, 0, and −0.5.

Two key results emerge from these simulations. First, three factors – the percentage of workers who choose the dangerous job, the relative uncertainty, and the population correlation – all substantially impact the VSL's overestimation of the population average value of reduced mortality risk. Correcting the bias in the VSL requires the researcher to account for all three determinants – no simple constant correction for VSL is likely to exist. The figures show that the properties of the VSL bias are complex, with surfaces that are both nonmonotonic and nonlinear. For instance, the VSL *underestimates* the population average value of risk reduction when few workers are employed in the dangerous job. For nonnegative population correlations, the population overestimation then increases monotonically with more workers in the dangerous job (Figures 7.1 and 7.2). But when the population correlation is negative, this relationship is no longer monotonic (Figure 7.3). The population correlation strongly impacts the shapes of

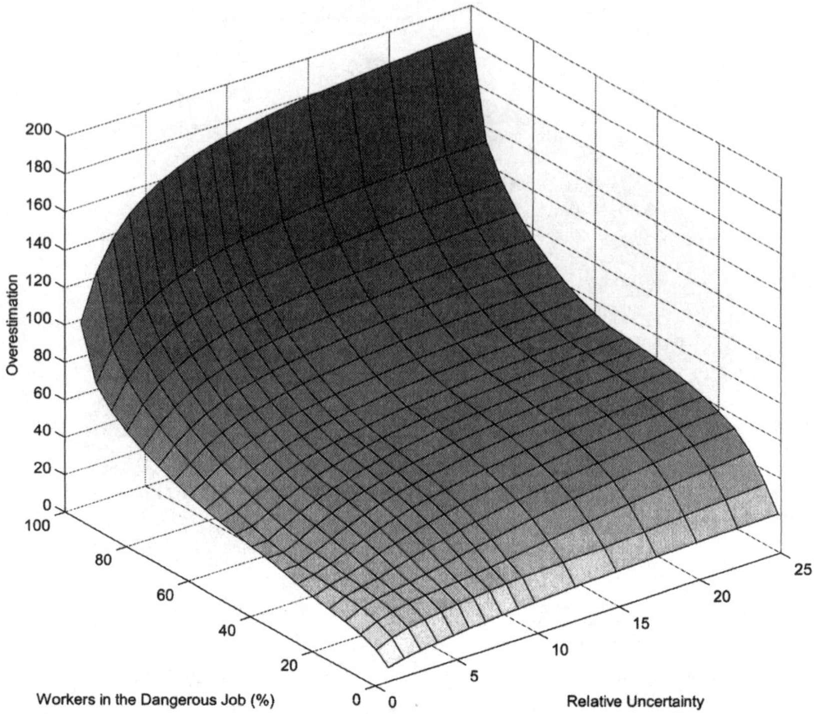

Figure 7.5. Overestimation of the job mean value of life population correlation = 0

these surfaces. The greater the correlation, the steeper is the increase in the overestimation as diversity rises. The impact of the relative uncertainty becomes more important – compared to the effect of worker diversity – as the population correlation decreases. A detailed empirical investigation of the VSL to further size up the consequences of this problem would be useful.

Second, the VSL systematically overestimates the average value of risk reduction for the workers in the dangerous job ('job overestimation'). Figures 7.1–7.3 show the VSL leans towards overestimating the population average value of reduced risk. Figures 7.4–7.6 reveal that this problem is accentuated when the VSL is compared to the average value of reduced risk of the workers in the dangerous job. For nonnegative population correlations, the VSL always overestimates this value revealing a systematic bias (see Figures 7.4 and 7.5).

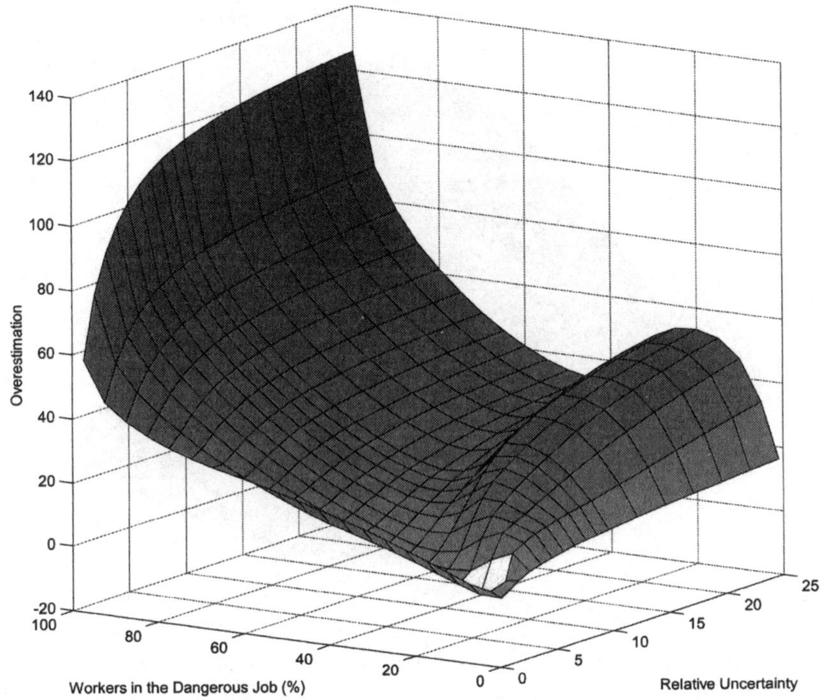

Figure 7.6. Overestimation of the job mean value of life population correlation $= -0.5$

Figure 7.6 shows that job underestimation is possible, although unlikely. Shogren and Stamland (2002) showed that the VSL will overestimate the value of reduced risk of the workers in the dangerous job *unless there is an inverse relationship between risk and the value of reduced mortality risk.* Across the simulations, we observe job underestimation on average only when the correlation between risk and the value of reduced risk for the workers in the dangerous job is -0.95 or lower on average, which is consistent with the upward VSL bias. The correlation need not be quite -1 since the inverse relationship need not be perfectly linear and need not be perfect in *every case* to get underestimation *on average.* We observe in Figure 7.6 that job *under*estimation may be obtained if the population correlation is negative, there are few workers in the dangerous job, and the relative uncertainty is low. But Figure 7.6 shows us that *over*estimation appears to be by far the most common case. We also see that the job overestimation, unlike the population overestimation, need not be monotonically increasing in the relative uncertainty.

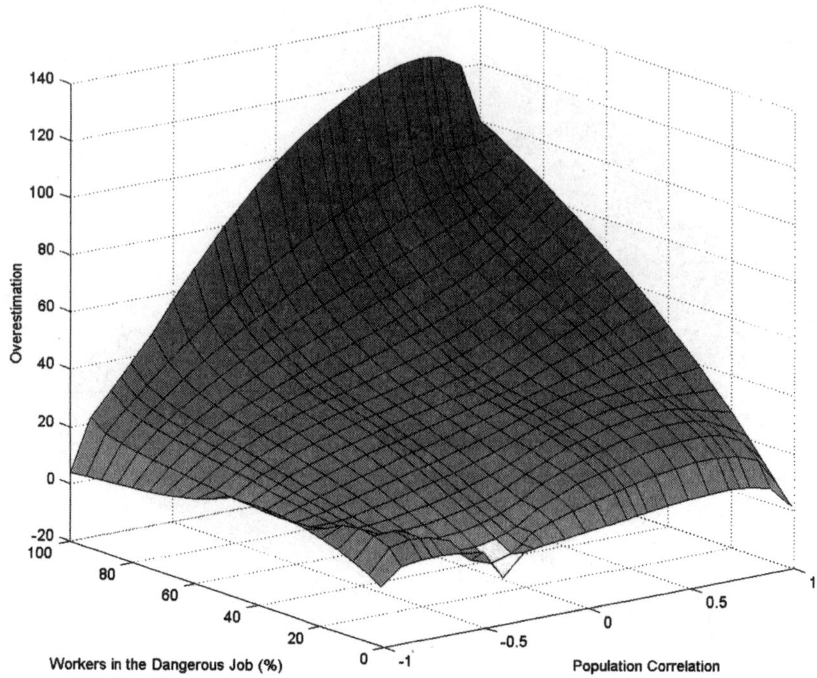

Figure 7.7. Overestimation of the job mean value of life risk in the interval [0.0001, 0.0002]

Figures 7.7–7.9 plot the population correlation rather than the relative uncertainty along the X-axis, and show the job overestimation for relative uncertainties of 1, 3 and 10. This yields another compelling view of the non-linearity and systematic upward bias of the VSL estimate. These figures show the importance of the population correlation and its interaction with the number of workers in the dangerous job. An increase in either of these variables tends to increase the bias in the VSL, and this increase is higher when both these variables are high.

Finally, Figure 7.10 shows how self-selection induces more negative correlation between risk and the value of reduced risk. Again, the relationship is nonlinear and nonmonotonic. The effect roughly tends to be larger the greater the population correlation and the fewer workers in the job. The job correlation and population correlation must necessarily be equal when the entire population works in the dangerous job – as shown by the 45-degree line above the Y-axis in Figure 7.10.

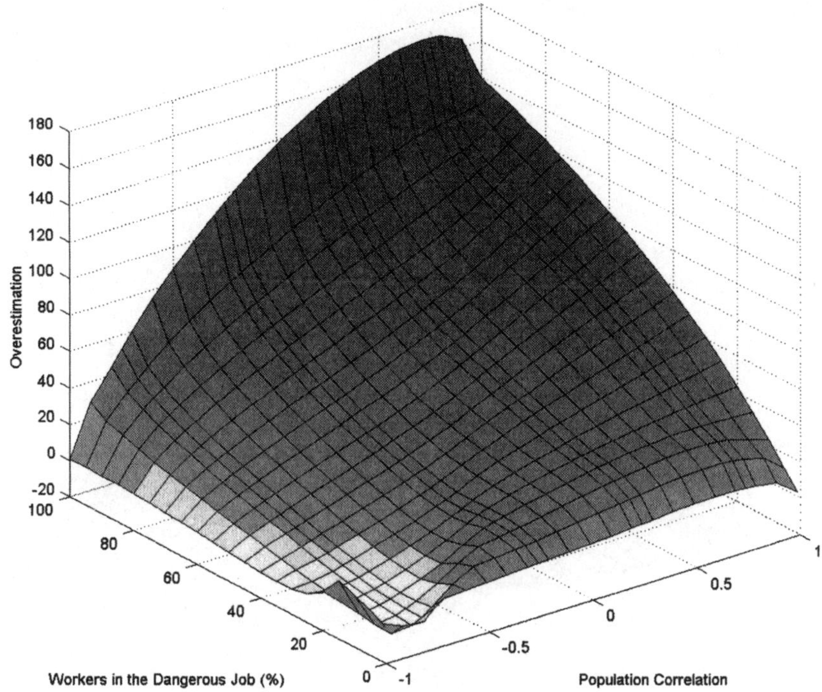

Figure 7.8. Overestimation of the job mean value of life risk in the interval [0.0001, 0.0004]

4. CONCLUDING COMMENTS

A problem with using wage–risk tradeoffs to infer private preferences about the value of lives saved is that workers' choices are not just driven by risk preferences. Workers can invest effort to protect themselves from risk, and their skill in doing so is often private information too. Workers select occupations of different inherent risks based on both their risk preference and their skill to reduce risk. And when a choice under risk is made based on two pieces of private information, the choice is unlikely to reveal perfectly either piece of information. This suggests inferences made from market or survey data might lead to biased estimates of the value of reduced mortality risk, if it does not account for private information about a worker's skill to reduce risk himself and his value of risk reduction.

This chapter shows that the value of statistical life (VSL) is still likely to be biased even if we allow workers to self-select into safe and risky jobs. Our overall conclusion about self-selection and job risk is that the VSL

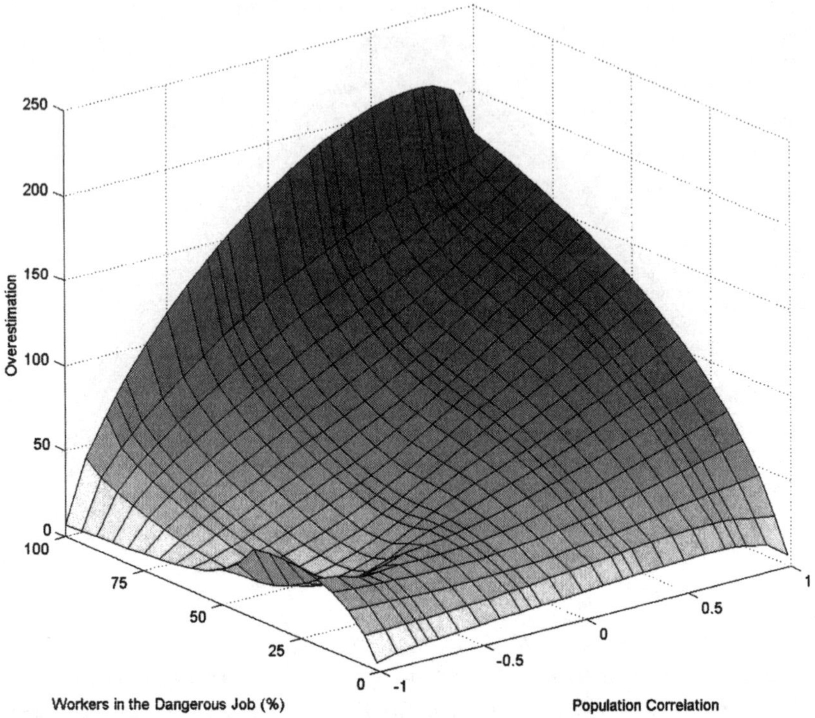

Figure 7.9. Overestimation of the job mean value of life risk in the interval [0.0001, 0.0011]

performs poorly in our simulations that were designed to provide a best-case scenario for the VSL estimator. Accounting for friction in the labor market will only make the VSL bias more severe. These results continue to support the idea that value of lives saved as estimated from wage–risk tradeoffs is likely to be biased upward when one accounts for the diversity of skill. This result holds even if workers self-select into dangerous and safe occupations. The VSL estimate still divides the highest required wage differential with the average risk differential so that a bias arises. Given the importance of the value of lives saved in major policy debates, future efforts to account for skill in the labor market to estimate the magnitude of the upward bias would be most welcome.

We conclude by offering a constructive direction for future research aimed at accounting for the VSL bias in wage–risk tradeoffs. Shogren and Stamland (2003) suggest using the General Method of Moments (GMM) approach to elicit consistent estimates of the value of reduced risk. GMM

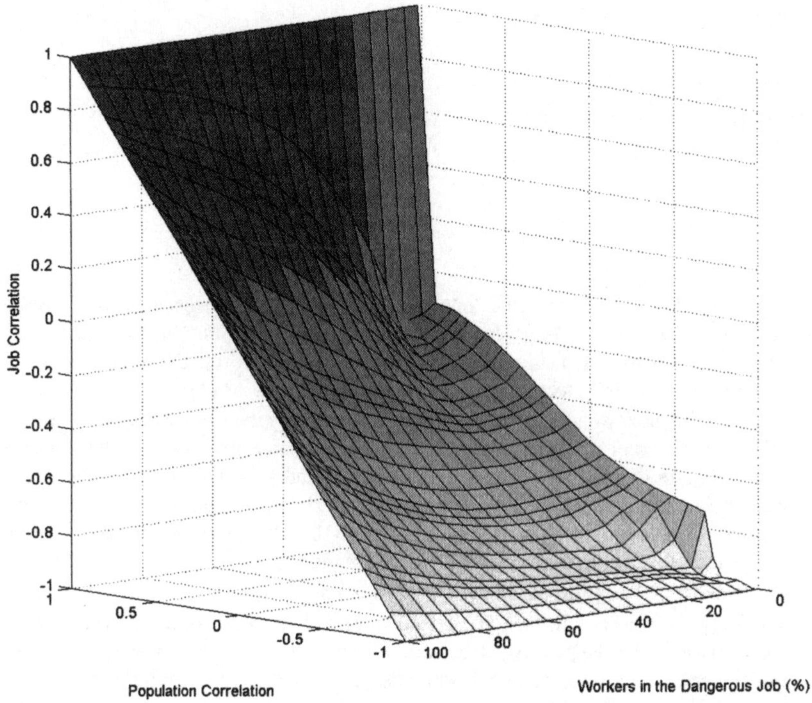

Figure 7.10. Correlation, in the dangerous job, between risk and the value of life risk in the interval [0.0001, 0.0004]

can combine data from several sources into a coherent framework that allows the estimation of one person's idiosyncratic utility parameters. Popular in macro-economic and finance research, the method creates a single estimate based on multidimensional data from different sources (also see Pagan and Wickens 1989). Although one might expect the method will have to operate with fewer observations due to costly data collection, our initial simulation results suggest that good estimates can still emerge. Future empirical research exploring the usefulness of applying GMM in the estimation of wage–risk data or any other risk reduction data (e.g., averting behavior) seems worthwhile, and is a next step in our research program.

ACKNOWLEDGEMENTS

Thanks to Tom Crocker, Randy Lutter, Laura Taylor, and Kip Viscusi for their helpful comments. We acknowledge the Economic Research Service/ USDA for their financial support. All views remain our own.

NOTES

1. Lipsey (1976, p. 302) says that 'one might guess that the presence of this personal-characteristics element [e.g., habits aside from risk aversion] in the risk measure produces a downward bias in the estimate of the price of occupational risk, additional to the bias from self-selection of less risk-averse workers'.
2. In discussing how wage–risk trade-offs are estimated by the wage differential between jobs with different risks, Viscusi (1993) suggests that worker heterogeneity can affect the value of reduced mortality risk. Viscusi notes the marginal worker sets the wage differential and hence the inferred value of risk reduction. And if this marginal worker's unobserved risk preference differs from the other workers, this local trade-off can be a misleading index of the required wage premium.
3. We relax the assumption of independence in our simulations.
4. The marginal worker has the highest product of risk and value of life, $q_t VOL_t$, among the workers in the dangerous job because this product alone determines the workers' ranking according to the wage demand, $w_d(t)$. So the marginal worker's realization of each of these characteristics must be large enough for the worker to have the highest product, $q_t VOL_t$, in the dangerous job. Therefore, the marginal worker can never be representative of the average worker in the dangerous job *unless* all workers share the same realizations of both risk and the value of life, or there is an inverse relationship between these characteristics.
5. The exception is when the entire population works in the dangerous job so that the true average value of life is the same in the job and in the population.
6. Kniesner and Leeth (1995) illustrated how numerical simulation can be used to examine econometric models of workplace safety. They explored how safety programs such as OSHA and Workers Compensation affect fatality risks, whereas in our related simulation work, we use simulations to quantify a fundamental problem with the VSL estimator revealed by our theoretical analysis (Shogren and Stamland 2002). Safety programs cause the fatality risk in a job to vary over time. Kniesner and Leeth also recognized the source of the risk variation could be the person in question.
7. We use two independent unit uniform random variables, u_1 and u_2, to generate the random draws of the risk and the value of life, with a population correlation of ρ between them, as follows:

$$q = 1 + u_1 RU \qquad \text{(in ten thousands)}$$

$$VOL = 2 - \rho + \sqrt{1-\rho^2} + 2\rho u_1 + 2\sqrt{1-\rho^2}u_2 \qquad \text{(in million dollars)}$$

Note the value of life's probability distribution changes shape when we induce correlation between the variables because this distribution is then a convolution of two uniform distributions. But we maintain a fixed variance of these distributions across all the population correlations, ρ.

8. The intervals the risk is drawn from imply that we shift the mean of the risk as we vary RU. This is necessary so that we do not allow negative probabilities.

REFERENCES

Ehrlich, I. and G. Becker (1972). 'Market insurance, self-insurance, and self-protection', *Journal of Political Economy*, 80, 623–648.

Freeman, A.M. III (1993), *The Measurement of Environmental and Resource Values: Theory and Methods*, Washington, DC: Resources for the Future.

Hammitt, J.K. (2000), 'Valuing mortality risk: Theory and practice', *Environmental Science and Technology*, 34, 1396–1400.

Kniesner, T. and J. Leeth (1995), 'Numerical simulation as a complement to econometric research on workplace safety', *Journal of Risk and Uncertainty*, 10, 99–126.

Lipsey, R. (1976), 'Comments on "The value of saving a life: Evidence from the labor market"', in N. Terleckyj (ed.), *Household Production and Consumption*, New York: NBER, pp. 301–302.

Pagan, A. and M. Wickens (1989), 'A survey of some recent econometric methods', *Economic Journal*, 99, 962–1025.

Schelling, T. (1968), 'The life you save may be your own', in *Choice and Consequence: Perspectives of an Errant Economist*, Cambridge, MA: Harvard University Press, pp. 113–146.

Shogren, J. and T. Crocker (1999), 'Risk and its consequences', *Journal of Environmental Economics and Management*, 37, 44–52.

Shogren, J. and T. Stamland (2002), 'Skill and the value of life', *Journal of Political Economy*, 110, 1168–1173.

Shogren, J. and T. Stamland (2003), 'Consistent estimation of the value of statistical life', Manuscript, University of Wyoming.

Thaler, R. and S. Rosen (1976), 'The value of saving a life: Evidence from the labor market', in N. Terleckyj (ed.), *Household Production and Consumption*, New York: NBER, pp. 265–298.

US Environmental Protection Agency (USEPA) (2000), 'Regulatory impact analysis: Heavy-duty engine and vehicle standards and highway diesel fuel sulfur control requirements', EPA420-R-00-026, Washington, DC.

Viscusi, W.K. (1992), *Fatal Tradeoffs: Public and Private Responsibilities for Risk*, New York: Oxford University Press.

Viscusi, W.K. (1993), 'The value of risks to life and health', *Journal of Economic Literature*, 31, 1912–1946.

8. International Fisheries Agreements: The Feasibility and Impacts of Partial Cooperation

Kim Hang Pham Do and Henk Folmer

1. INTRODUCTION

The oceans' fish stocks have been exploited as never before. Most of the world's marine fishing areas have already reached their maximum potential for fish captures (UN 2002). FAO (2000) shows that about 47 to 50 per cent of marine fish stocks are fully exploited and are, therefore, producing catches that have either reached or are very close to their maximum limits, with no room for further expansion. Another 15 to 18 per cent are overexploited and there is an increasing likelihood that catches from these stocks will decrease, if remedial action is not taken to reduce or revert overfishing conditions. The world catch of marine fish has continued to rise in spite of extensions of fisheries jurisdictions (Exclusive Economic Zone or EEZ) in the mid-1970s to 200 miles, though at a slower rate. To regulate the exploitation of the ocean's fish stocks further, several international agreements have been concluded. The relevant international law was codified, developed and enhanced through, *inter alia*, the entry into force of the UN Convention on the Law of the Sea in 1994, the adoption of the Convention on Straddling Fish Stocks and Highly Migratory Fish Stocks in 1995 (abbreviated as 1995 UN Fish Stocks Agreement), and the adoption of the FAO Code of Conduct for Responsible Fisheries in the same year. Moreover, an international jurisprudence on fisheries related issues is slowly emerging through the work of the International Tribunal on the Law of the Sea (for details, see Green Paper 2001).

The 1995 UN Fish Stocks Agreement calls for those nations who wish to participate in the harvesting of the fish resources in the high seas, but are not currently members of the relevant Regional Fisheries Management Organization (RFMO), to declare a willingness to join and to enter into negotiations over mutually acceptable terms of entry. Under the terms of the UN Convention on the Law of the Sea, which is of direct relevance to the 1995 UN Fish Stocks Agreement, coastal states (CSs) and distant water fishing nations (DWFNs) shall apply the precautionary approach to conservation, management and exploitation of straddling and highly migratory fish stocks in order to protect the living resources and preserve the marine environment. In addition, all states are obliged to take conservation and management measures necessary for the conservation of the living resources of the high seas (Article 117). Moreover, international cooperation and negotiations are required for all states involved in the exploitation of such resources (Article 118).

Although the 1995 UN Fish Stocks Agreement entered into force on 11 December 2001 (UN 2002), the precise meaning of the provisions describing these obligations is not clear nor the manner in which they will be applied. For example, Article 63 expresses that the states concerned should seek to agree on conservation measures applicable beyond the EEZs, either directly or through appropriate RFMOs. Article 64 requires that coastal and other states whose nationals fish in the region '*shall cooperate*' directly or through appropriate international organizations with a view to ensuring conservation and optimum utilization. Furthermore, Article 118 on high seas stocks, referring to the need to establish RFMOs, provides that states exploiting such stocks or different ones in the same area '*shall enter into negotiations*' with a view to taking the measures necessary for the conservation of the living resources concerned.

Due to *inter alia* its ambiguities, the 1995 UN Fish Stocks Agreement provides little or no guidance as to how cooperation, through a RFMO, is to be effected (Munro 2000). The lack of cooperation has resulted in conflicts between coastal states and distant water fishing states (Bjørndal and Munro 2003).[1] Moreover, overexploitation has continued and the need for a cooperative management regime is evident.[2]

The literature on the economic analysis of the 1995 UN Fish Stocks Agreement notes that the new member or participant problem is one of the most important problems in the high seas fishery management (Kaitala and Munro 1993, 1995; Bjørndal and Munro 2003), since the interests of current members of the RFMO and of the applicants are often strongly opposed: the current members face the likelihood of having to give up a portion of their present quotas to the newcomer, and the applicant believes that it may be better off by staying outside of the coalition and continuing harvesting while facing fewer constraints. According to Kaitala and Munro

(1997), the likelihood of achieving stable cooperation will be very low if the new member problem is mishandled. In addition, Datta and Miraman (1999) show that with an increasing number of countries, the inefficiency of the noncooperative equilibrium generated by the common access feature of high seas dominates and overharvesting increases. Although the nations involved in a regional fishery resource often recognize an advantage in cooperative management of the resource, on-going negotiations over harvest allotments often have proven to be arduous and frustrating, and interrupted by brief but astonishingly violent 'fish wars'.

This chapter examines how a RFMO might successfully achieve effective control of a high seas fishery in the context of partial cooperation. We consider the high seas fishery stock as common property and assume that all nations are allowed to exploit it. We view concluding a Regional Fishery Agreement (RFA) as a game, where countries freely decide whether or not to join a coalition (i.e. a RFMO).[3] That is, we consider a management situation where a coalition of countries, say S, cooperate and where one or several groups of countries stay outside S. The coalition member of S will coordinate their inputs so as to maximize their incomes. However, coalition S's income will be affected by a negative externality due to the input of those who do not belong to S.

The question that we deal with here is the feasibility of partial cooperation and its impacts on fishing efforts. Moreover, we analyse how to allocate property rights among fishing nations that have expressed an interest in sustainable exploitation of a fish stock in a partial cooperative setting. Particulary, we examine the feasible allocations of property rights among members of a given RFMO and coalitions of potential entrants.

In this chapter, the feasibility and impacts of partial cooperation are analysed by means of games in partition function form. This class of games was introduced in Thrall and Lucas (1963) and is a generalization of characteristic function form games. The partition function form game allows the complements to split into coalitions in an arbitrary manner, while the classical characteristic function form game is defined in terms of coalitions and their complements only. We apply the modified Shapley value as a device for the division of the gains from partial cooperation. We observe that the emphasis in this chapter is on the cost function rather than on the production function.

The chapter is organized as follows. The next section presents the basic model and introduces notations and definitions. Section 3 analyses the effects of partial cooperation in terms of fishing efforts. Section 4 demonstrates that the modified Shapley value is a feasible solution concept for RFMOs. Concluding remarks follow in the last section.

2. THE MODEL AND DEFINITIONS

We begin by specifying a static model[4] of a common fishery resource as an n-person game (cf. Funaki and Yamato 1999, Cornes and Hartley 2000). Let $N = \{1, 2, \ldots, n\}$ be the set of n fishing nations, with generic element $j \in N$. Let $e = (e_1, e_2, \ldots, e_n)$ be a vector of fishing efforts, where $e_j \geq 0$ is country j's fishing effort, and let $e_N = \sum_{j=1}^{n} e_j$ be the aggregate fishing effort of all countries.

We introduce the production function $f(e_N)$ that specifies the amount of fish caught for each value of the total effort e_N. We assume that effort as input is homogenous and that all countries are equally likely to catch a fish per unit of effort. This implies that the share of the total harvest obtained by country j is directly proportional to the share of country j's effort in total effort e_N. In other words, the harvest of country j is given by $(e_j/e_N)f(e_N)$ for a given fish stock.[5]

Different levels of technology efficiency among countries are represented by the cost functions $c_j(e_j)$. Normalizing the price of the resource to unity, the net rent or benefit of country j is given by

$$\pi_j(e_1, e_2, \ldots, e_n) = \frac{e_j}{e_N} f(e_N) - c_j(e_j), \tag{1}$$

where $\pi_j(0, 0, \ldots, 0) = 0$.

We make the following assumptions:

Assumption A1: $f(.)$ is twice continuously differentiable, $f''(.) < 0$ (i.e. strictly concave for $e_N > 0$),[6] and $f(0) = 0$.

Assumption A2: $c_j(.)$ is continuously differentiable, increasing and convex for every j.

To simplify the analysis, we assume that $c_j(e_j) = c_j e_j$, where $c_j > 0$ for every $j \in N$.

Assumption A3: $0 < c_j < f'(0)$, for every $j \in N$.

This assumption guarantees the existence of an interior solution.

For every $e = (e_1, e_2, \ldots, e_n)$, and $i \in N$ we define $e_{-i} = (e_1, \ldots, e_{i-1}, e_{i+1}, \ldots, e_n)$. In a similar vein, a vector $e = (e_1, e_2, \ldots, e_n)$ is written as $e = (e_i, e_{-i})$.

The above assumptions imply that the benefit function (1) is continuously differentiable and strictly concave on e_j. Particularly, the biological constraints that the benefit function is decreasing for e_N large enough is met.

- A vector of effort $e^* = (e_1^*, e_2^*, \ldots, e_n^*)$ is said to be a *competitive equilibrium* or Nash equilibrium (NE) if $\forall i \in N$, and $\forall\, e_i \geq 0$

$$\pi_i(e_i^*, e_{-i}^*) \geq \pi_i(e_i, e_{-i}^*), \tag{2}$$

where $e_i^* \geq 0$, $\forall i \in N$.

The assumptions A1–A3 guarantee the existence of a competitive equilibrium. Moreover, this equilibrium is unique (Theorem 1 and Corollary 1 in Watt 1996).

In addition to the above mathematical assumptions (A1–A3), we make the following behavioural assumptions A4–A5.

Assumption A4: A country is free to enter or leave a coalition. When a country defects from a coalition defectors either play as singletons or form a new coalition.

Assumption A5: When countries coordinate to form a coalition, their objective is to maximize the aggregate benefit, given the strategies of the others.

We introduce the following notions and definitions that will be used to analyse partial cooperation:

- A *coalition structure*, κ, is a partition of the set N of countries. Let $\mathbb{P}(N)$ be the set of all partitions of N. So, a coalition structure $\kappa \in \mathbb{P}(N)$ means that $\kappa = \{S_1, \ldots, S_m\}$, $N \supseteq S_j \neq \emptyset$, $S_j \cap S_k = \emptyset$, for all $j, k = 1, \ldots, m$, $j \neq k$ and $\cup_{j=1}^m S_j = N$.

For a given $\kappa \in \mathbb{P}(N)$, let $|\kappa|$ denote the cardinality of κ (i.e. if $\kappa = \{S_1, \ldots, S_m\}$ then $|\kappa| = m$). The partition which consists of singleton coalitions only, $\kappa = \{\{1\}, \{2\}, \ldots, \{n\}\}$, is denoted by $[N]$ whereas the partition which consists of the grand coalition only is denoted by $\{N\}$.

- A pair (S, κ) which consists of a coalition S and a partition κ of N to which S belongs is called an *embedded coalition.*

Let $\mathbb{E}(N)$ denote the set of embedded coalitions, i.e.

$$\mathbb{E}(N) = \{(S, \kappa) \in 2^N \times \mathbb{P}(N) \mid S \in \kappa\}.$$

DEFINITION 1. A mapping

$$w : \mathbb{E}(N) \longrightarrow R$$

that assigns a real value, $w(S, \kappa)$, to each embedded coalition (S, κ) is called a *partition function*. The ordered pair (N, w) is called a *partition function form game*.

The value $w(S, \kappa)$ represents the payoff of coalition S, given that coalition structure κ forms. For a given partition $\kappa = \{S_1, S_2, \ldots, S_m\}$ and a partition function w, let $\overline{w}(S_1, S_2, \ldots, S_m)$ denote the m-vector $(w(S_i, \kappa))_{i=1}^m$.

It will be convenient to economize on brackets and suppress the commas between elements of the same coalition. Thus, we will write, for example, $w(\{i, j, k\}, \{\{i, j, k\}, \{l, h\}\})$ as $w(ijk, \{ijk, lh\})$, and $\overline{w}(\{ikj\}, \{lh\})$ as $\overline{w}(ijk, lh)$. The set of partition function form games with player set N is denoted by $PFFG^N$.

DEFINITION 2. Let (N, w) be a partition function form game and $\kappa \in \mathbb{P}(N)$.

(i) coalition $S \in \kappa$ is *feasible under coalition structure* κ if

$$w(S, \kappa) \geq \sum_{i \in S} w(i, [N]),$$

(ii) a coalition structure $\kappa \in \mathbb{P}(N)$ is *a feasible structure* if all coalitions are feasible under coalition structure κ, i.e.

$$w(S, \kappa) \geq \sum_{i \in S} w(i, [N]), \text{ for all } S \in \kappa.$$

A feasible coalition implies that the worth of its members is at least as much as their worth under the stand-alone structure. In a similar vein, a coalition structure is feasible if the worth of each coalition in the coalition structure is at least as much as its stand-alone worth. A feasible coalition structure for a given game (N, w) is called a *partial cooperation.*

EXAMPLE 1. Consider the game (N, w), where $N = \{1, 2, 3, 4\}$, the players are identical and w is given as follows:

$$w(i, [N]) = 3, \quad w(i, \{i, j, N\backslash\{ij\}\} = 2, \quad w(i, \{i, jkl\}) = 3,$$

$$w(ij, \{ij, k, l\}) = 4, \quad w(ij, \{ij, kl\}) = 5, \quad w(ijk, \{ijk, l\}) = 10,$$

$$w(\{N\}) = 11.$$

In this example, every coalition formed by three players such as $\{i, j, k\}$, has

$$w(ijk, \{ijk, l\}) \geq w(i, [N]) + w(j, [N]) + w(k, [N]),$$

while the value for a singleton in this coalition structure is

$$w(l, \{ijk, l\}) = 3 = w(l, [N]).$$

For every coalition consisting of two players, we have two cases:

(i) if $\kappa = \{ij, kl\}$ then $w(\{ij\}, \kappa) < w(\{i\}, [N]) + w(\{j\}, [N])$,

(ii) if $\kappa = \{ij, k, l\}\}$ then $w(\{ij\}, \kappa) < w(\{i\}, [N]) + w(\{j\}, [N])$ and $w(i, \{i, j, N\backslash\{ij\}\} = 2 < w(i, [N])$.

In addition, $w(\{N\}) < \sum_{i=1}^{4} w(i, [N])$.

Hence, feasible coalition structures are: $\{i, jkl\}$.

DEFINITION 3. A *solution* of $PFFG^N$ is a function Ψ which associates with each game (N, w) in $PFFG^N$ a vector $\Psi(N, w)$ of individual payoffs in $\mathbb{R}^N$, i.e. $\Psi(N, w) = (\Psi_i(N, w))_{i \in N} \in \mathbb{R}^N$.

We now turn to the case that some countries agree to form a coalition S, $S \subseteq N$. Since countries have different technologies, and each country is free to enter or leave a coalition, we consider the case in which cooperation among countries is possible in term of *transferable technologies*[7] (cf. Norde et al. 2002). This implies that the cost function of coalition S, $c_S(.)$, is the cheapest cost function which is available among members in their coalition, i.e.

$$c_S(e_S) = \min_{j \in S}\{c_j(e_S)\}, \tag{3}$$

where $e_S = \sum_{j \in S} e_j$ is the total effort of S.

Suppose that a coalition structure $\kappa = \{S_1, S_2, \ldots, S_m\}$ is formed ($m \leq n$). Total effort for an admissible coalition structure S_i in κ is denoted by e_{S_i}. The benefit function of coalition S_i is defined by

$$\pi_{S_i}(e_{S_i}, e_{-S_i}) = \frac{e_{S_i}}{e_N} f(e_N) - c_{S_i}(e_{S_i}), \tag{4}$$

where $e_{-S_i} = (e_{S_1}, \ldots, e_{S_{i-1}}, e_{S_{i+1}}, \ldots, e_{S_m})$

- A nonnegative vector $e^* = (e^*_{S_1}, e^*_{S_2}, \ldots, e^*_{S_m})$ associated with coalition structure $\kappa = \{S_1, S_2, \ldots, S_m\}$, is called a *competitive equilibrium* under coalition structure κ (or *equilibrium under* κ) if for all $i \in \{1, 2, \ldots, m\}$, and $e_{S_i} \geq 0$

$$\pi_{S_i}(e^*_{S_i}, e^*_{-S_i}) \geq \pi_{S_i}(e_{S_i}, e^*_{-S_i}). \tag{5}$$

Note that if $m = n$, then (5) is the definition of Nash equilibrium, and if $m = 1$ then it presents Pareto efficiency.

The existence of a unique competitive equilibrium under a given coalition structure is obvious since the strategy sets are one-dimensional and the m-person game with payoff functions (4) is obtained[8] from the n-person game with payoff functions (1).

We are now in a position to define the fishery game in partition function form.

DEFINITION 4. A *fishery game in partition function form (FGPFF)* is an ordered pair (N, π), where N is the set of players and π is the partition (benefit) function derived from competitive equilibrium e^* under κ such that

$$\pi(S_i, \kappa) = \pi_{S_i}(e^*_{S_i}, e^*_{-S_i}) \quad \text{for all } (S, \kappa) \in \mathbb{E}(N), \tag{6}$$

with $\pi_{S_i}(e)$ defined by (4).

The set of fishery games in partition function form with player set N is denoted by $FGPFF^N$.

Let $\kappa(S_i)$ denote a coalition structure κ, which S_i belongs to. Note that $\pi(S_i, \kappa)$ may differ from $\pi(S_i, \kappa')$ since there exist many coalition structures which a coalition S_i may belong to, while the equilibria under coalition structures κ and κ' are different (cf. there is a presence of externalities).

In the remainder of this chapter, we use the notations $\pi(i, [N])$ and $\pi(S_i, \kappa)$ to denote the payoff of a single coalition $\{i\}$ in the Nash equilibrium and the payoff of a coalition S_i under coalition structure κ, respectively.

3. IMPLICATIONS OF PARTIAL COOPERATION

In this section we analyse various impacts of coalitions and coalition structures. For each coalition structure $\kappa = \{S_1, S_2, \ldots, S_k\}$, let $e^*(\kappa)$ be total effort associated with κ, i.e. $e^*(\kappa) = \sum_{j=1}^{k} e^*_{S_j}$, where $\{e^*_{S_1}, e^*_{S_2}, \ldots, e^*_{S_k}\}$ is the unique competitive equilibrium under κ. Let $\pi(e^*(\kappa)) = \sum_{j=1}^{k} \pi(S_j, \kappa)$ be total net rents or benefits associated with κ at equilibrium $e^*(\kappa)$, where $\pi(S_j, \kappa)$, defined by (6), is the net rent of coalition S_j under κ.

Without loss of generality, we assume that $c_1 \leq c_2 \leq \ldots \leq c_n$. Thus, condition A.2 implies: $0 \leq c_n < f'(0)$.

For each coalition structure κ, a straightforward result is that in the competitive equilibrium a coalition with lower c_{S_i} has a higher fishing effort level e_{S_i}.

PROPOSITION 1. *For every coalition structure κ, the lower the marginal cost c_{S_i}, the higher the effort level in the coalition structure equilibrium. That is, for every $S_i, S_j \in \kappa$, if $c_{S_i} \geq c_{S_j}$ then $e^*_{S_j} \geq e^*_{S_i}$ in the equilibrium.*

Proof. Observe that in a coalition structure equilibrium $e^* = (e^*_{S_1}, e^*_{S_2}, \ldots, e^*_{S_m})$, the first-order condition leads to

$$c_{S_i} = \frac{e^*_{S_i}}{[e^*(\kappa)]^2}[f'(e^*(\kappa))e^*(\kappa) - f(e^*(\kappa))] + \frac{f(e^*(\kappa))}{e^*(\kappa)}, \quad (7)$$

for all $i \in \{1, 2, \ldots, m\}$, and $e^*(\kappa) = \sum_{i \in I(\kappa)} e^*_{S_i}$.

From (7), it follows that

$$c_{S_i} - c_{S_j} = \frac{e^*_{S_i} - e^*_{S_j}}{[e^*(\kappa)]^2}[f'(e^*(\kappa))e^*(\kappa) - f(e^*(\kappa))].$$

Moreover, assumption A1 implies that

$$f'(e^*(\kappa))e^*(\kappa) - f(e^*(\kappa)) < 0$$

in the equilibrium under κ.[9]

Therefore, if $c_{S_i} - c_{S_j} \geq 0$ we have $e^*_{S_i} \leq e^*_{S_j}$. □

Summing up (7), it follows that total effort $e^*(\kappa)$ can be determined by the following equation:

$$f'(e^*(\kappa)) + (k-1)\frac{f(e^*(\kappa))}{e^*(\kappa)} = \sum_{j=1}^{k} c_{S_j}. \tag{8}$$

Furthermore, from (7) and (8),

$$e^*_{S_j} = \frac{e^*(\kappa)[c_{S_j} - \frac{f(e^*(\kappa))}{e^*(\kappa)}]}{f'(e^*(\kappa))e^*(\kappa) - f(e^*(\kappa))}$$

and

$$f'(e^*(\kappa))e^*(\kappa) - f(e^*(\kappa)) = \sum_{m=1}^{k} c_{S_m} - k\frac{f(e^*(\kappa))}{e^*(\kappa)}.$$

Then, for every coalition structure $\kappa = \{S_1, S_2, \ldots, S_k\}$,

$$e^*_{S_j} = e^*(\kappa)\left(\frac{\frac{f(e^*(\kappa))}{e^*(\kappa)} - c_{S_j}}{k\frac{f(e^*(\kappa))}{e^*(\kappa)} - \sum_{m=1}^{k} c_{S_m}}\right), \tag{9}$$

where $e^*(\kappa) = \sum_{j=1}^{k} e^*_{S_j}$, and $e^* = (e^*_{S_1}, e^*_{S_2}, \ldots, e^*_{S_k})$.

If the share of efforts of coalition S_j in the competitive equilibrium under structure κ is defined by $sh(S_j) = e^*_{S_j}/e^*(\kappa)$. Then from (9) it follows that

$$sh(S_j) = \frac{\frac{f(e^*(\kappa))}{e^*(\kappa)} - c_{S_j}}{k\frac{f(e^*(\kappa))}{e^*(\kappa)} - \sum_{m=1}^{k} c_{S_m}}. \tag{10}$$

Equations (8) and (9) above form an alternative to the proof of Proposition 1 and show how to calculate total effort and each coalition effort in coalition structures. Therefore, total effort can be predicted by the aggregate marginal cost and the number of coalitions k. In the following example we will illuminate how to calculate total effort and the effort of each coalition, under a given coalition structure in the competitive equilibrium.

EXAMPLE 2. Consider four countries, indexed by $i = 1, 2, 3, 4$, with the production function $f(e_N) = (60 - e_N)e_N$ and marginal costs $c_1 = 2$, $c_2 = 3$, $c_3 = 6$, $c_4 = 9$. Aggregate marginal costs, total effort and total benefits as calculated by means of (8) and (9) are presented in Table 8.1.

Consider, for example, the case $k = 3$ with $\kappa = \{12, 3, 4\}$. Aggregate marginal cost of this coalition structure is $2 + 6 + 9 = 17$.[10] Since

Table 8.1. The possible coalition structures for the four countries

Coalitions	κ	$\sum_{m=1}^{k} c_{S_m}$	$e^*(\kappa)$	$\pi(e^*(\kappa))$
$k=4$	$1-2-3-4$	20	44	514
$k=3$	$12-3-4$	17	40.75	548.18
$k=3$	$13-2-4$	14	41.50	602.75
$k=3$	$1-23-4$	14	41.50	602.75
$k=3$	$14-2-3$	11	42.25	603.68
$k=3$	$1-24-3$	11	42.25	603.68
$k=3$	$1-2-34$	11	42.25	603.68
$k=2$	$123-4$	11	36.33	684.51
$k=2$	$12-34$	8	37.33	704.81
$k=2$	$124-3$	8	37.33	704.81
$k=2$	$14-23$	5	38.33	735.71
$k=2$	$13-24$	5	38.33	735.71
$k=2$	$134-2$	5	38.33	735.71
$k=2$	$1-234$	5	38.33	735.71
$k=1$	1234	2	29	841

$f'(e^*(\kappa)) = 60 - 2e^*(\kappa)$ and $f(e^*(\kappa))/e^*(\kappa) = 60 - e^*(\kappa)$, Equation (8) implies that

$$60 - 2e^*(\kappa) + 2[60 - e^*(\kappa)] = 17.$$

Solving the above equation, the total effort in the competitive equilibrium is obtained by $e^*(\kappa) = (180 - 17)/4 = 40.75$.

Substituting $e^*(\kappa)$ into (9) we have

$$e^*_{\{12\}} = 40.75\left(\frac{60 - 40.75 - 2}{3(60 - 40.75) - 17}\right) = 17.25,$$

$$e^*_{\{3\}} = 40.75\left(\frac{60 - 40.75 - 6}{3(60 - 40.75) - 17}\right) = 13.25,$$

and

$$e^*_{\{4\}} = 40.75\left(\frac{60 - 40.75 - 9}{3(60 - 40.75) - 17}\right) = 10.25.$$

Similarly for all other coalition structures.

COROLLARY 1. *For every coalition structure κ, the lower the marginal cost c_{S_i}, the higher the net benefits in the coalition structure equilibrium.*

Proof. Let $e^* = (e^*_{S_1}, e^*_{S_2}, \ldots, e^*_{S_m})$ be a coalition structure equilibrium. By Proposition 1 above, if $c_{S_i} \geq c_{S_j}$, then $e^*_{S_i} \leq e^*_{S_j}$. Moreover, at this equilibrium, the difference in payoffs between coalitions S_i and S_j is:

$$\pi(S_i, \kappa) - \pi(S_j, \kappa) = \frac{f(e^*(\kappa))}{e^*(\kappa)}(e^*_{S_i} - e^*_{S_j}) - c_{S_i} \cdot e^*_{S_i} + c_{S_j} \cdot e^*_{S_j}$$

$$= \frac{f(e^*(\kappa))}{e^*(\kappa)}(e^*_{S_i} - e^*_{S_j}) - c_{S_i}(e^*_{S_i} - e^*_{S_j}) + e^*_{S_j}(c_{S_j} - c_{S_i})$$

$$= \underbrace{\left(\frac{f(e^*(\kappa))}{e^*(\kappa)} - c_{S_i}\right)}_{(+)} \underbrace{(e^*_{S_i} - e^*_{S_j})}_{(-)} + e^*_{S_j} \underbrace{(c_{S_j} - c_{S_i})}_{(-)}.$$

Since in the competitive equilibrium $f(e^*(\kappa))/e^*(\kappa) \geq c_{S_i}$ (i.e. by (7)), it follows that $\pi(S_i, \kappa) - \pi(S_j, \kappa) \leq 0$. □

PROPOSITION 2. *Let κ and κ' be two coalition structures of a game $(N, w) \in FGPFF^N$, where κ is formed by values c_{S_j}, $S_j \in \kappa$ and κ' is formed by $c_{S'_j}$, $S'_j \in \kappa'$, and $|\kappa| \geq |\kappa'|$. Then $e^*(\kappa) \geq e^*(\kappa')$ if $\sum_{j=1}^{k} c_{S_j} \leq \sum_{j=1}^{m} c_{S'_j}$.*

Proof. Let $|\kappa| = k$, $|\kappa'| = m$, and $k \geq m > 1$. Since $\sum_{j=1}^{k} c_{S_j} \leq \sum_{j=1}^{m} c_{S'_j}$ and (8), it follows that

$$f'(e^*(\kappa)) + (k-1)\frac{f(e^*(\kappa))}{e^*(\kappa)} \leq f'(e^*(\kappa')) + (m-1)\frac{f(e^*(\kappa'))}{e^*(\kappa')}.$$

Hence

$$f'(e^*(\kappa)) - f'(e^*(\kappa')) + (m-1)\left[\frac{f(e^*(\kappa))}{e^*(\kappa)} - \frac{f(e^*(\kappa'))}{e^*(\kappa')}\right] + (k-m)\frac{f(e^*(\kappa))}{e^*(\kappa)} \leq 0. \qquad (\star)$$

Assume to the contrary that $e^*(\kappa) < e^*(\kappa')$. Since $f(x)/x$ and $f'(x)$ are decreasing functions, it follows that

$$f'(e^*(\kappa)) > f'(e^*(\kappa')) \quad \text{and} \quad \frac{f(e^*(\kappa))}{e^*(\kappa)} > \frac{f(e^*(\kappa'))}{e^*(\kappa')}.$$

Moreover, $k - m \geq 0$. Therefore the left-hand side of inequation $(\star)$ is positive which is a contradiction. □

This proposition shows that total fishing effort for a coalition structure depends on the number of coalitions and aggregate marginal cost in the competitive equilibrium. However, for a given coalition structure, the forming of coalitions with lower total cost need not reduce the total effort, while for a given total cost, the total effort increases if the number of coalitions increases (i.e. if $\sum_{S\in\kappa} c_S = c(\kappa) = c(\kappa')$, and $|\kappa| > |\kappa'|$, then $e^*(\kappa) > e^*(\kappa')$).[11] These results are illuminated in Table 8.1:

(i) coalition structures $\{14, 2, 3\}$ and $\{123, 4\}$ have the same aggregate marginal cost, i.e. 11, but $e(3, \{14, 2, 3\}) > e(2, \{123, 4\})$.

(ii) coalition structures $\{123, 4\}$ and $\{124, 3\}$ have the same number of coalitions, i.e. $k = 2$, but aggregate marginal cost is 11 for $\{123, 4\}$ which is larger than aggregate marginal cost 8 for $\{124, 3\}$. Then the total effort $e(2, \{123, 4\}) < e(2, \{124, 3\})$.

Applying (6), the partition function form game (N, w) is obtained as follows:

$$\overline{\pi}(1, 2, 3, 4) = (196, 169, 100, 49);$$

$$\overline{\pi}(12, 3, 4) = (297.56, 175.56, 105.06);$$
$$\overline{\pi}(13, 2, 4) = \overline{\pi}(1, 23, 4) = (272.25, 240.25, 90.25);$$

$$\overline{\pi}(14, 2, 3) = \overline{\pi}(1, 24, 3) = \overline{\pi}(1, 2, 34) = (248.06, 217.56, 138.06);$$

$$\overline{\pi}(123, 4) = (469.59, 214.92);$$
$$\overline{\pi}(124, 3) = \overline{\pi}(12, 34) = (427.25, 277.56);$$

$$\overline{\pi}(1, 234) = \overline{\pi}(13, 24) = \overline{\pi}(14, 23) = \overline{\pi}(134, 2) = (386.91, 348.20);$$

$$\overline{\pi}(1234) = 841. \tag{G.1}$$

From this partition function, it follows that for the case of $k = 3$ coalition structure $\{14, 2, 3\}$ is the only feasible,[12] while every coalition structure consisting of two coalitions is feasible.

Observe that if countries are identical, i.e. $c_i = c_j$ for all $i \neq j$, Equations (8) and (9) in the unique equilibrium $e^* = (e^*_{S_i}, e^*_{S_2}, \ldots, e^*_{S_m})$ under κ satisfy:

$$f'(e^*(\kappa)) + (k-1)\frac{f(e^*(\kappa))}{e^*(\kappa)} = k \cdot c,$$

$$e^*_{S_j} = \frac{e^*(\kappa)}{k} > 0, \quad \text{for all } j = 1, 2, \ldots, k,$$

where $e^*(\kappa) = \sum_{j=1}^{k} e^*_{S_j}$.

Therefore, the effort of each coalition only depends on the number k of coalitions. Furthermore, for any coalition structure $\kappa = \{S_1, S_2, \ldots, S_k\}$, total fishing effort is an increasing function of the number of coalitions k, whereas total net rents and the net rent of each coalition are decreasing functions of k (Theorem 2 in Funaki and Yamato 1999).[13]

COROLLARY 2. *For the case of identical countries, it follows that*

(i) *the minimum and maximum value of a coalition $S \subseteq N$ are determined by*

$$\min_{\kappa:S\in\kappa} \pi(S,\kappa) = \pi(S, S \cup [N\backslash S]),$$

$$\max_{\kappa:S\in\kappa} \pi(S,\kappa) = \pi(S, S \cup \{N\backslash S\}).$$

(ii) *a coalition structure κ is feasible if the size of the largest coalition is feasible under the equal sharing rule.*

Proof. (i) We have $\min_{k:S\in\kappa} \pi(S,\kappa) \le \pi(S,\kappa') \le \max_{\kappa:S\in\kappa} \pi(S,\kappa)$ for all coalition structures $\kappa' \neq \kappa$. Moreover, from Proposition 2, i.e. that fishing effort is an increasing function of the number of coalitions, it follows that for any two coalition structures $\kappa = \{S_1, S_2, \ldots, S_k\}$ and $\kappa' = \{S'_1, S'_2, \ldots, S'_m\}$ such that $k < m$, $e^*(\kappa) < e^*(\kappa')$; $\pi(e^*(\kappa)) > \pi(e^*(\kappa'))$; and if $S \in \kappa$ and $S \in \kappa'$

$$\pi(S,\kappa) > \pi(S,\kappa'),$$

where $e^*(\kappa) = \sum_{j=1}^{k} e^*_{S_j}$, $e^*(\kappa') = \sum_{i=1}^{m} e^*_{S_i}$. Thus, result (i) is obtained.

(ii) In a Nash equilibrium, e^*, the net benefits are:

$$\pi(i, [N]) = \frac{[f(e^*_N) - c \cdot e^*_N]}{n} \quad \text{for all } i \in N,$$

and

$$\sum_{i\in S} \pi(i, [N]) = \frac{|S|[f(e^*_N) - c \cdot e^*_N]}{n}.$$

Then, if countries have prudent perceptions (pessimistic expectations), a vector $z = (z_1, z_2, \ldots, z_n)$ can be considered as a feasible payoff if

$$\sum_{j \in S} z_j \geq \frac{|S|[f(e_N^*) - c \cdot e_N^*]}{n}.$$

We observe that for a given coalition structure κ with k coalitions, a vector z is a feasible payoff vector if

$$z_j = \frac{c \cdot e^*(\kappa) - f(e^*(\kappa))}{|S|k} \geq \frac{[f(e_N^*) - c \cdot e_N^*]}{n} \quad \text{for all } j \in S,$$

where $e^*(\kappa)$ is the total effort in an equilibrium under κ, and e_N^* is the Nash equilibrium. Since

$$\pi(S, \kappa) = \frac{f(e^*(\kappa)) - c \cdot e^*(\kappa)}{k} \quad \text{for all } S \in \kappa,$$

then, if

$$\frac{f(e^*(\kappa)) - c \cdot e^*(\kappa)}{k|S_m|} \geq \frac{f(e_N^*) - c \cdot e_N^*}{n}$$

for the coalition S_m, where $|S_m| = \max_{j \in I(\kappa)} |S_j|$, it follows that

$$\frac{f(e^*(\kappa)) - c \cdot e^*(\kappa)}{k|S_j|} \geq \frac{f(e^*(\kappa)) - c \cdot e^*(\kappa)}{k|S_m|}$$

$$\geq \frac{f(e_N^*) - c \cdot e_N^*}{n} \quad \text{for all } S_j \in \kappa. \qquad \square$$

EXAMPLE 3. Consider four identical countries, $i = 1, 2, 3, 4$, with marginal cost $c = 9$ and production function $f(e) = (60 - e)e$. Since all countries are identical, there are only five types of coalition structures: $\kappa_1 = \{|1|, |1|, |1|, |1|\}$, $\kappa_2 = \{|1|, |1|, |2|\}$, $\kappa_3 = \{|2|, |2|\}$, $\kappa_4 = \{|1|, |3|\}$, and $\kappa_5 = \{|4|\}$, where $|i|$ denotes the number of countries. The game $(N, \pi) \in FGPFF^N$ is given by

$$\overline{\pi}(|1|, |1|, |1|, |1|) = (100.40, 100.40, 100.40, 100.40);$$

$$\overline{\pi}(|1|, |1|, |2|) = (162.56, 162.56, 162.56);$$

$$\overline{\pi}(|2|, |2|) = \overline{\pi}(|1|, |3|) = (289, 289); \quad \overline{\pi}(|4|) = 650.25.$$

The coalition structures κ_3 is feasible, since

$$\pi(|2|, \kappa_3) = 289 > 2 \cdot \pi(|1|, \kappa_1) = 200.80,$$

under the equal sharing rule. However, a coalition with two players for a coalition structure consisting of three coalitions is not feasible since $\pi(|2|, \kappa_2) = 162.56 < 2 \cdot \pi(|1|, \kappa_1) = 200.80$.

4. DISTRIBUTION OF PAYOFFS

This section considers the distribution of payoffs of partial cooperation that countries can agree upon. To simplify the analyses, suppose the production function takes the quadratic form $f(e) = (b - e)e$. The parameter b can be considered a critical (maximum) effort level where production cannot recover the total cost, i.e. $f(e_N) \leq c \cdot e_N$ if $e_N \geq b$, and $c \in [\min_{i \in N} c_i, \max_{i \in N} c_i]$.

Recall that $c_1 \leq c_2 \leq \ldots \leq c_n$. To ensure that all countries have the possibility to catch, i.e. $e_j^* \geq 0$ for all $j \in N$, we assume that $(b + \sum_{j=1}^{n} c_j)/(n+1) > c_n$.[14] The net benefit function of coalition S_i under coalition structure κ is:

$$\pi_{S_i}(e_{S_i}, e_{-S_i}) = (b - e_N)e_{S_i} - c_{S_i} \cdot e_{S_i}. \tag{11}$$

For each coalition structure κ, the value $\pi_{S_i}(e^*_{S_i}, e^*_{-S_i})$ of the coalition S_i (under κ) is defined by (11) at competitive equilibrium e^*. Denote the share of efforts of coalition S in the competitive equilibrium e^* under structure κ as $sh(S) = e^*_S / e^*(\kappa)$, where $e^*(\kappa) = \sum_{S \in \kappa} e^*_S$ and $e^*_S = \sum_{l \in S} e^*_l$. Moreover, let $\pi(e^*(\kappa)) = \sum_{S \in \kappa} \pi_S(e^*)$ be the total net benefit.

PROPOSITION 3. *For every coalition structure κ, the following results hold for every competitive equilibrium:*

(i) for any $i < j$, $c_{S_j} - c_{S_i} = e^*_{S_i} - e^*_{S_j} \geq 0$,

(ii) $\frac{\partial e^*_{Si}}{\partial c_{S_j}} = \begin{cases} -\frac{k}{k+1} < 0 \text{ if } i = j, \\ \frac{1}{k+1} > 0 \text{ if } i \neq j, \end{cases}$

(iii) $\frac{\partial \pi_{S_j}(e^*)}{\partial c_{S_i}} = \begin{cases} -\frac{2k}{k+1} e^*_{S_j} < 0 \text{ if } i = j, \\ \frac{2}{k+1} e^*_{S_j} > 0 \text{ if } i \neq j, \end{cases}$

(iv) $\frac{\partial \pi(e^*(\kappa))}{\partial c_{S_j}} > 0 \Longleftrightarrow sh(S_j) < 1/(k+1)$.

Proof. (i) From (7) and $f(e^*) = (b - e^*)e^*$ which implies (i).

(ii) Since $e_N^* = (kb - \sum_{i=1}^k c_{S_i})/(k+1)$ and $e_{S_i}^* = (b - e_N^*) - c_{S_j}$ it follows that

$$e_{S_i}^* = \frac{b - kc_{S_i} + \sum_{j \neq i} c_{S_j}}{k+1}$$

leading to (ii).

(iii) As $\pi_{S_j}(e^*) = (b - e_N^* - c_{S_j})e_{S_j}^* = (e_{S_j}^*)^2$, it follows that

$$\frac{\partial \pi_{S_j}(e^*)}{\partial c_{S_i}} = 2e_{S_j}^* \frac{\partial e_{Sj}^*}{\partial c_{S_i}} = \begin{cases} -\frac{2k}{k+1} e_{S_j}^* < 0 \ \textit{if } i = j, \\ \frac{2}{k+1} e_{S_j}^* > 0 \ \textit{if } i \neq j, \end{cases}$$

leading to (iii).

(iv) Since $\pi(e^*(\kappa)) = \sum_{j=1}^k \pi_{S_j}(e^*)$ and (iii), it follows that

$$\begin{aligned} \frac{\partial \pi(e^*(\kappa))}{\partial c_{S_i}} &= \sum_{j=1}^{k} \frac{\partial \pi_{S_j}(e^*)}{\partial c_{S_i}} \\ &= \frac{\partial \pi_{S_i}(e^*)}{\partial c_{S_i}} + \sum_{j \neq i} \frac{\partial \pi_{S_j}(e^*)}{\partial c_{S_i}} \\ &= 2\left[\frac{-k}{k+1} e_{S_i}^* + \frac{1}{k+1} \sum_{j \neq i} e_{S_j}^*\right] \\ &= \frac{2}{k+1}\left\{-ke_{S_i}^* + \left[\sum_{m=1}^{k} e_{S_m}^* - e_{S_i}^*\right]\right\} \\ &= \frac{2\sum_{m=1}^k e_{S_m}^*}{k+1}\left[1 - \frac{(k+1)e_{S_i}^*}{\sum_{m=1}^k e_{S_m}^*}\right] > 0 \\ &\Leftrightarrow 1 - \frac{(k+1)e_{S_i}^*}{\sum_{m=1}^k e_{S_m}^*} > 0 \\ &\Leftrightarrow sh(S_i) < \frac{1}{k+1}, \end{aligned}$$

which implies (iv). □

Proposition 3 shows the relationship between marginal costs, fishing efforts and net benefits for coalitions in the competitive equilibrium.[15] To illuminate Proposition 3 consider a coalition structure κ consisting of k coalitions ($|\kappa| = k$) and the case where one member i leaves its coalition $S_{\kappa(i)}$ ($\in \kappa$) and joins another coalition, say $S_{\kappa(j)} \in \kappa$. If the marginal cost c_i of this member is larger than the marginal cost $c_{S_{\kappa(i)}}$ of its former coalition $S_{\kappa(i)}$ but smaller than the cost $c_{S_{\kappa(j)}}$ of its new coalition $S_{\kappa(j)}$, then the joining of this member will lead to a cost reduction of coalition $S_{\kappa(j)}$. Moreover, the marginal cost of the coalition to which i used to belong does not change. Therefore, although the number of a new coalition structure κ' does not change (i.e. $|\kappa'| = k$, since only i changes coalitions), the cost structure does change. In a similar vein, (ii) and (iii) describe the impacts on coalition efforts and coalition net benefits. If own marginal costs of a coalition increase, own efforts and net benefits decrease, whereas if the marginal costs of another coalition increase own efforts and net benefits increase. According to (iv), the forming of a new coalition structure may cause a reduction of total net benefit if at least one of the effort shares is larger than $1/k + 1$.

The above Propositions 1, 2 and 3 imply that although an outcome depends on both the marginal cost c_{S_j} and cardinality of κ, countries with high costs have an incentive to cooperate since they will take advantage by reducing costs when joining a coalition with lower costs. The following example illuminates this:

EXAMPLE 4. Consider Example 2. The benefits of free-riding for each coalition structure are presented in Table 8.2. The number of coalitions is presented in the first column and the benefit of each free-rider follows in the next columns.

In Table 8.2 the second row represents noncooperative net benefits. The third and fourth rows represent free-riding benefits for countries i, j, $i \neq j$ when countries k and l form a coalition $\{kl\}$, $k, l \in N\backslash\{i, j\}$. For example, for $k = 3$, 272.25 and 248.06 are the payoffs of country 1 in the coalition structures $\kappa = \{1, 4, 23\}$ with aggregate marginal cost 14 and $\kappa = \{1, 3, 24\}$ with aggregate marginal cost 11, respectively (see Table 8.1). The last row represents free-riding benefits for country i when $N\backslash\{i\}$ forms a coalition.

If only two countries form a coalition (i.e. $k = 3$) then, relative to the noncooperative situation a free-rider country, for example, country 4, gains $90.25 - 49 = 41.25$ (84 per cent) in the low cost cases (i.e. coalition structures $\{13, 2, 4\}$ or $\{1, 23, 4\}$), and $105.06 - 49 = 56.06$ (114 per cent) in the high cost case (i.e. coalition structure $\{12, 3, 4\}$). In a similar vein, country 1 gains $248.06 - 196 = 52.06$ (27 per cent) in coalition structure

Table 8.2. The benefits of free-riding

$\lvert\kappa\rvert$	$\pi(\{1\},\kappa)$	$\pi(\{2\},\kappa)$	$\pi(\{3\},\kappa)$	$\pi(\{4\},\kappa)$
$k = 4$	196	169	100	49
$k = 3$ (free-riders with high costs)	272.25	240.25	175.56	105.06
$k = 3$ (free-riders with low costs)	248.06	217.56	138.06	90.25
$k = 2$	386.91	348.20	277.56	214.92

$\{1, 24, 3\}$ and $272.25 - 196 = 76.25$ (39 per cent) in coalition structure $\{1, 23, 4\}$.

In Example 4, although country 4 with the highest marginal cost has the smallest net benefit in the noncooperative situation (Corollary 1), it will gain relatively more from free-riding than the other countries. For example, consider the case of only one free-rider (i.e. $k = 2$). In this situation, if countries 1, 2 and 3 form a coalition $\{123\}$, then in the coalition structure $\{123, 4\}$ country 4 gains $214.92 - 49 = 165.92$ (337 per cent). The gains are 177.56 (177 per cent) in $\{124, 3\}$ for country 3, 179.20 (106 per cent) in $\{134, 2\}$ for country 2 and 190.91 (97 per cent) for country 1 in $\{234, 1\}$. Moreover, in coalition structure $\{123, 4\}$ country 4 gains more than in coalitions with two free-riders (cf. $\{1, 4, 23\}$ or $\{13, 2, 4\}$ with gains 56.06 (114 per cent) and $\{12, 3, 4\}$ with gains 41.25 (84 per cent) for country 4).

Observe that although all coalition structures with two coalitions in Example 4 are feasible under the equal sharing rule (see Section 3), the total benefits of coalition structures with two coalitions will increase if country 4 forms a coalition such that the lowest cost coalition materializes (because it reduces the total cost of the coalition structure). For example, consider $\kappa_1 = \{12, 34\}$, $\kappa_2 = \{14, 23\}$, $\kappa_3 = \{13, 24\}$, $\kappa_4 = \{123, 4\}$, $\kappa_5 = \{124, 3\}$, $\kappa_6 = \{134, 2\}$ and $\kappa_7 = \{234, 1\}$. From the last column in Table 8.1, it follows that:[16]

$$\pi(e^*(2, \kappa_2)) = 735.71 > 704.81 = \pi(e^*(2, \kappa_1)),$$

and

$$\begin{aligned}\pi(e^*(2, \kappa_7)) &= 735.71 > 704.81 = \pi(e^*(2, \kappa_5)) > 648.51 \\ &= \pi(e^*(2, \kappa_4)).\end{aligned}$$

In coalition structures κ_4, κ_5, κ_6 and κ_7 there is free-riding by countries 4, 3, 2 and 1, respectively.[17] The total effort and total net benefit are affected by the marginal cost of the free-rider. For example, Table 8.1 shows that if country 1 or 2 free-rides, then total effort is 38.33 and the total net benefit is 735.71. If country 3 free-rides, then the total effort is 37.33 and the total net benefit is 704.81, whereas the total effort reduces to 36.33 and total net benefit is 684.51 if country 4 free-rides.

The smallest effort (29) and highest net benefit (841) materialize for the grand coalition only. Therefore, although there exist some feasible partial coalition structures, the grand coalition is optimal efficiency.

The question arises what sharing rule of the net benefits should be adopted to stimulate the fishing nations to join the grand coalition. We propose the modified Shapley value, developed by Pham Do and Norde (2005).[18] The reason to consider the modified Shapley value rather than the original value developed by Shapley[19] (1953) is that the latter cannot be applied to games in partition function form such as the present game $(N, w) \in PFFG^N$, since in this class of games the contributions of each player to the grand coalition differ among coalition structures, due to the presence of externalities among coalitions.

Pham Do and Norde (2005) show that the modified Shapley value (see Appendix) is a unique and efficient solution for a $PFFG^N$. Moreover, they point out that for a class of oligopoly games in partition function form such as a $(N, w) \in FGPFF^N$, where the net benefit function (11) is determined in a competitive equilibrium under coalition structures, the modified Shapley value keeps the same ordering for every player in the Nash situation. Applying this result to a fishery game in partition function form, the following proposition is obtained.

PROPOSITION 4. *Let ψ be the modified Shapley value for a $(N, \pi) \in FGPFF^N$, where the net benefit function (11) is determined in a competitive equilibrium under coalition structures. It follows that if $c_1 \leq c_2 \leq \ldots \leq c_n$ then*

(i) $\pi(1, [N]) \geq \pi(2, [N]) \geq \ldots \geq \pi(n, [N])$,

(ii) $\psi_1(\pi) \geq \psi_2(\pi) \geq \ldots, \geq \psi_n(\pi)$, *and*

(iii) $\pi(N, \{N\}) = \sum_{i=1}^{n} \psi_i(\pi)$.

Proof. See section 6 in Pham Do and Norde (2005). □

It is obvious that stable cooperation results if $\psi_i(\pi) \geq \pi(i, [N])$ for every $i \in N$.

EXAMPLE 5. Consider the fishery game in partition function form (N, π) in Example 2, where w is given by (G.1). In this game, we have

$$\begin{aligned}\pi(1, [N]) &= 196 > \pi(2, [N]) = 169 > \pi(3, [N]) \\ &= 100 > \pi(4, [N]) = 49.\end{aligned}$$

Using the Appendix the modified Shapley value is obtained as

$$\psi(\pi) = (271.18, 238.86, 184.94, 146.02).$$

Additionally, $\pi(4, \{4\}) = \sum_{i=1}^{4} \psi_i(\pi) = 841$.

The modified Shapley value allocates the payoffs such that the contributions of each country in the grand coalition as determined by its marginal cost are rewarded. The surplus gained from full cooperation is (75.18, 69.86, 84.94, 97.02). Each country has thus a different gain in the grand cooperation, due to its contribution. We observe that this distribution differs from the values that are obtained by applying other division rules such as the equal sharing rule. For example, the transition from the noncooperative to the cooperative situation yields the surplus 327 (= 841 − 514). The equal sharing rule gives the outcomes (277.75, 250.75, 181.75, 130.75), where each player gains 81.75.

This example indicates that although the equal sharing rule can be applied for any feasible coalition structure, the modified Shapley value has more potential to induce full cooperation.

Finally, we observe that although each country is better off in the grand coalition than in the competitive outcome, individual countries can do even better by free-riding under certain circumstances, as illustrated in the last row of Table 8.2. This implies that application of the modified Shapley value is not sufficient to discourage free-riding. Therefore, additional measures are needed to deter free-riding; e.g. linking a fishery problem to another problem in which the players are involved (see Folmer et al. 1993, Kroeze-Gil 2003, and the references therein).

5. CONCLUDING REMARKS

The objective of regional fishery agreements is to develop rules for joint decision making to use common fishery resources efficiently to avoid inefficient outcomes, and the collapse of fish stocks resulting from noncooperative behaviour. Furthermore, a better balance must be reached between fishing effort and the quantities of fish that can be removed from the sea without endangering the future of the fish stocks or ecosystems.

This chapter has addressed the formation of coalitions smaller than the grand coalition. Particularly, attention has been paid to the feasibility of coalition structures and their impacts on reducing harvest levels. We have shown that for every coalition structure in a competitive equilibrium a coalition with lower marginal cost has a higher effort level, and total fishing effort is an increasing function of the number of coalitions. Moreover, the lower the marginal costs, the higher the net benefits in the coalition structures.

In order to induce countries to cooperate the modified Shapley value adopted to games in partition function form has been considered. This is a unique and efficient division rule of gains from cooperation that preserves the ordering of players in the Nash outcome. This device can be applied to develop a profit allocation scheme such as a reasonable compromise and compensation for both the potential entrants and the charter members. However, allocation of the gains from cooperation on the basic of the modified Shapley value is not sufficient to discourage free-riding since under certain coalition structures the latter option may result in a higher payoff than is attainable on the basic of the modified Shapley value.

APPENDIX

In order to introduce the modified Shapley value for games in partition function form, we need some additional notations. Let $\Pi(N)$ be the set of all *bijections* $\sigma : \{1, 2, \ldots, n\} \rightarrow N$ of N. For a given $\sigma \in \Pi(N)$ and $i \in I([N])$ we define $S_i^\sigma = \{\sigma(1), \sigma(2), \ldots, \sigma(i)\}$, and $S_0^\sigma = \emptyset$. For a given $\sigma \in \Pi(N)$ and $i \in I([N])$, we define the partition κ_i^σ associated with σ and i, by $\kappa_i^\sigma = \{S_i^\sigma\} \cup [N \backslash S_i^\sigma]$. So, in κ_i^σ the coalition S_i^σ has already formed, whereas all other players still form singleton coalitions. Furthermore, we define $\kappa_0^\sigma = [N]$.

Let (N, w) be a partition function form game, and $\sigma \in \Pi(N)$. We define the marginal contribution of the ith player $\sigma(i)$ to coalition S_i^σ such as

$$m_{\sigma(i)}^\sigma(w) := w(S_i^\sigma, \kappa_i^\sigma) - w(S_{i-1}^\sigma, \kappa_{i-1}^\sigma).$$

Based on these marginal vectors $\{m^\sigma(w)\}_{\sigma \in \pi(N)}$, we define the modified *Shapley value* ψ of the partition function form game (N,w) as the average of the $n!$ marginal vectors,[20]

$$\psi(w) = \frac{1}{n!} \sum_{\sigma \in \Pi(N)} m^{\sigma}(w).^{21}$$

EXAMPLE. Consider the partition function form game (N, w) defined by

$$\overline{w}(1, 2, 3) = (0, 0, 0), \quad \overline{w}(12, 3) = (2, 0),$$
$$\overline{w}(23, 1) = (3, 2), \quad \overline{w}(13, 2) = (2, 1), \quad \overline{w}(123) = 10.$$

The marginal vectors associated[22] with σ are:

$$\text{if} \quad \sigma_1 = (1, 2, 3) \text{ then } m^{\sigma_1}(w) = (0, 2, 8),$$
$$\text{if} \quad \sigma_2 = (2, 1, 3) \text{ then } m^{\sigma_2}(w) = (2, 0, 8),$$
$$\text{if} \quad \sigma_3 = (1, 3, 2) \text{ then } m^{\sigma_3}(w) = (0, 8, 2),$$
$$\text{if} \quad \sigma_4 = (2, 3, 1) \text{ then } m^{\sigma_4}(w) = (7, 0, 3),$$
$$\text{if} \quad \sigma_5 = (3, 1, 2) \text{ then } m^{\sigma_5}(w) = (2, 8, 0),$$
$$\text{if} \quad \sigma_6 = (3, 2, 1) \text{ then } m^{\sigma_6}(w) = (7, 3, 0).$$

So, the modified Shapley value $\psi(w) = (3, 3.5, 3.5)$.

ACKNOWLEDGEMENT

We thank Henk Norde for valuable and helpful comments.

NOTES

1. According to these authors, the inadequacies of Part VII, section 2 (Articles 116–120), of the UN Convention pertaining to the management of high seas fisheries are the source of the lack of cooperation and conflicts.
2. For a review of the history of the 1995 UN Fish Stocks Agreement as well as its implementation, see Bjørndal and Munro (2003).
3. For related applications of cooperative game theoretic approaches to high seas fishery management, see, for example, Li (1998), Lindroos (2000), Bjørndal et al. (2000) and Pintassilgo (2003).
4. That is, we assume a situation where the fishing nations choose across different possible steady states, ignoring the transitional dynamics.
5. Note that the distribution of fish is not a result of negotiations among fishing countries; it is simply a reflection of the dependence of harvesting on its effort level e_j and e_N.

6. This assumption implies that the additional catch from an extra unit of effort will clearly decrease as the total effort expended increseases, i.e. there are decreasing returns to fishing effort.
7. For example, cooperation may lead to an exchange of vessels or labor among coalition partners.
8. The assumptions A1–A3 still hold for this game.
9. Since $f(0) = 0$, and $f'(x)x - f(x)$ is decreasing and nonpositive.
10. Observe that transferable technology within a coalition is assumed.
11. These results imply that the forming of coalitions will determine the situation of a fish stock. Moreover, aggregate effort under a given coalition structure depends strongly upon how coalitions are formed by the marginal costs. For a given number of coalitions, the coalition structure with lower aggregate marginal cost has higher total effort.
12. This is because $\pi(14, \{14, 2, 3\}) = 248.06 > \pi(1, [N]) + \pi(4, [N]) = 245$, $\pi(2, \{14, 2, 3\}) > \pi(2, [N])$ and $\pi(3, \{14, 2, 3\}) > \pi(3, [N])$.
13. This result can be easily extended to the asymmetric case such as a refinement of the coalition structure: for a given coalition structure, the broken coalition will increase both total cost and total effort (related to the original coalition structure).
14. This assumption is considered as the requirement of positive shares at the equilibrium for all players (for details, see Zhao 2001).
15. Coalitions mean both individuals and groups of individuals in a given coalition structure.
16. Note that $\pi(e^*(2, \kappa_2)) = \pi(e^*(2, \kappa_3))$ and $\pi(e^*(2, \kappa_7)) = \pi(e^*(2, \kappa_6))$ since the total cost of κ_2 and κ_3 as well as κ_7 and κ_6 are equal.
17. It is a reason why the full cooperation may not stable if a distribution of benefits can not be accepted by several countries.
18. An alternative is the equal sharing rule. However, this rule does not take into account the contributions of each player to the grand cooperation, whereas the Shapley value does.
19. For the introduction to the Shapley value, its extensions and applications, see, for example, chapters 53–58 in Aumann and Hart (2002).
20. For more details, see Pham Do and Norde (2005).
21. Observe the similarity to TU-games (cf. Shapley 1953).
22. For example, the marginal vector of σ_2 is computed as follows. As $\sigma_2 = (2, 1, 3)$ then $m^{\sigma_2}_{\sigma_2(1)}(w) = w(21, \{21, 3\}) - w(2, [N]) = 2$, $m^{\sigma_2}_{\sigma_2(2)}(w) = w(2, [N]) = 0$, $m^{\sigma_2}_{\sigma_2(3)}(w) = w(213, \{N\}) - w(21, \{21, 3\}) = 10 - 2 = 8$. Hence, $m^{\sigma_2}(w) = (2, 0, 8)$.

REFERENCES

Aumann, R.J. and S. Hart (2002), *Handbook of Game Theory with Economic Applications, Vol. 3*, Amsterdam: Elsevier Science Publishers.

Bjorndal, T., V. Kaitala, M. Lindroos and G. Munro (2000), 'The management of high seas fisheries', *Annals of Operations Research*, 94, 183–196.

Bjørndal, T. and G. Munro (2003), 'The management of high seas fisheries resources and the implementation of the U.N. fish stocks agreement of 1995', in T. Tietenberg and H. Folmer (eds), *The International Yearbook of Environmental and Resource Economics 2003–2004*, Cheltenham, UK and Brookfield, US: Edward Elgar, pp. 1–35.

Cornes, R. and R. Hartley (2000), 'Joint production games and share functions', Discussion Paper, School of Economics, University of Nottingham, UK.

Datta, M. and L. Miraman (1999), 'Externalities, market power and resource extraction', *Journal of Environmental Economics and Management*, 37, 233–255.

FAO (2000), *The Status of World Fisheries and Aquaculture*, (SOFIA, 2000), Food and Agricultural Organization.

Folmer, H., P. von Mouch and S. Ragland (1993), 'Interconnected games and environmental problems', *Environmental and Resource Economics*, 3, 313–335.

Funaki Y. and T. Yamato (1999), 'The core of an economy with a common pool resource: A partition function form approach', *International Journal of Game Theory*, 28, 157–171.

Green Paper (2001), 'On the future of the common fisheries policy', Commission of the European Communities in http://europa.eu.int/comm/fisheries/greenpaper/green/volume1_en.pdf.

Kaitala, V. and G. Munro (1993), 'The management of high seas fisheries', *Marine Resource Economics*, 8, 313–329.

Kaitala, V. and G. Munro (1995), 'The economic management of high sea fishery resources: A game theoretic aspects', in J.A. Filar and C. Carraro (eds), *Control and Game Theoretic Models of the Environment*, Annals of the International Society of Dynamic Games, Vol. 2, Boston, MA: Birkhäuser, pp. 299–318.

Kaitala, V. and G. Munro (1997), 'The conservation and management of high seas fishery resources under the new law of the sea', *Natural Resource Modeling*, 10(2), 87–108.

Kroeze-Gil, J. (2003), 'International environmental problems, issue linkage and the European Union', Ph.D. Thesis, Tilburg University.

Li, E. (1998), 'Cooperative high-seas straddling stock agreement as a characteristic function game', *Marine Resource Economics*, 13, 247–256.

Lindroos, M. (2000), *Cooperation and Conflicts in High Seas Fisheries*, Helsinki: Helsinki School of Economics and Business Administration.

Munro, G.R. (2000), 'The management of transboundary fishery resources and property rights', in B.L. Gowley (ed.), *Taking Ownership: Property Rights and Fishery Management on the Atlantic Coast*, Atlantic Institute for Market Studies, AIMS, Canada.

Norde, H., K.H. Pham Do and S. Tijs (2002), 'Oligopoly games with and without transferable technologies', *Mathematical Social Sciences*, 43, 187–207.

Pham Do, K.H. and H. Norde (2005), 'The Shapley value for partition function form games', *International Game Theory Review*, to appear.

Pintassilgo, P. (2003), 'A coalition approach to the management of high seas fisheries in the presence of externalities', *Natural Resource Modeling*, 16(2), 175–197.

Shapley, L. (1953), 'A value for n-person games', in H.W. Kuhn and A.W. Tucker (eds), *Contributions to the Theory of Games II, Annals of Mathematics Studies*, Vol. 28, Princeton University Press, pp. 307–312.

Thrall, R.M. and W.F. Lucas (1963), 'n-person games in partition function form', *Naval Research Logistic Quarterly*, 10, 281–293.

UN (2002), *Oceans: The Lifeline of Our Planet – Anniversary of the United Nations Convention on the Law of the Sea: 20 Years of Law and Order on the Oceans and Seas (1982–2002).*

Watt, A. (1996), 'On the uniqueness of equilibrium in Cournot oligopoly and other games', *Game and Economic Behavior*, 13, 269–285.

Zhao, J. (2001), 'A characterization for the negative welfare effects of cost reduction in Cournot oligopoly', *International Journal of Industrial Organization*, 19, 455–469.

9. Salmon and Hydropower: Dynamic Cost–Benefit Analysis

Cecilia Håkansson, Per-Olov Johansson and Bengt Kriström

1. INTRODUCTION

Natural resource conflicts present a challenging task for cost–benefit analysis, mainly because of the intricate dynamic issues such resources raise. Karl-Gustaf Löfgren has been a front figure in structuring the economic analysis pertaining to dynamic cost–benefit analysis of natural resources. In this homage to Professor Löfgren, we use some of the tools that he has developed together with his students and colleagues. We touch historical base with a cost–benefit analysis that Professor Löfgren carried out in 1979 (Löfgren and Johansson 1979), regarding timber passage in the same river and power plant as in the present study. We present a framework for dynamic cost–benefit analysis of hydropower–fish passage conflicts. The approach is illustrated with data from an ongoing project regarding the salmon–hydropower conflict in a river in northern Sweden (Umeälven/Vindelälven). Daily water flow data is combined with daily data on the number of salmon that pass the hydropower plant Stornorrfors, located about 40 km up-river. Data covers the period 1974 to 2000 and are used to study the opportunity costs of releasing more water to the potential benefit of salmon migration (at the cost of electricity production).

The chapter is structured as follows. In Section 2 we detail the theoretical framework, including cost–benefit rules for the salmon–hydropower case. Section 3 provides background information about the wild salmon case under study. Section 4 has details on a pilot study carried out to measure the benefits of increasing the salmon stock. Section 5 includes a preliminary assessment of the opportunity costs of diverting water from the hydropower plant to improve fish passage conditions. Section 6 presents concluding remarks.

2. COST–BENEFIT ANALYSIS OF THE SALMON–HYDROPOWER CASE

In this section, drawing on contributions by Karl-Gustaf Löfgren (see e.g. Johansson and Löfgren 1996, Löfgren 2003), we derive a simple dynamic cost–benefit rule. In so doing, we develop a model that covers the salmon–hydropower case. Let us consider a society that values both its consumption of a numeraire good and its consumption of salmon. In addition society attributes a value to the stock of salmon. We interpret the stock of salmon as an indicator of an existence value. Abstracting from distributional concerns, the society under consideration aims at maximizing the present value utility of a representative individual:

$$\int_0^\infty u\,(c(t), c_L(t), s_L(t))\ \mathrm{e}^{-\delta t}\,\mathrm{d}t, \tag{1}$$

where $u(.)$ is an instantaneous utility function, $c(t)$ denotes consumption of the numeraire good at time t, $c_L(t)$ denotes consumption of salmon at time t, $s_L(t)$ denotes the stock of salmon at time t, and δ is a discount rate, for simplicity assumed to be constant across time.

For simplicity, we assume that the numeraire commodity is produced using electricity as the sole input. In turn, the amount of electricity is a function of the flow of water through the power station. Thus we have:

$$c(t) = f(\dot{s}_w(t)), \tag{2}$$

where $\dot{s}_w(t)$ is the time t flow of water through the power station (a dot refers to a time derivative). This flow is determined by natural conditions (precipitation, etc.), and the amount of water diverted from electricity production in order to promote the possibility of salmon to pass the power station and reach their spawning-grounds:

$$\dot{s}_w(t) = k(t) - A(t), \tag{3}$$

where $k(t)$ refers to the flow of water as determined by natural conditions, and $A(t)$ denotes the amount of water diverted from electricity production. The policy variable of our model is $A(t)$, because it directly controls the production of goods from water/electricity, and indirectly controls the amount of salmon.

The change of the stock of salmon is determined as follows:

$$\dot{s}_L(t) = g(s_L(t), A(t)) - c_L(t), \tag{4}$$

where $g(.)$ is a generic growth function. This formulation is based on the idea that $A(t)$, i.e. the amount of water diverted from electricity production, affects the number of salmon that makes it upstream through the power station. Thus the natural growth of the stock of salmon is a function of $A(t)$ and the size of the stock itself at time t. Equation (4) shows that the change of the salmon stock at time t is equal to the natural growth of the stock at time t less the catch of salmon at time t. For simplicity, it is assumed that the catch of salmon at time t is equal to the consumption of salmon at time t.

Equations (3) and (4) make it clear that diversion of water from electricity production has two effects. First, there is an immediate impact on production of the numeraire good such that $c(t)$ is reduced. Second, there is an indirect impact on the growth of salmon such that the stock of salmon will be larger in the future (given the catch of salmon). The cost–benefit analysis looks at these benefits and costs. Thus we can use a change in $A(t)$ to generate the principal terms in a cost–benefit analysis of the salmon–hydropower 'conflict'.

This interpretation seems to be at odds with the empirical finding that electricity and salmon are 'complements' rather than 'substitutes'. However, at the margin the two 'goods' might still be substitutes. Assume that it is optimal for electricity production to divest more water during weekends than during weekdays since electricity demand is higher during weekdays. However, from the point of view of reproduction of salmon it might be optimal to have a constant $A(t)$ over the week, i.e. a constant electricity production independently of how demand varies over time. For this reason we continue to speak in this section of a conflict between the two uses of water.

Given $A(t)$ society is assumed to maximize Equation (1) with respect to $c_L(t)$ subject to Equation (4) and some initial conditions and transversality conditions. Note that given $A(t)$, consumption of the numeraire good is completely determined by the flow of water, which in turn is determined by natural conditions. This can be seen from Equations (2) and (3).

The present value Hamiltonian of this problem can be written as follows:

$$H(t) = u(c(t), c_L(t), s_L(t))e^{-\delta t} + \lambda_L(t)(g(s_L(t), A(t)) - c_L(t)), \quad (5)$$

where $\lambda_L(t)$ is a present value costate variable.

First-order conditions for optimality can be summarized as follows:

$$\frac{\partial u(.)}{\partial c_L(t)} e^{-\delta t} = \lambda_L(t), \tag{6}$$

$$\dot{\lambda}_L(t) = -\frac{\partial u(.)}{\partial s_L(t)} e^{-\delta t} - \lambda_L(t)\frac{\partial g(.)}{\partial s_L(t)}. \tag{7}$$

Equation (6) states that in optimum the present value marginal utility of consumption of salmon at time t is equal to the shadow price of the stock of salmon at that time. Equation (7) relates the change over time of the costate variable to the sum of the present value marginal utility of the stock of salmon plus the utility value (in present value terms) of a change in the growth rate of salmon caused by a marginal increase in the stock of salmon.

In order to arrive at a simple cost–benefit rule we assume that $A(t)$ is a parameter whose value is constant over the planning horizon; $A(t) = A, \forall t$. Consider then a small uniform increase in A. This can be interpreted as an increase of the water flow in the bypass channel at the power station. In turn, this increase causes an increase in the number of salmon that survive the passing of the power station. It is one of the technologies discussed in relation to the contingent valuation study presented in Section 4.

The total effect on the objective function, i.e. Equation (1), of an infinitesimally small change in a parameter is obtained by taking the partial derivative of the present value Hamiltonian (or more generally the Lagrangean) with respect to the parameter and integrating along the optimal path over the planning horizon. Thus we obtain:

$$\int_0^\infty \frac{\partial H(t)}{\partial A(t)} = \int_0^\infty \left[-\frac{\partial u(.)}{\partial c(t)} \frac{\partial f(.)}{\partial A(t)} + \lambda_L^{c*}(t) \frac{\partial g(.)}{\partial A(t)} \right] \mathrm{e}^{-\delta t}\, \mathrm{d}t, \tag{8}$$

where an asterisk refers to an optimal value, and $\lambda_L^{c*}(t)$ is a current value costate variable. The first term within brackets on the right-hand side of Equation (8) reflects the marginal cost (in units of utility) of diverting marginally more water from electricity production. This cost is equal to the loss of consumption of the numeraire good, as less electricity for its production is available. Note that the magnitude of this cost might vary from year to year due to variations in $k(t)$, the natural flow of water; recall that $f(.)$ in Equation (8) is a function of the difference between $k(t)$ and $A(t)$. The second term within brackets yields the marginal benefit of divesting marginally more water from electricity production. This marginal benefit is equal to the optimal current value costate variable of the stock of salmon times the impact on the growth rate of the stock of salmon of diverting marginally more water from electricity production. It is here assumed that the last effect, i.e. $\partial g(.)/\partial A(t)$, is strictly positive. It can be shown that the current value costate variable $\lambda_L^{c*}(t)$ is equal to the present value sum (integral) from time t and onwards of the marginal utility of the stock of salmon plus the marginal utility of consuming salmon times the marginal effect on growth of the stock of salmon; see the Appendix to this chapter for details. This fact indicates that existence values as well as use values should be accounted for in the valuation study.

Dividing through by the marginal utility of consumption of the numeraire good converts the expression in Equation (7) from units of utility to monetary units. Thus the following expression represents a simple cost–benefit rule (CBR) for the project under consideration:

$$CBR = \int_0^{\infty} \left[\frac{\lambda_L^{c*}(t)}{\lambda_m^{c*}(t)} \frac{\partial g(.)}{\partial A(t)} - \frac{\partial f(.)}{\partial A(t)} \right] e^{-\delta t} dt, \tag{9}$$

where $\lambda_m^{c*}(t) = \partial u(.)/\partial c(t)$ denotes the optimal current value marginal utility of consumption of the numeraire good at time t. The first term within brackets is equal to the time t marginal WTP for an increase in the stock of salmon times the impact on growth of salmon of a marginal increase in $A(t)$. In the valuation question in Section 4 the number of wild salmon initially increases from 3000 to 4000. After ten years the number has increased to 9000 due to natural reproduction, i.e. through growth as captured by the growth function in Equation (4). The second term within brackets yields the marginal cost at time t in terms of the value of the loss of production of the numeraire good as marginally more water is used to 'transport' salmon. The policy implication is that we should divert more water from electricity production as long as the present value of the sum of marginal benefits over the time horizon exceeds the present value of the sum of marginal costs over the time horizon.

Let us next assume that it is possible to use different technologies to 'transport' salmon beyond the power plant; see Section 4 for further details. These different technologies require different amounts of water. For simplicity, let us model this by rewriting Equation (4) as follows:

$$\dot{s}_L(t) = g(s_L(t), A(t) \cdot \alpha) - c_L(t), \tag{10}$$

where $\alpha > 0$. Thus, the less water a technology requires in order to allow a particular number of salmon to pass the power plant, the larger is its α value.

In order to model the cost of an α-technology, we rewrite Equation (3) as:

$$\dot{s}_w(t) = k(t) - A(t) - I(\alpha), \tag{11}$$

where $I(.)$ is an 'investment' function with $\partial I(.)/\partial\alpha > 0$. Thus it is assumed that the more efficient a technology is in terms of its ability to transport salmon, the more costly is the technology in terms of the reduction it causes in the production of the numeraire good. Equation (10) implicitly assumes that more efficient technologies require more inputs in terms of the numeraire good. However, due to the nature of the simple model employed here there is no other way of modelling this than through detracting water from the production of the numeraire commodity.

Proceeding as before, we obtain the following cost–benefit rule:

$$CBR_\alpha = \int_0^\infty \left[\frac{\lambda_L^{c*}(t)}{\lambda_m^{c*}(t)}\frac{\partial g(.)}{\partial\alpha}A(t) - \frac{\partial f(.)}{\partial\alpha}\frac{\partial I(.)}{\partial\alpha}\right] \mathrm{e}^{-\delta t}\,\mathrm{d}t. \tag{12}$$

The first term within brackets represents the time t marginal benefits of an increase in the magnitude of α. These marginal benefits are equal to the marginal WTP for the stock of salmon times the impact on the growth of salmon of a marginal increase in α. The second term within brackets represents the instantaneous marginal cost, i.e. the loss of production of the numeraire good as resources are diverted to the 'production' of more α. The sum of discounted marginal benefits less the sum of discounted marginal costs is an indicator of the social profitability of a small increase in α.

Having outlined this framework, we now turn to our empirical application. We begin by presenting some useful biological background information and then turn to the benefits and costs.

3. SALMON AND HYDROPOWER

Fish passage problems related to migrations through flow controlled areas in regulated rivers are global. In Sweden, these problems arise in larger rivers where fish spawn in upriver areas while critical migration passages such as bypass channels and fish ladders are situated in the downriver areas. In the completely flow-controlled Umeälven, and its natural largest tributary Vindelälven, Rivinoja et al. (2001) show that about 75 per cent of the salmon do not pass upriver through the flow controlled area around the Stornorrfors power station.[1]

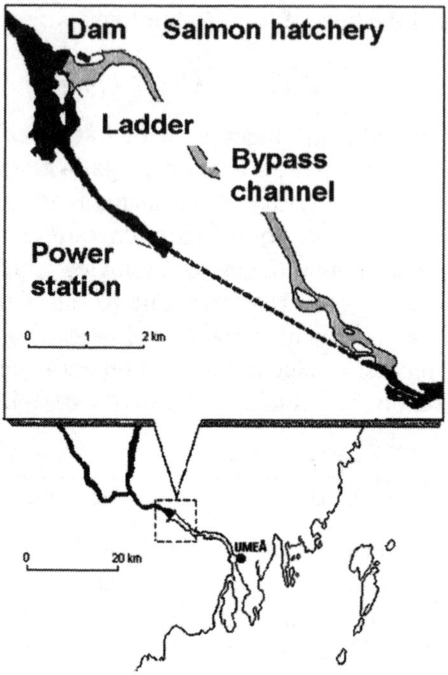

Figure 9.1. Study area

Wild salmon undertake their spawning migration in the lower Umeälven in early summer and migrate upstream till early October. Daily and weekly control of the water flow through the hydropower station and over the dam in Norrfors has given rise to a concern that the salmon migration is hindered by low daily flow regimes during the spawning migration.[2]

Our study area is presented in Figure 9.1. The salmon enter an area in which the water from the turbines and the bypass channel come together. The amount of water in each pathway depends on electricity generation (i.e. electricity demand) and stipulated flow in the bypass channel. We have data on the total flow, i.e. the sum of turbine and bypass channel flows (SMHI 2003), see Figure 9.2.

A salmon ladder, located 32 km from the estuary, generates detailed information on the hatchery (adipose fin cut) and wild (adipose fin intact) salmon and sea trout stocks reaching the Vindelälven. About 70 per cent of all fish observed in the fish ladder is of wild origin (McKinnell et al. 1994). Figure 9.3 presents data from the ladder, using observations on the yearly averages from 1974 to 2000.

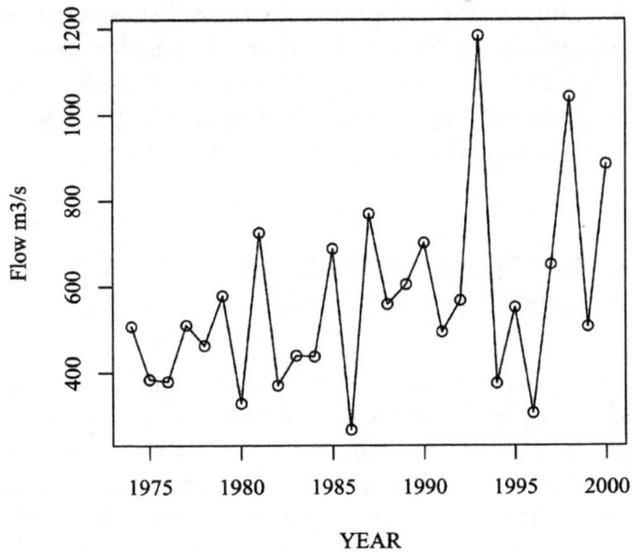

Figure 9.2. Water flow during salmon runs, yearly averages

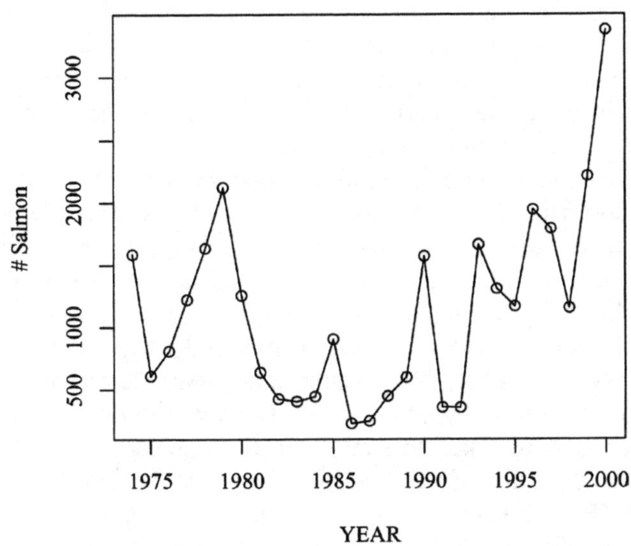

Figure 9.3. Number of salmon in the Stornorrfors ladder, yearly averages 1974–2000

Turning to daily data, an estimate of the density shows that the distribution is markedly skewed towards the origin. The median is about 8 and the mean around 15 salmon per day. If we piece the above information together, we obtain a relation between flow and the number of salmon. We will, however, undertake this analysis in Section 5.

4. MEASURING PREFERENCES FOR SALMON IN VINDELÄLVEN: A PILOT STUDY

A pilot study was carried out in May 2003 to obtain more information about Swedes' sentiments towards the wild salmon in Vindelälven. Questionnaires were mailed to 250 randomly selected Swedes[3] and 200 were mailed to randomly selected Swedish anglers.[4] Twenty-eight per cent returned the questionnaire. The main purpose of the pilot study was to identify problems that can be of importance when designing the survey for the main study.

The survey was structured in a conventional manner. It initially provides general information about the current situation for wild salmon globally and specific information concerning the wild salmon in the river Vindelälven. The respondents were also made aware of the fact that increasing the number of wild salmon typically comes at an opportunity cost. In addition, the background part of the questionnaire included information about the present and future fishing situation in the river.

Different methods can be used to improve the fish passage associated with the Stornorrfors Power Station in the Umeälven. One method is to build a fish ladder leading from the turbine discharge tunnel outlet to the bypass area so fish can migrate upstream and find the existing ladder, leading the returning fish to approach the spawning areas in Vindelälven. Another method is to increase the water flow in the bypass channel (Ferguson and Williams 2002). We assume that migration is increased due to increased flow in the bypass channel. However, in our questionnaire, the respondents were asked to state their willingness-to-pay (WTP) for increasing the migration of wild salmon with a new fish ladder.

Since WTP might vary across the methods proposed to increase migration, the following question was included in the questionnaire:

> One way to increase the number of wild salmon that reach their spawning places, is to build a new fish ladder. A fish ladder already exists today, but a more efficient one could be constructed. Suppose that any method to increase migration of wild salmon

is equally successful in terms of the number of migrating salmon and that the cost is the same. Does it then matter to you which method that is being used?

The respondents could answer 'yes', 'no' or 'do not know'. Space was also included for comments. Sixty-two per cent of the respondents did not care which method that was used, as long as the costs and the increase of wild salmon were the same for all methods. Nine per cent answered 'do not know'. Twenty-nine per cent of the respondents answered that it did matter for them which method was used, even if the costs and the increase of wild salmon were the same for all methods. The comments given by the yes-respondents indicate that it is of significance to this group whether or not the method used increases the number of salmon in a natural way. An example of a nonnatural increase would be to catch all salmon below the power station and then transport them to their spawning places above the power station. A new fish ladder and an increase of water flow in the old river basin are examples of methods that would increase the number of wild salmon in the river Vindelälven in a natural way.

We assume that a cost–benefit analysis can be carried out for all natural methods for increasing the number of wild salmon in the river Vindelälven, notwithstanding the fact that we asked only about one of a number of possible approaches. We will continue to explore preferences over different approaches in the main survey.

4.1. Willingness-to-Pay over Time

In recent years, a number of papers have inquired into WTP over time. This issue has several dimensions, including but not limited to: the difference between using lump sum or by-period payments (see Johansson 1987), implied discount rates (see Harrison et al. 2001) and the credibility of the payment vehicle. In our case, the dynamics enter in a natural way, because measures carried out 'today' will have an impact on the number of salmon 'tomorrow', via the growth function (see Equation (4)).

We began our analysis of this issue by examining if respondents were sensitive to different profiles of salmon development over time. Thus, half of the respondents (sample A) were asked the following WTP question:

During the last ten years, an average of 3000 wild salmon have reached the river Vindelälven each year. Assume that the number of wild salmon that reach the river increase to 4000 this year due to a new fish ladder. The new fish ladder will, together with the salmon's natural reproduction, result in approximately 6000 wild salmon reaching the spawning areas five years from now and approximately 9000 ten years from now. After ten years, the number of wild salmon in the river Vindelälven will stay at 9000 each year.

> Question (2): Would you be willing to pay the following lump sum for this increase of the number of wild salmon in the river Vindelälven?

The other half of the sample (sample B) answered a similar question, the difference being that the number of wild salmon was assumed to increase to 9000 already after five years, and was then held constant at that level. In summary, the difference between the scenarios for samples A and B is that 3000 additional salmon become available in year 5 in the case of sample B. We pictured the increase of wild salmon over time by using a diagram.

The different bids varied between 10–20 SEK and 300–400 SEK. At this point of the study, we have not invoked the results available from design theory regarding the choice of bids. The pilot study provides some indications of useful ranges. Yet, the number of bids, their spacing and so on and so forth are considerations not independent of the optimal design criterion used. This matter will be handled in a more satisfactory manner in the coming main study.

To make sure that the respondents distinguished between the different quantities of wild salmon, and between getting more wild salmon today and getting more wild salmon tomorrow, another WTP question was asked before question (2). Fifty per cent of the respondents were asked to reveal their WTP (lump sum) for an increase of salmon from 3000 to 4000 *this year*. The other 50 per cent were asked to state their WTP (lump sum) for an increase of salmon from 3000 to 9000 *this year*.

The results suggest that people are willing to pay more for a larger increase of salmon than for a smaller. In other words, people seem to perceive the difference between quantities and do express an opinion about them. This is important, given the discussion about insensitivity to scope that has taken place in the literature on valuation, cf. the discussion following the Exxon Valdez studies.[5]

Twenty-nine per cent of those with a positive WTP answered that they had the same WTP in both WTP questions.[6]

Due to the small sample size, the low respondent rate and the unsatisfactory answers to the second WTP question, little, if anything, can reliably be said about WTP for an increase of wild salmon over time. We will therefore modify our approach in the main study. First of all, we need to think of other ways of presenting the scenarios. Secondly, we will split the questions that are now asked within the same questionnaire. Some questionnaires will then include a question similar to the first WTP question in the pilot study, and some questionnaires will include a question similar to the second WTP question in the pilot study.

4.2. Interpretations of the Results

The question that we wanted survey participants to answer is how much their gross WTP is for increasing the amount of wild salmon that reach their spawning places in the river Vindelälven. In the survey, the respondents are told that the hydropower station is partly owned by the state and partly owned by the Umeå municipality. This raises questions about interpretation. For example, some people might believe that since the hydropower station has caused the passage problems, the owners of the station must also pay for the ladder. Some respondents might then conclude that this cost would be passed on to them through an increase of the electricity price or through the tax bill, since the state/municipality owns the hydropower station. These people might then state their WTP above what they believe that the state (municipality) will charge them anyhow. In other words, some respondents might actually carry out their own cost–benefit analysis of the project.

Observe that this problem arises quite generally. In the Exxon Valdez case (Carson et al. 2003), respondents might well be willing to pay for reducing the risk of future disasters. Yet, they might also perceive a risk for having to carry the costs anyway – quite a correct assessment! In some ways, this is an issue of scenario misspecification, such that it may not be clear which variables are to be kept constant from the individual's point of view. Is he or she to value the cost of preventing future oil spills with gasoline prices constant?

How can we then make sure that the respondents answered to the scenario we intended them to consider? One possible approach is to ask about increasing the water flow in the passage, rather than building a new ladder. Many would, however, realize that there is a cost for an increase of water flow, due to less electricity production, and a benefit from increasing the amount of salmon. Consequently, they might state their net WTP, rather than their gross WTP.

There are some indications in the survey that some respondents report their net WTP. Those who are not willing to pay are given eight possible reasons for this sentiment. Fifteen per cent of the respondents gave the following type of explanation for their zero response:

> I am willing to pay, but I believe that I would have to pay for the project through the tax bill anyway. Because the project is not important to me, I am not willing to pay more than what I will have to pay anyway.

The interpretation of this answer could be that some people state their net WTP rather than their gross WTP. A possible reason is that there is an

Table 9.1. Salmon count at the ladder and total flow (m^3/s)

	N	Salmon
Flow		
[144, 371)	504	11.61
[371, 482)	501	13.15
[482, 644)	502	15.63
[644, 2380]	502	20.24
Weekend		
No	1551	15.47
Yes	458	14.09
Overall	2009	15.16

uncertainty among the respondents about how the results from the study will be used. For example, as stated earlier, some of the respondents might believe that all Swedes must pay for the project through taxes. Some might also believe that they will be asked to pay an additional amount, collected through another system, such as more expensive fishing licenses in the river Vindelälven. In other words, our survey instrument probably failed on this account, by not making it crystal clear how the project should be financed. This is another issue that has to be taken care of in the main study.

5. MEASURING OPPORTUNITY COSTS

Our model postulates that there is an opportunity cost of releasing water to the salmon. The relationship between flow and salmon passage is, however, an empirical question. Recall that we have measures of the total water flow, i.e. the sum of water that passes the turbines and the water diverted to the salmon passage. We also know that there is a regulation, implying that there is more water diverted to the salmon on weekends.

To explore the relationship further, it is useful to display the underlying data. Table 9.1 shows a very clear pattern; an increased *total* flow of water implies more salmon in the ladder. This is intuitively plausible (given, of course, that there is enough water in the old river bed so that the salmon can move). What is more surprising is the fact that *less* salmon make it through the ladder on weekends. This could be due to the fact that

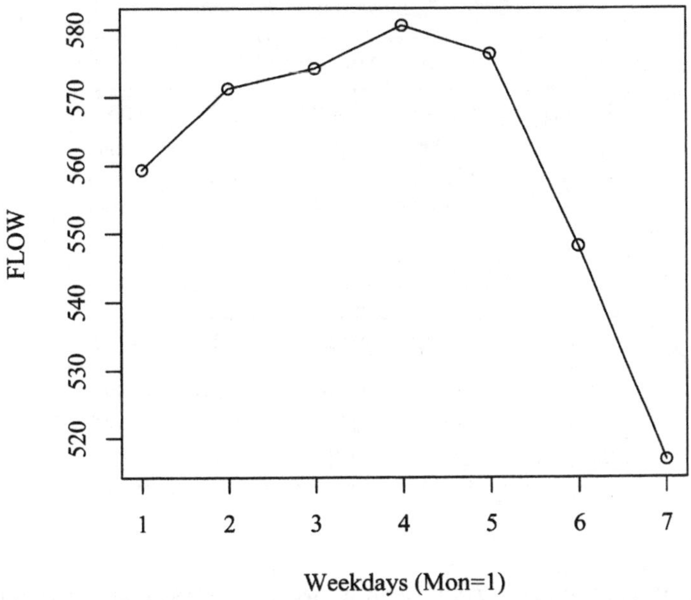

Figure 9.4. Average total daily flows during the salmon season, 1974–2000

total flow is lower during weekends, due to varying electricity demand. A simple (Welch 2 sample) t-test of this hypothesis gives a t value of 2.54, so that mean flow on Monday–Friday (572.3 m^3/s) appears to be significantly higher than flow on weekends (532.14 m^3/s). As a matter of fact, there is an interesting daily variation of total water flow through the week, as displayed in Figure 9.4.

Figure 9.4 is a mirror of electricity demand, as perceived by the managers of the Stornorrfors power station. When economic activity picks up on Monday, the flow increases through the turbines, and as we have seen, so does the number of salmon in the ladder. We must, however, reject the hypothesis that the salmon takes the weekends off. At this point, we are unable to provide an explanation of the 'weekend effect'. Possible explanations include an increased fishing pressure downstream during the weekends or some type of measurement error yet to be explained. There may also be complex time-lags in the data that we have not accounted for. Yet, at this stage, our working hypothesis is that the total flow is more important than the flow diverted to salmon.

We proceed to explore our working hypothesis by estimating some very simple regression models. Because salmon is a count variable, poisson re-

Table 9.2. Linear regression model

	Estimate	Std. Error	t value	Pr(> $\|t\|$)
(Intercept)	9.9689	1.0197	9.78	0.0000
Flow	0.0096	0.0015	6.27	0.0000
Weekend	−0.9943	1.0922	−0.91	0.3627

Table 9.3. Log-linear regression model

	Estimate	Std. Error	t value	Pr(> $\|t\|$)
(Intercept)	0.1961	0.3624	0.54	0.5884
Log. flow	0.3007	0.0578	5.20	0.0000
Weekend	0.0612	0.0621	0.99	0.3246

gression is a natural approach. Even so, we will use ordinary least squares.[7] The results of a simple ordinary regression model is given in Table 9.2. A Box–Cox transformation suggested transforming to a log-scale. The results are presented in Table 9.3.

Finally, given the potential sensitivity to extreme observations, we also used an M-estimator, as implemented in the statistical package R (see Table 9.4).

In each model, the weekend dummy is insignificant. We are thus unable to reject the hypothesis that the effect of increasing the total water flow on weekends has no effect on the number of salmon.

5.1. Opportunity Costs Estimates

In order to estimate the opportunity costs of diverting water from electricity production, we first need to estimate the value of production at the plant. We do not have official data on output per day at the plant, nor any plant-specific economic data. However, we know that the municipality owns 26 per cent of the revenues from the plant. In 2001, this was reported to be 118 MSEK, suggesting that the total revenue from the plant was about 453 MSEK.[8]

These data provide an idea of the economic values generated at the Stornorrfors plant. We do not claim to provide any exactness in these estimates. Yet, they can give us some idea of the values involved.

Table 9.4. Robust regression with an M-estimator

	Estimate	Std. Error	*t* value
(Intercept)	0.1942	0.3939	0.4929
Log. flow	0.3037	0.0628	4.8324
Weekend	0.0575	0.0675	0.8519

The current regulation at Stornorrfors during the salmon's migration season is that 20 m^3/s must be diverted from electricity production during weekdays, and 50 m^3/s must be diverted from electricity production during weekends. Given the data of Stornorrfors' revenue from year 2001 we assume that the daily production of electricity generates a value of approximately 1 MSEK per day. The current regulation of a larger diversion in the weekends translates to a loss of roughly 5 per cent of daily production, given that the average flow is about 600 m^3/s during June to September. Further, the larger diversion in the weekends translates to about 0.05 MSEK loss per day. Suppose there are 30 days of loss in production in this way (i.e. 15 weekends, or roughly the salmon season). Hence, the yearly loss is 1.5 MSEK. With a discount rate of 5 per cent and an infinite time horizon this gives a present value of 30 MSEK. A change in current regulation to a larger diversion of water from electricity production would make this number even bigger. Again, these numbers are based on rudimentary calculations, but suggest the scale of the values involved in regulations of the water flow through the power station.

6. CONCLUSIONS

This chapter presents a framework for dynamic cost–benefit analysis and applies it to a salmon passage–hydropower production conflict. The approach has wider applicability than suggested here and should be useful in similar contexts as well. It is based on the methods propelled by Karl-Gustaf Löfgren, who, as noted, carried out a rather similar project in 1979, concerning timber passage problem in the Umeälven. Our contribution certainly does not reflect all the developments of cost–benefit analysis since 1979. However, we believe it shows the usefulness and power of the approach that finds one of its leading proponents in Professor Löfgren.

Our application includes an interesting feature of the problem under study. Indeed, it is easy to take for granted that salmon and hydropower production are 'substitutes', not 'complements'. Yet, a first pass at the data is sufficient to excite further interest into the complex natural resource dynamics of the wild salmon and its intricate link with hydropower production. Indeed, we are unable to establish that the current regulation actually increases the number of salmon. It remains a fascinating topic for further research. Feynman's optimistic remark about science immediately comes to mind:

> With more knowledge comes a deeper, more wonderful mystery, luring one on to penetrate deeper still. Never concerned that the answer may prove disappointing ..., we turn over each new stone ... leading on to more wonderful questions and mysteries – [it is] certainly a great adventure! (Feynman 2001, p. XX)

Feynman's remark captures in a nutshell the driving force behind Professor Löfgren's ebullience and unfailing interest into the problems of economics. We hope that this chapter has whetted his appetite and that we can lure him into continuing his explorations into dynamic cost–benefit analysis.

APPENDIX

The relationship between the present value and current value costate variables is as follows:

$$\lambda_L(t) = \lambda_L^c(t) \cdot \mathrm{e}^{-\delta t}. \tag{13}$$

Using this relationship and integrating forward along the optimal path yields:

$$\lambda_L^{c*}(t) = \int_t^{\infty} \left[-\frac{\partial u(.)}{\partial s_L(\tau)} + \frac{\partial u(.)}{\partial c_L(\tau)} \frac{\partial g(.)}{\partial s_L(\tau)} \right] \mathrm{e}^{-\delta(\tau - t)}\, \mathrm{d}\tau. \tag{14}$$

Thus the current value costate variable $\lambda_L^{c*}(t)$ is equal to the present value sum (integral) from time t and onwards of the marginal utility of the stock of salmon plus the marginal utility of consuming salmon times the marginal effect on growth of the stock of salmon.

NOTES

1. The river enters the Bothnian bay (63°50′N 20°05′E) just south of Umeå and stems from the mountain areas ca. 450 km from the coast. The unexploited Vindelälven joins the Umeälven ca. 40 km from the estuary and ca. 8 km upriver of the dam in Norrfors. The wild salmon population in the Umeälven was destroyed during the 1950s by power exploitation while the Vindelälven still has wild salmon and trout. Releases of smolts from the Norrfors hatchery compensate the loss of naturally produced salmon from the Umeälven.
2. See Perä and Karlström (1996), Rivinoja and Lundqvist (1998) and Rivinoja et al. (2001) for detailed discussions about this issue.
3. Two hundred and fifty Swedes were randomly selected from the Swedish telephone directory.
4. Two hundred Swedish anglers were randomly selected from the register of members of the largest Swedish angle association.
5. A recent summary of the literature on 'scope' can be found in Veisten et al. (2003).
6. There are a number of possible explanations for these finding. First of all, the respondents may not be interested enough in the questionnaire to read, understand, and think through their preferences for two scenarios. Another possibility is that the respondents do not think that they should be willing to pay more in the second scenario since the cost of building a fish ladder should not differ between the two scenarios. Possibly, the respondents also start to think about why the amount of salmon is not allowed to increase with the help of natural reproduction in the first question.
7. We have estimated simple poisson regression models and they tend to give even stronger support for our working hypothesis.
8. The source for this information is the yearly report from the Umeå municipality in 2001 (see Umeå Kommun 2003).

REFERENCES

Carson, R.T. et al. (2003), 'Contingent valuation and lost passive use: Damages from the Exxon Valdez oil spill', *Environmental and Resource Economics*, 25(3), 257–286.

Ferguson, J. and J. Williams (2002), 'Recommendations for improving fish passage at the Stornorrfors power station on the Umeälven Umeå, Sweden', Report submitted to the Vindel River Fishery Advisory Board Umeå, Sweden.

Feynman, R.P. (2001), *What Do You Care What Other People Think*, New York: W.W. Norton.

Harrison, G.W., I.M. Lau and M.B. Williams (2001), 'Estimating individual discount rates in Denmark: A field experiment', *American Economic Review*, 5, 1606–1617.

Johansson, P.-O. (1987), *The Economic Theory and Measurement of Environmental Benefits*, Cambridge, UK: Cambridge University Press.

Johansson, P.-O. and K.-G. Löfgren (1996), 'On the interpretation of "green" NNP measures as cost–benefit rules', *Environmental and Resource Economics*, 7, 243–250.

Löfgren, K.-G. (2003), 'Evaluating projects in a dynamic economy: Some new envelope results', Mimeo, Department of Economics, University of Umeå.

Löfgren, K.-G. and P.-O. Johansson (1979), 'River driving along the Uman-River; A cost benefit analysis' (Virkestransporter längs Uman – samhällsekonomiska synpunkter på valet av transportsätt), Department of Forest Economics, SLU, Report No. 28 [in Swedish].

McKinnell, S., H. Lundqvist and H. Johansson (1994), 'Biological characteristics of the upstream migration of naturally and hatchery-reared Baltic salmon (Salmo salar)', *Aquaculture and Fisheries Management*, 25, Suppl. 2, 46–63.

Perä, I. and Ö. Karlström (1996), 'Undersökning av laxuppvandringen till Ume- Vindelälven vid Stornorrfors kraftverk 1996', Fiskeriverket Utredningskont (Luleå), Rapport 1996-12-23 [in Swedish].

Rivinoja, P. and H. Lundqvist (1998), 'Laxens lekvandring i nedre Umeälven: Redovisning av telemetriförsök år 1997', Mimeo, SLU, Vattenbruksinstitutionen, 980125 [in Swedish].

Rivinoja, P., S. McKinnell and H. Lundqvist (2001), 'Hindrances to upstream migration of Atlantic Salmon (Salmo salar) in a northern Swedish river caused by a hydroelectric power-station', *Regulated Rivers: Research and Management*, 17, 101–115.

SMHI (2003), Flowdata from the Stornorrfors power station obtained electronically on file from Eva.Edquist@smhi.se.

Umeå Kommun (2003), http://www.umea.se/net/Ume%e5+Kommun/innehe5llsmeny/Fakta+om+Ume%e5/Ekonomi/Redovisning/Bokslut+2001

Veisten, K., H.F. Hoen, S. Navrud and J. Strand (2003), 'Scope insensitivity in contingent valuation of complex environmental amenities', Working Paper, Institute of Transport Economics, University of Oslo.

10. Trees vs. Fish, or Discrete vs. Continuous Harvesting

Martin L. Weitzman

1. KARL-GUSTAF LÖFGREN AND THE HARVESTING OF RENEWABLE NATURAL RESOURCES

Karl-Gustaf Löfgren has been one of the early pioneers in developing and applying dynamic economic tools (in particular, optimal control theory) to the analysis of how best to develop and harvest natural resources. At the same time, he has maintained a special interest in forestry economics. The topic of this chapter may thus be relevant for a celebration of his sixtieth birthday.

I have a suspicion that Kalle was, at a young age, attracted to the interface between human beings and the natural environment that surrounds and nurtures them. That is to say, I am guessing that early on he was relatively most interested in the part of environmental economics having to do with the combining of economics with 'nature', as opposed to, say, the combining of economics with pollution–health issues, which might be called 'Environmental Protection Agency-type' environmental economics. What then could be a more 'natural' (no pun intended) field for Kalle to specialize in than the harvesting of renewable natural resources.

This is not to say that Kalle has not done outstanding work in lots of other areas of economics. It is just that I think that the 'love of his life' has been in this area of how to balance human interests and the interests of 'nature'.

When Kalle first entered the field, back in the 1960s, the economic harvesting of natural resources was still in its murky infancy. The basic ideas were 'out there', for sure, but they were far from being in the nicely-packaged reduced form we now know and teach to students. Every model seemed special, and disconnected from every other. It was not clear what were the basic unifying underlying principles. Were they just specific particularly-exotic examples of capital theory, or was there some deeper connection with the rest of dynamic economics?

I think it is fair to say that Pontryagin's maximum principle, which was just then beginning to be applied to economics, and which Kalle latched on to very early, forced us economists to 'see' the capital-theoretic unity of all such natural resource problems. First of all, just using the maximum principle made us put all dynamic problems into a canonical form that was almost automatically a useful way of seeing the underlying unity. More importantly, the maximum principle itself is a set of duality conditions with a natural, and very important, economic interpretation centered on the co-state variables, which are competitive-like prices to us. The maximum principle has a direct economic interpretation as describing a dynamic competitive equilibrium, while other forms of dynamic optimality conditions (for example, Euler-type equations) essentially must be transformed into a maximum principle-like form to give them economic meaning.

Thus, by using the maximum principle, we economists were led to a rich understanding of the connections between the optimal regulation of a renewable fishery resource, the optimal extraction of an exhaustible mineral resource, and the neoclassical theory of optimal growth – to name just three famous models that thereby became interconnected. However, one famous and very important model that we natural-resource economists knew and loved remained somehow outside this maximum principle-contained orbit of (almost) all other dynamic resource allocation models. This was the famous Faustmann–Wicksell model of optimal forestry rotation. I would think that Kalle is perhaps the world's expert on the history of economic thought surrounding the Faustmann–Wicksell model (or models), since he has been especially concerned with the theory (and practice) of forestry economics throughout his career and has written on the intellectual history of just such a class of aging and growth models.

Forestry models seemed somehow 'different' from the other models of natural resource harvesting or extraction. The forestry models focus sharply on the age structure of a cohort, and are essentially discrete. The 'harvesting' of a tree or forest is the discrete act of cutting it down and bringing it to market. The 'renewal' of a tree or forest is the discrete act of planting seedlings. This seems very different from the continuous harvesting and renewal that characterizes, say, the classical model of the fishery.

There is an air of intellectual disappointment in not being able to combine fishery and forestry models under some unifying umbrella. At least this was the case for me. Kalle, I believe, may have also been intellectually puzzled about this seeming dichotomy between the continual harvesting and renewal of the fishery and the discontinuous harvesting and renewal of the forest. Why should these two core models of the economics of renewable resources seem so different in structure?

What I want to show in this chapter is that there exists a way to connect the two models by turning the classical Faustmann–Wicksell forestry model into an equivalent continuous-harvesting version. We will then be able to see how the maximum principle applied to this equivalent continuous-harvesting version of the forestry rotation problem is just another form of the famous Faustmann–Wicksell first-order conditions telling us when to cut down the tree.

In the next section, we recapitulate the problem of the sole owner of the fishery as an optimal control problem that is linear in net investment, and hence supports a most rapid approach bang-bang solution. Then, the more interesting and novel part, which follows in the third section, shows that the classical forestry problem is also an optimal control problem that is linear in net investment, and hence this problem also supports a most rapid approach bang-bang solution. In this way, we show that the mathematical structure of these two famous problems of the harvesting of natural resources is essentially isomorphic. Both are linear in investment optimal control problems whose solution is the most rapid approach to their respective stationary states.

2. OPTIMAL MANAGEMENT OF THE FISHERY

The classical dynamic economic problem of optimal fishery management is typically presented as if seen through the eyes of a fictitious 'sole owner', who may be conceptualized as being either a private firm or a government regulatory agency. The sole owner is assumed to be seeking a harvesting policy that maximizes net present discounted profits.

The problem here is which form to choose for the harvesting flow rate $\{h(t)\}$ to

$$\text{maximize} \int_0^\infty \pi(x)h(t)\,\mathrm{e}^{-\rho t}\,\mathrm{d}t \tag{1}$$

subject to

$$\dot{x}(t) = F(x(t)) - h(t), \tag{2}$$

and

$$\underline{h} \leq h(t) \leq \bar{h}, \tag{3}$$

and with the given initial condition

$$x(0) = x_0. \tag{4}$$

For this model, $x(t)$ represents the stock of fish at time t, and $h(t)$ is the harvest flow taken at time t. In condition (3), $\hat{h}$ is some more or less arbitrary upper bound on harvesting; the lower bound $\underline{h}$ is perhaps somewhat less arbitrary because $\underline{h} \equiv 0$, at least, has a natural interpretation. (The upper and lower bounds are needed to make sense of the problem for technical reasons, so in a way it does not matter what they are.) The function $F(x)$ represents the net biological increase of the fish population, in the absence of any harvesting. The function $\pi(x)$ gives the net profits per fish caught when the stock of fish is x.

In the fisheries literature it is standard to take as unit profit the difference between price and catch cost, so that

$$\pi(x) = P - c(x), \tag{5}$$

where P represents the exogenously-given price of fish and $c(x)$ represents per unit 'locating and harvesting cost' as a function of fish density x. A reader typically sees the form of the right-hand side of (5), rather than our more concise notation $\pi(x)$.

To reduce the problem of the sole owner of the fishery to a canonical form, it is useful to reformulate it in terms of net investment. In this situation, net investment is the natural biological increment of the fish population *minus* the amount of fish being caught or harvested. (It is perhaps not yet entirely clear why we might want to take a problem out of the form in which it naturally suggests itself and recast it in the form of a prototype economic problem where net investment is considered to be the control variable – the reason is that this canonical form always permits the solution to be understood quickly, easily, and in the most economically intuitive way.)

With the change of variables $K \equiv x$ and $I \equiv F(x) - h$, and specifying $m(K) \equiv F(K) - \hat{h}$ and $M(K) \equiv F(K) - \underline{h}$, the optimal fishery harvesting problem is a prototype-economic problem with gain function

$$G(K, I) = \pi(K)[F(K) - I]. \tag{6}$$

The stationary rate of return on capital is defined to be

$$R(K) \equiv \frac{G_1(K, 0)}{-G_2(K, 0)}. \tag{7}$$

It can readily be shown that net investment should be positive if $R(K) > \rho$, negative if $R(K) < \rho$, and zero if $R(K) = \rho$. Once the stationary rate of return on capital has been calculated, the qualitative direction of investment (positive, negative, or zero) is determined. The only remaining question is how fast to go to a stationary state. For the linear in investment renewable resource problems under investigation here, the answer is 'as fast as possible'.

From applying formulae (7) to (6) (and remembering to evaluate at $I = 0$), the stationary rate of return on capital for this model of optimal fishery management is

$$R(K) = F'(K) + F(K)\frac{\pi'(K)}{\pi(K)}. \tag{8}$$

Equation (8) can be interpreted as saying that the stationary rate of return $R(K)$ consists of two terms representing the two economic effects that come from having a higher amount of fish capital here. The first effect, $F'(K)$, represents the increment of new fish population that comes with a higher parent fish stock. The second term on the right-hand side of (8) represents the additional profit from the lower unit harvesting cost that attends a larger fish population, since it is easier to locate and catch fish when there are more of them.

Let $\hat{K}$ represent the stationary solution where

$$R(\hat{K}) = \rho. \tag{9}$$

As is well known for a problem linear in net investment, the optimal policy is a most rapid approach to the stationary solution $\hat{K}$.

This description of the management of the fishery is familiar, because we are (by now) accustomed to seeing the classical fishery model as a linear in investment optimal control problem with a bang-bang solution. What is less familiar, and less obvious, is that the optimal forest rotation problem is also a linear in investment optimal control problem with a bang-bang solution. Hence, the mathematical structure of the two renewable resource harvesting problems is essentially the same.

3. OPTIMAL TREE HARVESTING AS A CONTROL PROBLEM

Another model whose gain function is linear in investment is the *optimal tree harvesting model*. This problem can be posed and solved directly, without invoking optimal control theory – so a formulation in terms of optimal control theory serves more to enrich an intuitive understanding of the maximum principle (as capital theory) than to serve as a mechanism for actually solving a problem that could not otherwise be solved.

Suppose that, when it is cut down and brought to market, a tree of age T yields a net value given by the function

$$F(T). \tag{10}$$

Frequently in the forestry literature, $F(T)$ is specified in the form

$$F(T) = Pf(T) - c + \nu, \tag{11}$$

where P is the given market price of wood and $f(T)$ is (in forestry terminology) the 'merchantable volume' of wood yielded by a tree of age T. The parameter c represents the total economic cost of cutting down the tree, processing it for sale, and bringing the wood to market. (In the forestry literature, the expression $Pf(T) - c$ is called the *net stumpage value* of the tree.) The parameter ν stands for the *opportunity value* (in lumbering terminology the *land expectation* or *site value*) of the land being freed for its best subsequent economic use after the tree is felled – which 'best subsequent economic use' might well be the replanting of a sapling to start the tree-growing cycle anew.

The famous *Wicksell problem* of capital theory is to choose the time of cutting T to

$$\text{maximize } \mathrm{e}^{-\rho T} F(T). \tag{12}$$

It might seem perverse to force such a direct statement as (12) into the seemingly more arcane form of an optimal control problem. However, an optimal control formulation will serve to reinforce economic intuition and to highlight quite dramatically the underlying unity of *all* time and capital problems. In particular, it will allow us to see sharply the relationship between the two most famous models of renewable resources – optimal harvesting of the fishery and optimal harvesting of the forest.

In the optimal control version of the Wicksell problem, the 'capital stock' is the *age of the tree* (more precisely, it is the tree of that age). The corresponding 'investment' here means allowing the tree to grow older by a year.

Suppose we fancifully imagined that 'the forest' could be continuously harvested in the spirit of 'the fishery'. For this fishery-like forest, the 'harvest-flow' generalization of the Wicksell problem in capital theory is to control the 'investment rate' $\{I(t)\}$ to

$$\text{maximize} \int_0^{\infty} \rho F(K(t))[1 - I(t)]\, \mathrm{e}^{-\rho t}\, \mathrm{d}t \tag{13}$$

subject to

$$\dot{K}(t) = I(t), \tag{14}$$

and

$$0 \leq I(t) \leq 1, \tag{15}$$

and with the given initial condition

$$K(0) = 0. \tag{16}$$

The original Wicksell formulation in effect limits the investment $I(t)$ to be a step function, which takes on value one when the tree is growing (or until it is cut), and takes on value zero thereafter. As we will see, the above 'harvest-flow' generalization yields the Wicksell solution anyway. For now it suffices to note that the Wicksell problem is a special case of (13)–(16); therefore, if the optimal solution of (13)–(16) is a step function, as will turn out to be the case, then it must also represent the solution of the more restricted Wicksell problem (12).

It is useful to pose the Wicksell model formally as an optimal control model of capital accumulation because it highlights the underlying connection between growth and aging processes where *capital is time* (aging of wine is another well-known example) and the bulk of *all other* capital-theoretic models that can be formulated as simple optimal control problems where capital is *not* time. Posing the problem this way allows us to see rigorously what we otherwise can only intuit in models of tree cutting, wine aging, animal raising, and many other problems of growth and aging – the important idea that in many situations *age is capital*, but that otherwise the same general principles of capital theory apply.

So, for this Wicksell problem, let us identify 'capital' with 'age'. Applying definition (12) to the gain function

$$G(K, I) = \rho F(K)[1 - I], \tag{17}$$

which appears in (13), the stationary rate of return on capital in the optimal tree cutting problem is

$$R(K) = \frac{F'(K)}{F(K)}. \tag{18}$$

From the general consideration that the gain function of the Wicksell problem is linear in investment, we know that the optimal solution involves a most rapid approach to the stationary state $\hat{K}$ where $R(\hat{K}) = \rho$, which by (19) is equivalent to the condition

$$\frac{F'(\hat{K})}{F(\hat{K})} = \rho. \tag{19}$$

Let us see what is happening specifically in this particular optimal control problem by formally applying the maximum principle. The Hamiltonian here is

$$H = \rho F(K)[1 - I] + pI. \tag{20}$$

where p stands for the marginal value of letting a tree of age K grow for one more year.

The next step is to calculate the maximum value of the Hamiltonian over all feasible values of I. This part is easy because we are maximizing a linear function over the unit interval. With $\tilde{I}(p)$ denoting the Hamiltonian-maximizing value of investment as a function of its price, from (20) there are three possibilities:

$$p > \rho F(K) \Rightarrow \tilde{I}(p) = 1 \Rightarrow \tilde{H}(K, p) = p, \tag{21}$$

or

$$p < \rho F(K) \Rightarrow \tilde{I}(p) = 0 \Rightarrow \tilde{H}(K, p) = F(K), \tag{22}$$

or, the case of an indeterminate solution where $\tilde{I}(p)$ can be *any* feasible value,

$$p = \rho F(K) \Rightarrow 0 \leq \tilde{I}(p) \leq 1 \Rightarrow \tilde{H}(K, p) = F(K). \tag{23}$$

It is now not difficult to guess at the form of an optimal policy. Just from glancing at (21), (22), and (23), an intuitive chain of reasoning is that

$$K < \hat{K} \Rightarrow \frac{F'(K)}{F(K)} > \rho \Rightarrow p > \rho F(K) \Rightarrow \tilde{I}(p) = 1 \Rightarrow \tilde{H}(K, p) = p, \tag{24}$$

in which case we have

$$-\frac{\partial \tilde{H}}{\partial K} = 0, \tag{25}$$

and therefore the dual differential equation condition here becomes

$$\dot{p}(t) = \rho p(t), \tag{26}$$

with the 'terminal condition'

$$p(\hat{K}) = \rho F(\hat{K}). \tag{27}$$

Combining (26) with (27), yields

$$p(t) = \rho F(\hat{K})\, \mathrm{e}^{\rho(t-\hat{K})}. \tag{28}$$

By the optimality of $\hat{K}$ for the problem (12), we must then have for $K(t) < \hat{K}$ that

$$F(K(t))\, \mathrm{e}^{-\rho t} < F(\hat{K})\, \mathrm{e}^{-\rho\hat{K}}. \tag{29}$$

Combining (29) with (28), we obtain the basic result that for $K(t) < \hat{K}$

$$p(t) > \rho F(K(t)). \tag{30}$$

From (30) we can say that the signal *not* to cut down the tree is that the shadow indirect value of allowing the tree to grow exceeds the direct value of harvesting it. (It is never optimal to allow a tree to grow to an age T where $F'(T)/F(T) < \rho$, but if we acquired such an 'economically overripe tree' having $T > K'$ from a nonprofit-maximizing owner, the signal to cut it down immediately would be that the shadow indirect value of allowing the tree to grow is less than the direct value of harvesting it.)

We now make some important observations about the role of the hitherto obscure parameter ν, which stands for the *opportunity value* of the land being freed for its best subsequent economic use after the tree is felled. Suppose that, instead of being concerned about the fate of an individual tree, which is the Wicksell problem, we are interested in the infinite horizon optimal rotation of a one-tree lot (or, more realistically, of a woodlot consisting of a stand of cohort trees). In this case, the opportunity value ν of the land being freed for its best subsequent economic use after the tree is felled is the present discounted value of a infinite-horizon rotation policy beginning with the replanting of a sapling to start the tree-growing cycle anew.

Suppose the parameter c now includes all costs of replanting (as well as logging, processing, and transportation costs). The competitive market value ν of the land (in forestry terminology the land expectation or the site value), right after it has been cleared and a new sapling has just been replanted, satisfies in competitive equilibrium the recursive equation

$$\nu = \mathrm{e}^{-\rho\hat{K}}[Pf(\hat{K}) - c - \nu], \tag{31}$$

which is equivalent, after rearrangement, to

$$\nu = \frac{e^{-\rho \hat{K}}[Pf(\hat{K}) - c]}{1 - e^{-\rho \hat{K}}}. \tag{32}$$

If $\hat{K}$ is the optimal age to cut down a tree given the competitive market value ν of the site, then it seems plausible that $\hat{K}$ is chosen to maximize present site value, so that

$$\nu = \text{maximum}_K \frac{e^{-\rho K}[Pf(K) - c]}{1 - e^{-\rho K}}, \tag{33}$$

which yields the first-order condition

$$\frac{Pf'(\hat{K})}{Pf(\hat{K}) - c} = \frac{\rho}{1 - e^{-\rho \hat{K}}}. \tag{34}$$

Equation (34) is the famous *Faustmann formula* for the optimal rotation length $\hat{K}$.

Rewriting the optimization problem (33) in the equivalent form of an infinite geometric series, we have

$$\nu = \text{maximum}_K \sum_{j=1}^{\infty} e^{-jK}[Pf(K) - c]. \tag{35}$$

In effect, Equation (35) defines the *Faustmann model* of optimal forest rotation, whose solution satisfies the Faustman formula (34).

In the forestry literature, the Faustmann model and the Faustmann formula are typically contrasted with the Wicksell model and the Wicksell formula. In a serious sense, this is a false dichotomy, as Kalle has known and emphasized in his writings. The Wicksell model ostensibly takes the site value as exogenously given, often as zero, although there is evidence that Wicksell himself understood that it would be fallacious to perform comparative statics when treating ν as if it were constant. The *Faustmann and Wicksell models are identical* when proper account is taken of the market site value of forest land. We showed above that the Wicksell model with competitive market site value yields the Faustmann solution; the converse can readily be shown by substituting the Faustman formula for site value into the Wicksell formulation and confirming directly that the Wicksell-optimal cutting time satisfying condition (19) is exactly the Faustmann-optimal cutting time satisfying condition (34). The two models represent two equivalent ways of looking at optimal forestry management. The Wicksell approach emphasizes how to think about harvesting an individual tree. The Faustmann approach emphasizes how to think about the harvesting cycle of an ongoing stand of trees. So long as the opportunity value of the wood-lot is properly assessed and included, both models yield identical conclusions. It is essentially a case of looking at two sides of a single problem that more properly should be called 'the' *Faustmann–Wicksell model* of forestry management.

4. SUMMARY AND CONCLUSION

What has been shown here is that the Faustmann–Wicksell model of optimal tree harvesting has essentially the same form as the standard model of the sole owner of the fishery. Both can be seen as optimal control models linear in net investment, and both have the same form of most rapid approach to their respective stationary solution.

Of course the Faustmann–Wicksell model can be developed without optimal control theory. But applying the maximum principle to the forestry rotation problem allows us to see it as a harvesting problem of the same generic form as the standard fishery model. Thus, the two most famous models in the economics of renewable resources – the fishery and the forest – are essentially two forms of the same underlying optimal control problem. The same capital theoretic principle of most rapid approach to the stationary state underlies their solution, since both models can be expressed as optimal control problems with an objective function that is linear in net investment.

ACKNOWLEDGEMENTS

This chapter was prepared for the volume in honor of Karl-Gustaf Löfgren and it is essentially a repackaged version (with different emphases) of some material contained in my book *Income, Wealth, and the Maximum Principle* (Harvard University Press, 2003).

11. Differentiating at the Speed of Light in a Universe of Trees and Moose[1]

Olvar Bergland, Richard Ready and Eirik Romstad[2]

1. INTRODUCTION

The population of European moose (*Alces alces*) in Sweden and Norway has increased manifold since World War II. In Norway the annual harvest varied between one and two thousand animals in the early parts of the nineteenth century, but has increased steadily since 1945. The increase has been particularly profound since the 1970s. In the 1990s the annual Norwegian moose harvest exceeded 35 000 animals per year (Andersen and Sæther, 1996). There are several reasons for this increase. First, the Norwegian hunting policy has changed so that more young animals are shot, thereby leaving a larger share of the productive animals in the forest. Second, and possibly even more important, there has been a large growth in the acreage of clear cuts and hence forest regeneration areas. These forest types provide more feed for the moose, thereby increasing their reproductivity rate.

Scots pine (*Pinus silvestris*) is one of the three most important commercial tree species in Norway. Commercial forests in Norway are primarily owned as part of family farms, and the scale of the average operation is small. The average individual clear cut is only 1.4 hectares. This creates a patchy environment that is well suited as moose habitat.

In winter, when snow covers the moose's preferred forage, young pine trees are an important food source (Sæther et al. 1992). Moose browsing on the young pine damages the trees, reducing the tree growth rate, and the future commercial value of the pine. Browsing may damage more than 10 per cent of the young pine trees in high density moose regions. On less productive forest tracts, high moose densities can make pine production unprofitable.

While the presence of moose clearly is damaging to the pine production, the presence of young pines provides additional winter feed for the moose. This is particularly the case in years with much snow, when young pines may be the only suitable moose feed. With ample winter forage, female calves grow faster, and reach sexual maturity at younger age. This increases the reproduction rate of the moose population.

Under previous Norwegian wildlife law, the state determined how many animals could be shot each season in each management area, resulting in a quota to the land owners in the area. These land owners then decided among themselves how to harvest and share the quota within the limits of the law. In many places in Norway, the moose migrate during the year and are located in different areas during the hunting season and the winter forage season. Under this regime it was possible that the pine tree owner who suffers the damage from the browsing during the winter season may not be the same person as the land owner who benefits from harvesting the animals.

Since 2000, the land owners who join into a management area that is sufficiently large to encompass a distinct moose population are now free to set the overall moose hunting quota for the management area, and to distribute these moose among the land owners. In most management areas that have been founded, the overall quota and its distribution among the various land owners are determined by majority rule.

Regardless of the management regime, the risk remains that pine production provides a positive externality for moose production, while moose stocks provide a negative externality for pine production. This is important not only because of the fairness issues involved, but because pine owners may not consider the positive impacts on moose populations that occurs after their stand is harvested, and may therefore make pine cutting decisions that are socially sub-optimal. The challenge is to design institutional arrangements that wil induce the pine owner to make socially optimal cutting decisions. These arrangements must be perceived as fair, or they will not be implemented.

The purpose of this chapter is to model the joint moose/pine system, and characterize its optimal management. Using this model, we explore two issues. First, we characterize the optimal joint management of moose and pine. Second, we explore the optimal schedule of harvests in a multi-stand forest.

Several studies explore interactions among multiple forest stands, i.e., determining when it is preferable to synchronize harvest of adjacent stands, and when it is preferable to increase the difference in harvest times across stands (Swallow and Wear 1993, Swallow et al. 1997, Koskela and Ollikainen 1999, Tahvonen and Salo 1999). When a single wildlife stock's range includes multiple stands, it will introduce interdependencies among the stands. If, for example, a wildlife stock benefits from having at least some part of its range covered by young forest that provides forage, then adjacent forest stands may serve as 'substitutes' in providing this age-dependent externality. In such a case, it may be socially optimal to stagger harvest of adjacent stands, maximizing the total time that forage is available, and minimizing temporal overlap among stands in providing this externality.

To date, these studies have all modeled the externalities generated by the forest stand as unilateral. In this chapter we have already seen that in the case for moose and pine in Norway, these externalities go both ways. Younger stands of pine provide important winter browse for moose, increasing the productivity of the moose stock. In return, the moose browse down the pine, slowing growth and decreasing eventual timber harvest values.

What are the implications of this second externality on the management of a multiple stand forest? Forest management can no longer be considered in isolation of how the wildlife stock is managed. We have already shown that optimal management of the wildlife stock will involve a tradeoff between wildlife productivity and tree revenues. While the Hartman (1976) result – that the forest rotation length should be shortened relative the rotation length that maximizes timber values – still holds in most situations, this chapter identifies settings where this is not the case. We also show that, in a multi-stand forest, it may be optimal to synchronize harvests of adjacent stands.

The chapter proceeds as follows: the model framework is developed (building on Ready et al. 2000, 2001) and is then used to evaluate several management regimes, and to provide policy insights.

2. MODEL FORMULATION

Our model follows the general structure of that developed by Tahvonen and Salo (1999), with adjustments to include the moose stock's influences on forest growth. The forest or management area consists of K tree stands (sections) that were planted at times $t_0^1, \ldots, t_0^K$ so that at time t, their ages are $s_0^1, \ldots, s_0^K = t - t_0^1, \ldots, t - t_0^K$. The sizes of the stands are $z_0^1, \ldots, z_0^K$, with a total acreage of $Z = \sum_{k=1}^{K} z_0^k$.

The standing volume of lumber in tree stand k, per unit area (hectare), is measured by $x^k(t)$, so that the total volume is given by the product $x^k(t)z^k$. For older trees, this measures the saleable volume after harvest. For young trees, this should be thought of more as an index of biomass than as an actual measure of volume. When a stand is harvested, natural regeneration supplies an initial biomass of x_0^k per hectare, which may differ among stands due to differences in the natural productivity of the land.[3] Tree growth adds to $x^k(t)$ over time, while browsing by moose decreases $x^k(t)$.

A single tree's vulnerability to browsing depends on its size. It is high during the early years, but decreases sharply when the tree reaches a height of about three meters. At that stage, the moose can no longer reach the top of the tree. Let the tree's vulnerability to browsing be given by $v(t) = v(x(t))$.

The actual browsing pressure that a given stand experiences depends on: (i) its vulnerability, (ii) the number of moose in the area, and (iii) the amount of other forage available to the moose, f_0. For stand k the total moose forage becomes $f_k(t) = x_k(t)v_k(t) + f_0$. As moose are not restricted to browsing a single stand, the average moose forage availability becomes

$$\bar{f} = \frac{1}{Z} \sum_{k=1}^{K} z^k f^k(t). \tag{1}$$

The density of moose in the area is given by $m(t)$. If moose target pine and other forage equally, the young pines receive the following browsing pressure:

$$b^k(t) = m(t) \frac{x^k(t)v^k(t)}{\bar{f}(t)}. \tag{2}$$

At lower moose densities, the dominant impact of browsing is lost biomass (i.e., delayed growth). Tree biomass per unit area changes according to

$$\dot{x}^k(t) = F(x^k(t), b^k(t)), \tag{3}$$

where the function $F(\cdot)$ includes both natural tree growth and biomass loss due to browsing. At higher browsing densities, however, moose can damage trees to the point where they loose commercial value or even die. Let $d^k(t)$ denote the percentage of the tree stand area that is undamaged. Then $d^k(t_0) = 1$, and $d^k(t)$ decreases over time due to moose browsing as a function of the size of the trees and the browsing pressure they are subject to:

$$\dot{d}^k(t) = D(x^k(t), b^k(t)). \tag{4}$$

Technically, $d^k(t)$ can never go below zero. We assume that it never gets small enough that this constraint becomes binding.

At any given point in time, the moose population (density), $m(t)$, increases due to natural growth, which depends on the amount of forage available, and decreases due to moose harvest, h, so that

$$\dot{m} = g(m(t), \bar{f}(t)) - h, \tag{5}$$

where $g(\cdot)$ denotes the natural growth of the moose stock, and h is the biomass of harvested moose. The moose stock is measured as 'moose equivalent' units, a moose-size neutral entity.

The value of killing one moose equivalent equals j, and includes both the meat and recreational value to the hunter. The wildlife management entity sets the allowed harvest level, $h(t)$ within the interval $[0, m(t)]$.

The per hectare net value of harvesting the timber from stand k at time t is $d^k(t)r(x^k(t))$, where $r(x^k(t))$ is the net revenue the owner receives from harvesting one hectare with tree volume $x^k(t)$, and zero tree mortality due to moose browsing. The expression $r(x^k(t))$ includes both harvesting costs and any costs of replanting. One expects the net timber revenue function to be highest for mature timber, and possibly negative for very young stands. Tree stand k is harvested at times $t_1^k, t_1^k, \ldots$, with N_k possibly infinite. The social discount rate is δ.

This gives a maximization problem with two types of control variables: the continuous harvest rate for moose, $h(t)$, and the discrete timing of the tree harvests. Society's objective function includes the joint present values of timber cuttings plus the value of the moose harvests:

$$\max_{t_i^k, h} W = \sum_{k=1}^{K} \sum_{i=1} N_k [z^k r(x^k(t_i^k)) d^k(t_i^k) \,\mathrm{e}^{-\delta t_i^k}] + \int_0^{\infty} jh(t) \,\mathrm{e}^{-\delta t} \,\mathrm{d}t \tag{6}$$

subject to:

$$x^k(0) = x_0^k,$$
$$\dot{x}_k = F^k[x^k(t), b^k(t)] \quad \text{when } t \neq t_i^k,$$
$$x^k(t_i^{k+}) = x_0,$$

$$
\begin{aligned}
& m(0) = m_0, \\
& \dot{m} = g(m(t), \bar{f}(t)) - h, \\
& d^k(0) = d_0^k, \\
& \dot{d}^k(t) = D[x^k(t), b^k(t)] \quad \text{when } t \neq t_i^k, \\
& d^k(t_1^{k+}) = 1.
\end{aligned} \tag{6'}
$$

This gives the following state variables: $m(t)$, $x^k(t)$ and $d^k(t)$ for $k = 1, 2, \ldots, K$. The vulnerability indices $v^k(t)$, browsing pressure measures $b^k(t)$ and $f^k(t)$ are all functions of $x^k(t)$ and $m(t)$, and do not represent new state variables.

3. OPTIMAL MOOSE HARVEST

The solution follows the approach of Seierstad and Sydsæther (1987), except that the current-valued Hamiltonians are used. Note that there are $2K$ multipliers, K growth multipliers (one for each stand), and K damage multipliers (one for each stand). The current-valued Hamiltonian becomes

$$H = jh - \lambda_m(g(m, \bar{f}) - h) + \sum_{k=1}^{K} \lambda_x^k F(x, b) + \sum_{k=1}^{K} \lambda_d^k D(x, b). \tag{7}$$

The first-order condition for moose harvest is

$$\left(\frac{\mathrm{d}H}{\mathrm{d}h} = j - \lambda_m \leq 0, \quad h(t) \geq 0, \quad h(t)(1 - \lambda_m) = 0\right) \Rightarrow \lambda_m \geq j, \tag{8}$$

where λ_m measures the current value of one additional moose in the stock at time t. The current value of harvesting one moose at time t always equals j. Any time λ_m exceeds j, it makes sense to expand the moose stock by halting all moose harvest. If $\lambda_m < j$, moose should be harvested at the maximum possible rate until $\lambda_m = j$. Thus, if the moose stock is above (below) this limit, one harvests (saves) moose until the singular solution is reached. The adjoint equation for moose becomes

$$
\begin{aligned}
\dot{\lambda}_m &= \delta\lambda_m - \frac{\partial H}{\partial m} \\
&= \lambda_m\left(\delta - \frac{\partial g(m, \bar{f})}{\partial m}\right) - \sum_{k=1}^{K}\left[\lambda_x^k \frac{\partial F(x^k, b^k)}{\partial m} - \lambda_d^k \frac{\partial D(x^k, b^k)}{\partial m}\right].
\end{aligned} \tag{9}
$$

At the singular solution, where $\lambda_m = j$, $\dot{\lambda}_m = 0$, it is possible to simplify (9) into

$$\delta = \frac{\partial g(m, f)}{\partial m} + \sum_{k=1}^{K} \frac{\lambda_x^k}{j} \frac{\partial F(x, b)}{\partial m} + \sum_{k=1}^{K} \frac{\lambda_k^k}{j} \frac{\partial D(x, b)}{\partial m} \tag{10}$$

which implicitly can be solved for the optimal value of m.

Equation (10) corresponds to the standard result that (without harvest cost effects) the growth rate of a renewable stock should be set equal to the interest rate. Note that there are $2K$ extra terms in (10) that capture the impact of the moose stock on future tree harvests. The ratios λ_x^k/j and λ_d^k/j trade off the value of more moose with the value of more wood. Both these terms are negative, so that $m(t)$ is set at a level where $\partial g(m, f)/\partial m > \delta$. The impact of moose browsing on forests is therefore that moose populations should be held lower than they would be without browsing impacts.

4. OPTIMAL TREE HARVEST TIMING

The costate equation for timber, x, is:

$$\begin{aligned} \dot{\lambda}_x^k &= \delta\lambda_x^k - \frac{\partial H}{\partial x^k} \\ &= \delta\lambda_x^k - \lambda_m \frac{\partial g(m, \bar{f})}{\partial \bar{f}} - \frac{\mathrm{d}\bar{f}}{\mathrm{d}x^k} + \\ &\quad + \sum_{j=1}^{K} \left[-\lambda_x^j \frac{\mathrm{d}F(x, b)}{\mathrm{d}x} - \lambda_d^j \frac{\mathrm{d}D(x^j, b^j)}{\mathrm{d}x^j} \right]. \end{aligned} \tag{11}$$

A change in x^k will change both f^k and $\bar{f}$. In turn, that influences $g(\cdot)$, and indirectly $F(\cdot)$ and $D(\cdot)$ for each stand through the associated change in b^k, i.e., the shadow value of the additional timber volume in stand k depends on its impacts on the browsing pressure in the other stands. The costate equation for d is indexed for the stands, d^k, and becomes

$$\dot{\lambda}_d^k = \delta\lambda_d^k - \frac{\partial H}{\partial d^k} = \delta\lambda_d^k. \tag{12}$$

Observe that d^k does not feed back into any other process. Hence, the only reason for wanting more d^k is to increase the saleable timber volume. The current value of the saleable timber volume grows at the discount rate, so its present value $\lambda_d^k e^{-\delta t}$ remains constant over time.

The state variables x^k and d^k jump instantaneously at the tree cutting time. Consequently, the wildlife management agency may want to adjust the moose stock instantaneously as well. The size of the jumps in x^k and d^k are determined by the biological processes governing tree growth. Regarding the moose jump, we know that in optimum $\lambda_m = j$ both before and after the jump as long as $h > 0$. The size of the moose stock jump is therefore just sufficient to bring λ_m back to the right condition as defined by (9).

The following must hold immediately before the ith cutting of stand k, that is at time t_i^{k-}:

$$\lambda_x^k(t_i^{k-}) = z^k d^k(t_i^{k-}) \frac{\mathrm{d}r(x^k(t_i^{k-}))}{\mathrm{d}x^k(t_i^{k-})}, \tag{13a}$$

$$\lambda_d^k(t_i^{k-}) = z^k r(x^k(t_i^{k-})). \tag{13b}$$

Equations (13a) and (13b) yield the end points for the differential equations controlling $\dot{\lambda}_x$ and $\dot{\lambda}_d$. The intuition is the same as for the single stand case: The shadow values for these two state variables are then simply the extra revenues at cutting time from marginal increases in x^k or d^k.

Finally, consider the timing of the tree cutting. At the cutting time society receives a discrete payoff equal to the net cash flow generated by the timber sale, plus the value of the instantaneous adjustment in the moose population. The necessary condition for the optimal timing of a tree harvest in stand k is

$$H(t_i^{k+}) = H(t_i^{k-}) - \delta\{z^k r(x(t_i^{k-}))d^k(t_i^{k-}) + j[m(t_i^{k-}) - m(t_i^{k+})]\}. \tag{14}$$

This arbitrage condition states that the gains from delaying the cut, which equal the rate of payoff prior to the cut minus the financial opportunity cost of delaying the discrete payoff from the cut, must equal the rate of the payoff after the cut. If the left-hand side of (14) is greater than the right side, it is optimal to cut immediately.

5. NUMERICAL SIMULATION

To simulate the system, functional forms must be chosen for $g(\cdot)$, $F(\cdot)$, $D(\cdot)$, $v(\cdot)$ and $r(\cdot)$ functions, and the parameter values must be set. For the moose growth function, we assume that the moose population grows logistically, with a growth rate and carrying capacity that depend on the availability of young pine:

$$g(m(t), \bar{f}(t)) = r_m(\bar{f})m\left[1 - \frac{m}{G_m(\bar{f})}\right], \tag{15}$$

where $g(\cdot)$ denotes the growth function for moose, $m(t)$ denotes the moose population, $f(t)$ is feed availability, $r_m(\bar{f})$ denotes the growth rate for moose given the area weighted mean forage availability, $\bar{f}$, and $G_m(\bar{f})$ denotes the carrying capacity for a given forage availability.

The basic functions used for the moose growth rate and the carrying capacity are linear in $\bar{f}$:

$$\begin{aligned} r_m(\bar{f}) &= r_m^0 + r_m^1 \bar{f}, \\ G_m(\bar{f}) &= G_m^0 + G_m^1 \bar{f}, \end{aligned} \tag{16}$$

where f_m^0 and G_m^0 are the growth rate and carrying capacity of an area with no browsing, and r_m^1 and G_m^1 are the slopes of these respective functions of feed availability. This linear specification may not be realistic for all levels of forage, in particular in winter when moose survival may hinge on some minimum feed availability, while at times abundant forage will not have that large impact on the moose population. Still, for a well-managed moose population, however, the linear specification in (16) is most likely reasonably realistic.

Trees are also assumed to grow logistically, but with browsing losses, where browsing pressure is a function of the moose population and how susceptible the stand is to browsing;

$$\dot{x} = F(x, b) = r_p x\left[1 - \frac{x}{G_p}\right] - cb, \tag{17}$$

where c is the amount of forage consumed by one moose, r_p is the tree (pin) growth parameter, and G_p is the maximum possible tree volume. A tree is browsed at the rate cb.

Trees die if browsed too intensively. Large trees tolerate more browsing than small trees, i.e., the smaller the tree, the more damaging the browsing. A functional form that captures this is

$$d(t) = D(x(t), b(t)) = -\gamma\left(\frac{\beta}{x}\right)^{\sigma}. \tag{18}$$

This functional form implies that the tree death rate declines slowly until the tree biomass is so large that the moose cannot reach the top branches. With $\sigma > 1$ the marginal damage from one moose is increasing in the number of moose. $\sigma = 2$ is a reasonable value, as well as computationally convenient.

The stand vulnerability index, $v = v(x)$ starts out close to one when x is small, and decreases asymptotically to zero as the pine biomass increases. A computationally simple functional form that captures these effects is

$$v(x) = 1 - \frac{1}{1 + e^{(\alpha_v^0 - \alpha_v^1 x)}}. \tag{19}$$

The land owner's net timber value per unit area is likely to be negative for young stands (to cover clearing and eventual planting costs), but increases at a decreasing rate as the forest matures. One functional form that captures timber price–timber volume relationships well is:

$$p(x) = \alpha_0 + \frac{\alpha_1}{1 + e^{\alpha_2 + \alpha_3 \ln(x)}}. \tag{20}$$

6. PARAMETER VALUES

The parameter values used for the simulations are given in Table 11.1. The parameters for the pine growth function (17) and the price function (20) were estimated based on data from Norwegian commercial forests with the productivity grade H11.0.[4] The harvest value of a moose is based on a contingent valuation study of moose hunters (Sødal, 1989).

The parameters for the vulnerability function (19) were chosen so that the vulnerability falls most rapidly when the tree volume reaches 15 m^3 per hectare. For the pine growth function used here, that occurs when the tree stand is about 10 years.

Parameters in the damage function (18) were set to capture actual tree mortality over a stand's life in heavily browsed areas of Norway. Unfortunately, not much is known about the quantitative relationship between moose density and tree mortality. Moose growth and carrying capacity parameters (16) were chosen such that simulation results matched measured densities and calving rates. Again, lack of data causes difficulties in terms of getting high quality parameter estimates (and having a good empirical basis for choosing functional form) on the relationship between carrying

Table 11.1. Baseline parameter values

Symbol	Value	Description
δ	0.025	Discount rate
J	5400	Harvest value of one moose equivalent
G_p	403.737	Maximum pine biomass
r_p	0.469	Pine growth rate
X^0	9.805	Initial pine biomass
C	0.5	Forage quantity consumed by one moose equivalent
r_m^0	0.75	Moose baseline growth rate[(a)]
r_m^1	0.03	Increase in moose growth rate with forage[(a)]
G_m^0	0.75	Moose baseline carrying capacity[(a)]
G_m^1	0.03	Increase in moose carrying capacity with forage[(a)]
α_v^0	15	Intercept in vulnerability function, $v(x)$[(a)]
α_v^1	1	Slope term in vulnerability function, $v(x)$[(a)]
β	500	Scale parameter in damage function, $D(x)$
σ	2	Exponent in damage function, $D(x)$
α_0	–1000	Intercept in price function, $p(x)$
α_1	125 007	Scale parameter in price function, $p(x)$
α_2	16.026	Intercept exponent in price function, $p(x)$
α_3	10	Constant term in exponent in price function, $p(x)$
f	10	Baseline forage available

Note: [(a)] Values shown are for the linear model. See text for sensitivity analysis using the log model.

capacity and forage availability. Our results are therefore illustrative, and should not be seen as exact guidelines for moose management in the pine growing areas of Norway.

7. SIMULATION RESULTS

Simulations were run with the Gauss add-on package SIMGAUSS, using a variable-step Runge–Kutta method. For our initial results, the linear moose growth model is used. We assume an initial moose population of 0.05 animals per hectare. This figure is immediately adjusted according to the arbitrage condition (14).

In the multiple stand simulations the above parameters remain unchanged. The multiple stand aspects are stylized by two forest stands of equal size. At the beginning of the simulation, both forest stands contain volume equal to the long-run maximum possible (G_x). Forest stand 1 is harvested at time 0. Forest stand 2 is harvested after a fixed amount of time. Thus, after forest stand 2 is harvested, we have two stands of unequal age. The initial difference in ages is called the lag between the two stands. The research question is whether, over time, the optimal strategy is to push the two stands 'into synch', i.e., increase the lag, or further 'out of synch', i.e., decrease the lag.

The model can be either partially or fully optimized. For a given series of cutting times, a partial optimization involves finding the correct values of the costate variables λ_x and λ_d for each forest stand, and for each harvest rotation. These costate variables determine the correct time path for moose harvests, to maintain the optimal moose density over the lifetimes of the forests.

In the simulations presented below, this approach is used to determine the fixed rotation length that gives highest social benefits. More broadly, the optimal set of cutting times can be found. These can then be compared to the best fixed rotation length. In all simulations, optimal cutting times are determined to the nearest 0.1 years.

8. OPTIMAL MOOSE MANAGEMENT

8.1. The Single Stand Case

Joint moose-forest management is only relevant if trees are vulnerable to browsing. Then and only then is there feedback from moose onto the forest so that moose stocks influence timber harvest values, and has feedback onto itself besides the self evident impact of initial moose stock and calving rates.

The optimal moose stock when trees are large (zero browsing vulnerability) is constant over time, and is only a function of the moose stock growth parameter, the moose stock carrying capacity, and the discount rate. In our baseline simulations this 'no-interaction' optimal moose size is 0.0512 moose equivalents per hectare.

The important interaction between moose and pine occurs when the stand is young, i.e., when the browsing-vulnerability is the highest. Management then involves trading off two competing objectives: The younger the forest, the higher the moose growth rate and the carrying capacity. This effect gives an incentive to increase the moose stock size to take advantage

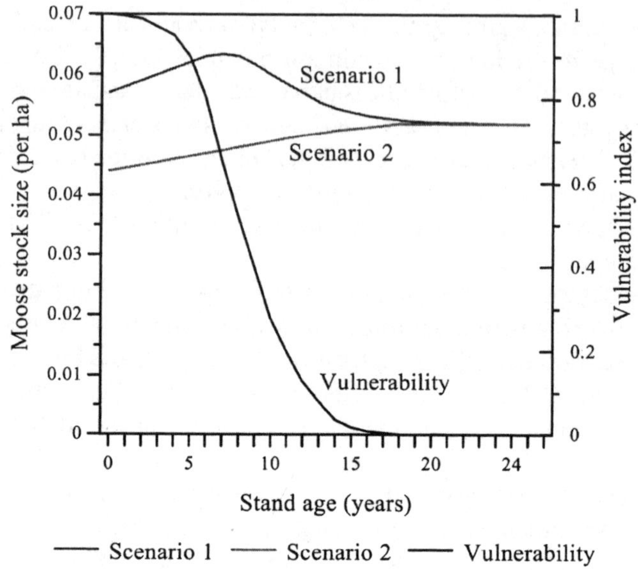

Figure 11.1. Time path for moose stocks when tree vulnerability changes over time

of the higher productivity. On the other hand, high moose stocks when the pine trees are young increases browsing damages on trees, and hence also tree mortality.

The optimal moose stock balances these two conflicting effects. Depending on which effect that dominates, the optimal moose stock could be higher or lower than the no-interaction solution described at the beginning of this section. If the moose value is high relative to the timber value, or if the damages to young trees are small, the optimal stock size is higher when the forest is young. Conversely, if damages to young trees are large, the optimal stock size is lower when trees are young. Figure 11.1 depicts the time path for optimal moose stocks for these two scenarios: Scenario 1 is the baseline scenario, and scenario 2 differs from the baseline by decreasing the harvest value per moose by half ($J = 2700$), and doubling the tree mortality.

In scenario 1 the moose productivity effect outweighs the browsing damage effects, so moose stocks are kept above the no-intervention level to utilize the higher forage production when trees are young and vulnerable. Scenario 2 depicts the opposite effects. The lower value per moose equivalent and higher mortality suggests that stocks should be kept lower when the stand is young and vulnerable.

8.2. The Multiple Stand Case

As in the single stand case, the relative importance of increased moose productivity when trees are young and browsing damages determines the optimal moose stock in a multiple stand forest. Depending on the age distribution of the forest stands and damages, the optimal moose stock could either be above or below the 'no interaction' level. As age and damage distributions vary from one forest to another, the short run optimal moose stock is site-specific. It is through synchronizing tree harvests that the forest manager has real opportunities of jointly optimizing moose and timber production beyond the insights from the single stand case.

9. OPTIMAL ROTATION TIMES AND HARVEST TIMING

9.1. Single Stand Insights

Society's objective function involves two competing objectives, moose and trees. This competition therefore tends to be non-convex in the control variable, t_i. The socially optimal rotation length for a single stand forest could be either long or short, depending on the relative value of moose and trees, but it is never intermediate. In contrast, the rotation length that maximizes timber values only, as would be the case when the land owner does not share in the moose harvest, is always long. Figure 11.2 shows both the socially and privately (timber-only) optimal solutions for the baseline scenario, with varying moose harvest values.

For the base scenario parameter values Figure 11.2 shows that when the moose equivalent value exceeds about 11 000, it becomes socially optimal to grow pine to feed the moose (short rotation). This is, however, not privately optimal unless the land owner gets to harvest all of the moose he/she has been feeding. Consequently, the private solution with the base parameter values is long rotation.

Increases in the moose value reduce the socially optimal rotation age, and may even make it optimal to change from timber to moose forage production, particularly on the lower quality timber lands. For low quality forest lands, the switch to short rotations occurs at moose values down to NOK 7750. Other factors that work in the same direction are low timber prices, and high tree mortality rates from browsing.

Using the baseline set of parameters, then, the socially optimal rotation length is shorter than the privately optimal rotation length, sometimes

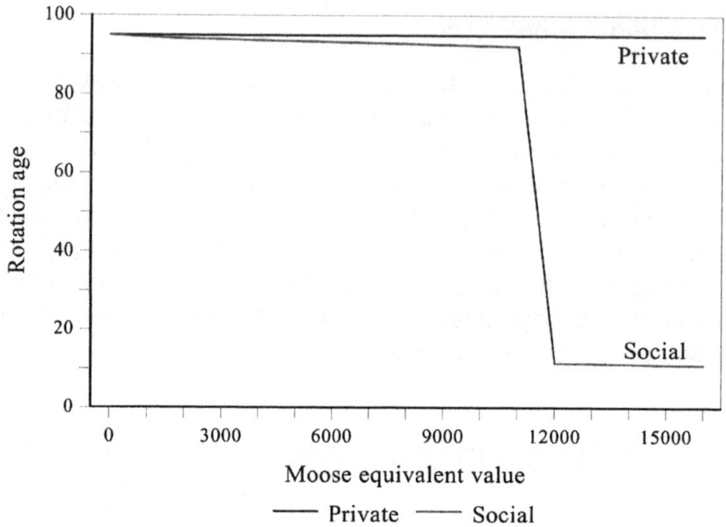

Figure 11.2. Optimal rotation age over moose equivalent values

much shorter. This result is consistent with the one of Hartman (1976) and Swallow et al. (1990). However, with the addition of moose browse impacts on pine, it is no longer always the case that the socially optimal rotation length will be shorter than the privately optimal length. If the damage by moose to trees is large, the optimal response of the wildlife management agency is to reduce moose density while trees are small. If the availability of young trees does not boost moose productivity enough, then the rate of moose harvest will be lower when trees are vulnerable. In that case, society suffers a loss in moose harvest values each time trees are harvested, and it is socially optimal to delay these occasions.

9.2. Multiple Stand Extensions

We first find the fixed rotation length that gives highest social benefits, given that moose are managed optimally for that rotation pattern. If the two stands are initially synchronized, i.e., the initial lag = 0, or if the initial lag is less than seven years, the fixed rotation length that generates highest total benefits from moose and pine is 93.6 years. If the initial lag is greater than seven years, the best fixed rotation length is 93.7 years. For practical purposes there is no difference between these two settings.

Next we determine whether this fixed rotation strategy maximizes total social benefits, or if it is desirable to change the synchronization of the two stands. We have the following possibilities in addition to the status quo: lengthen the rotation period (postponing tree harvests) or shortening the rotation period (cut earlier than optimal when only timber production is concerned) for either of the two stands. This is done by evaluating the first-order condition governing timing of the tree harvests (14). Doing so shows that if the initial lag is 0, i.e., if the forests are already synchronized, then the optimal strategy is to keep them synchronized, and the fixed rotation strategy is the welfare maximizing strategy. Similarly, if the initial lag between the two stands is large (14.6 years or larger), so that the two stands are never vulnerable simultaneously, then the fixed rotation strategy is again optimal. For lags between 0.1 and 14.5 years inclusive, however, evaluation of the first-order conditions shows that the fixed rotation strategy is not optimal. If the two stands are vulnerable simultaneously, then the optimal strategy is to adjust the lag over time by harvesting the two stands each at a different stand age.

The lag adjustment at each harvest and the direction of the adjustment were determined using backward optimization, starting with the stationary solutions with lag $= 0$ and lag $= 14.6$. For initial lags between 0.1 and 14.5 years inclusive, we found that the optimal strategy is to synchronize the stands, but to do so gradually, possibly over several rotations.

Figure 11.3 provides a graphical illustration of how two stands should be synchronized. The curved line in Figure 11.3 shows the optimal lag between harvests in the $i + 1$st rotation, given the lag between harvests in the ith rotation. The 45° line depicts no adjustment, and the optimal lag reduction is the difference between these two lines. The lag reduction at each rotation depends on the lag size at the beginning of that rotation. Both the moose productivity boost and browsing damage depend on the amount of available pine forage, $x_k v(x^k)$. Not surprisingly, this peaks at about stand ages 7 to 8. If the lag between the stands is between 5.5 and 8.8, the optimal strategy is to reduce the lag by 1.2 years during the next rotation. So, if the initial lag between the stands is 7 years, the harvest time should be adjusted so that the lag after the next harvest is 5.8 years. For initial lags less than 5.5 years, or greater than 8.8 years, the optimal strategy is to reduce the lag by less than that amount. For very high lags, greater than 14.6 years, the optimal strategy is again the fixed-rotation strategy. With these lags, the two stands are never vulnerable at the same time. Hence, they do not influence each other.

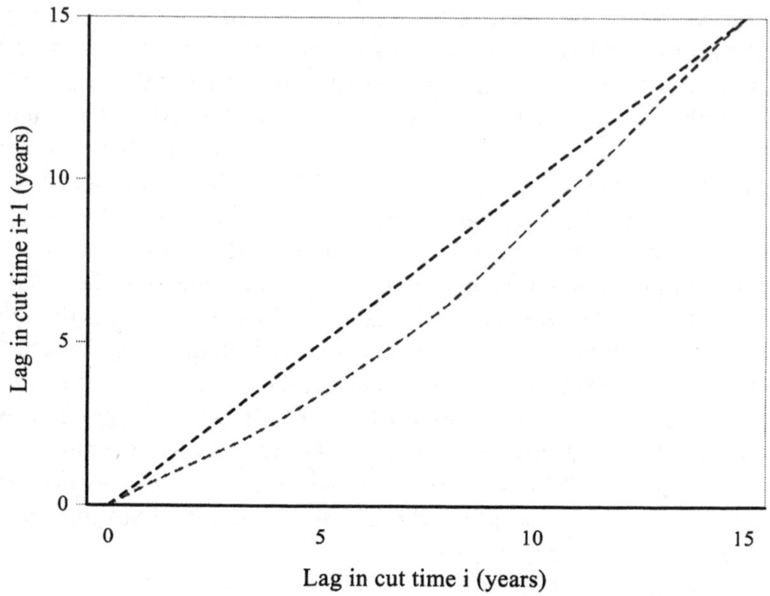

Figure 11.3. Optimal lag time adjustment

9.3. Factors Motivating Stand Convergence

Why is synchronizing the stands the preferred strategy? The only interaction between the two forest stands is through the moose stock. Therefore, the answer must lie in the interactions between pine and moose. There are two interactions between moose and pine – the increase in moose productivity that comes from increased forage availability (captured by the parameters r_m^1 and G_m^1), and the damage to pine growth and survival caused by browsing (captured by the parameters γ and c). Both of these interactions are sensitive to the amount of pine that is available for browsing in each stand, $x^k v(x^k)$. When both stands are vulnerable at the same time the following effects emerge: (i) it spreads out the browsing pressure over a larger area, and (ii) it shortens the amount of time that forage is available to the moose, but concentrates that forage.

The impact of the first effect is clear. From the perspective of a single stand of trees, it is better to be vulnerable to browsing at the same time that neighboring stands are vulnerable, spreading the browsing pressure over a larger area. Magnifying this tendency is the fact that tree mortality occurs as a squared function of browsing pressure. This browsing dilution effect can be isolated by removing the moose productivity enhancement (setting r_m^1 and G_m^1 equal to zero). When only the browsing damage effects are included in the model, the optimal strategy is still to bring the two stands into synch over time, showing that the browsing damage effects alone are enough to bring the two stands into convergence. Moreover, either component of browsing damage, taken by itself, is enough to generate this result. When the impact on the growth rate of pine is removed (by setting c equal to 0), the mortality effect is sufficient to encourage convergence. Similarly, when the mortality effect is removed, by setting γ equal to zero, the growth rate effect alone encourages convergence.

The impact of the second effect is less clear. From the perspective of the moose stock, is it better to have all of the pine forage available at the same time, or spread out over a longer period? The answer depends on the exact form of the relationship between forage availability and moose productivity.

For a fixed moose stock, the rate of growth of the stock increases linearly with the amount of forage available. Lacking any adjustment to the moose stock, there is no advantage to concentrating the forage into a short period of time. However, when the wildlife management agency's behavior is included, the relationship becomes nonlinear. As previously shown, it is socially optimal to increase moose stocks when forage availability is high. This enhances the moose productivity effect. The result is a nonlinear, convex relationship between forage availability and moose production. Figure 11.4 shows moose productivity as a function of various scenarios for forage availability.

Suppose the moose stock productivity is concave with respect to available winter forage, as depicted in the two lower curves in Figure 11.4. This is achieved by keeping the marginal increase in productivity from an increase in forage at $\bar{f} = 10$, i.e. as with the linear model, and with the following parameter values used: $r_m^0 = 1.05$, $r_m^1 = 0.03$, $G_m^0 = 0.105$, $G_m^1 = 0.003$, and $f_{\min} = 9$. The browsing damage effect was eliminated by setting γ and c equal to zero. For lags less than 15 years, the optimal strategy is to increase the lag between the two rotations. Even if the initial lag is zero, so that the forest is comprised of one even-age stand, the optimal strategy is to split the stand into smaller pieces, and bring those smaller stands out of synch over time. This result holds regardless of whether the wildlife management agency adjusts moose stocks as the trees age. The benefit from pushing the two stands out of synch is that the moose productivity boost that occurs after each rotation will be stretched

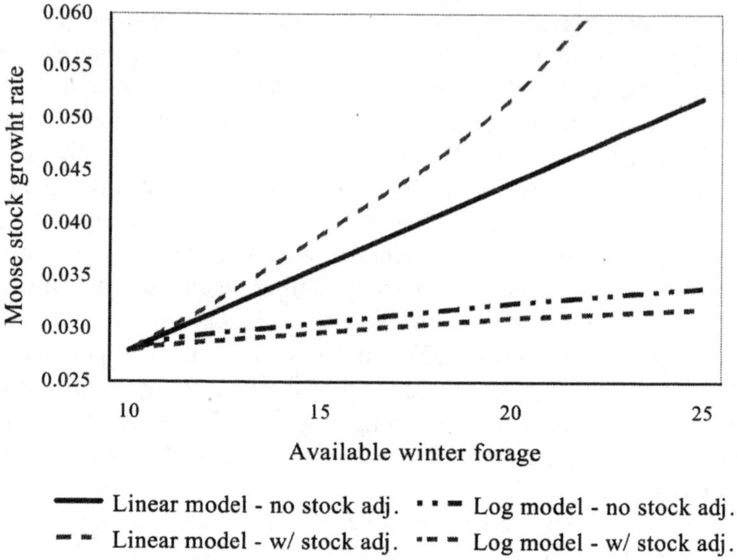

Figure 11.4. Moose stock growth rate (g) as a function of winter forage availability ($\bar{f}$)

out over a longer period of time, avoiding a concentrated period when the marginal benefit from additional forage is low.

As mentioned earlier the assumed linear relationship between forage availability and moose productivity may not hold. Suppose it is concave, i.e., there are decreasing marginal productivity returns to forage? The parameters were adjusted so that the marginal increase in productivity from an increase in forage was the same at $\bar{f} = 10$, as with the linear model. The specific parameter values used were $r_m^0 = 1.05$, $r_m^1 = 0.03$, $G_m^0 = 0.105$, $G_m^1 = 0.003$, and $f_{\min} = 9$. The browsing damage effect was eliminated by setting γ and c equal to zero. For lags less than 15 years, the optimal strategy is to increase the lag between the two rotations. Even if the initial lag is zero, so that the forest is comprised of one even-age stand, the optimal strategy is to split the stand into smaller pieces, and bring those smaller stands out of synch over time. This result holds regardless of whether the wildlife management agency adjusts moose stocks as the trees age. The benefit from pushing the two stands out of synch is that the moose productivity boost that occurs after each rotation will be stretched out over a longer period of time, avoiding a concentrated period when the marginal benefit from additional forage is low.

This last result is similar to situations investigated in previous studies. Swallow et al. (1997) assumed that the marginal value of forage decreases as the total supply of forage increases (similar to our log model). They found that stands age should diverge over time. Tahvonen and Salo (1999) arrived at a similar conclusion. Koskela and Ollikainen (2000) showed that the influence of an adjacent stand on optimal harvest time depends on whether the stands are 'substitutes' or 'complements' in generating non-timber benefits.[5] In our models the two forest stands could be considered complements in generating moose productivity in the linear model, and substitutes in the log model. One relationship of particular interest in our work is how non-timber benefits change as the quantity of a forest output (forage) changes. This separates our chapter from previous studies, where the focus has been on how timber benefits change as the forest matures.

The browsing dilution effect favors synchronization of stands. If this effect is combined with a less-than-proportional moose productivity enhancement – favoring divergence among stands – which effect will dominate? For the parameters chosen here, the browsing dilution effect is stronger. Hence, the optimal strategy is to synchronize the two stands.

10. MANAGEMENT INFERENCES

The relationship between moose and pine is bilateral – young pine enhances moose growth, while moose damage young pine. Both of these relationships have implications for forest management.

The browsing damage impact unambiguously encourages synchronization of nearby forest stands. This allows the browsing pressure to be spread out over a larger area during the time when the trees are vulnerable to damage, keeping the pressure below the level where serious harm is done. It is important, though, to manage the moose stock correctly during this vulnerable period, to take advantage of the enhanced moose productivity without allowing too much damage to occur.

The implications of the moose productivity impact are not so clear cut. If the marginal increase in moose productivity from additional forage is increasing in the amount of forage available, the optimal strategy is to concentrate the forage into a short period of time, by cutting adjacent forest stands at the same time. This results in a short period with very high forage availability, and even higher moose productivity, followed by a long time with no productivity boost. If the marginal increase in moose productivity from additional forage is decreasing in the amount of forage available, then the optimal strategy is to stretch out the forage over as long as possible. This is done by spacing out harvests of adjacent stands, so that there is at least one stand providing forage for as long a period as possible.

Clearly, the actual solution will vary depending not only on the form of the relationship chosen for modeling the moose productivity impact, but also on aspects such as the amount of nonpine forage available as well as other factors limiting moose stock size. Whether forest stands should be synchronized, or pushed out of synch, may vary between locations, particularly due to differences in the quality of the land, as reflected in differences in the growth rate of the pine trees.

This study adds to previous investigations on the interactions between wildlife and multiple stand forests by incorporating damage to trees due to browsing. This effect by itself is enough to generate inter-stand dependencies, and encourages the synchronization of harvesting adjacent stands. This study differs from previous investigations in that an explicit model is specified of the interactions between the wildlife stock and the tree stands. This specificity clarifies the assumptions necessary to drive the divergence result. Finally, our study shows that forest management cannot be done in isolation of wildlife management. Whether the optimal forest management strategy is synchronization or divergence depends on how the wildlife stock is managed over time.

Finally, our study provides some general insights. The divergence between the private (only maximizing timber harvest value) and social optima (joint maximization of timber and moose use values) is more likely to be reduced if the forest owner is more certain to reap the benefits of moose forage investments. This is more easily achieved when:

(1) There is joint ownership of hunting rights and timber.

(2) The moose does not move from the property where the browsing damage occurs. This implies that the larger the forest property, the more likely it is that joint maximization of moose and timber profits will take place.[6]

The majority of the Norwegian (and Nordic) forest properties are small. Creating sufficiently large moose management regions so that the extent of migrating moose is reduced, and side payment schemes within these entities, appear as the most obvious measures to achieve joint maximization of moose and timber harvest values. There are immense informational requirements associated with side payment schemes that sustain voluntary moose management regions of the needed size. Following Seabright (1993) it is not unreaonable to assume that land owners have better reciprocal information about moose habitat qualities and improvements in moose habitats undertaken on nearby properties. This eases the informational issues somewhat, but does not resolve them.

NOTES

1. Our title is inspired by Kalle Löfgren's frequently used statement at conference presentations '... and then we differentiate at the speed of light'.
2. Senior authorship is not assigned. Olvar Bergland and Eirik Romstad are Associate Professor and Sr. Research Fellow respectively at the Department of Economics and Resource Management, Norwegian University of Life Sciences, while Richard Ready is Assistant Professor at the Department of Agricultural Economics and Rural Sociology, Penn State University. Corresponding author is Eirik Romstad, e-mail: eirik.romstad@umb.no.
3. In Norway, the more productive forest tracts are replanted after harvest, in which case x_0^k measures biomass of the planted seedlings. The main effect of planting is that it shortens the rotation period of the stand.
4. Data for pine growth and timber prices were obtained from the *Handbok for planlegging i skogbruket* (English title: *Handbook for Forestry Planning*), published by the Norwegian Forest Research Institute (Skogforsk).
5. More formally – using their terminology – the result depends on whether the degree of substitutability or complementarity is increasing or decreasing over time.
6. This is also consistent with observations, where large forest owners appear more willing to undertake moose forage investments.

REFERENCES

Andersen, R. and B.-E. Sæther (1996), *Elg i Norge: Biologi, Atferd og Forvaltning*, Oslo: N.W. Damm and Sønn – Teknologisk forlag.

Hartman, R. (1976), 'The harvesting decision when a standing forest has value', *Economic Inquiry*, 14, 52–58.

Koskela, E. and M. Ollikainen (1999), 'Optimal public harvesting under the interdependence of public and private forests', *Forest Science*, 45(2), 259–271.

Ready, R., O. Bergland and E. Romstad (2000), 'Optimal management of two interlinked renewable resources: Moose and pine in Norway', Discussion Paper D-23/2000, Department of Economics and Social Sciences, Agricultural University of Norway, Ås, Norway (http://www.umb.no/ior/publikasjoner/diskusjonsnotat2000.23.html as of 15 February 2005).

Ready, R., O. Bergland and E. Romstad (2001), 'Optimal management of a forest/wildlife system with bilateral externalities', Discussion Paper D-05/2001, Department of

Economics and Social Sciences, Agricultural University of Norway, Ås, Norway (http://www.umb.no/ior/publikasjoner/diskusjonsnotat2001.5.html as of 15 February 2005).

Sæther, B.-E., K. Solbraa, D.P. Sødal and O. Hjeljord (1992), 'The final report from the project "Moose – Forest – Society"', Research Report #28, Norwegian Institute for Nature Research, Oslo.

Seabright, P. (1993), 'Managing local commons: Theoretical issues in incentive design', *Journal of Economic Perspectives*, 7(4), 113–134.

Seierstad, K. and A. Sydsæther (1987), *Optimal Control Theory with Economic Applications*, Amsterdam: North-Holland.

Sødal, D.P. (1989), 'Economic valuation of moose hunting', Report No. 1/89, Department of Forest Economics, Agricultural University of Norway, Ås.

Swallow, S.K. and D.N. Wear (1993), 'Spatial interactions in multiple-use forestry and substitution and wealth effects for the single stand', *Journal of Environmental Economics and Management*, 25(2), 103–120.

Swallow, S.K., P.J. Parks and D.N. Wear (1990), 'Policy-relevant nonconvexities in the production of multiple forest benefits', *Journal of Environmental Economics and Management*, 19(3), 264–280.

Swallow, S.K., P. Talukdar and D.N. Wear (1997), 'Spatial and temporal specialization in forest ecosystem management under sole ownership', *American Journal of Agricultural Economics*, 79(2), 311–326.

Tahvonen, O. and S. Salo (1999), 'Optimal forest rotation with in situ preferences', *Journal of Environmental Economics and Management*, 37(1), 106–128.

12. Empirical Behaviour Models on Timber Supply

Jari Kuuluvainen, Ibrahim Moulifla Favada and Jussi Uusivuori

1. INTRODUCTION

In empirical econometric studies on timber supply there has been a continuous interest in building models for pragmatic forecasting of timber market development at an aggregate level. Research has concentrated mainly in North America and Scandinavia (for example, Leuschner 1973, Robinson 1974, Adams 1975, Adams and Haynes 1980, Korpinen 1981, Cardellichio and Veltkamp 1981, Binkley and Cardellichio 1985, Newman 1987, Brännlund et al. 1985, Kuuluvainen et al. 1988, Toppinen 1998; see also Ruist and Svennilsson 1948, Seppälä 1974, Wear and Newman 1991 and Newmann and Wear 1993). Binkley (1987) offers a comprehensive review of early studies that used aggregate time series to model timber supply.

A model introduced by Binkley (1981), of a utility maximizing forest owner who values both consumption as well as forests *in situ*, inspired interest in the empirical testing of positive models on NIPF owner behaviour using micro-level data. The model of the utility-maximizing forest owner and its extensions to utility-based dynamic biomass harvesting models (Lohmander 1983) have been frequently used since then as a starting point, when deriving reduced form supply relationships for empirical testing. Only recently, some studies have used rotation models to derive testable hypotheses to empirically study the timber supply of private forest owners (Hyberg and Holthausen 1989, Provencher 1995a, 1995b, 1997, Kuuluvainen and Tahvonen 1999, Prestemon and Wear 2000).

In this survey study we will focus on the literature covering econometric studies of timber supply, which use individual forest and forest-owner level observations. A broader review of econometric studies on NIPF owner's forest management behaviour is in Amacher et al. (2003). Our focus will be on the links between the predictions of the theory and the received empirical evidence as well as on the limitations of the used models and data. In empirical studies on timber supply one of the basic tests has concerned the question of how forest owners react to changing prices. Therefore, we will present hypotheses on the effects of timber prices derived using the basic theoretical timber supply models and discuss their implications for empirical testing. For any empirical study to produce relevant results for policy analysis, it is important to be aware of what the empirically estimated effects of exogenous variables actually describe. The type of used data is crucial in terms of the conclusions that can be drawn from an empirical study, and hence we will discuss the issue of compatibility between the theoretical models and the data.

In Section 2, we present the theoretical approaches to NIPF timber supply and clarify the relationship between biomass harvesting model and the rotation model. Section 3 reviews the empirical studies and in Section 4 the empirical results are interpreted and summarized. We will also discuss the structural estimations, as a potentially useful route to gain insight into the forest owners' decision-making process.

2. TIMBER SUPPLY, THEORETICAL APPROACHES

2.1. Optimal Rotation and Biomass Harvesting Models

Theoretical studies on the optimal rotation periods have evolved since the work of Faustmann (1849) to determine the optimal time to harvest an even-aged stand. The model determining the optimal rotation age of an even-aged stand has been augmented to include for example, (1) nontimber values (e.g. Hartman 1976, Calish et al. 1978, Strang 1983); (2) management intensity (e.g. Hyde 1980; Chang 1983) and (3) forest taxation (e.g. Chang 1982, 1983). Important recent theoretical extensions are the model of a tree farm by Mitra and Wan (1985), generalized in Salo and Tahvonen (2001, 2002a, 2002b) to study the optimality of normal forest convergence with endogenous timber prices and, for example, land allocation between agriculture and forestry.

Despite the large body of theoretical studies on the Faustmann rotation model, empirical literature on testing the forest owner behaviour against the hypotheses of the rotation model is small. An obvious practical reason for this is the lack of suitable micro data, which would be expensive to collect. At least two reasons lie behind the fact that forest economists seldom have considered the investment into laborious data collection worthwhile. First, the extensions of the Faustmann model to account for market imperfections are recent (Tahvonen 1998), and the assumptions of the basic deterministic rotation model have been considered to be too stringent for a valid positive description of forest owner behaviour. However, this argument can be disputed based on the fact that much of the empirical work on consumer behaviour and labour supply is based on equally stringent assumptions. The other explanation is the nature of the hypotheses produced by the basic Faustmann rotation model. The basic rotation model as a positive description of forest owner behaviour determines a static long-run equilibrium. One could claim that empirical observations are never able to tract changes in the equilibrium harvest levels predicted by the rotation model. However, if we are not able to test our theoretical hypotheses against the empirical evidence, the reliability of policy recommendations based on the theoretical or even numerical models using the rotation framework is greatly reduced.

The 'two-period critique' of the Faustmann model, and the empirical studies based on it, attempted to bring economic 'realism' to studies on NIPF owner behaviour at the cost of 'biological realism' by simplifying the description of forest dynamics. This line of modelling timber supply behaviour, established in the 1980s (e.g., Lohmander 1983, Koskela 1989a, 1989b), uses a lumped parameter biomass growth function ignoring the age-class structure of growing timber and a Fisherian consumption-saving model of a utility maximizing forest owner. The forest owner's problem is formulated as that of maximizing utility from consumption with endogenous timber income that can be obtained either now or in the future. The lumped parameter biomass growth function and the fact that any portion of the growing timber can be harvested has been suggested as describing regulated uneven-aged forest management at the woodlot level (Kuuluvainen and Salo 1991, Montgomery and Adams 1995).

While capturing many important characteristics of forest growth, the biomass harvesting model ignores important aspects related to the age structure of stands (however, see Uusivuori and Kuuluvainen 2001). The problem is that most biological information on forest dynamics relates to the age structure (Binkley 1987). Recent studies on utility based rotation models by Tahvonen (1998), Tahvonen and Salo (1999) and Tahvonen et al. (2001) have moved the originally management-orientated Faustmann rotation model towards a positive description of a forest owner's behaviour. Thus, they have been able to combine the 'biological realism' of the rotation model with the 'economic realism' of the two-period model in a theoretically consistent manner.

The empirical models on timber supply have used these theoretical models mainly to determine which variables to include into estimable behavioural timber supply equations. The gap between the theoretically sophisticated models, especially the utility-based rotation model, and the estimated reduced form equations still seems to be large. The structural empirical models accounting for uncertainty, introduced to forest economics by Provencher (1995a, 1995b, 1997), may provide an alternative route if detailed enough data are available and the computational difficulties can be overcome. However, if the theory were used to guide the data collection, the ability of reduced form models in testing out the theory could also be considerably increased.

2.2. Implications of Theory for Empirical Testing

The lumped parameter biomass-harvesting model and the rotation model imply different descriptions of forests and the way they are harvested. To clarify the ideas and the empirical implications, we will present the basic versions of the Faustmann rotation model and the two-period biomass harvesting model to understand to what extent these two models describe the same phenomena.

The basic rotation model approaches the timber supply problem by determining the steady state rotation age. Denoting timber price with p, the volume of the stand which depends on the stand's age, t, with $q(t)$, interest rate with r, optimal rotation age with t^* and the maximized land value with $V(t^*)$, the equilibrium condition for optimal rotation age for an infinite cycle of rotations under perfect markets and certainty (e.g., Johansson and Löfgren, 1985)

$$pq'(t^*) = rpq(t^*) + rV(t^*) \tag{1}$$

states that the marginal benefit from letting the stand grow, $pq'(t^*)$, has to equal the opportunity cost of capital in timber, $rpq(t^*)$, and land, $rV(t^*)$. Because price, p, regeneration cost, w, and the interest rate, r, are assumed to be constant, the comparative static effects must be interpreted as once-and-for-all changes in the levels of the exogenous variables. The implicit equation for the long-run equilibrium harvest, $h(t^*)$, is

$$h(t^*) = q(t^*)/t^*(r, w/p), \tag{2}$$

where the interest rate and timber price have a negative effect and planting cost a positive effect on the steady state optimal rotation age, t^*. The effect on the equilibrium harvest depends on whether rotations initially are under or above the maximum sustained yield rotation.

The intertemporal variation of prices, absent in the basic rotation model, is an important determinant of the timing of harvest. The two-period model allows timber prices to change between the periods. It has been used both in empirical and in theoretical research (e.g., Lohmander 1983, Koskela 1989a, 1989b, Kuuluvainen 1990, Ovaskainen 1992). The equilibrium condition of the basic two-period model is

$$q_1(1+r) = (p_2/p_1)q_2, \tag{3}$$

where p_1 and p_2 are timber prices in the present period and in the future, r is the interest rate, q_1 and q_2 are the first period after harvest timber volume and second period timber volumes per unit of land area respectively ($q_2 = q_1[1 + F'(q_1)]$, $q_1 = q_0 - H_1$). Forest growth as a function of the stock, $F(q_1)$, is strictly concave. The short-run behavioural function for the first period harvest, H_1, is

$$H_1 = H(p_2/p_1, r, q_0), \tag{4}$$

where the first period price, the interest rate and the initial timber volume have an increasing impact, while the second period price has a decreasing impact on the first period timber supply. Because the basic two-period biomass harvesting model ignores the land allocation between present and future stands, regeneration costs do not affect the optimal harvest levels in the model. In the two-period model, relative prices over time matter. For this reason, the two-period model has often been interpreted as describing forest owners' short-term arbitrage between present and future harvest, while the Faustmann model is interpreted as describing the long-term equilibrium behaviour. In spite of this, Equation (2) also has short-term supply implications due to immediate adjustment to the observed once-and-for-all change in relative prices or the interest rate (e.g., Clark 1976). On the other hand, Equation (4) has long-term implications through the stock remaining after the first period harvest (Ovaskainen 1992).

As there is no *a priori* reason why a forest owner would believe that timber price relative to regeneration costs are likely to stay constant in the near (or distant) future, intertemporal price changes should clearly be incorporated in the rotation framework. However, this should be done without sacrificing the land allocation problem, as is done in the biomass harvesting model. As stumpage prices are highly volatile, especially periodic temporary changes in w/p may have a strong effect on the profitability of harvest. The analysis of changing prices in an infinite horizon Faustmann model is involved, but some intuition can be obtained by using a two-period rotation model which is consistent with the Faustmann model (Salo and Tahvonen 2002a, Uusivuori and Kuuluvainen 2005, Viitala 2003).[1] If the forest owner is maximizing the present value of harvest over two periods and can have two age classes, the equilibrium condition corresponding to the Faustmann rule is written as follows:

$$(q_1 - w/p_1)(1+r) + (p_2/p_1)q_1 \geq (p_2/p_1)q_2, \tag{5}$$

where $q_1 < q_2$ are now (constant) per land unit timber volumes of age classes 1 and 2. Because timber volumes are constant, either the first or second age class is (or both age classes are) at the Faustmann rotation. Expression (5) depicts the condition for the first age class to represent the Faustmann rotation. The optimal timing of harvest depends on both the price level relative to planting costs as well as on the price change between periods. If the second period price increases sufficiently, the second period becomes the optimal Faustmann rotation. The difference between the two-period biomass harvesting model and the rotation model can be seen by comparing the equilibrium condition of the two-period rotation model (5) without planting costs, $p_1q_1(1+r) + p_2q_1 \geq p_2q_2$ to the equilibrium condition (3). The second term, p_2q_1, on the left-hand side accounts for the bare land value, which is ignored in the two-period biomass harvesting model. The behavioural equation for optimal first period harvest under perfect markets becomes

$$H_1 = H(w/p_1, p_2/p_1, r, x), \tag{6}$$

where x is the forest land area. The effect of price level on harvest is negative, as in the basic Faustmann model below maximum sustained yield rotations. A parametric increase in the stumpage price level leaves p_2/p_1 unaffected but decreases w/p_1 making the first age class to be more likely the Faustmann period, i.e., shortens the rotation and reduces the long-run timber supply below MSY rotations.

Only a few studies exist allowing time trends in prices in continuous time Faustmann model. Newman et al. (1985) studied the effects of constant price trends in the Faustmann framework, and used numerical simulations to demonstrate the effects. Kuuluvainen and Tahvonen (1999), allowed timber price to change over time in a finite lived forest owner's utility maximizing framework, and concluded that forest owners observing increasing (decreasing) prices (with constant regeneration cost) will postpone the harvest (harvest earlier) even if the price level itself might indicate that the stand is (not) financially mature. Therefore, harvests tend to gather around price peaks, and the sign of the price change is unambiguously positive. However, due to fluctuating timber prices, multiple solutions to forest owners' maximization problem cannot be ruled out.

As noted by Brazee and Mendelsohn (1988) (see also Lohmander 1987), the traditional Faustmann model ignores uncertainty. Including price uncertainty in the rotation model affects the rotation ages and the land value. However, the implications for the reduced form estimable timber supply equation do not really change in any empirically observable way, as long as price process can be assumed stationary (see note 4) and forest owners' other economy is ignored. The probability of harvest increases as timber prices are high, the interest rate and planting costs, which are assumed to be known with perfect certainty in Brazee and Mendelsohn (1988), have similar effects on the rotation age as in the case of perfect certainty.

The introduction of nonmarketable *in situ* valuations, capital market imperfections or uncertainties may cause inseparability of harvesting and consumption decisions as initially demonstrated in a two-period framework by Lohmander (1983) (see also Koskela 1989a, 1989b, Kuuluvainen 1990, Ovaskainen 1992). Tahvonen (1998) showed that market imperfections or *in situ* value in forest owners' life cycle utility maximization problem make the optimal rotation periods to depend on forest owners' (permanent) income and wealth as well as on other owner characteristics. As a result the preference-related variables enter the behavioural reduced form equations of timber supply. Both in the age-class rotation model as well as in the two-period biomass harvesting model with age classes, nonseparability makes an interior solution possible, so that it may be optimal to harvest an age class only partially (Uusivuori and Kuuluvainen 2001, 2005).

The implications of uncertainty for reduced form models can be conjectured to be similar to those of other market imperfections. However, a structural estimation of forest owners' problem with explicit account, for example, of price uncertainty may be an alternative method of gaining information on forest owner behaviour, as will be discussed below. The theoretical bases of these structural estimations rest on the rotation framework (e.g., Provencher 1995a).

3. EMPIRICAL STUDIES ON TIMBER SUPPLY

3.1. Reduced Form Logit and Probit Probability Models

For empirical studies to produce relevant results for policy analysis, it is important to be aware of what the empirically estimated effects of exogenous variables actually describe. The interest of a policy maker is often in the long-term equilibrium relationships. However, data available to the researcher may mainly describe short-term dynamics.

The data on NIPF owner behaviour often records only harvest in m^3/year, or merely the qualitative binary information on whether the owner has harvested or not. The area harvested and the stand age at the time of harvest have not been recorded in the survey data used by any of studies to be cited later. In contrast, stand ages at the time of harvest are more commonly recorded in forest inventory data, which on the other hand normally provide little or no information on owner characteristics.

In empirical studies on consumer behaviour or labour supply, the cross-section variation of the data is interpreted to measure long-run equilibrium behaviour. The intertemporal variation, on the other hand, can be used to measure the short-run adjustment (McCurdy 1981, Heckmann and McCurdy 1980). Analogously, one could argue that a cross-sectional variation in harvest and prices and other explanatory variables describes the long-run equilibrium behaviour of forest owners.

Several empirical studies have modelled the probability of harvest using micro data on forest owners harvesting decision (harvest vs. no harvest) at the woodlot level (see Table 12.1).[2] Binkley (1981) justified the use of explanatory variables in a sales probability model using a static utility maximization problem of the forest owner. Latent unobservable propensity to harvest was assumed to be a linear function of exogenous variables in the forest owner's utility maximization problem. The supply equations were estimated using cross-sectional data and a logit model. A similar approach was used, for example, by Boyd (1983) and Jamnick and Beckett (1988). In Binkley (1981) and Boyd (1983), the effect of price on probability of harvest was found to be positive, while the effect of nonforestry income on harvesting probability was negative in all three studies.

The empirical results obtained in these three studies could be interpreted through the long-run equilibrium effects obtainable from the utility based rotation model, because cross-sectional data were used. According to the utility-based rotation model, assuming a normal-forest structure and homogenous population of forest owners, high observed prices in a

Table 12.1. Comparison of empirical household production models

	Estimation method	Data type	Price	Income/ wealth	Inventory
Binkley 1981	Logit model Cross-section, Pooled	Cross-section and Cross-section time-series N=232, 27 years	3.84[a] 2.03[b] 0.82[b]	-0.34[a] -0.31[b] -0.52[b]	None
Jamnick & Becknett 1988	Logit	Cross-section N=8790	None	-0.02836	None
Dennis 1989	Tobit model	Cross-section N=58	7.73	-2.81	1.06
Hyberg & Holthausen 1989	Logit model Pooled	Cross-section time-series N= not reported	-0.05	-0.002	None
Kuuluvainen and Salo 1991	Tobit model Pooled	Cross-section time-series N=1570, 5 years	2.16	-0.25/ (0.15, wealth)	0.40
Dennis 1990	Probit model Pooled	Cross-section time-series N=706, 11 years	3.94	-1.292	0.351
Carlén 1990	Tobit model Pooled	Cross-section time-series N=7028, 5 years	1.72 1.92[c]	None	0.84 0.84[c]
Aronsson 1990	Tobit model	Cross-section N=858	1.67[d]	None	0.16
Wear and Newman 1991	System MLE	Regional cross-section N=not reported	[e]	None	[e]
Newman and Wear 1993	System MLE	Regional cross-section N=132	[e]	None	[e]
Kuuluvainen et al. 1996	Tobit model Pooled	Cross-section time-series data N=730	0.41	-0.13/ (0.25 wealth)	0.99
Kuuluvainen & Tahvonen 1999	Tobit model, Panel, Cross-section	Cross-section time-series N=1071 (119)[n]	1.93[f] -2.90[g]	-0.31[f] 0.10[g]	Not reported
Prestemon & Wear 2000	Probit model,	Cross-section time-series N[o]: NIPF 541 Industry 268 Government 112	1.96[h] 0.12[h] 1.13[i] 0.08[i]	None	Not reported
Lee 1997	Probability of harvest, MLE	Cross-section time series, 2799	-0.0085[j] 0.0063[j]	None	None
Bolkesjø and Baardsen 2002	Tobit model, MLE, Panel	Cross-section time series data[k] N=3413 (160)[n]	0.49 0.44	-0.05[l] -0.01[l] 0.48[m] 0.54[m]	0.69 0.73

a) Elasticities for 1973 sample based on cross-sectional data. b) Elasticities based on pooled data. c) Probit elasticities. d) Based on price difference. e) Supply elasticities for restricted short-run supply were estimated and unrestricted long-run elasticities are calculated for industrial and nonindustrial private forest owners using the properties of the profit function for saw timber and pulpwood. For quasi-fixed growing stock only the long-run unrestricted elasticities were calculated. f) Intertemporal elasticities, time-section variation. g) Parametric elasticities, cross-section variation. h) Sawtimber and pulpwood price elasticities of supply, respectively, under temporal price increases for NIPF owners. i) Sawtimber and pulpwood price elasticities of supply, respectively, under permanent price increases for NIPFowners. j) Marginal effects of the estimated marginal costs and marginal benefits of timber. k) Bolkesjø and Baardsen estimated both the standard fixed effects tobit model and a specification to account for the simultaneity of harvest level and tax rate (upper elasticities are those from the standard tobit model). l) Agricultural income. m) Other income. n) Cross-section units. o) Sampled stands were measured in 1983 and the second time in 1989.

region imply shorter rotations and consequently higher frequency of sales. Higher nonforest income on the other hand means that forest owners who value forest amenities, as assumed by Binkley, can afford longer rotations (Tahvonen and Salo 1999). Therefore, the frequency of sales decreases as nonforest income increases.

Hyberg and Holthausen (1989) explicitly stated these hypotheses using a static rotation model, where the owner valued both the utility of consumption and of the forest amenities. Hyberg and Holthausen (1989) used a logit model to test individual data on frequency of sales of forest owners in Georgia during 1977–1984. The estimated effect of nonforest income on harvest probability was negative, as expected, but also the stumpage price had a negative effect on harvesting frequency. The authors attributed this unexpected result to dominating income effect of prices and to problems of measurement in stumpage prices observed by the forest owners. Dennis (1990) used pooled data from New Hampshire to estimate a sales probability model. Problems in interpreting the estimated effects from a pooled data are related to the possibly opposite short-run and equilibrium effects of the model's exogenous variables on timber supply. These will be discussed below.

3.2. Reduced Form Limited Dependent Variables Models

Given the information on harvested timber volumes, the tobit model has typically been applied in timber supply studies. Nevertheless, normal forest structure and homogeneity of the sampled population of forest owners must still be assumed in order to interpret the elasticities. Using the tobit model to identify the determinants of harvest (≥ 0, mbf/ha) from cross-sectional data of individual landowners in New Hampshire, Dennis (1989) found timber price to have a positive but not significant effect on timber supply while the effect of nonforest income was negative. The nonsignificant effect of the stumpage price is not surprising, if interpreted as a long-run equilibrium effect, as cross-sectional variation on only 58 observations was used. Dennis (1989) related the negative effect of nontimber income to decreasing marginal utility of consumption in the static utility maximization problem of the representative forest owner. However, in the rotation model, the expected sign would actually be positive, as wealthier forest owners can afford longer rotation (or larger timber stocks in biomass harvesting model) leading to larger harvested volumes per hectare if the owner eventually harvests.

Aronsson (1990) used the tobit model to analyse timber supply and non-linear income taxation. He used cross-sectional data on 858 forest owners in Sweden. Instead of the price level, year-to-year price changes were used. This is theoretically correct since Aronsson (1990) assumed perfect capital markets, and accordingly the short-run supply was homogenous of degree zero in prices, as explicitly stated by Aronsson (1990). Carlén (1990) also investigated the harvesting behaviour of NIPF owners. Carlén estimated a tobit model using cross-section time-series data of NIPF owners in Sweden over the cutting seasons 75/76–79/80. Regional stumpage price series (four regions) were used. The empirical results indicated, as in Aronsson (1990), that stumpage prices have a positive short-term effect on timber supply.

Kuuluvainen and Salo (1991) and Kuuluvainen et al. (1996) used a tobit model to identify the determinants of NIPF timber supply in Finland. In the first study cross-section time-series data from 1982 to 1995 and in the second study a similar data set from 1986 to 1990 were used. In Kuuluvainen and Salo (1991) stumpage prices had temporal variation only, thus only short-term effects could be estimated. Exogenous nonforest income had both individual and temporal variation. The negative effect of exogenous nonforest income was interpreted in the two-period biomass-harvesting model to indicate liquidity constrained harvesting behaviour due to credit rationing. However, forest owners' wealth had a positive effect.

The results were similar in Kuuluvainen et al. (1996), who included both the price change (aggregate data) to measure the short-run price effects and the individual price level (prices recorded for each forest owner) to measure the long-term effect of prices. However, because of dominating intertemporal variation in the price series, the effect of price level could not be interpreted as parallel to the effects of parametric changes in a rotation model. The effect of price level was positive but not significant. The same concerns the results of Bolkesjø and Baardsen (2002), who also had access to individual price observations. According to their results based on a panel tobit model and cross-section time-series data of 160 Norwegian forest owners, prices, costs and taxes were found to have statistically significant effects on timber supply over time (see also Bolkesjø and Solberg 2003).

Kuuluvainen and Tahvonen (1999) elaborated the empirical approach of Hyberg and Holthausen (1989) investigating both the impacts of intertemporal and cross-sectional variation in prices and other exogenous variables on timber supply. They estimated a panel tobit model and a linear regression model using a small data set of forest owners in Southern Finland in 1982–1990. Thus, this study explicitly considered the cross-section and over time variation in the data in order to empirically measure both the short-term and the long-term effects on harvest of the exogenous variables. The empirical results were in accordance with the utility based rotation model with *in situ* values of forests predicting a negative long-run price effect on volume per hectare harvested but a positive short-run price effect. However, probably due to the inefficiency of the two stage estimation method and a small number of regional price observations, the long-run elasticity of the supply with respect to price was unrealistically large absolute terms. The short-run effect of nonforest income was negative but the long-run effect was positive. This result is analogous to Kuuluvainen and Salo (1991) and Kuuluvainen et al. (1996), who obtained a positive elasticity of supply with respect to forest owners' wealth.

3.3. Structural Harvest Decision Models

The above studies suggest that, in addition to timber prices, also owner characteristics, and nonforest income in particular, affect NIPF harvesting behaviour. However, the measured effects of prices are, to an extent, contradictory. As noted by Provencher (1995a, 1995b, 1997), the problem with the reduced form probability models is that the results obtained can only be linked indirectly to actual harvesting decisions. To overcome this, Provencher (1995a) formulated industrial forest owners' harvesting decision directly into the econometric model used to estimate the parameters of the decision problem in a rotation framework with stochastic prices and growth.[3] In this case, estimation of ML parameters of the harvest probability function requires custom programming because stochastic dynamic programming problem (DP) for a harvesting decision problem constrained by volume growth and price process has to be solved for every set of parameters. The formulation produces a direct link between forest owners' intertemporal decision problem and the parameters of price and growth processes to be estimated.

Provencher (1995b) used a similar approach but explicitly considered the value of standing timber to the industrial forest owner, caused by timber units contribution to assure that the mill operates at desired levels and that production plans are not disrupted. The results indicate that profitability of harvesting a given stand by industrial forest owners may be more dependent on a reliable supply of timber to a production unit than on attempts to forecast the price development correctly. The results in Provencher (1995b) have an interesting similarity to the reduced form models allowing market imperfections in the sense that uncertainty makes the optimal harvesting decisions dependent, not only on relative prices and the interest rate, but also on forest owners' other economy.

Using a Monte Carlo analysis, Provencher (1997) demonstrated that a structural model could substantially outperform the standard reduced form estimations in explaining qualitative harvest choices. Based on Monte Carlo results, Provencher (1997) also proposed a reduced form probability model better capable of approximating the results of the structural estimation. The difference with standard formulations used in the above-cited studies is the inclusion of independent variables for the interaction between price and the stand volume, age of the stand, and age squared. The interaction term measures the revenues from harvest while the stand age variables measure the expected revenue, if harvest is postponed. Provencher (1995a, 1995b, 1997) did not explicitly calculate the short- or long-run effects of prices on expected harvest, but these could be obtained via simulations.[4]

The study by Prestemon and Wear (2000) is a standard reduced form estimation of a discrete harvest choice, but it utilizes the idea of Provencher (1997) in linking the harvest choices directly to harvest revenue rather than prices. Prestemon and Wear (2000) define the decision to harvest a stand as a function of net benefits of harvesting at the beginning of the present period and net benefits from harvesting the stand in the future. In addition to prices, timber volume, harvesting costs and bare land value, the net benefits are assumed to depend on money metric measure of nontimber values of the stand as in Hartman (1976).

The probability of harvest equation was estimated using the data for the Coastal Plain of North Carolina. Probability to harvest as a function of present and future value of the stand (a function of timber price, volume and quality of the stand), plot's distance from the road and timber content was estimated using a probit model for nonindustrial, industrial and government forests. Using inventory information on representative plots and the predicted probabilities of harvest, Prestemon and Wear (2000) were able to calculate, for example, the effects of temporary (short-run) and permanent (long-run) price changes on the supply of timber for different owner categories. The short-run elasticities of supply were typically larger than the effects of permanent long-run price changes (which in some cases were negative). The results are consistent with the theoretical expectations from the rotation model.

Lee (1997) used USDA Forest Service inventory data and Timber Mart South price surveys from North Carolina to study the effects of on-site forest amenity characteristics on harvest probability and on the marginal opportunity cost of timber. She used the inventory information, ages of stands harvested and regional prices to obtain implied individual interest rates and the marginal opportunity costs and benefits of timber at the time of harvest. This is one way to, at least partly, answer the 'Provencher critique' above when estimating a reduced form harvesting probability model if the required stand level information is available.

4. INTERPRETATIONS AND POLICY IMPLICATIONS

According to the above-cited studies, the most important factor determining timber supply is the timber price. However, the long-term policy implications that can be drawn from the studies are limited and in some cases contradictory. In most studies on qualitative harvesting decisions, prices have a positive effect both on the probability of harvest as well as on the quantity harvested. Due to the lack of data, the effects of interest rates and silvicultural costs are often ignored in the estimated models, causing a possible omitted variables bias.

When the probability of harvesting is studied using cross-sectional data, the interpretation of a positive effect of timber price level is that shorter rotations are used in those cross-sectional units where prices are high, resulting in more frequent harvests in these units (Hyberg and Holthausen 1989). However, this interpretation is based on the assumption that harvests come from a normal-forest structure, where the oldest age classes are the first ones to be harvested. It must also be assumed that observations are from a homogenous sample of forest owners. The homogeneity assumption also concerns the independent variables of the model. For example, for the long-run interpretation of price effects to be valid when estimated using a cross-sectional variation in the data, business cycles or possible trends in prices in different regions must move in phase. If this is not the case, the effect of a price on probability of harvest may not be related to the average rotation length at all.

When the probability of harvesting is studied using pooled cross-section time-series data, a positive price effect is more likely to be due to the intertemporal than cross-section variation in prices. In this case the price effect is related to the participation to timber market over business cycles, and the effect is not likely to have long-term policy relevance, except for measuring transitional impacts of forest policy changes, such as those of an anticipated change in forest taxation regime, tax rates or temporary subsidies. According to Provencher (1997), it is these short-term market reactions that can be most reliably predicted by the reduced-form models on probability of harvest, but the quantitative effects on timber supply cannot be evaluated without information on stands that are harvested.

For evaluating the long-term effects of forest taxation on probability of harvest (or the rotation age) and timber supply structural estimations could provide a potentially more useful approach (Provencher 1997). However, the problem with structural models is that they are computationally demanding and the decision rules for optimal stopping problem must be highly simplified. Presently, experience on structural estimations are limited to a few small data sets on industrial forest owners' quarterly harvesting decisions in the Eastern United States. An intermediate approach by Prestemon and Wear (2000) and Lee (1997) estimating reduced form discrete choice models for harvesting decision but accounting for a specific information on harvested stands and the revenues from harvest seems promising.

When harvest volumes are available the models are more immune to the problems of discrete choice models, as the revenue is directly related to the dependent variable. Furthermore, the estimated parameters also relate directly to the timber supply, which is useful in forecasting and policy planning. Also in this case, the most reliable estimates are the short-term effects obtained using the intertemporal variation in the data (e.g., Aronsson 1990, Carlén 1990, Kuuluvainen and Tahvonen 1999, Bolkesjø and Baardsen 2002). A problem in interpreting the cross-sectional variation in prices, as a policy relevant long-run phenomenon, is that harvested volumes are usually recorded either as cubic metres per year and forest owner, or as cubic metres per year and per total forest land area of the woodlot. In the former case the price effect cannot be interpreted using the rotation model. In the latter, normal-forest structure and homogenous population must be assumed (Kuuluvainen and Tahvonen 1999). For more valid inference, either the ages of the stands harvested or the actual hectares harvested and their timber volumes should be measured. Such data could also be used in constructing structural models. A remaining important empirical problem will be the usually low cross-sectional variation in prices and costs.

The results concerning the effects of nonforestry income in the above studies seem to be theoretically more easily interpretable than the effects of timber prices. In all discrete choice models nonforest income has a negative effect on timber supply. The cross-sectional interpretation (Binkley 1981, Jamnick and Becket 1988, Hyberg and Holthausen 1989) would be longer rotations used by wealthy forest owners due to nontimber amenities increasing with stand volume. A positive effect of forest owners' wealth or permanent income measured using cross-sectional variation (Kuuluvainen and Salo 1991, Kuuluvainen et al. 1996, Kuuluvainen and Tahvonen 1999) has a similar interpretation as the negative income effect in cross-section models for harvesting probability. Wealthy forest owners use longer rotations than the less wealthy ones. Under MSY, this implies higher harvested equilibrium volumes. However, in absolute terms the effects are small, and may have limited policy relevance.

5. CONCLUSIONS

In this survey, we have presented a brief summary of the existing empirical models on private timber supply and harvesting models. The general conclusion is that, as expected, prices in particular play an important role in private forest owners' harvesting decisions. Quantitatively, forest-owner and woodlot characteristics play a less important role, and therefore the possible changes in ownership structures may in fact have only a modest role in predicting the future timber supply.

However, the results of the studies based on survey data seem to give the most consistent results relating to short-term transitional effects of prices on supply, while the policy-relevant quantitative measures on the long-term effects of prices, costs and the interest rate are largely missing or they are contradictory. A general feature concerning most studies cited in this survey is also the fact that little attention has been paid to the statistical validity of the estimated models. Both more detailed data as well as more sophisticated empirical models and statistical inference, with a more explicit relation to theory, could further increase our understanding of the harvesting behaviour of private forest owners.

ACKNOWLEDGEMENT

We thank the Academy of Finland (project 48795) for its financial support.

NOTES

1. The landowner maximizes utility over two periods:

$$\text{Max } U = u(c_1) + (1/(1+r))u(c_2)$$

subject to

$$\begin{aligned} c_1 &= ax(p_1q_1 - w) + s_0 - s_1, \\ c_2 &= ax(p_2q_1 - w) + (1-a)x(p_2q_2 - w) + (1+r)s_1, \\ a &\geq 0, \quad 1 - a \geq 0, \end{aligned}$$

where c_t ($t = 1, 2$) is periodic consumption, q_i ($i = 1, 2$) is the per hectare timber volume in the two age classes, describing a concave growth function, s is external assets, r is interest rate, p_t ($t = 1, 2$) is timber price per volume unit, x is the initial forest land area, w is regeneration cost per hectare and a is the share of the forest land that is harvested in the first period (Uusivuori and Kuuluvainen 2005, Viitala 2003). It is assumed that initially forest is in the first age class. This model can be generalized to consider multiple age classes and an infinite planning horizon (e.g., Salo and Tahvonen 2002b, Uusivuori and Kuuluvainen 2005).

2. Information on studies quoted below has been collected in Table 12.1, except for the studies using structural estimations (Provencher 1995a, 1995b, 1997).
3. A firm's decision to harvest a stand is assumed to be based on maximizing expected profit, which is a function of net present value of per stem of timber conditional on the decision to harvest the timber either now, or in the future. Forest owners' maximization problem at time t can be expressed as

$$J(p_t, v_t, \theta_t) = \max\{\pi^0(p_t, v_t, \theta_t), \pi^1(p_t, v_t, \theta_t)\},$$

subject to a stochastic price process for p_t and volume growth function for v_t with

$$\pi^0(\cdot) = \beta E\{J(p_{t+1}, v_{t+1}, \theta_{t+1})\},$$

$$\pi^1(\cdot) = p_t x_t + \gamma + \theta_t,$$

where π^0 is the expected profit of postponing the harvest and π^1 is the profit from harvest in the present period, β is a discount factor, γ is the expected value of bare land and θ_t is the IID random term with constant variance, σ_θ^2, in the tree growth per stem, $v_{t+1} = f(v_t)$ with f monotonically increasing in v_t, and $p_{t+1} = \alpha_0 + \alpha_1 p_t + \varepsilon_t$ is a first order Markov process for prices and ε_t is an IID random term with constant variance, σ_ε^2. The stand is harvested if $\pi^1 > \pi^0$.
4. Provencher (1997) discusses also the possible effects of different price processes, i.e. random walk versus stationary AR1 prices, on the estimated price effects in discrete choice models. There is some evidences from Scandinavia indicating stationarity of annual price series (e.g., Lohmander 1987, Hultkrantz 1995, 1999, Huhtala et al. 2001), the results of Abildtrup et al. (1997) are mixed. In contrast, monthly prices in Scandinavia seem to be random walks (Toppinen and Toivonen 1998, Toppinen 1998, Nyrud 2002) and stationary in first differences. The results in the United States are mixed (e.g., Washburn and Binkley 1990, Yin and Newman 1996). If stumpage prices are random walks, trading rules based on historical prices alone cannot succeed on average. However, even in this case other public and/or private information may help in predicting price development (Fama 1970).

REFERENCES

Abildtrup, J., J. Riis and B.J. Thorsen (1997), 'The reservation price approach and informationally efficient markets', *Journal of Forest Economics*, 3, 229–246.

Adams, D.M. (1975), 'A model of pulpwood production and trade in Wisconsin and the Lake States', *Forest Science*, 21, 301–312.

Adams, D.M. and R.W. Haynes (1980), 'The 1980 softwood timber assessment market model: Structure, projections and policy simulations', *Forest Science Monographs*, Vol. 22.

Amacher, G.S., M.C. Conway and J. Sullivan (2003), 'Econometric analysis of nonindustrial forest landowners: Is there anything left to study?', *Journal of Forest Economics*, 9, 137–164.

Aronsson T. (1990), 'The short-run supply of roundwood under nonlinear income taxation. Theory, estimation methods and empirical results based on Swedish data', Umeå Economic Studies, No. 220, University of Umeå, 166 pp.

Binkley, C.S. (1981), 'Timber supply from private forests', Bulletin No. 92, Yale University, School of Forestry and Environmental Studies, 97 pp.

Binkley, C.S. (1987), 'Economic models of timber supply', in M. Kallio et al. (eds), *The Global Forest Sector, An Analytical Perspective*, New York: John Wiley & Sons, pp. 109–136.

Binkley, C.S. and P.A. Cardellichio (1985), 'The hardwood assessment market model: Structure, historical simulations and preliminary projections', Report to the USDA Forest Service, Pacific Northwest Forest and Range Experiment Station under Cooperative Agreement PNW 81-137.

Bolkesjø, T.F. and S. Baardsen (2002), 'Roundwood supply in Norway: Micro-level analysis of self-employed forest owners', *Forest Policy and Economics*, 4, 55–64.

Bolkesjø, T.F. and B. Solberg (2003), 'A panel data analysis of nonindustrial private roundwood supply with emphasis on the price elasticity', *Forest Science*, 49(4), 530–538.

Boyd, R. (1983), 'The effects of FIP and Forester Assistance on nonindustrial private forests', in J.P. Royer and C.D. Risbrudt (eds), *Nonindustrial Private Forests*, Symposium Proceedings, April 19–20, 1983, Duke University, North Carolina, pp. 189–203.

Brännlund, R., P.-O. Johansson and K.G. Löfgren (1985), 'An econometric analysis of aggregate sawtimber and pulpwood supply in Sweden', *Forest Science*, 31, 595–606.

Brazee, R. and R. Mendelsohn (1988), 'Timber harvesting with fluctuating prices', *Forest Science*, 34(2), 359–372.

Cardellichio, P.A. and J. Veltcamp (1981), 'Demand for Pacific Northwest timber and timber products. Module II – A report for the Pacific Northwest Regional', Commission Forest Policy Project.

Carlén, O. (1990), 'Private nonindustrial forest owners' management behaviour: An economic analysis based on empirical data', Report 92, Swedish University of Agricultural Sciences, Department of Forest Economics, 104 pp.

Calish, S., R.D. Fight and D.E. Teeguarden (1978), 'How do non-timber values affect Douglas-fir rotations', *Journal of Forestry*, 76, 217–221.

Chang, S.J. (1982), 'An economic analysis of forest taxation's impact on optimal rotation age', *Land Economies*, 58(3), 293–309.

Chang, S.J. (1983), 'Rotation age, management intensity, and the economic factors of timber production: Do changes in stumpage price, interest rate, regeneration cost, and forest taxation matter?', *Forest Science*, 29, 267–277.

Clark, C.W. (1976), *Mathematical Bioeconomics*, New York: Wiley Interscience, 352 pp.

Dennis, D. (1989), 'An econometric analysis of harvest behavior: Integrating ownership and forest characteristics', *Forest Science*, 35, 1088–1104.

Dennis, D. (1990), 'A probit analysis of harvest decisions using pooled time-series and cross-sectional data', *Journal of Environmental Economics and Management*, 18, 176–187.

Fama, E.F. (1970), 'Efficient capital markets: A review of theory and empirical work', *Journal of Finance*, 25, 383–417.

Faustmann, M. (1849), 'Berechnung des Werthes, welchen Waldboden, sowie noch nicht haubare Holzbestände für die Waldwirthschaft besitsen', *Algemeine Forst und Jagd-Zeitung*, December, 441–455.

Hartman, R. (1976), 'The harvesting decision when a standing forest has value', *Economic Inquiry*, 81(1), 8–38.

Heckman, J.J. and T.M. McCurdy (1980), 'A life cycle model of female labor supply', *Review of Economic Studies*, XLVII, 47–74.

Huhtala, A., A. Toppinen and M. Boman (2001), 'An environmental account's dilemma: Are stumpage prices reliable indicators of resource scarcity', Working Paper 77, National Institute of Economic Research, Stockholm, 33 pp.

Hultkrantz, L. (1995), 'The behaviour of the timber rents in Sweden 1909–1990', *Journal of Forest Economics*, 1, 165–180.

Hultkrantz, L. (1999), 'Informational efficiency of markets for stumpage: Comment', *American Journal of Agricultural Economics*, 75, 234–238.

Hyberg, B.T. and D.M. Holthausen (1989), 'The behavior of nonindustrial private forest landowners', *Canadian Journal of Forest Research*, 19, 1014–1023.

Hyde, W.F. (1980), *Timber Supply, Land Allocation, and Economic Efficiency*, Baltimore, MD: Johns Hopkins/Resource for the Future, 224 pp.

Jamnick, M.S. and D.R. Beckett (1988), 'A logit analysis of private woodlot owners' harvesting decisions in New Brunswick', *Canadian Journal of Forest Research*, 18, 330–336.

Johansson, P.O. and K.G. Löfgren (1985), *The Economics of Forestry and Natural Resources*, London: Basil Blackwell, 292 pp.

Korpinen, P. (1981), 'Raakapuumarkkinoiden hinnanmuodostuksesta Suomessa', Esitelmä Taloustieteellisen Seuran kokouksessa 29.1.1981, Taloustieteellisen Seuran Vuosikirja 1980/1981, pp. 250–257.

Koskela, E. (1989a), 'Forest taxation and timber supply under price uncertainty: Perfect capital markets', *Forest Science*, 35, 150–159.

Koskela, E. (1989b), 'Forest taxation and timber supply under price uncertainty: Credit rationing in the capital markets', *Forest Science*, 35, 160–172.

Kuuluvainen, J. (1989), 'Nonindustrial private timber supply and credit rationing, microeconomic foundations with empirical evidence from the Finnish case', Report 85, Department of Forest Economics, Swedish University of Agricultural Sciences, Umeå.

Kuuluvainen, J. (1990), 'Virtual price approach to short-term timber supply under credit rationing', *Journal of Environmental Economics and Management*, 19, 109–126.

Kuuluvainen, J. and J. Salo (1991), 'Timber supply and life cycle harvest of nonindustrial private forest owners, An empirical analysis of the Finnish case', *Forest Science*, 37, 1011–1029.

Kuuluvainen, J. and O. Tahvonen (1999), 'Testing the forest rotation model: Evidence from panel data', *Forest Science*, 45(4), 539–551.

Kuuluvainen, J., L. Hetemäki, P. Ollonqvist, V. Ovaskainen, H. Pajuoja, J. Salo, H. Seppälä and M. Tervo (1988), 'The Finnish roundwood market: An econometric analysis', *Finnish Economic Papers*, 1, 191–201.

Kuuluvainen, J., H. Karppinen and V. Ovaskainen (1996), 'Landowner objectives and nonindustrial private timber supply', *Forest Science*, 42, 300–309.

Lee, K.J. (1997), 'Hedonic estimation of forest amenity values of nonindustrial private landowners', Doctoral Dissertation, North Carolina State University, Forestry and Economics, 80 pp.

Leuschner, W.A. (1973), 'An econometric analysis of the Wisconsin Aspen pulpwood market', *Forest Science*, 19(1), 41–46.

Lohmander, P. (1983), 'Optimal harvest policy under the influence of imperfections and uncertainty', Working Paper 22, College of Forestry, Department of Forest Economics, Umeå, 75 pp.

Lohmander, P. (1987), 'The economics of forest management under risk', Report 79, College of Forestry, Department of Forest Economics, Umeå,

Lyon, K.S. and R.A. Sedjo (1983), 'An optimal control theory model to estimate the regional long-term supply of timber', *Forest Science*, 29(4), 798–812.

McCurdy, E. (1981), 'An empirical model of labor supply in a life-cycle setting', *Journal of Political Economy*, 89, 1059–1085.

Mitra, T. and H.Y. Wan (1985), 'Some theoretical results on the economics of forestry', *Review of Economic Studies*, LII, 263–282.

Montgomery, C.A. and D.M. Adams (1995), 'Optimal timber management policies', in D.W. Bromley (ed.), *Handbook of Environmental Economics*, London: Basil Blackwell, pp. 379–404.

Newman, D. (1987), 'An econometric analysis of southern softwood stumpage market: 1950–1980', *Forest Science*, 33, 932–945.

Newman, D.H. and D.N. Wear (1993), 'Production economics of private forestry: A comparison of industrial and nonindustrial forest owners', *American Journal of Agricultural Economics*, 75(3), 674–684.

Newman, D.H., C.B. Gilbert and W.F. Hyde (1985), 'The optimal forest rotation with evolving prices', *Land Economics*, 61(4), 347–353.

Nyrud, A.Q. (2002), 'Integration in the Norwegian pulpwood market: Domestic prices versus external trade', *Journal of Forest Economics*, 8, 213–225.

Ovaskainen, V. (1992), 'Forest taxation, timber supply, and economic efficiency. Seloste: Metsäverotus, puun tarjonta ja taloudellinen tehokkuus', *Acta Forestalia Fennica*, 233, 88 pp.

Prestemon, J.P. and D.N. Wear (2000), 'Linking harvest choices to timber supply', *Forest Science*, 46(3), 377–389.

Provencher, B. (1995a), 'Structural estimation of the stochastic dynamic decision problems of resource users: An application to the timber harvest decision', *Journal of Environmental Economics and Management*, 29, 321–338.

Provencher, B. (1995b), 'An investigation of the harvest decisions of timber firms in the South-East United States', *Journal of Applied Econometrics*, 10, 57–74.

Provencher, B. (1997), 'Structural versus reduced-form estimation of optimal stopping problems', *American Journal of Agricultural Economics*, 79, 357–368.

Robinson, V.L. (1974), 'An econometric model of softwood and stumpage markets, 1947–1967', *Forest Sciece*, 20(2), 171–179.

Ruist, E. and I. Svennilsson (1948), *Den norrländska skogsnäringens konjukturkänslighet under mellankrigsperioden*, Stockholm: IUI.

Salo, S. and O. Tahvonen (2001), 'Optimal evolution of forest age-classes and land allocation between forestry and agriculture', Working papers W-286, Helsinki School of Economics and Business Administration.

Salo, S. and O. Tahvonen (2002a), 'On equilibrium cycles and normal forests in optimal harvesting of tree vintages', *Journal of Environmental Economics and Management*, 44(1), 1–22.

Salo, S. and O. Tahvonen (2002b), 'On the optimality of a normal forest with multiple land classes', *Forest Science*, 48(3), 530–542.

Seppälä, R. (1974), 'Raakapuun tarjonnasta Suomessa', *Folia Forestalia*, 190.

Størdahl, S. and A. Nyrud (2003), 'Testing roundwood market efficiency using a multivariate cointegration estimator', *Forest Policy and Economics*, 5, 57–68.

Strang, W.J. (1983), 'On the optimal harvesting decision', *Economic Inquiry*, 21 (October), 577–583.

Tahvonen, O. (1998), 'Bequests, credit rationing and in situ values in the Faustmann–Pressler–Ohlin forestry model', *Scandinavian Journal of Economics*, 100, 781–800.

Tahvonen, O. and S. Salo (1999), 'Optimal forest rotation with in situ preferences', *Journal of Environmental Economics Management*, 37, 106–128.

Tahvonen, O., S. Salo and J. Kuuluvainen (2001), 'Optimal forest rotation and land values under borrowing constraint', *Journal of Economic Dynamics and Control*, 25, 1595–1627.

Toppinen, A. (1998), 'Incorporating cointegration relations in a short-run model of the Finnish sawlog market', *Canadian Journal of Forest Research*, 28, 291–298.

Toppinen, A. and R. Toivonen (1998), 'Roundwood market integration in Finland. A multivariate cointegration analysis', *Journal of Forest Economics*, 4, 241–263.

Uusivuori, J. and J. Kuuluvainen (2001), 'Benefits of forest-owner collaboration and imperfect capital markets', *Forest Science*, 47(3), 428–436.

Uusivuori, J. and J. Kuuluvainen (2005), 'The harvesting decisions when a standing forest with multiple age classes has value', *American Journal of Agricultural Economics*, 87(1), 61–77.

Viitala, E-J. (2003), 'Normaalimetsän optimaalisuudesta' (On the optimality of normal forest), Metsäntutkimuslaitoksen tiedonantoja, 895, 59 pp. [in Finnish].

Washburn, C.L. and C.S. Binkley (1990), 'Informational efficiency of markets for stumpage', *American Journal of Agricultural Economics*, 72, 394–405.

Wear, D.N. and D.H. Newman (1991), 'The structure of forestry production: Short-run and long-run results', *Forest Science*, 37, 540–551.

Yin, R. and D.H. Newman (1996), 'Are markets for stumpage informationally efficient', *Canadian Journal of Forest Research*, 26, 1032–1039.

13. Travelling Waves in a Modified Hotelling Population Model

Tönu Puu

1. THE ORIGINAL HOTELLING MODEL

In an unpublished MA thesis in 1921, Hotelling invented a model for population dynamics, combining nonlinear growth with dispersal through space. This short contribution was published as an article in 1978 through the initiative of Wilson, but it made no success in economics, neither before, nor after the publication. It was reinvented several times. In 1937, Fisher applied it to the 'advance of advantageous genes' and in 1951, Skellam applied it to 'random dispersal' in theoretical animal populations.

The setup of the model contained a nonlinear growth part:

$$\dot{p} = p(1 - p), \tag{1}$$

where p denotes the population variable, 1 denotes a constant sustainable population which nature can support, and the dot denotes differentiation with respect to time. Normally one would have a speed coefficient and a nonunitary sustainable population, but we can always re-scale the population variable and time so as to make both coefficients unitary. Standing alone this is a logistic growth equation which can be easily solved by variable separation and expansion in partial fractions:

$$\frac{\mathrm{d}p}{p} - \frac{\mathrm{d}p}{1 - p} = \mathrm{d}t. \tag{2}$$

This integrates to

$$\ln p - \ln(1 - p) = -\ln K + t \tag{3}$$

or exponentiating to

$$\frac{p}{1 - p} = \frac{1}{K} \mathrm{e}^t. \tag{4}$$

Solving for p we have the closed-form solution

$$p = \frac{1}{1 + K\,\mathrm{e}^{-t}}. \tag{5}$$

In substance this growth process is thought to mimic a Malthusian setting where population grows exponentially when its size is small compared to the sustainable size, but bends off once the latter is approached. Should population initially exceed the sustainable size, then it starts to decrease according to the Malthusian 'positive and moral' checks.

The Hotelling model adds diffusion through the Laplacian operator, i.e. the process is changed to

$$\dot{p} = p(1 - p) + \nabla^2 p, \tag{6}$$

where

$$\nabla^2 p = \frac{\partial^2 p}{\partial x^2} + \frac{\partial^2 p}{\partial y^2} \tag{7}$$

and x, y are the space coordinates. (In 1D we just retain the first term.) The statement assumes a flow in the reverse direction of the gradient.

$$\phi = (\phi_1, \phi_2) = -\nabla p = -\left(\frac{\partial p}{\partial x}, \frac{\partial p}{\partial y}\right), \tag{8}$$

where the negative of the divergence

$$-\nabla \cdot \phi = -\frac{\partial \phi_1}{\partial x} - \frac{\partial \phi_2}{\partial y} = \frac{\partial^2 p}{\partial x^2} + \frac{\partial^2 p}{\partial y^2} \tag{9}$$

indicates the volume withdrawn from such a flow at any given location. This chained operator $\nabla^2 p = \nabla \cdot \nabla p$, the Laplacian, is the basis of all linear diffusion processes. In the present application population diffuses away from relatively densely to relatively sparsely populated regions. In animal populations the effect arises from mere probability: if any animal is likely to move in any direction a certain distance per unit of time, then more animals move out from than in to dense locations, whereas the reverse holds in sparse locations. In Hotelling's case the action is deliberate, due to people looking for locations of better living conditions, which are the sparsely populated ones as production is carried out under decreasing returns.

Though it is very simple, the complete model does not have a known closed-form solution. In the case of one-dimensional space it is however possible to study at least the stationary cases:

$$p(1 - p) + \nabla^2 p = 0, \tag{10}$$

where now $\nabla^2 p \doteq \partial^2 p/\partial x^2$. If we multiply the equation through by the first derivative $\partial p/\partial x$ and integrate, then we obtain the first integral

$$\frac{1}{2}p^2 - \frac{1}{3}p^3 + \frac{1}{2}\left(\frac{\mathrm{d}p}{\mathrm{d}x}\right)^2 = \text{constant}. \tag{11}$$

By varying the constant, we obtain a set of integral curves in $p, \partial p/\partial x$-phase space. There are two fixed points with spatially invariant populations $p \equiv 0$ and $p \equiv 1$, the former unstable, the latter stable, as a linearization of the dynamic equations (1) or (6) would show. In phase space the former represents a centre, the latter a saddle point. Except for the fixed points there are integral curves with population varying over the space, some of them closed orbits, which indicate a possibility of stationary patterns of undulating population density. Such solutions are only possible over limited intervals less than a complete cycle, as otherwise population becomes negative. Ecologists call such intervals 'habitats', i.e. isolated population communities. The solutions for the nonlinear dynamic model have however never been obtained. For more details, the reader is referred to Okubo (1980), Beckmann and Puu (1990), and Grindrod (1996).

2. A MODEL WITH PRODUCTION

One of the reasons why the Hotelling model never became a success in economics no doubt is that humankind produces its own means of subsistence, which can hence not be taken as given, especially not independent of population itself in its capacity of humanpower. It is fortunate that the introduction of a production function, which actually increases the degree of nonlinearity, also makes it possible to obtain more precise results. The author tried his hands on this before, but did not come up with a model with this fortunate property (see Puu 1985).

Suppose that we replace the given sustainable population level by a function which depends on population itself:

$$q = 2\alpha\beta p^2 - \alpha p^3. \tag{12}$$

This is the simplest type of a production function with increasing/decreasing returns. Here α is a techological efficiency factor, and β denotes the technologically optimal scale of operation, as the shift from increasing to decreasing returns occurs for $p = \beta$. The reader can easily see this by calculating average and marginal productivities, equating them, and solving for the population (= humanpower) variable.

Now, the potential for population growth is production per capita, as a measure of living standard, multiplied by population in its capacity of the reproducing mass. The product is production according to the above expression. To convert it into an increase through nativity we just need a multiplicative factor, but we can absorb it in the technological efficiency factor α already present.

Given a mortality rate δ, we have the pure growth equation

$$\dot{p} = 2\alpha\beta p^2 - \alpha p^3 - \delta p. \tag{13}$$

The growth equation has three distinct, or just one (real) root, only depending on the value of the composite parameter

$$\rho = \frac{\alpha\beta^2}{\delta}. \tag{14}$$

From (13), writing $\dot{p} = f(p) = 2\alpha\beta p^2 - \alpha p^3 - \delta p$, it is possible by using an easy calculation to obtain that $f(p) = f'(p) = 0$ for $\rho = 1$. This is a point of bifurcation, so we have three distinct roots when $\rho < 1$ and just one when $\rho > 1$. As we will shortly see the composite parameter ρ controls other things as well.

Before continuing, we will convert (13) to a more handy form, by rescaling population $hp \to p$ and time $kt \to t$, using $h = \beta(1 + \sqrt{1 - 1/\rho})$ and $k = (\sqrt{\rho} - \sqrt{\rho - 1})^2/\delta$ as scaling factors. Then we can write

$$\dot{p} = p(1 - p)(p - a), \tag{15}$$

where

$$a = (\sqrt{\rho} - \sqrt{\rho - 1})^2. \tag{16}$$

Note that the new parameter a only depends on ρ, and that it is a decreasing function. From (14), ρ is high, i.e. a is low, if technological efficiency α (including the absorbed nativity coefficient) or the scale constant β are high and the mortality coefficient δ is low. We will see that a, which from (16) has a positive value less than unity, provides an unstable steady state (a basin separatrix) between the stable zero and unitary staedy states of the growth equation.

The growth equation (15) only differs from the original Hotelling model through appearance of the factor $(p - a)$.

To complete the model, we add diffusion as before. It would again be preceded by a diffusivity constant, but we can now re-scale the space

Figure 13.1. Evolution curves for population p over time t

variable by the square root of the diffusivity factor to reduce it to unity. So, finally, we obtain

$$\dot{p} = p(1-p)(p-a) + \nabla^2 p. \tag{17}$$

Note that we do not lose any information by such changes of scale; we can measure population in individuals or in millions, time in seconds or millennia, space in millimetres or light years. The formulae and derivations become simpler, and we retain the right number of independent coefficients.

3. PURE GROWTH

Let us start with the pure growth system, Equation (15), and in order to get a nice solution let the remaining coefficient $a = 0.5$, i.e.

$$\dot{p} = p(1-p)(p-0.5). \tag{18}$$

Separating variables we have

$$2\frac{\mathrm{d}p}{p(1-p)(2p-1)} = \mathrm{d}t, \tag{19}$$

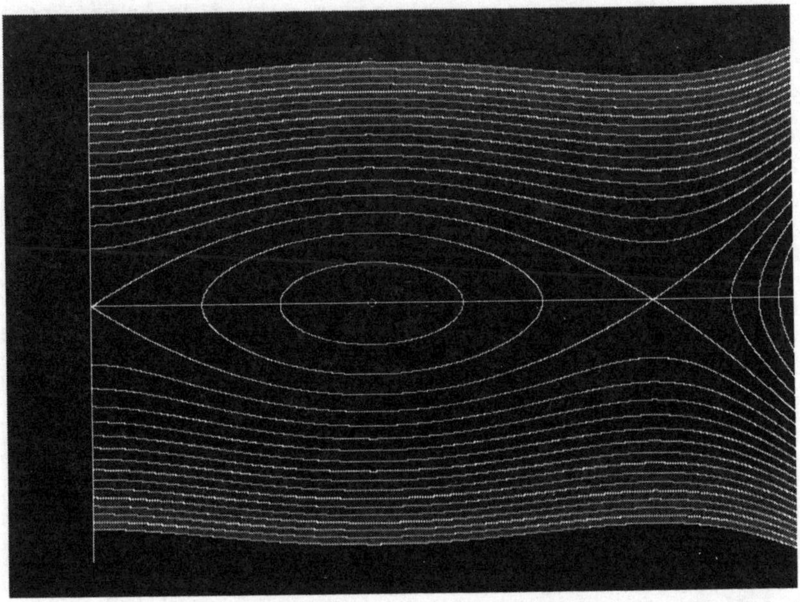

Figure 13.2. Phase space for population p (horizontal) and its space derivative $\partial p/\partial x$ (vertical)

or, expanding in partial fractions,

$$8\frac{\mathrm{d}p}{2p-1} - 2\frac{\mathrm{d}p}{p-1} - 2\frac{\mathrm{d}p}{p} = \mathrm{d}t. \tag{20}$$

Equation (20) is readily integrated into

$$4\ln(2p-1) - 2\ln(1-p) - 2\ln(p) = t - 2\ln(K/4), \tag{21}$$

where $-2\ln(K/4)$ denotes the integration constant. The reason for this style for the constant will soon become apparent. Exponentiating (21), we obtain

$$\frac{(2p-1)^4}{p^2(1-p)^2} = \left(\frac{4}{K}\right)^2 \mathrm{e}^t. \tag{22}$$

Taking the square root, we can rearrange this as a quadratic equation in p:

$$p^2 - p + \frac{1}{4}\frac{K}{K+\mathrm{e}^{t/2}} = 0, \tag{23}$$

which has the roots

$$p = \frac{1}{2} \pm \frac{1}{2}\frac{1}{\sqrt{1+K\,\mathrm{e}^{-t/2}}}. \tag{24}$$

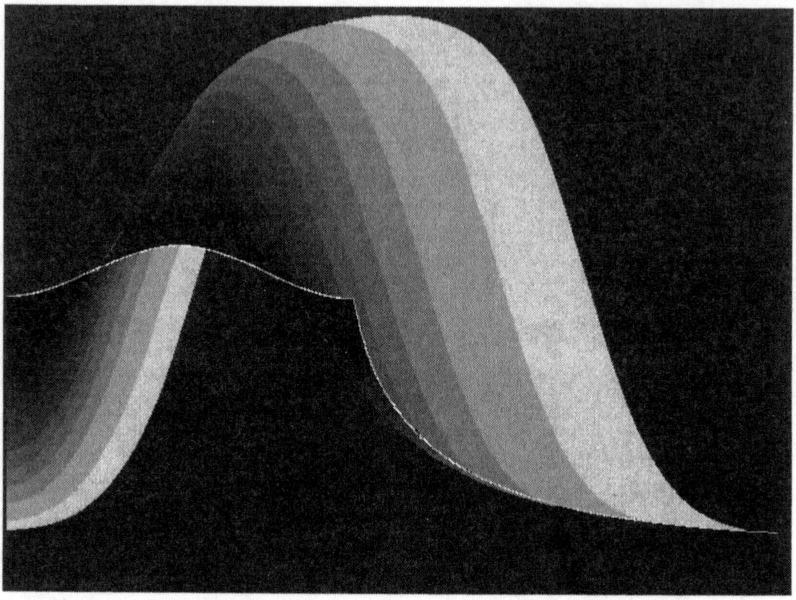

Figure 13.3. Stack of solution curves population p (vertical) as functions of space variable x (horizontal), with K increasing from 0 to 0.5 (foreground to background)

We immediately see that $p = 0$ and $p = 1$ are the stable solutions, approached as $t \to \infty$, whereas $p = a = 0.5$ is unstable. Figure 13.1 displays the population growth curves over time, and we see how they converge at the two stable equilibria, whereas $p = a = 0.5$ provides a watershed between their basins.

4. THE STATIONARY SOLUTIONS

Let us now focus on space instead of time. Take the complete Equation (17), retain the numerical value $a = 0.5$, and put the temporal derivative $\dot{p} = 0$. Further, suppose, that space is one-dimensional, so that $\nabla^2 p = \partial^2 p/\partial x^2$. Accordingly, we have

$$p(1-p)(p-0.5) + \frac{\partial^2 p}{\partial x^2} = 0. \tag{25}$$

Multiplying through by the first derivative and expanding the polynomial, we have

$$-p^3\frac{\partial p}{\partial x} + \frac{3}{2}p^2\frac{\partial p}{\partial x} - \frac{1}{2}p\frac{\partial p}{\partial x} + \frac{\partial p}{\partial x}\frac{\partial^2 p}{\partial x^2} = 0, \tag{26}$$

which integrates to

$$-\frac{1}{4}p^4 + \frac{1}{2}p^3 - \frac{1}{4}p^2 + \frac{1}{2}\left(\frac{\partial p}{\partial x}\right)^2 = \frac{K}{2}. \tag{27}$$

The p terms make a perfect square, so we may write

$$-\frac{1}{4}p^2(1-p)^2 + \frac{1}{2}\left(\frac{\partial p}{\partial x}\right)^2 = \frac{K}{2} \tag{28}$$

or

$$\frac{\partial p}{\partial x} = \pm\sqrt{K + \frac{p^2(1-p)^2}{2}}. \tag{29}$$

For various values of K we can construct the integral curves in phase space (see Figure 13.2). Note however that the phase space is made up of the population variable and its first *space* derivative, as we are studying stationary structures. Again we have two trivial equilibria with spatially constant population, obtainable for $K = 0$, i.e. for $p \equiv 0$ and $p \equiv 1$. Both are now saddle points, due to the higher order of nonlinearity, whereas $p \equiv a = 0.5$ represents a centre point in the phase portrait, obtainable for $K = -1/32$, which is the negative of the highest value the expression of p in the square root can take.

We can derive the closed-form solution $p(x)$ at least if we put $K = 0$ in (29). Then, obviously:

$$\frac{\partial p}{\partial x} = \pm\frac{p(1-p)}{\sqrt{2}}, \tag{30}$$

which can be written with the variables separated as

$$\frac{\partial p}{p(1-p)} = \pm\frac{\partial x}{\sqrt{2}} \tag{31}$$

or, again,

$$\frac{\partial p}{p} - \frac{\partial p}{(1-p)} = \pm\frac{\partial x}{\sqrt{2}} \tag{32}$$

so, integrating, exponentiating, and solving for p, as in Section 1, we have

$$p = \frac{1}{1 + K\,\mathrm{e}^{\pm x/\sqrt{2}}}. \tag{33}$$

This solution refers to integration along either the upper or lower branch of the heteroclinic saddle trajectory in Figure 13.2, and the shapes are similar

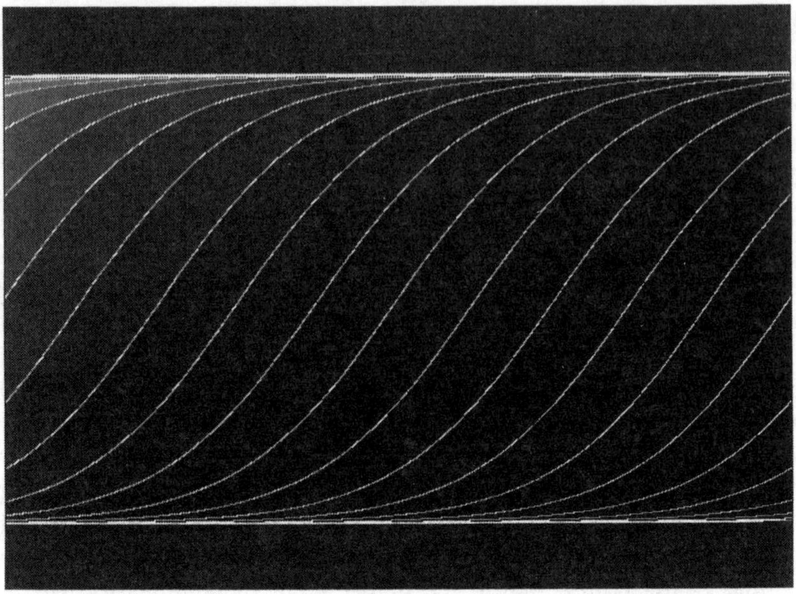

Figure 13.4. Travelling population wave front function at various time points

to the curves shown in the middle section of Figure 13.1. By numerical integration we can also calculate $p(x)$ from (29) for the closed elliptic inner curves of Figure 13.2. These correspond to oscillatory solutions, i.e. (stationary) waves over space. A selection of such solutions is shown in Figure 13.3. We see that there is a definite relation between (spatial) wavelength and population amplitude (between the most densely and the most sparsely populated locations) – the longer the wave the larger the amplitude.

We also see that our closed-form solution (33) fits nicely into this picture, as it represents a maximum population density range (between 0 and 1) and has infinite wavelength. The complete logistic function to infinity represents just one half of a wave as shown in Figure 13.3.

Each wave such as shown in Figure 13.3, has a certain connection to the ecological concept of a 'habitat', though population does not quite drop to zero at its boundries. We understand that each such type of wave can be chained into a smooth train with alternating maxima and minima. This is possible because each of the wave profiles starts and ends with a horizontal slope.

It is noteworthy in Figure 13.3 that the wavelength does not seem to go to zero as the amplitude collapses. This is in fact true, the wave bifurcates off with a certain finite wavelength from the spatially homogeneous solution, the centrepoint in Figure 13.2.

5. TRAVELLING WAVES: ONE-DIMENSIONAL

What is nice with the present model is that, unlike the original Hotelling model, it is possible to say something about the evolution of spatial patterns. Suppose we have a travelling wave solution to (17), and suppose again that we deal with a one-dimensional space, so that we may write

$$\frac{\partial p}{\partial t} = p(1-p)(p-a) + \frac{\partial^2 p}{\partial x^2}. \tag{34}$$

Note that we reintroduced the general constant a, and wrote out the (partial) time derivative, which before was just indicated by a dot. If we now have

$$p = p(x + ct), \tag{35}$$

where c is some constant indicating the speed of wave propagation, then obviously

$$\frac{\partial p}{\partial t} = cp' \tag{36}$$

and

$$\frac{\partial^2 p}{\partial x^2} = p'', \tag{37}$$

where the dashes indicate differentiation with respect to the compound variable $z = x + ct$. Using (36)–(37) in (34) we get:

$$p'' - cp' + p(1-p)(p-a) = 0. \tag{38}$$

This equation actually has a closed-form solution. Defining

$$z = x + ct, \tag{39}$$

the solution is

$$p = \frac{1}{1 + \mathrm{e}^{-z/\sqrt{2}}}. \tag{40}$$

We can calculate the derivates from (40):

$$p' = \frac{\mathrm{e}^{-z/\sqrt{2}}(1 + \mathrm{e}^{-z\sqrt{2}})}{\sqrt{2}(1 + \mathrm{e}^{-z/\sqrt{2}})^3} \tag{41}$$

and

$$p'' = \frac{e^{-z/\sqrt{2}}(e^{-z/\sqrt{2}} - 1)}{2(1 + e^{-z/\sqrt{2}})^3} \tag{42}$$

and substitute (40) in the growth term of (38):

$$p(1-p)(p-a) = \frac{e^{-z/\sqrt{2}}(1 - a(1 + e^{-z/\sqrt{2}}))}{2(1 + e^{-z/\sqrt{2}})^3}. \tag{43}$$

Substituting (41)–(43) back into (38) we obtain:

$$p'' - cp' + p(1-p)(p-a) = \frac{e^{-z/\sqrt{2}}(1 + e^{-z/\sqrt{2}})(1 - 2a - \sqrt{2}c)}{2(1 + e^{-z/\sqrt{2}})^3} \tag{44}$$

which is zero provided that

$$c = \sqrt{2}(0.5 - a). \tag{45}$$

This means that the travelling wave

$$p = \frac{1}{1 + e^{-(x+ct)/\sqrt{2}}} \tag{46}$$

is a solution provided (45) is fulfilled. We see that each constant a determines one unique speed of propagation. For the special case $a = 0.5$ we see that $c = 0$, i.e. the wave profile is stillstanding. Note how this fits the stationary solution obtained in (33) above. For $a < 0.5$ the profile is translated in the negative direction of x, whereas for $a > 0.5$ it moves in the positive direction of x.

We also note that $\lim_{x\to\infty} = 1$ and $\lim_{x\to-\infty} = 0$, so the wave profile connects the two stable spatially homogeneous solutions. The moving wave hence transfers the entire population from one stable stationary level to the other, whether extinguishing it or saturating it at the highest possible homogeneous stationary level, depends on the sign of c, and hence ultimately on the value of a. This moving wave profile would have been highly interesting for Hotelling, who originally wanted to model the westward migration of the American population.

Hence a critical value of $a = 0.5$ decides whether a travelling wave moves left or right in space. As the wave extends from zero to unitary population, a movement to the right means that population grows, whereas a movement to the left means that population decreases. The association to the technological and demographic parameters noted above makes this intuitively plausable.

6. ON INITIAL GROWTH

We may regard it as a disadvantage that zero population is one of the *stable* spatially homogeneous equilibrium solutions, whereas it was *unstable* in the original Hotelling model. If the zero is stable, then population will never spontaneously start growing. We may, however, easily change the situation by reintroducing the given (nonproduced) means of subsistence as an additive constant to production in the growth equation, so that (13) reads

$$\dot{p} = 1 + 2\alpha\beta p^2 - \alpha p^3 - \delta p. \tag{47}$$

We can then find the lowest root $\bar{p}$ for (47) which satisfies the stationarity condition:

$$1 + 2\alpha\beta\bar{p}^2 - \alpha\bar{p}^3 - \delta\bar{p} = 0. \tag{48}$$

This lowest (positive) root replaces the zero population, so that we now have two stable positive solutions, one small and one large, separated by one intermediate unstable root. Of course we have to take care to choose the coefficients α, β, δ so that (48) indeed has three real zeros. We can now change the variable to $\bar{p} + p \to p$ by substituting $\bar{p} + p$ in (47) and then subtracting (48). Hence

$$\dot{p} = \alpha(2\beta - 2\bar{p})p^2 - \alpha p^3 - (\delta - 4\alpha\beta\bar{p} + 3\alpha\bar{p}^2)p \tag{49}$$

which is of the same form as (13) though the coefficients are different. We can then again use the coordinate change (14) to get the equation in the form of (15). We just have to recall that the p variable everywhere now measures the *deviation* of the population size from this lowest equilibrium value.

As for diffusion the Laplacian operator is linear and $\bar{p}$ is spatially constant with zero Laplacian, so (16) still holds.

The 1985 attempt by Puu at solving this problem essentially dealt with (47), though all terms of the polynomial were one degree higher, as in the original Hotelling model. But then, of course, the analysis of travelling waves was not so easy.

7. TRAVELLING WAVES: TWO-DIMENSIONAL

Note that the travelling wave solution works equally well in two-dimensional space, and needs no alteration for the case of a wave propagating in the direction normal to some given straight line in the plane.

Suppose we try the solution $p(x\cos\theta + y\sin\theta + ct)$, where x and y are coordinates in twospace and θ is constant. We have $\nabla p = f'(\cos\theta, \sin\theta)$ and $\nabla^2 p = \nabla \cdot (f'(\cos\theta, \sin\theta)) = f''(\cos\theta, \sin\theta)^2 = f''$. Hence (16) still applies, and we have the travelling wave solution

$$p = \frac{1}{1 + \mathrm{e}^{-(x\cos\theta + y\sin\theta + ct)/\sqrt{2}}}. \tag{50}$$

More interesting possibilities arise with radial or spiral waves, a hot topic of research in chemistry, relating to the Beluosov–Zhabotinsky reaction, which is responsible for the creation of interesting spatial patterns. Things become much more complicated in those cases as the temporal velocity of propagation cannot then be a constant throughout space.

To give just a flavour of the radial case, suppose we consider travelling wave solutions of circular symmetry in 2D. If so in the style of (35) we now attempt the solution

$$p(r + ct) \quad \text{with} \quad r = \sqrt{x^2 + y^2}. \tag{51}$$

Calculating the derivatives for (17) we have

$$\dot{p} = cp' \tag{52}$$

and

$$\nabla^2 p = \nabla \cdot \nabla p = \nabla \cdot (p'\nabla r) = p''(\nabla r)^2 + p'\nabla^2 r, \tag{53}$$

where, as before, the dashes indicate the derivatives of the attempted solution function (51). From the definition $r = \sqrt{x^2 + y^2}$ and elementary vector analysis we have $(\nabla r)^2 = 1$ and $\nabla^2 r = 1/r$, so (53) can be written as

$$\nabla^2 p = p'' + \frac{1}{r}p'. \tag{54}$$

Substituting from (52) and (54) into (16), we then have

$$p'' - \left(c - \frac{1}{r}\right)p' + p(1 - p)(p - a) = 0. \tag{55}$$

Note that this is of the same form as (38). This is the case, provided we can consider the factor $(c - 1/r)$ as a constant, which is the case if we consider the situation at a certain given distance r from the origin in twospace. The argument

$$z = r + ct \tag{56}$$

can still vary due to the variation of t even when $r = \sqrt{x^2 + y^2}$ is kept fixed. Accordingly,

$$p = \frac{1}{1 + e^{-z/\sqrt{2}}} \tag{57}$$

is a travelling wave solution to (55), provided the dispersion relation:

$$c = \frac{1}{r} = \sqrt{2}(0.5 - a) \tag{58}$$

holds. We immediately see that the speed of propagation c is no longer constant throughout space. Also, when piecing together the solution from (56), (57) and (58) we see that in case the right-hand side of (58) is negative, then time affects the compound variable z through terms of opposite sign, of which one may dominate for small radii, and another for large radii

REFERENCES

Ball, P. (1999), *The Self-Made Tapestry*, Oxford: Oxford University Pres.

Beckmann, M.J. and T. Puu (1990), *Spatial Structures*, Berlin: Springer-Verlag.

Fisher, R.A. (1937), 'The wave of advance of advantageous genes', *Annals of Eugenics*, 7, 355–369.

Grindrod, P. (1996), *The Theory and Applications of Reaction-Diffusion Equations*, Oxford: Clarendon Press.

Hilborn, R.C. (1994), *Chaos and Nonlinear Dynamics*, Oxford: Oxford University Press.

Hotelling, H. (1921), 'A mathematical theory of migration', *Environment and Planning A*, 10, 1223–1239.

Jackson, E.A. (1991), *Perspectives of Nonlinear Dynamics*, Cambridge: Cambridge University Press.

Okubo, A. (1980), *Diffusion and Ecological Problems*, Berlin: Springer-Verlag.

Puu, T. (1985), 'A simplified model of spatiotemporal population dynamics', *Environment and Planning A*, 17, 1263–1269.

Volterra (1940), *Human Biology*.

14. The Optimal Control of a Stock Pollutant with Sunk Capital and Endogenous Risk of Catastrophic Damages

Urvashi Narain and Anthony Fisher

1. INTRODUCTION

In this chapter we characterize the optimal rate of emission of a pollutant whose stock poses a threat of damages of an unknown magnitude in the future, when abatement capital is sunk, the stock of pollutant is nondegradable, and there is an endogenous risk of catastrophic damages. These are features of the decision problem with regard to a number of different environmental threats. Policymakers in charge of nuclear waste management must decide whether to sink resources into building underground nuclear waste repositories or to leave the radioactive waste at the plant site where people will be exposed to low levels of radiation. This decision must take into account the fact that radioactive waste decays slowly, that there is uncertainty about whether or not exposure to low levels of radiation over a long period of time can result in radiation poisoning, and that the risk of radiation poisoning is avoidable (Makhijani 2000). Policymakers concerned with the as yet uncertain threat posed by global climate change need to decide whether to invest more heavily in abatement capital or to allow a further buildup of a stock of greenhouse gases. This decision must allow for the possibility that climate change events may lead to catastrophic damages. Finally, since anthropogenic sources are leading to the accumulation of the stock of greenhouse gases in the atmosphere, the risk posed by global climate change is endogenous. This fact too must enter the decision calculus. Similar issues arise with the management of toxic chemicals and with the control of emissions of pollutants that deplete stratospheric ozone.

Abatement capital is considered to be sunk if resources, once invested, cannot be converted to consumption or other forms of capital. The stock of pollutant is said to be nondegradable if it cannot be reduced through abatement and if it does not decay naturally. Policymakers want to avoid two situations: (i) building up a large stock of abatement capital when damages turn out to be negligible; (ii) allowing too large a buildup in the stock of a nondegradable pollutant when damages are revealed to be catastrophic. Unfortunately, the stock of pollutant cannot be reduced unless policymakers invest in abatement capital. Sunk capital and nondegradable pollutant stocks thus confront policymakers with a trade-off. A third important concern is the extent to which the risk of potentially catastrophic damages is endogenous. If the probability of damages occurring depends on the behavior of economic agents, then the risk should be considered to be endogenous. The effect of endogenous risk and the potential for catastrophic impacts on the optimal rate of emission are a major focus of our chapter.

In order to characterize the optimal rate of emission, we develop a multi-period stochastic model that incorporates the three features of the decision-making environment that we have drawn attention to – sunk capital, nondegradable stocks of pollutant, and endogenous risk of catastrophic damages. The main differences from earlier studies of the optimal control of stock pollutants are our focus on rigidities, or irreversibilities, in both investment and pollution, and the joining of these rigidities with endogenous risk of catastrophic impact. Conrad (1992) studies the effect of nondegradable pollutant stocks on the optimal rate of emissions, but his model does not include capital, the potential for catastrophic damages, or endogenous risk. Clarke and Reed (1994) consider what we have called endogenous risk, in a model of an accumulating pollutant that can trigger an irreversible environmental catastrophe, but both capital and the stock of the pollutant are assumed to be fully reversible. A similar model is developed by Aronsson et al. (1997), with catastrophic damages, endogenous risk and two types of capital – trees and production capital. However, their model does not include abatement capital or the sorts of irreversibilities we emphasize here.

Our model does not allow agents to act on new information, but nonetheless generates changes in the optimal steady-state rate of emission. Although we do find an 'irreversibility effect' (defined as a change in the optimal rate of emissions caused by capital and pollutant stock rigidities) even in the absence of learning, we recognize that a model with learning would perhaps be more realistic. Adding learning to our model, which already has two state variables, capital and the stock of pollutant, would however make the analytics intractable. In order to incorporate learning we would have to either restrict ourselves to a two-period model or to numerical simulations, as in recent contributions to the literature on control of greenhouse gases (Kolstad 1996a, 1996b, Ulph and Ulph, 1997). Although we mentioned this application earlier, our view is that the primary issue with respect to control of greenhouse gases is essentially how soon, and how stringently, to control emissions. The steady state, which may be well in the future, is probably of less concern. Elsewhere we develop a two-period analytical model and a multi-period numerical simulation model, a revised and extended version of Nordhaus' 1994 DICE model, to address the question of whether and how stringently to control greenhouse gases today and in the near future. Learning about future damages is a feature of both models.

Briefly, in the present contribution we find that with abatement capital and nondegradable pollutant stocks, an increase in the degree of capital 'sunkness' does not affect the optimal steady-state rate of investment while an increase in the degree of stock nondegradability calls for an increase in the optimal steady-state rate of investment. These results continue to hold, under certain sufficient conditions, when the risk of a catastrophe is endogenous, but not under alternative definitions for sunk abatement capital and nondegradable pollutant stocks that have been applied in the literature.

The rest of the chapter is organized as follows. The next section contains a description of the theoretical model. Section 3 considers the effect of sunk capital, and Section 4 the effect of a nondegradable pollutant stock on the optimal rate of investment. Section 5 repeats the analysis in Sections 3 and 4 with the added feature that the risk of a catastrophe is endogenous. Conclusions are presented in Section 6.

2. THEORETICAL MODEL

Agents derive utility from consumption and disutility from the stock of pollutant so long as a catastrophe does not occur. If and when a catastrophe occurs utility is driven to zero for ever.[1] Catastrophic damages are therefore irreversible; once catastrophic damages have occurred they exist forever and at the same magnitude as at the time of their occurrence. The only source of uncertainty in the model is whether or not a catastrophe will occur. The extent of catastrophic damages, should a catastrophe occur, are known in advance.

The agent receives a fixed endowment of resources in every period that she allocates between consumption and investment in capital used to abate the flow of the pollutant. Abatement capital is either convertible or sunk. Only the former can be converted back into consumption, though at a cost. If not abated, emissions, a byproduct of consumption, add to the stock of pollutant which is either degradable or nondegradable. Only degradable stocks decay naturally over time, and neither type of stock can be abated.[2] In addition to causing disutility in every period up until a catastrophe occurs, the stock of pollutant also affects the probability that a catastrophe will occur when the risk of a catastrophe is endogenous.

2.1. Primitives

Up until a catastrophe occurs, a representative agent derives utility from consumption, C, and disutility from the stock of pollutant, M. Let the momentary utility function $U = U(C, M)$ satisfy the conditions

$$U_1(C, M) > 0, \quad U_{11}(C, M) < 0, \quad U_{12}(C, M) < 0,$$
$$U_2(C, M) < 0, \quad U_{22}(C, M) < 0$$

where subscripts denote differentiation. As long as there is no catastrophe, catastrophic damages are zero and the utility function is unaffected. After a catastrophe, however, utility goes to zero forever.

A fixed amount of output, R, is available each period for either consumption or investment, I, in abatement capital. The budget constraint is thus $C + I = R$. Abatement capital, K, changes from one period to the next as a result of investment and depreciation according to

$$\dot{K} = I - \delta_K K, \tag{1}$$

where δ_K is the rate of depreciation of capital. For the base model we assume that capital is reversible. This means that at any time consumption can be greater than the fixed amount of resource R or that investment can be negative. Specifically,

$$C \leq R + \Phi K, \tag{2}$$

where Φ is a parameter that governs the cost of converting capital into consumption. When $\Phi = 0$ it is infinitely costly to convert capital into consumption and when $\Phi \geq 0$ capital can be converted into consumption, though at a cost.[3]

Emissions are a byproduct of consumption. Let $g(C)$ be the emissions function where $g_1(C) > 0$ and $g_{11}(C) = 0$. If unabated, emissions increase the stock of pollutant. Let $H(K)$ be the abatement function where $H_1(K) > 0$ and $H_{11}(K) \leq 0$. Capital abates only the flow and not the stock of pollutant, implying that the amount of pollutant abated in a period cannot exceed the amount emitted in that period. The abatement function $H(K)$ thus lies between zero and one. The stock also decays naturally. Consequently, the law of motion for the stock of pollutant is given by[4]

$$\dot{M} = g(C)\big(1 - H(K)\big) - \delta_M M, \tag{3}$$

where $g(C)(1 - H(K))$ are net emissions and δ_M is the natural decay rate of the pollutant. If the rate of decay is close to zero, then the stock of pollutant is considered to be nondegradable.

Finally, there always exists the possibility of a catastrophe occurring. The occurrence of a catastrophe is captured by a jump process as

$$\mathrm{d}D = \begin{cases} 1 & \text{with probability } p\,\mathrm{d}t, \\ 0 & \text{with probability } (1 - p\,\mathrm{d}t). \end{cases} \tag{4}$$

where D is an indicator of the catastrophe (initially $D = 0$) and p is the conditional probability for an immediate occurrence of a catastrophe. If the risk of a catastrophe is exogenous then p is a constant. With endogenous catastrophic risk the conditional probability for an immediate occurrence of a catastrophe is an increasing and convex function of the stock of pollutant. That is, $p = p(M)$ with $p_1(M) > 0$ and $p_{11}(M) > 0$.[5]

2.2. Objective

The agent chooses a stream of consumption to maximize expected intertemporal utility subject to Equations (1)–(4). The only source of uncertainty is whether or not a catastrophe will occur. The Bellman–Hamilton–Jacobi equation for this problem is

$$(r + p)V(K, M) = \max_{C \leq R + \Phi K} \big[U(C, M) + \mu_1 \dot{K} + \mu_2 \dot{M}\big], \tag{5}$$

where $V(K, M)$ is the value function, r is the discount rate, μ_1 is the co-state variable associated with the stock of abatement capital and μ_2 is the co-state variable associated with the stock of pollutant.[6]

2.3. Optimality Conditions

In this subsection we establish optimality conditions for consumption, capital, and the stock of pollutant. For now we assume that risk is exogenous and so p is a constant. We begin by differentiating Equation (5) with respect to the choice variable – consumption. This gives the following first-order condition:

$$U_1(C, M) - \lambda - \mu_1 + \mu_2 g_1(C)\big(1 - H(K)\big) = 0 \tag{6}$$

where λ is the Lagrange multiplier on the consumption constraint given by Equation (2). The co-state equations of motion, obtained by differentiating Equation (5) with respect to the state variables, K and M, are

$$\dot{\mu}_1 = \mu_1(r + \delta_K + p) - \lambda\Phi + \mu_2 g(C) H_1(K) \tag{7}$$

$$\dot{\mu}_2 = \mu_2(r + \delta_M + p) - U_2(C, M) \tag{8}$$

We are now in a position to characterize the steady state.

2.4. Steady State

Equation (6), and Equations (7) and (8) at the steady state, combine to give the Euler equation, which in turn with the steady-state laws of motion gives a system of equations that determines the steady-state level of consumption, capital, and stock of pollutant (the arguments are suppressed for compactness)

$$\begin{aligned} U_1 &= -\frac{U_2}{(r + \delta_M + p)}\left(g_1(1 - H) + \frac{gH_1}{r + \delta_K + p}\right) \\ &\quad + \lambda\left(\frac{\Phi}{(r + \delta_K + p)} + 1\right), \end{aligned} \tag{9}$$

$$K^* = \frac{R - C^*}{\delta_K}, \tag{10}$$

$$M^* = \frac{g(1 - H)}{\delta_M}, \tag{11}$$

where stars denote steady-state levels. When the constraint on consumption is not binding, $\lambda = 0$ and the Euler equation states that along the steady-state consumption trajectory there is nothing to gain by increasing consumption. Equation (10) states that at the steady state, investment is equal to capital depreciation while Equation (11) states that net emissions are equal to the decay in the steady-state stock of pollutant.

When the constraint on consumption is binding, $\lambda > 0$ and steady-state consumption is equal to $C^* = R + \Phi K^*$. Since negative investment period after period drives the steady-state capital stock to zero, steady-state consumption is in fact equal to R.

2.5. Stability of the Steady State

To analyse the stability properties of the steady state we use the necessary and sufficient conditions identified by Dockner (1985). The first step in this process is to express the necessary conditions for optimality (Equations (1), (3), (6), (7) and (8)) in terms of the state and the co-state variables only. From Equation (6) and the assumption that the second derivative of Equation (5) with respect to the control is nonzero, we can, using the implicit function theorem, express consumption as a function of the state and co-state variables. Substituting this expression into the co-state and state variables yields the necessary modified dynamic system (equations of motion for the state and the co-state variables).

By a theorem due to Lyapunov (Coddington and Levinson 1955), the stability behavior of the nonlinear dynamic system can be studied by analysing the stability properties of the first approximation of the system around the steady state. Let $J(K^*, M^*, \mu_1^*, \mu_2^*)$ denote the Jacobian matrix of the modified system, evaluated at the steady state.

$$J = \begin{bmatrix} \frac{\partial \dot{K}}{\partial K} & \frac{\partial \dot{K}}{\partial M} & \frac{\partial \dot{K}}{\partial \mu_1} & \frac{\partial \dot{K}}{\partial \mu_2} \\ \frac{\partial \dot{M}}{\partial K} & \frac{\partial \dot{M}}{\partial M} & \frac{\partial \dot{M}}{\partial \mu_1} & \frac{\partial \dot{M}}{\partial \mu_2} \\ \frac{\partial \dot{\mu}_1}{\partial K} & \frac{\partial \dot{\mu}_1}{\partial M} & \frac{\partial \dot{\mu}_1}{\partial \mu_1} & \frac{\partial \dot{\mu}_1}{\partial \mu_2} \\ \frac{\partial \dot{\mu}_2}{\partial K} & \frac{\partial \dot{\mu}_2}{\partial M} & \frac{\partial \dot{\mu}_2}{\partial \mu_1} & \frac{\partial \dot{\mu}_2}{\partial \mu_2} \end{bmatrix}. \tag{12}$$

2.5.1. *Saddle Point*

We are interested in establishing conditions under which the steady state is a saddle point. If the steady state is a saddle point then there exists a two-dimensional (local) manifold consisting of the steady state and all solutions that converge towards the steady state. This implies that given the initial stock of capital and greenhouse gases, it is possible to pick the initial co-state variables for both capital and greenhouse gases to ensure that the system converges to the steady state.

Under the assumption that $(r + p) \geq 0$, the necessary and sufficient conditions for the steady state to be a saddle point are: (i) $L < 0$; (ii) det $J > 0$; and (iii) det $J < (L/2)^2$, where

$$L = \begin{vmatrix} \frac{\partial \dot{K}}{\partial K} & \frac{\partial \dot{K}}{\partial \mu_1} \\ \frac{\partial \dot{\mu}_1}{\partial K} & \frac{\partial \dot{\mu}_1}{\partial \mu_1} \end{vmatrix} + \begin{vmatrix} \frac{\partial \dot{M}}{\partial M} & \frac{\partial \dot{M}}{\partial \mu_2} \\ \frac{\partial \dot{\mu}_2}{\partial M} & \frac{\partial \dot{\mu}_2}{\partial \mu_2} \end{vmatrix} + 2 \begin{vmatrix} \frac{\partial \dot{K}}{\partial M} & \frac{\partial \dot{K}}{\partial \mu_2} \\ \frac{\partial \dot{\mu}_1}{\partial M} & \frac{\partial \dot{\mu}_1}{\partial \mu_2} \end{vmatrix}. \tag{13}$$

Since we have a four-dimensional system, two state variables and two co-state variables, it is hard to further study these stability properties analytically. Instead, we impose functional forms for the utility, emissions, and abatement functions and analyse the stability properties numerically.[7]

2.5.2. *Functional Forms*

We assume that agents have quadratic preferences over consumption, and the stock of greenhouse gases.

$$U(C_t, M_t) = \frac{-1}{2}\left((C_t - b)^2 + M_t^2\right), \tag{14}$$

where b is the bliss point. Greenhouse gases are produced as a result of consumption with a linear technology $E_t = \sigma C_t$, where E_t denotes emissions and σ is a constant denoting the emissions to consumption ratio. Finally, the abatement function is given by

$$A_t = H(K_t) = \frac{2}{1 + \exp(-\rho K_t)} - 1, \tag{15}$$

where A_t is the amount of abatement in period t and ρ is the slope of the modified logistic function. We use a modified logistic function to limit abatement to be a fraction that lies between zero and one.

2.5.3. *Results*

We now look for parameter values that ensure that the steady state is a saddle point. The results of a five-dimensional grid search, using the parameters δ_k, δ_m, σ, ρ and p, are summarized in Figure 14.1. The stars signify parameter values for which the steady state is a saddle point. The maximum and minimum values for each of these parameters over which the search was conducted are given in Table 14.1.[8] Each of these subplots hold irrespective of the value of p.

The first subplot shows that for low values of the rate of capital depreciation, δ_k, and capital productivity, ρ, if the rate of decay of greenhouse

Table 14.1. Parameter values used for saddle point search

Parameter	Minimum Value	Maximum Value
δ_k	0.1	0.9
δ_m	0.01	0.5
σ	0.5	5
ρ	0.1	0.9
p	0.002	0.02

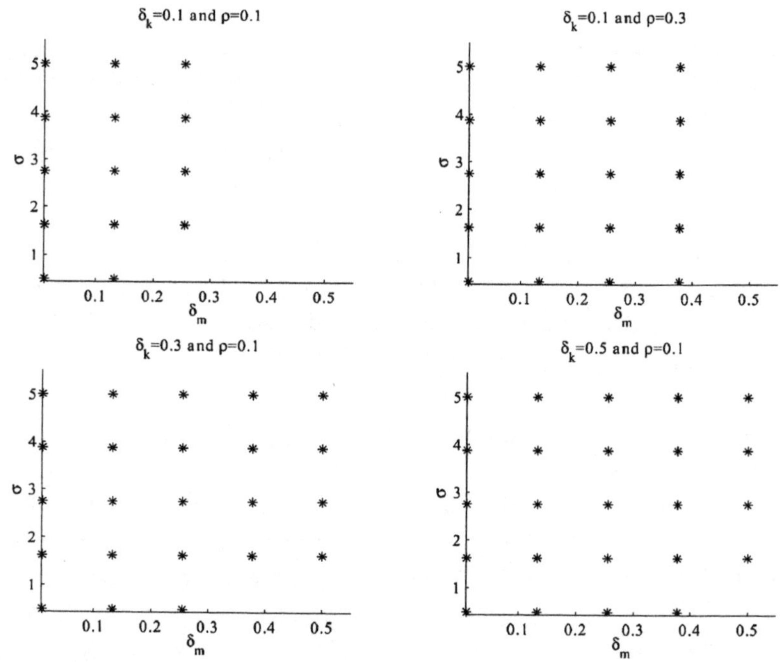

Figure 14.1. Parameter values for saddle point steady state

gases is high (between 0.3 and 0.5), then, irrespective of the value of the emission to consumption ratio, the steady state is not a saddle point. Increasing capital productivity, moving from subplot 1 to subplot 2, gives the result that higher values of the rate of decay now support a saddle point. If the rate of capital depreciation is increased instead, say moving from subplot 1 to either subplot 3 or 4, still larger values of the rate of decay support a saddle point. Consequently, the higher the values of δ_k, σ and ρ and the lower the value of δ_m, the more likely is the steady state to be a saddle point.

2.5.4. *Monotonicity*

If the steady state is a saddle point then it is easy to show that the state variables, K and M, evolve monotonically. For this we first restrict ourselves to the state plane of the linearized stable manifold, that is, to the submatrix of the Jacobian J

$$J_s = \begin{bmatrix} \frac{\partial \dot{K}}{\partial K} & \frac{\partial \dot{K}}{\partial M} \\ \frac{\partial \dot{M}}{\partial K} & \frac{\partial \dot{M}}{\partial M} \end{bmatrix}. \tag{16}$$

For the analytical model described in this section, the J_s matrix is given by (the arguments are suppressed),

$$J_s = \begin{bmatrix} -\frac{U_2 H_1 g_1}{U_{11}(r+p+\delta_m)} - \delta_k & \frac{U_{12}}{U_{11}} \\ \frac{(1-H) g_1^2 U_2 H_1}{U_{11}(r+p+\delta_m)} - g H_1 & -\frac{(1-H) g_1 U_{12}}{U_{11}} - \delta_m \end{bmatrix}. \tag{17}$$

The trace of this matrix is negative, its determinant is positive and its discriminant is positive. This implies that the related phase-plane diagram is characterized by an improper stable node. Thus the optimal trajectory is locally monotonic (Dockner 1985).

3. SUNK CAPITAL

In this section we explore the implications of capital being sunk. We find that these are weaker under our suggested definition than they are under an alternative definition employed in related literature.

3.1. Defining Sunk Capital

One possible definition of sunk capital is that capital is sunk if it is durable, that is, if it has a low rate of depreciation (Kolstad 1996a, 1996b). In our judgment this definition fails to capture the essential problem faced by policymakers, who we assume wish to avoid a situation where resources invested in abatement capital cannot be converted back into some productive use in the future, or into consumption, if damages turn out to be negligible. What matters is the cost of conversion, not depreciation.

Durable capital may still have a low conversion cost. We therefore prefer to define sunk capital as capital that is prohibitively costly to convert into consumption.[9] Or, capital is considered to be sunk if investment is constrained to be positive in every period.

3.2. Positive Investment

We now show that, under our definition, a decrease in capital convertibility has no effect on the optimal steady-state rate of investment. We capture convertibility through the parameter Φ, with an increase in Φ implying greater convertibility. Capital is perfectly sunk when $\Phi = 0$.

The parameter Φ enters the steady-state system of equations only as part of the coefficient on the consumption multiplier, λ. This implies that if the constraint on consumption is not binding then Φ does not affect the steady-state level of consumption or investment. The constraint on consumption is less likely to bind the greater is the disutility associated with the stock of pollutant because agents will want to undertake investment to reduce the disutility from the stock of pollutant.

In fact, this result holds even when the constraint on consumption is binding at the steady state. Recall that when the constraint binds, the steady-state level of consumption is in fact equal to R and is thus independent of Φ. Out of steady state and when the consumption constraint binds, Φ may have an effect on the rate of consumption. So long as $\Phi > 0$, agents will drive the inherited capital stock to zero very quickly. The level of investment, while the system is out of steady state, remains independent of the level of Φ at zero. Out of steady state, the level of consumption (and thus emissions) however now depends on Φ. This is because the level of Φ determines how much consumption can be had from a given amount of capital. When the consumption constraint binds and $\Phi = 0$, agents have no option but to wait for capital depreciation to drive the stock of capital to zero. Once again, there is no effect on the level of investment out of steady state. Even the level of consumption out of steady state is unaffected. Capital cannot add to consumption since it is perfectly sunk.

Simulations based on a simple parameterization of the model presented in Section 2 help illustrate these results.[10] The first subplot in Figure 14.2 shows that when the initial stock of abatement capital is low, the ratio of consumption under convertible capital to consumption under sunk capital is one during the transition to and at the steady state. However, if the initial stock of capital is high then consumption is at first higher and then lower under convertible capital as compared to consumption under sunk capital

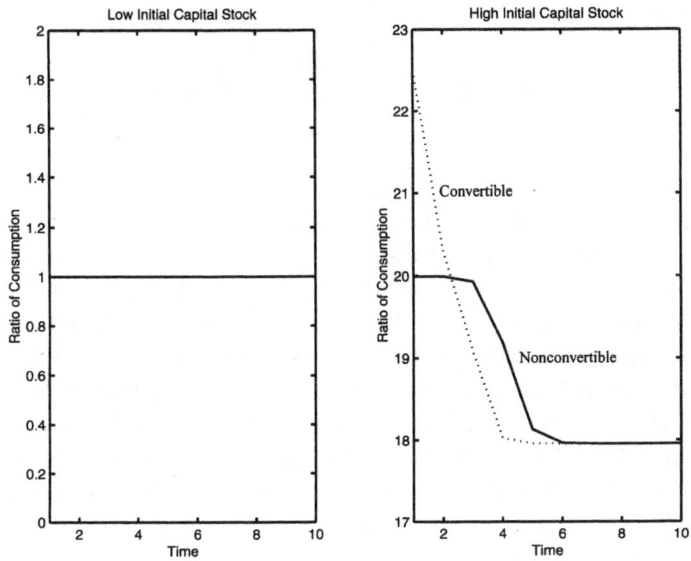

Figure 14.2. Consumption paths for convertible and nonconvertible stocks of capital with exogenous risk

(see subplot 2 of Figure 14.2). This is because consumption is constrained to be less than or equal to R (for the simulations $R = 20$) when capital is perfectly sunk. The steady-state level of consumption is the same for both types of capital. That said, the first subplot is usually more reflective of the policy environment facing the policymaker. Rarely does the policymaker have to worry about there being too much abatement capital.

3.3. Durable Capital

We now explore the impact of durable capital on the optimal rate of investment. We begin by writing the Euler equation, Equation (9), as a function of steady-state consumption and system parameters (steady-state capital and stock of pollutant gases are both functions of steady-state consumption and system parameters from Equations (10) and (11), respectively).[11] With this simplification the effect of a change in the degree of durability of capital on consumption is given by differentiating the Euler equation with respect to the rate of depreciation. The result is formalized in the following proposition.[12]

PROPOSITION 1. *If*

$$-H_{11}(K^*)\frac{K^*}{H_1(K^*)} \geq \frac{\delta_K}{(r+\delta_k+p)},$$

then $dC^*d\delta_K < 0$.

In words the proposition states that steady-state consumption will increase (and steady-state investment will decrease) as capital becomes more durable if the gain from the increase in capital, caused by the decline in the rate of depreciation, is greater than the loss caused by the decline in the marginal product of capital. This result is fairly straightforward since the presence of durable capital reduces the need for new investment.

The effect of capital becoming more durable on steady-state stocks of capital and the stock of pollutant is ambiguous. Consequently, the effect on the optimal rate of net emissions, $g(C^*)(1 - H(K^*))$, of a change in the durability of capital is unknown.

4. NONDEGRADABLE POLLUTANT STOCK

We next explore whether or not there is a change in the optimal rate of investment associated with a change in the degree of degradability of the pollutant stock. We find that the effect is stronger under our preferred definition of nondegradablility than under definitions employed in the literature.

4.1. Defining Nondegradable Stock

We require a near-zero decay rate and capital to abate only the flow of emissions for the stock of gases to be considered nondegradable. If the stock decays or if emissions are permitted to be negative, then the stock will dissipate over time and cannot be considered nondegradable. Conrad (1992) defines a nondegradable pollutant stock as one that has a near-zero decay rate but since his model does not allow for abatement he does not impose the additional requirement that capital abate only the flow of emissions. Kolstad (1996a) and Ulph and Ulph (1997) define a nondegradable stock of greenhouse gases as one where emissions are restricted to be nonnegative and place no restriction on the rate of decay. Since Clarke and Reed (1994) and Aronsson et al. (1997) do not consider stock irreversibilities, they do not define nondegradable pollutant stocks.

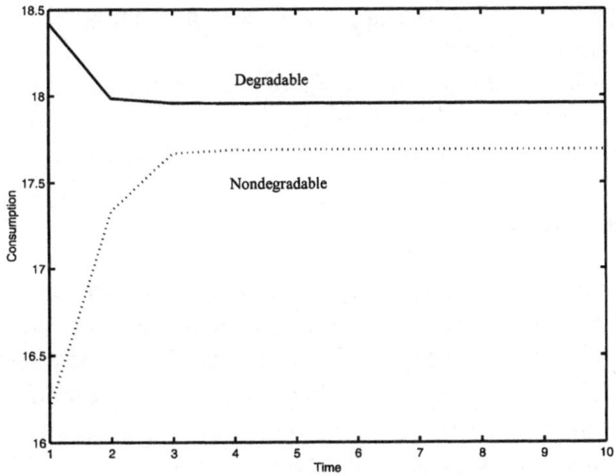

Figure 14.3. Consumption paths for degradable and nondegradable pollutant stocks with exogenous risk

4.2. Rate of Decay

We capture nondegradability of the stock of pollutant through the parameter δ_m with a decline in δ_m implying an increase in stock nondegradability. The effect, then, of a change in the degree of stock nondegradability can be studied by differentiating the Euler equation (expressed in terms of consumption and system parameters) with respect to the rate of decay. This yields the following proposition:

PROPOSITION 2. *Steady-state consumption is an increasing function of the rate of decay of the stock pollutant.*

As the stock of pollutant becomes nondegradable, consumption decreases while investment in abatement capital increases. A lower rate of decay implies that any emissions that are released into the atmosphere remain for a longer period of time. This in turn implies that agents have to incur the disutility of these emissions for a longer period. Agents thus choose to reduce consumption, the source of these emissions, and increase investment to reduce the stock of pollutant.

Figure 14.3 illustrates this result. The rate of decay is higher for the solid line and lower for the dotted line, though for both curves the rate of decay is positive. For our simulation model, under nondegradable pollutant stocks, not only is the steady-state level of consumption lower, but so is consumption along the approach path, as compared to that under degradable pollutant stocks.

Along with investment the stock of capital increases and the level of net emissions decreases. However, the effect of an increase in the nondegradability on the stock of pollutant itself is ambiguous.

4.3. Nonnegative Emissions

If instead stock nondegradability is defined in terms of nonnegative emissions with no restriction on the rate of decay, then an increase in nondegradability has no effect on the steady-state level of consumption or investment. The constraint on emissions simply does not bind at the steady state. This can be seen from the following equation for the steady-state stock of pollutant (assuming an interior solution):

$$M^* = \frac{g(C^*)(1 - H(K^*))}{\delta_M} \geq 0. \tag{18}$$

The steady stock of pollutant is restricted to be nonnegative which in turn implies that steady-state emissions will be nonnegative (positive if the stock is positive and zero if the stock is zero). The constraint on emissions simply does not bind. A change in the degree of degradability does not affect steady-state consumption or investment.

If agents choose to reduce the stock of pollutant to zero and want to do so quickly, then in the transition to steady state the nonnegativity constraint will bind. This situation will also arise when agents inherit a large stock of pollutant and want to reduce the stock quickly. In both these situations agents will prefer to emit negative amounts of the stock to reduce the stock as fast as possible. This will not be possible if the stock is nondegradable. Consequently, stock nondegradability may have an effect away from the steady state. However, for this effect to hold it must be true that a drastic reduction of the stock is optimal or that agents begin with a large endowment of the stock of pollutant.

5. ENDOGENOUS RISK

If it is true that the probability of catastrophe is increased with an increase in the stock of pollutant, then the threat can be mitigated by reducing the stock, that is, by economic agents changing their behavior. In other words, the risk of a catastrophe is endogenous. We now explore the implications of adding endogenous risk to the model.

5.1. Optimality Conditions

As with exogenous risk, we begin by differentiating equation (5) with respect to the choice variable – consumption. This gives the first-order condition

$$U_1(C, M) - \lambda - \mu_1 + \mu_2 g_1(C)(1 - H(K)) = 0. \qquad (19)$$

The equations of motion for the co-state equations, obtained by differentiating Equation (5) with respect to the state variables, K and M, are

$$\dot{\mu}_1 = \mu_1\big(r + \delta_K + p(M)\big) - \lambda\Phi + \mu_2 g(C) H_1(K), \qquad (20)$$

$$\dot{\mu}_2 = \mu_2\big(r + \delta_M + p(M)\big) - U_2(C, M) - V(K, M) p_1(M). \qquad (21)$$

To allow for endogenous risk, the conditional probability for an immediate occurrence of the catastrophe, p, is now a function of the stock of pollutant.

5.2. Steady State

Since Equation (21) contains $V(K, M)$, to obtain the Euler equation we need an additional equation that relates the value function to the primitives of the economy. This additional equation is obtained by evaluating the Bellman–Hamilton–Jacobi equation, Equation (5), at the steady state.

$$(r + p(M))\, V(K, M) = U(C, M) + \lambda(R + \Phi K - C). \qquad (22)$$

Now Equations (19) and (22), and Equations (20) and (21), evaluated at the steady state, combine to give the Euler equation, which in turn with the steady-state laws of motion gives a system of equations that determine the steady-state level of consumption, capital, and stock of pollutant.

$$U_1 = \frac{(U + \lambda(R + \Phi K - C))\, p_1 - (r + p) U_2}{(r + p)(r + \delta_M + p)} \times \left(g_1(1 - H) + \frac{g H_1}{(r + \delta_K + p)}\right) + \\ + \lambda\left(\frac{\Phi}{(r + \delta_K + p)} + 1\right), \qquad (23)$$

Table 14.2. Parameter values used for saddle point search

Parameter	Minimum Value	Maximum Value
δ_k	0.1	0.5
δ_m	0.05	0.3
σ	0.5	5
ρ	0.01	0.05
ω	0.0001	0.0005

$$K^* = \frac{R - C^*}{\delta_K}, \tag{24}$$

$$M^* = \frac{g(1 - H)}{\delta_M}. \tag{25}$$

When $\lambda = 0$ (the constraint on consumption is not binding) the Euler equation states that, along the optimal consumption path, net utility from an increase in consumption is zero. Equations (24) and (25) give arbitrage conditions for optimal stocks of capital and the pollutant. When the consumption constraint is binding ($\lambda > 0$), steady-state consumption is once again equal to R.

5.3. Saddle Point

Once again we use the necessary and sufficient conditions outlined by Dockner (1985) to establish the conditions for the steady state to be a saddle point. The complexity of the dynamic system limits us to a numerical analysis. Before we do that we specify one additional functional form for the probability of catastrophe function.

5.3.1. *Functional Forms*

The probability function is assumed to be the modified logistic function

$$p_t = \frac{2}{(1 + \exp(-\omega M_t))} - 1, \tag{26}$$

where ω is a parameter that captures the sensitivity of p_t to the stock of greenhouse gases. The modified logistic restricts p_t to lie between zero and one.

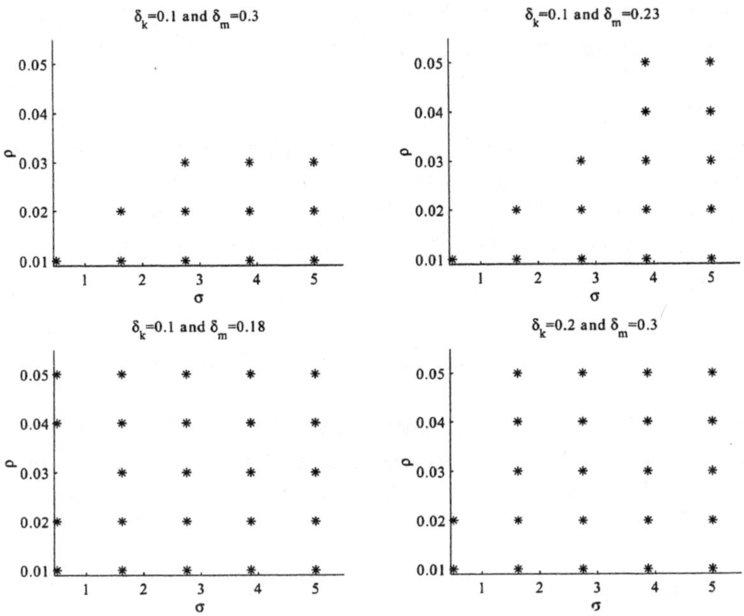

Figure 14.4. Parameter values for saddle point steady state

5.3.2. *Results*

We now look for parameter values that ensure that the steady state is a saddle point. The results of a five-dimensional grid search, using the parameters δ_k, δ_m, σ, ρ, and ω, are summarized in Figure 14.4. The maximum and minimum values for each of these parameters over which the search was conducted are given in Table 14.2.[13] Each of these subplots hold irrespective of the value of ω and the stars signify parameter values for which the steady state is a saddle point.

The first subplot shows that for a low value of the rate of capital depreciation, δ_k, and a high value for the rate of decay of greenhouse gases, δ_m, if the parameter affecting capital productivity, ρ, is high (between 0.03 and 0.05), then, for most values of the emission to consumption ratio, σ, the steady state is not a saddle point. Increasing the rate of capital depreciation, moving from subplot 1 to subplot 4, gives the result that higher values of ρ now support a saddle point. If the rate of decay of greenhouse gases is decreased instead, say moving from subplot 1 to either subplot 2 or 3, still larger values of ρ support support a saddle point. Consequently, the higher the values of δ_k and σ, and the lower the values of δ_m and ρ, the more likely is the steady state to be a saddle point.

5.3.3. *Monotonicity*

Having established that the steady state is a saddle point we now show that the state variables, K and M, evolve monotonically. As was done in Section 2.5.4, we establish monotonicity by looking at the trace, determinant, and discriminant of the submatrix of the Jacobian, specifically at

$$J_s = \begin{bmatrix} -\frac{\mu_2^* H_1 g_1}{U_{11}} - \delta_k & \frac{U_{12}}{U_{11}} \\ \frac{(1-H) g_1^2 \mu_2^* H_1}{U_{11}} - g H_1 & -\frac{(1-H) g_1 U_{12}}{U_{11}} - \delta_m \end{bmatrix}. \tag{27}$$

The trace of this matrix is negative and its determinant and discriminant are both positive. This implies that the related phase-plane diagram is characterized by an improper stable node and that the optimal trajectory is locally monotonic.

5.4. Positive Investment

With or without a binding constraint on consumption, Φ, the parameter governing the cost of converting capital to consumption, does not affect steady state consumption, capital, or stock of pollutant. Away from the steady state too, Φ does not affect investment decisions. If agents choose to consume all their endowment and devote nothing to investment then they will run down the capital stock at a rate dictated by Φ (quickly if Φ is high and slowly if Φ is low). However, Φ does not affect an agent's decision to invest nothing and consume all. As with exogenous risk, the degree of convertibility of abatement capital does not affect decisions to consume or emit the pollutant.

Figure 14.5 illustrates this result. The ratio of consumption under a convertible stock of abatement capital to consumption under a sunk stock is one. For our numerical model, at the steady state and away from it, a change in the degree of convertibility of capital does not affect the level of consumption or investment.

5.5. Durable Capital

Now let us consider the case where risk is endogenous and the rate of depreciation is used to capture capital convertibility. Once again steady-state capital can be expressed as a linearly decreasing function of steady-state

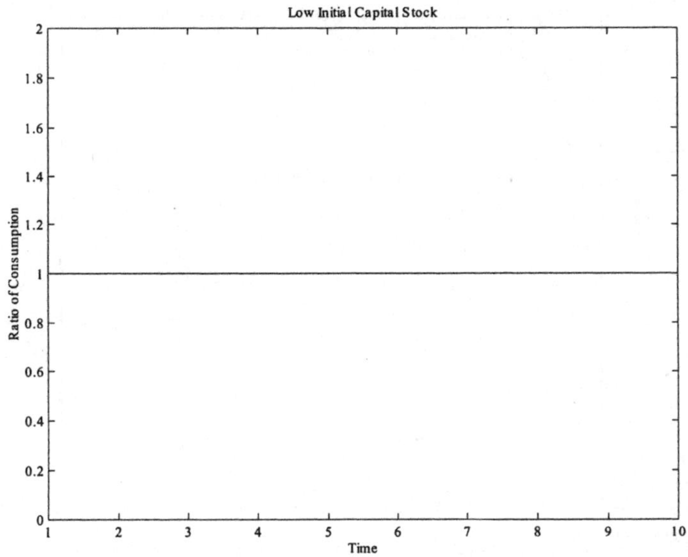

Figure 14.5. Consumption paths for convertible and sunk stocks of capital with endogenous risk

consumption, Equation (24), and the steady-state stock of the pollutant as an increasing function, Equation (25). This in turn implies that we can write the steady-state Euler equation as a function of steady-state consumption and some parameters.

To analyse the effect on the optimal rate of consumption of a change in the degree of durability of capital, we differentiate the Euler equation, Equation (23), with respect to the rate of depreciation. The differentiation yields a complicated expression with an ambiguous sign. Adding endogenous risk thus dilutes the result that durable capital leads to a decrease in investment. Individuals may choose to increase investment in order to reduce the risk of the catastrophe. This counters the need to decrease investment as capital becomes more durable. Models that do not account for endogenous risk will find a stronger effect of durable capital on the optimal rate of emissions.

5.6. Decay Rate

Now let us consider how consumption at the steady state changes with a change in the degree of degradability of the stock of pollutant. This result

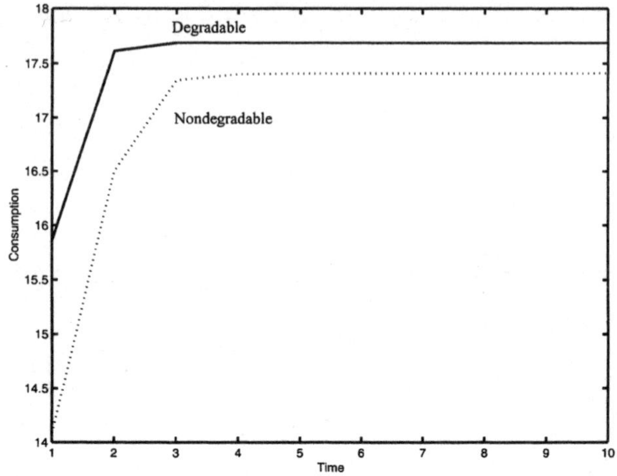

Figure 14.6. Consumption paths for degradable and nondegradable stocks of pollutant with endogenous risk

is obtained by differentiating the Euler equation with respect to the rate of decay of the pollutant stock.

PROPOSITION 3. *If*

$$\frac{-\partial p}{\partial M}\frac{\partial M}{\partial \delta_M}\left(\frac{(r+\delta_M+p)}{(r+\delta_K+p)}+\frac{(2r+2p+\delta_M)}{(r+p)}\right)<1,$$

then $\mathrm{d}C^*/\mathrm{d}\delta_M > 0$.

In words, as the stock of pollutant become nondegradable, consumption decreases while investment increases if a reduction in the rate of decay leads to a relatively small increase in the conditional probability of a catastrophe. Consequently, an increase in the degree of degradability of the stock of pollutant lowers consumption when the risk is endogenous so long as the increase in nondegradability does not cause a large increase in the conditional probability of catastrophe. If risk does increase rapidly, then it may be optimal to increase consumption today rather than wait for a tomorrow that may never come.

Figure 14.6 illustrates that a change in the degree of stock degradability can affect the level of consumption at, as well as away from, the steady state. The solid line corresponds to a higher rate of decay while the dotted line to a lower rate of decay. An increase in the degree of nondegradability decreases the amount of resources devoted to consumption and thereby increases the amount devoted to investment.

5.7. Nonnegative Emissions

Once again the nonnegativity constraint does not bind at the steady state or during the transition to the steady state unless the agents begin with a large stock of pollutant that they want to reduce drastically. Consequently, defining nondegradability of the stock of pollutant in terms of nonnegative emissions weakens the effect of the stock of pollutant on the optimal rate of emissions.

6. CONCLUSIONS

We have shown that under our definitions of sunk abatement capital and a nondegradable stock of pollutant, a decrease in the degree of capital convertibility has no impact on the optimal steady-state rate of investment while an increase in the degree of pollutant stock nondegradability leads to an increase in the optimal steady-state rate of investment. These results hold even when the conditional probability for an immediate occurrence of a catastrophe is endogenous, though under sufficient conditions. The upshot of these results is that for an environmental problem characterized by sunk abatement capital, nondegradable pollutant stocks, and endogenous risk of catastrophic damages, the optimal steady-state rate of investment in abatement capital is increased.

With different definitions of sunk abatement capital and nondegradable stocks of pollutant, as we show, the policymaker would come to a different conclusion. When sunk capital is equivalent to durable capital, an increase in durability leads to a decrease in the optimal steady-state level of investment. On the other hand, when pollutant stock nondegradability is captured by a nonnegativity restriction on emissions then an increase in the degree of stock nondegradability has no effect on the optimal steady-state rate of investment. A policymaker using these alternative definitions and faced with sunk capital, nondegradable pollutant stocks, and potentially catastrophic damages would decrease steady-state investment. This result is opposite to the one we reach with the definitions that we have argued better reflect both physical realities and the decision-making environment. Adding endogenous risk corrects for some of the bias introduced by the alternative definitions, but these can still give misleading results.

APPENDIX A. DERIVATION OF THE BELLMAN–HAMILTON–JACOBI EQUATION

An agent chooses a stream of consumption to maximize expected intertemporal utility subject to Equations (1)–(4).

$$\max_C E_t \int_t^\infty S(C, M, D, \tau)\, \mathrm{d}\tau,$$

where $S(C, M, D, t)$ is the momentary utility function. Let $J(K, M, D, t)$ denote the corresponding value function. To derive the appropriate Bellman–Hamilton–Jacobi equation we begin by breaking up the dynamic program into two parts[14]

$$J(K, M, D, t) = \max_C E_t \left[\int_t^{t+\mathrm{d}t} S(C, M, D, \tau)\, \mathrm{d}\tau + \int_{t+\mathrm{d}t}^\infty S(C, M, D, \tau)\, \mathrm{d}\tau \right]. \quad (28)$$

Since

$$E_{t+\mathrm{d}t} \int_{t+\mathrm{d}t}^\infty S(C, M, D, \tau)\, \mathrm{d}\tau = E_{t+\mathrm{d}t} J(K+\mathrm{d}K, M+\mathrm{d}M, D+\mathrm{d}D, t+\mathrm{d}t),$$

Equation (28) simplifies to

$$J(K, M, D, t) = \max_C \Big[S(C, M, D, t)\, \mathrm{d}t + J(K + \mathrm{d}K, M + \mathrm{d}M, D + a, t + \mathrm{d}t) p\, \mathrm{d}t + $$
$$+ J(K + \mathrm{d}K, M + \mathrm{d}M, D, t + \mathrm{d}t)(1 - p\, \mathrm{d}t) \Big]. \quad (29)$$

Next we take a first-order Taylor series expansion of the last two terms on the right-hand side of Equation (29) around $\mathrm{d}t = 0$. This gives the following expression:

$$J(K, M, D, t) = \max_C \Big[S(C, M, D, t)\, \mathrm{d}t + J(K, M, D + a, t) p\, \mathrm{d}t + J(K, M, D, t) +$$
$$+ J_1(K, M, D, t)(R - C - \delta_K K)\, \mathrm{d}t +$$
$$+ J_2(K, M, D, t)\big(g(C)(1 - H(K)) - \delta_M M\big)\, \mathrm{d}t +$$
$$+ J_4(K, M, D, t)\, \mathrm{d}t - J(K, M, D, t) p\, \mathrm{d}t + \text{h.o.t.} \Big],$$

where $J_1(K, M, D, t)$ is the derivative of the value function with respect to its first argument. $J_2(K, M, D, t)$ and $J_4(K, M, D, t)$ are similarly defined and h.o.t. denotes higher-order terms in the Taylor expansion.[15] Subtracting $J(K, M, D, t)$ from both sides, dividing through by $\mathrm{d}t$ and letting $\mathrm{d}t$ approach zero with the added assumption that $\lim_{\mathrm{d}t\to 0}(\text{h.o.t.}/\mathrm{d}t) = 0$ gives

$$\begin{aligned} 0 = \max_C \Big[& S(C, M, D, t) + \big(J(K, M, D + a, t) - J(K, M, D, t)\big)p + \\ & + J_1(K, M, D, t)(R - C - \delta_K K) + \\ & + J_2(K, M, D, t)\big(g(C)(1 - H(K)) - \delta_M M\big) + \\ & + J_4(K, M, D, t)\Big]. \end{aligned} \tag{30}$$

For the autonomous problem the value function $J(K, M, D, t)$ can be written as $\mathrm{e}^{-rt}W(K, M, D)$. Making this substitution into Equation (30) and multiplying through by e^{rt} gives the following version of the Bellman–Hamilton–Jacobi equation

$$\begin{aligned} & rW(K, M, D) = \\ & \max_C \Big[S(C, M, D) + \big(W(K, M, D + a) - W(K, M, D)\big)p + \\ & \quad + W_1(K, M, D)(R - C - \delta_K K) + \\ & \quad + W_2(K, M, D)\big(g(C)(1 - H(K)) - \delta_M M\big)\Big]. \end{aligned}$$

Up until the time when the catastrophe occurs $D = 0$ and once the catastrophe has occurred utility goes to zero forever, or that, $W(K, M, a) = 0$. With these and the final simplification that $W(K, M, 0) = V(K, M)$ and $S(C, M, D) = U(C, M)$ the Bellman–Hamilton–Jacobi equation can be written as

$$\begin{aligned} & rV(K, M) = \\ & \max_C \Big[U(C, M) + V_1(K, M)(R - C - \delta_K K) + \\ & \quad + V_2(K, M)\big(g(C)(1 - H(K)) - \delta_M M\big) - V(K, M)p\Big]. \end{aligned}$$

APPENDIX B. PROOFS FOR PROPOSITIONS AND COROLLARIES

B.1. Proof of Proposition 1

Differentiating the Euler equation with respect to δ_K yields the condition that

$$\frac{\mathrm{d}C^*}{\mathrm{d}\delta_K} < 0 \quad \text{if} \quad -H_{11}(K^*)\frac{K^*}{H_1(K^*)} \geq \frac{\delta_K}{(r + \delta_K + p)}.$$

B.2. Proof of Proposition 2

Differentiate Equation (9) with respect to δ_M. This gives the result that $\mathrm{d}C^*/\mathrm{d}\delta_M > 0$.

B.3. Proof of Proposition 3

Differentiate Equation (23) with respect to δ_M. This expression is omitted here because of its complexity. Its denominator is negative while its numerator is negative if

$$\frac{-\partial p}{\partial M}\frac{\partial M}{\partial \delta_M}\left(\frac{(r + \delta_M + p)}{(r + \delta_K + p)} + \frac{(2r + 2p + \delta_M)}{(r + p)}\right) < 1.$$

ACKNOWLEDGEMENTS

We are grateful to Larry Karp and Hossein Farzin for suggestions and comments on earlier drafts.

NOTES

1. The assumption that the catastrophe drives utility to zero does not significantly affect our results. Any constant, nonzero level of utility could be substituted instead with no effect on results. We can show that a weaker, and perhaps more plausible, assumption, that utility after the catastrophe is a concave function of the levels of the stock of abatement capital and the stock of pollutant at the time of the catastrophe, leads to a similar (though a bit messier) result. For simplicity of exposition we use the assumption of zero utility.

2. We do not allow the stock of pollutant to be abated in order to simplify our analysis. This assumption allows us to move from a model where the stock of pollutant is degradable to one where the stock is nondegradable by simply changing the rate of decay of the stock of pollutant. In the absence of this assumption we would have to introduce a different equation of motion for degradable stock of pollutant and thus a new set of optimality conditions. Our results are not affected by this simplification.
3. Our representation of sunk capital assumes symmetric but increasing adjustment costs. Irrespective of whether investment is positive or negative a unit of investment can be exchanged for a unit of consumption. This implies that adjustment costs are symmetric. However, depending on the magnitude of Φ adjustment costs are low when a small amount of capital is converted into consumption and infinitely large as the amount converted increases. An alternative formulation would be to have asymmetric but constant adjustment costs. Asymmetric adjustment costs imply that when investment is positive a unit of consumption can be exchanged for a unit of investment and when investment is negative a unit of investment gives less than a unit of consumption. However, irrespective of the quantity of capital converted into consumption, the adjustment costs remain constant. We feel both formulations are valid representations of sunk capital. We have chosen to use the former for its mathematical tractability.
4. By restricting the decay rate to be a linear function of the stock of pollutant we are in fact assuming that there is a unique steady state for the stock of pollutant. See Tahvonen and Salo (1996) for a discussion of multiple steady states with nonconvex decay functions.
5. Tsur and Zemel (1996) consider the effect of a different type of catastrophic risk on the optimal rate of emissions. In their model uncertainty stems from not knowing what is the exact level of stock needed to trigger a catastrophe. They call this risk endogenous and contrast it with the stochastic process we consider which they refer to as an exogenous risk. We consider a situation where there is a lag between stock buildup and the time when the effects of that level of stock are felt. Consequently, we believe that modeling the risk as a stochastic process is appropriate.
6. μ_1 is in fact equal to $V_1(K, M)$ while $\mu_2 = V_2(K, M)$. The derivation of the Bellman–Hamilton–Jacobi equation is given in Appendix A.
7. With the added assumption that $U_{12}(C, M) = 0$, the first two necessary and sufficient conditions for a saddle point can in fact be established analytically. It is hard to establish condition (iii) and for this reason we move to a numerical analysis.
8. The other parameters used in the simulations took on the following values: (i) $r = 0.03$; (ii) $R = 20$; and (iii) $b = 50$.
9. Pindyck (1991) defines capital to be sunk if it cannot be used productively by a different industry. To avoid having to add another state variable we define nonconvertibility in terms of the ability to switch between capital and consumption. Otherwise our definition matches that of Pindyck.
10. The details of the simulation model and the Matlab code used for the simulation are available from the authors.
11. We consider only an interior solution.
12. Proofs for all the propositions are in Appendix B.
13. The other parameters used in the simulations took on the following values: (i) $r = 0.03$; (ii) $R = 20$; and (iii) $b = 50$.

14. This derivation draws heavily on Mangel (1985) and Karp (1997).
15. Note that because damages take on integer values we do not differentiate the value function with respect to damages.

REFERENCES

Aronsson, T., P.-O. Johansson and K.-G. Löfgren (1997), *Welfare Measurement, Sustainability and Green National Accounting: A Growth Theoretical Approach*, Cheltenham, UK and Lyme, USA: Edward Elgar.

Clarke, H.R. and W.J. Reed (1994), 'Consumption/pollution tradeoffs in an environment vulnerable to pollution-related catastrophic collapse', *Journal of Economic Dynamics and Control*, 18, 991–1010.

Coddington, E.A. and N. Levinson (1955), *Theory of Ordinary Differential Equations*, New York: McGraw-Hill.

Conrad, J.M. (1992), 'Stopping rules and the control of stock pollutants', *Natural Resource Modeling*, 6(3), 315–327.

Dockner, E. (1985), 'Local stability analysis in optimal control problems with two state variables', in G. Feichtinger (ed.), *Optimal Control Theory and Economic Analysis*, Vol. 2, Amsterdam: Elsevier Science Publishers (North Holland), pp. 89–103.

Karp, L. (1997), 'Methods of dynamic analysis and control', Class Notes, Department of Agricultural and Resource Economics, University of California, Berkeley.

Kolstad, C.D. (1996a), 'Learning and stock effects in environmental regulations: The case of greenhouse gas emissions', *Journal of Environmental Economics and Management*, 31, 1–18.

Kolstad, C.D. (1996b), 'Fundamental irreversibilities in stock externalities', *Journal of Public Economics*, 60, 221–233.

Makhijani, A. (2000), 'Decommissioned but dangerous? The nuclear industry starts a difficult new chapter', *The Washington Post*.

Mangel, M. (1985), *Decision and Control in Uncertain Resource Systems*, New York: Academic Press.

Nordhaus, W.D. (1994), *Managing the Global Commons: The Economics of Climate Change*, Cambridge, MA: MIT Press.

Pindyck, R.S. (1991), 'Irreversibility, uncertainty, and investment', *Journal of Economic Literature*, 29, 1110–1148.

Tahvonen, O. and S. Salo (1996), 'Nonconvexities in optimal pollution accumulation', *Journal of Environmental Economics and Management*, 31, 160–177.

Tsur, Y. and A. Zemel (1996), 'Accounting for global warming risks: Resource management under event uncertainty', *Journal of Economic Dynamics and Control*, 20, 1289–1305.

Ulph, A. and D. Ulph (1997), 'Global warming, irreversibility and learning', *The Economic Journal*, 107, 636–650.

15. Environmental Performance in Swedish Manufacturing, 1913–1990

Bert M. Balk, Runar Brännlund, Rolf Färe, Shawna Grosskopf and Magnus Lindmark

1. INTRODUCTION

The purpose of this study is to investigate how environmental performance in the Swedish manufacturing sector has evolved in a historical perspective, and how this is related to economic development in Sweden. The issue in this study is closely related to the discussion about the possibility of an Environmental Kuznets Curve (EKC).

The contribution of this chapter is twofold; first, we derive an indicator based in axiomatic production theory that can be used to measure environmental performance. Second, we apply our performance measure to a historical data set including input/output data for eight Swedish manufacturing sectors over the period 1913–1990. The data set is unique in the sense that it includes not only 'good' outputs, but also 'bad' outputs in the form of emissions of CO_2 and SO_2.

The relationship between environmental performance and economic development has been the subject of discussion for a long time. Usually the discussion is focused on the relation between emissions of various pollutants and economic growth. One line of argument, the Malthusian view, has been that economic growth inevitably leads to more emissions and ultimately degradation of the natural environment (Meadows et al. 1972, 1992). Another line of argument, the neo-classical view, is that economic growth is necessary for improving the environment. This latter argument can be found in, for example, Grossman and Krueger (1991, 1995), and in a report from the World Bank (1992). The basic argument is that the Malthusian view does not take proper account of the market mechanism. That is, as resource scarcity increases with growth, incentives to find substitutes will also increase. In Grossman and Krueger (1991, 1995) and the

World Bank Report it was shown that for some emissions there appears to be an inverted U-shaped relationship between emissions and income. Countries with relatively low income appear to have relatively low emissions, middle income countries have relatively high emissions, while high income countries tend to have relatively low emissions. Thus the conclusion would be that as a poor country gets richer, emissions rise. However, when income passes a certain critical level emissions starts to fall. This inverted U-shaped relationship between emissions and income has been dubbed the Environmental Kuznets Curve (EKC).

The discovery of this potential relationship triggered substantial research efforts in this area, theoretical as well as empirical. The theoretical literature has focused mainly on the assumptions required with respect to technology/preferences and emissions (Lopez 1994, Selden and Song 1995, McConell 1997) for an EKC relationship to exist. However, the empirical literature differs substantially from the theoretical. In general the empirical models are of a reduced form type using cross-country data over relatively short time periods. A typical empirical model specifies emissions as a nonlinear function of income, income distribution, as well as some country-specific characteristics such as population density, trade intensity and openness to trade (see Grossman and Krueger 1991, 1995, Shafik and Bandyopadhyay 1992). One conclusion from these studies is that openness seems to be beneficial to the environment.[1] Another conclusion from more recent studies is that it is not only average income that matters, but also how that income is distributed. According to Torras and Boyce (1998) and Bimonte (2002) an increase in equity, measured by the Gini coefficient, shifts the EKC curve downwards, implying a turning point at a lower income level. An apparent drawback in many of these empirical models is that they can only describe the relationship, not explain it. Another drawback with most of the previous empirical studies is that they use rather short cross-country panels, which means that most of the intra-country dynamics inherent in the EKC hypothesis cannot be accounted for.

The purpose of this study is to investigate more directly how changes in environmental performance over time have contributed to the Kuznets curve, using a long-term perspective. This requires that we explicitly model technology, including emissions, and study the development of environmental performance over time. Here we measure the environmental performance in Swedish manufacturing using an indicator approach, which allows us to specify joint production of good output and emissions, accounting also for input usage. In contrast to the bulk of earlier empirical tests of the EKC, we focus on a single country over a long time period. We have data for eight manufacturing industries over the 1913–1990 time period. This allows us to analyse the relation between environmental performance over time as well as differences across industries.

2. THE BAD-OUTPUT QUANTITY INDICATOR

In this study environmental performance is measured by means of a quantity indicator based on a directional distance function.

Before we introduce the directional subvector output distance function, following Chung et al. (1997),[2] we formulate an environmental production technology. This technology uses inputs $x \in \mathcal{R}_+^N$ to produce good (desirable) outputs $y \in \mathcal{R}_+^M$ and bad (undesirable) outputs $u \in \mathcal{R}_+^J$ in accordance with

$$S = \{(x, y, u) \mid x \text{ can produce } (y, u)\}. \tag{1}$$

We require S to satisfy certain minimal regularity conditions: S is a closed nonempty set with freely disposable inputs, i.e., if $(x, y, u) \in S$ and $x' \geq x$ then $(x', y, u) \in S$.

In order to call S an environmental technology we impose the following two axioms

$$\text{if } (x, y, u) \in S \text{ and } 0 \leq \theta \leq 1 \text{ then } (x, \theta y, \theta u) \in S, \tag{2}$$

$$\text{if } (x, y, u) \in S \text{ and } u = 0_j \text{ then } y = 0_M. \tag{3}$$

The first condition says that proportional contraction of good and bad outputs simultaneously is feasible. This condition was called weak disposability of outputs by Shephard (1970). The second condition tells us that if no undesirable outputs are produced, then it is not possible to produce any good outputs, or conversely, if good outputs are produced then some undesirable byproducts must also be produced. This was called null-jointness by Shephard and Färe (1974).

In our empirical formulation of S some additional conditions will be imposed. These are however not required for the definition of the distance function.

Let $g_u \in \mathcal{R}_+^J$, $g_u \neq 0_J$ be a directional vector in the space of bad outputs. For the technology S the directional bad output distance function is defined as

$$\vec{D}_S(x, y, u; g_u) \equiv \max\{\beta \mid (x, y, u - \beta g_u) \in S\}. \tag{4}$$

This function measures the distance of the point (x, y, u) to the frontier of the technology in terms of units of the directional vector g_u. The function inherits the properties of the technology and under some additional conditions it fully describes S, i.e.,

$$\vec{D}_S(x, y, u; g_u) \geq 0 \quad \text{if and only if} \quad (x, y, u) \in S. \tag{5}$$

The function is increasing in u, satisfies the translation property

$$\vec{D}_S(x, y, u - \alpha g_u; g_u) = \vec{D}_S(x, y, u; g_u) - \alpha \qquad (\alpha \in \mathcal{R}), \tag{6}$$

and can be shown to be independent of the units of measurement of the bad outputs.[3]

Conditional on (x^0, y^0), the difference

$$\vec{D}_S(x^0, y^0, u; g_u) - \vec{D}_S(x^0, y^0, u'; g_u) \tag{7}$$

is a bad-output quantity indicator. It exhibits properties similar to those of the input quantity indicator as discussed by Balk et al. (2004).[4] It can be shown that the bad-output quantity indicator is independent of (x^0, y^0) if and only if

$$\vec{D}_S(x, y, u; g_u) = \vec{D}_S(x, y, 1; g_u) + \vec{D}_S(1, 1, u; g_u) - \vec{D}_S(1, 1, 1; g_u) \tag{8}$$

holds.[5]

Given data (x^{kt}, y^{kt}, u^{kt}), where $k = 1, \ldots, K$ indexes the 'sectors' and $t = 1, \ldots, T$ indexes the time periods, let us introduce the shorthand notation:

$$D(k, t) \equiv \vec{D}_S(x^0, y^0, u^{kt}; g_u), \tag{9}$$

where (x^0, y^0) is a certain reference input and good-output quantity combination. Using this notation it is clear that

$$q(k, t, t') \equiv D(k, t) - D(k, t') \tag{10}$$

measures the bad-output quantity change for sector k, going from time period t' to t. The aggregate bad-output quantity change is obtained as

$$\sum_{k=1}^{K} q(k, t, t'). \tag{11}$$

Notice also that

$$Q(k, k', t, t') \equiv q(k, t, t') - q(k', t, t') \tag{12}$$

measures the bad-output quantity change, between periods t' and t, for sector k relative to sector k'.

Alternatively,

$$r(k, k', t) \equiv D(k, t) - D(k', t) \tag{13}$$

measures the bad-output quantity difference between sectors k and k' at period t. The average difference over time can be measured by

$$(1/T)\sum_{t=1}^{T} r(k, k', t). \tag{14}$$

Notice that

$$r(k, k', t) - r(k, k', t') = Q(k, k', t, t'), \tag{15}$$

which can thus also be interpreted as the change of the bad-output quantity difference between sectors k and k' when time proceeds from period t' to t.

Rather than imposing the above mentioned separability structure on the distance function we use a specific reference vector (x^0, y^0), constructed using an idea of 'lattice' theory. Specifically we choose coordinate-wise

$$\begin{aligned} x_n^0 &\equiv \max\{x_n^{kt} \mid k = 1, \ldots, K; t = 1, \ldots, T\} \quad \text{and} \\ y_m^0 &\equiv \min\{y_m^{kt} \mid k = 1, \ldots, K; t = 1, \ldots, T\}, \end{aligned} \tag{16}$$

that is, the maximum input quantities and minimum good-output quantities in the sample. This has the advantage of ensuring that our linear programming problems have feasible solutions. In particular we compute the distance function value for any observation (k', t') as

$$D(k', t') = \max \beta$$

$$\text{subject to} \sum_{k=1}^{K}\sum_{t=1}^{T} z^{kt}\, y_m^{kt} \geq y_m^0, \quad m = 1, \ldots, M,$$

$$\sum_{k=1}^{K}\sum_{t=1}^{T} z^{kt}\, u_j^{kt} = u_j^{k't'} - \beta, \quad j = 1, \ldots, J,$$

$$\sum_{k=1}^{K}\sum_{t=1}^{T} z^{kt}\, x_n^{kt} \leq x_n^0, \quad n = 1, \ldots, N,$$

$$\sum_{k=1}^{K}\sum_{t=1}^{T} z^{kt} \leq 1$$

$$z^{kt} \geq 0, \quad k = 1, \ldots, K; \quad t = 1, \ldots, T. \tag{17}$$

We have chosen a directional vector of ones in this formulation.[6] By using an equality constraint for the undesirable outputs, good and bad outputs are together weakly disposable. The nonnegativity condition in conjunction with the sum less than or equal to unity on the intensity variables z^{kt} makes the technology into a nonincreasing returns to scale technology. To satisfy the null-joint condition, the data is required to satisfy

$$\sum_{k=1}^{K}\sum_{t=1}^{T} u_j^{kt} > 0, \quad j = 1, \ldots, J$$

$$\sum_{j=1}^{J} u_j^{kt} > 0, \quad k = 1, \ldots, K; \quad t = 1, \ldots, T. \tag{18}$$

The first of these conditions says that each undesirable output is produced by at least one observation (k, t), and the second inequality states that each (k, t) produces at least one bad output.

3. DATA AND MODEL SPECIFICATION

The sectoral division used in the Historical National Accounts for Sweden (SHNA) dictates the organization of the data in this study. In practice this classification is fairly consistent with the two-digit ISIC level. Some reclassifications have, however, been necessary in order to assure compatibility with the older data. The high level of aggregation naturally leads to heterogeneity in some sectors.

3.1. Value Added and Labour

Value added data is directly obtained from Schön's (1988) SHNA estimates. Labour inputs, measured as number of employees and self-employed company owners, have been elaborated by Lindmark and Vikström (2002) on the basis of the National Accounts from 1960. Gunnarsson and Lindh's (1997) estimates were used for 1950–1960. For 1870 to 1950 Jungenfeldt's (1959) estimates, completed with reconstructions based on Schön's (1988) estimates of those employed in handicrafts, have been used as a variation index.

3.2. Capital Inputs

Capital inputs at the sectoral level are comparatively difficult to obtain. The SHNA includes primarily estimates of investments for the manufacturing industry sector that subsequently may be used for Perpetual Inventory Method (PIM) estimates of stocks. This means that two approaches can be considered. Either one can try to estimate the investments or one can try to estimate the stocks by piecing together various sources of information and by using proxy indicators. For this study the latter approach was taken. Firstly, the so-called Socialization investigation of 1929 provides data on fixed assets for a large sample of companies during the period 1913–1925. The data in the investigation was collected from the companies' balance sheets. Obviously the firms' accounting practices for fixed assets are not formally consistent with the accounting principles for the National Accounts. It is also known that companies sometimes deliberately overestimated the value of their fixed assets in order to present a positive net worth in the annual report. A test of the reliability of the figures could, however, be obtained by comparing the trends in the total stock of fixed assets according to the balance sheets to the trends in the stock of fixed assets in the manufacturing industry, as obtained from a PIM estimate (Lindmark and Vikström 2002).

The next step was to calculate stocks from 1956, when investment data on an appropriate level of aggregation were included in the official statistics. In the National Accounts capital stocks are constituted as accumulated investments that are gradually phased out as they age. This phasing-out process is known as discards of capital ('scrapping'). The time during which the capital is in use, or is ready to be used in a production process, is called its service life. To estimate the gross capital stock, the investments are accumulated and removed after the capital has reached the end of its service life. Capital is, however, also consumed, which is known as depreciation. Depreciation is reflected in falling asset values with increasing age due to physical deterioration, normal obsolescence or normal accidental damage. When the accumulated consumption of capital is deducted from the gross capital stock, the net capital stock is obtained, which is the relevant stock for the computation of multifactor productivity. In conclusion, the accumulation and deduction process will create a vastly exaggerated estimate of the development of stocks, unless there are long enough time series to allow the first investments to leave the stock at the appropriate time, in this case 1956. This problem was approached by using the average investment to value added ratio for the whole manufacturing industry sector and applying this ratio to the value added series for each branch from 1900 to 1956. In 1956 these proximate series were linked to the official investment data. Since the first investments have left the stock in 1956, this means that the total value of the stocks in each branch should be reasonably accurate and that the subsequent development of the stocks, affected by scrapping of previous investments, should also be fairly accurate.

For interpolation between 1925 and 1956 we used installed motor power as a variation index, and then distributed the error between the estimates and the PIM stock, over the sectors in order to ensure compatibility with stocks based on investment data. Furthermore, the estimated stocks were linked to the official real capital stocks in 1980 (SCB 1992), thus forming a continuous series to 1990.

3.3. Energy Inputs

Energy inputs have largely been collected from the official statistics with complements from other sources. The first comprehensive study of fuel consumption inputs in the manufacturing industry in Sweden covered the period 1913–1917 (Kommerskollegium 1918). Energy inputs were included in the official statistics (SOS Industri) in 1924. This means that interpolations were necessary for the first part of the 1920s. Estimating a linearly changing trend of the fuel-to-output ratio between the benchmark years was the first step in these interpolations. Secondly, the fuel-to-output ratio was multiplied with the annual output data. For gas and liquid fuels, interpolations were necessary for the period 1917–1930. Here, a similar procedure was employed, with the exception that a linearly changing coal-to-fuel ratio was estimated and subsequently applied to the annual coal consumption data. It is also worth noticing that coal used for the manufacturing of gas and coke was removed from the series. Also nuclear fuel is included from the early 1970s.

Concerning electricity, the total production in power plants is included in the official statistics from the beginning of the period. The total electricity use in the manufacturing industry sectors is also shown. The use at the branch level was, however, not included until 1935. Interpolations were therefore necessary also in this case. Benchmarks for branch level electricity use was collected from Kommerskollegium (1918) and the official statistics, while installed electrical motor power was used as a variation index. Also the production of electro-steel and calcium carbide was used for estimating the electricity use in interpolation in metallurgical and electrochemical processes. Finally, the sector shares in the estimated series were used for distributing the actual electricity use in the manufacturing industries to the various sectors.

3.4. Bad Outputs

The bad outputs include sulphur dioxide (SO_2) and carbon dioxide (CO_2). Emissions of sulphur dioxide were calculated on the basis of estimates of total sulphur emissions from energy use by Kindbom et al. (1993). Boliden AB provided additional emissions data. The main difficulty is the distribution of the emissions over the respective sectors. This could, however, be done by estimating historical emission factors for coal and liquid fuels and then applying the emission factors to the fuel input data. Secondly, process emissions were allocated to the sectors. It is worth pointing out that the Rönnskär metal melting plant from 1931/32 significantly affects the aggregated emissions.

The CO_2 emissions were calculated on the basis of Statistics Sweden's emission factors for various fuels. The CO_2 emissions also include process emissions from concrete manufacturing. In practice the CO_2 emissions are nearly linearly dependent on the use of fossil fuels, affected only by composition changes.

3.5. Descriptive Statistics

The data we use span the period 1913–1990 and cover eight Swedish manufacturing sectors,[7] which are given below:

G1: Mining and metal industry
G2: Stone, clay and glass industry
G3: Wood products industry
G4: Paper and printing industry
G5: Food processing industry
G6: Textile and clothing industry
G7: Leather, hair and rubber industry
G8: Chemical industry

Our data include information on input and output quantities, including emissions, according to Table 15.1.

In Figures 15.1–15.4 we give a brief description of some of the data used. Figure 15.1 shows the development over time of aggregate (over sectors) value added, as well as emissions of CO_2 and SO_2. Here we can

Table 15.1. Input and output variables

Variable	Description
Output:	
y	value added, 1913 prices
Emissions:	
$u1$	sulfur dioxide (SO_2)
$u2$	carbon dioxide (CO_2)
Inputs:	
$x1$	capital stock, 1956 prices
$x2$	electricity, kWh
$x3$	fossil fuels, coal tons
$x4$	biological fuels, coal tons
$x5$	labor, number of employees

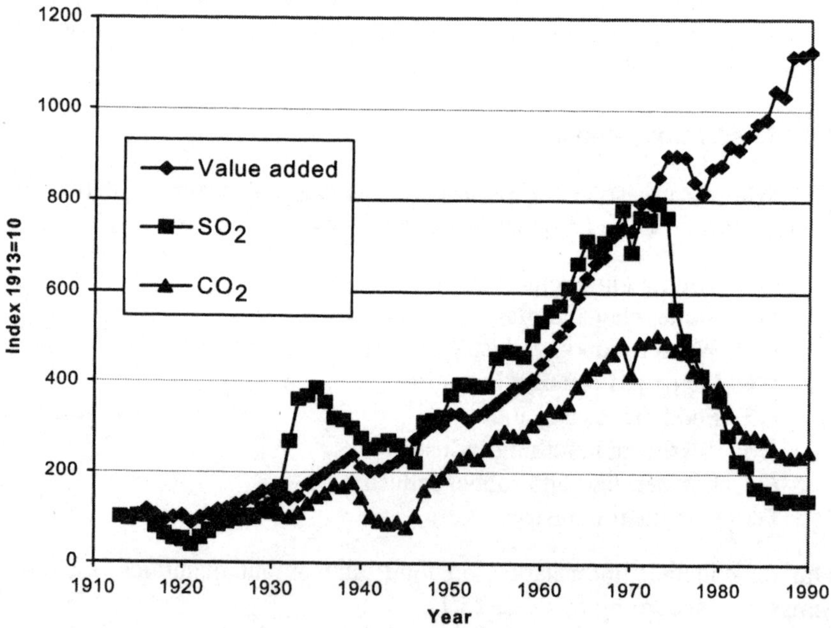

Figure 15.1. Value added, SO_2, and CO_2 emissions in Swedish manufacturing 1913–1990

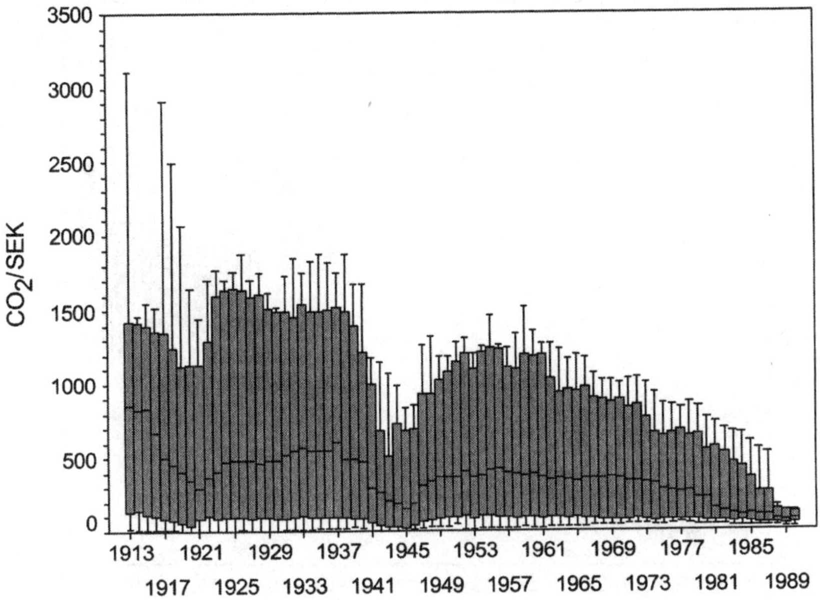

Figure 15.2. CO_2 emissions. 1000 kg/million SEK value added

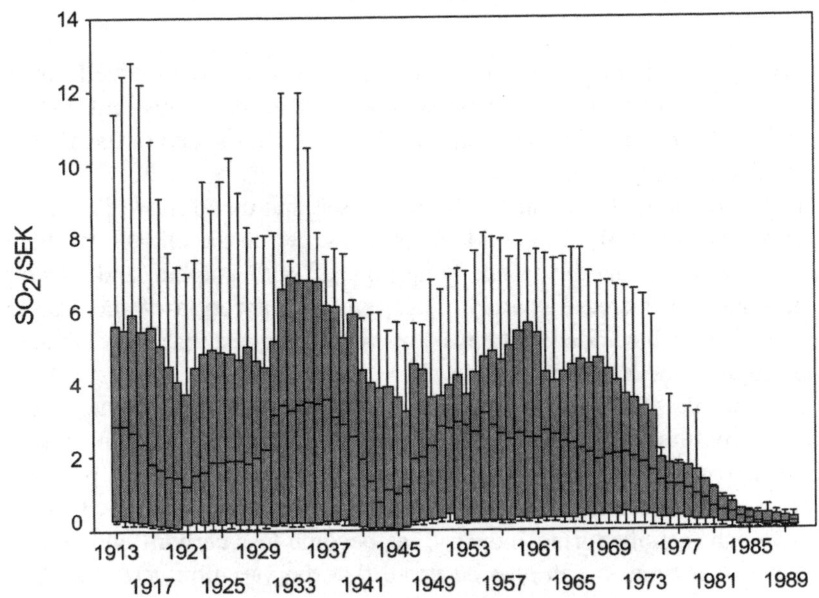

Figure 15.3. SO_2 emissions 1000 kg/million SEK value added

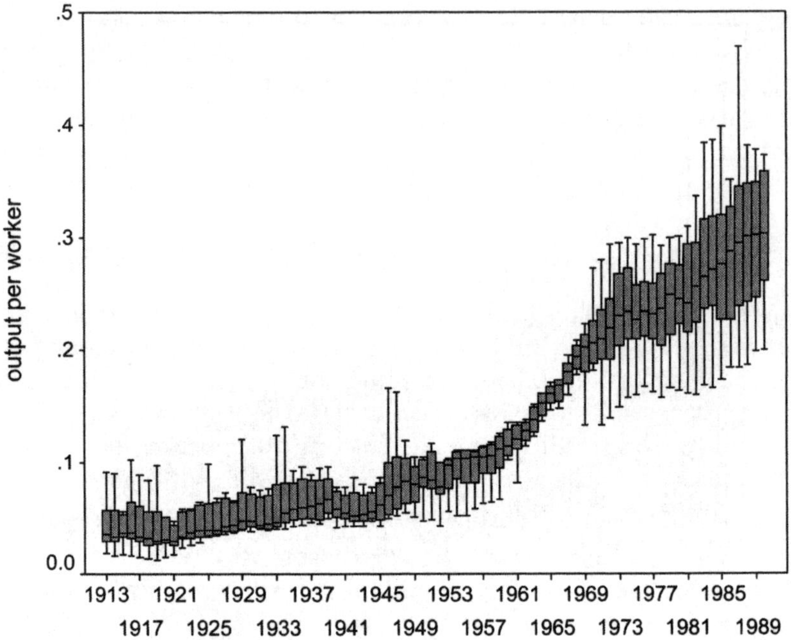

Figure 15.4. Value added per worker, million SEK/worker

see that value added has been increasing more or less monotonically over the whole time period. An exception though is in the 1930s and during World War II. We can also see a dip in value added at the end of the 1970s, mostly due to the oil crisis.

If we look at the trends in emissions we see that they follow the value-added series closely until the mid 1970s. However, in the mid 1970s there is a sudden break in the trend; emissions of both sulphur and carbon dioxide start to decrease sharply. Thus, casual inspection of the simple time trends in value added and emissions would suggest that Swedish data trends support the EKC hypothesis.

The box-plots in Figures 15.2 and 15.3 describe the development over time of emissions per unit of value added, including the mean and distribution across sectors. These figures show that mean emissions per unit of value added for both CO_2 and SO_2 have decreased over time. That is, the Swedish manufacturing industry has become less carbon- and sulfur-intensive over time. It can also be noted that the variation across sectors

Table 15.2. Environmental performance, 1913–1990

Industry	D (k, 1913)	D (k, 1990)	Change
G1	0.75	1.29	0.54
G2	0.71	0.51	–0.20
G3	0.05	0.09	0.04
G4	0.36	0.98	0.62
G5	0.12	0.07	–0.05
G6	0.04	0.01	–0.03
G7	0.07	0.02	–0.05
G8	0.26	0.36	0.10
TOT	2.36	3.32	0.96

has decreased substantially. One possible interpretation of the latter is that there has been a convergence in abatement technology over time.

Finally, in Figure 15.4 we see that labor productivity, in terms of value added per worker, has increased sharply over time. Interesting, however, is the fact that the variance (across sectors) seems to have increased slightly.

To summarize: the data show that there has been a clear trend in Swedish manufacturing in the sense that output, both in absolute value and in terms of output per unit of worker, has increased over time. Furthermore it is apparent that the Swedish manufacturing industry has become significantly less carbon- and sulphur-intensive.

4. RESULTS

We calculated the directional distance function values for each sector and each time period in our sample. Recall that the same reference technology is imposed on all the observations in the data set.

As a first summary of our results, we include the overall change from 1913 to 1990 for each sector as well as the aggregate change. Recall that a zero value of the distance function means that the observation is on the grand frontier. Values greater than zero represent inefficient points, which means that a negative change between 1990 and 1913 implies an improvement in environmental performance. From Table 15.2 we see that performance has declined between 1990 and 1913 overall, but that there is some variation across sectors.

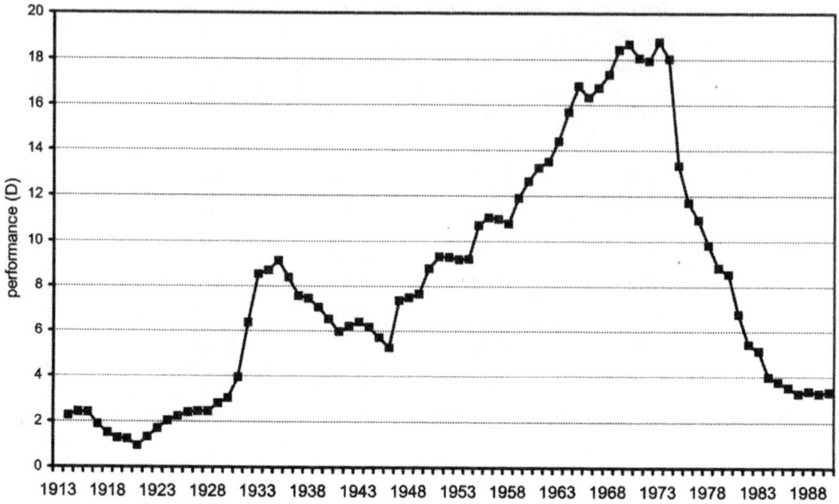

Figure 15.5. Aggregated environmental performance, 1913–1990

According to these results environmental performance has improved in the stone, clay and glass industry, the food processing industry, the textile and clothing industry, and the leather, hair and rubber industry. Overall, however, environmental performance is worse in 1990 than in 1913. This can partly be explained by the fact that fossil fuel intensity is higher in 1990 than 1913.

The development over time of the aggregate environmental performance indicator is shown in Figure 15.5. In this figure we can see an interesting pattern. Environmental performance deteriorates almost monotonically from 1913 to 1974. After 1974, however, there is a sharp improvement in environmental performance.

One interpretation would thus be that environmental considerations had very little impact on the Swedish manufacturing industry until the mid 1970s, but became important after that. One conclusion is then that environmental performance has changed considerably over time.

In order to relate our findings to the EKC idea we can compare our environmental performance indicator to the time trend of a measure of income in Sweden over the same period. In Table 15.3 we report the results from a simple regression analysis where our environmental indicator is the dependent variable, and GDP per capita and GDP per capita squared are the independent variables. According to the EKC hypothesis we then would expect a positive estimate of the coefficient representing GDP, and a neg-

Table 15.3. Environmental performance/income relation, 1913–1990

	OLS	*t*-ratio	AR1	*t*-ratio
C	–11.78	–9.18	–3.29	–0.75
GDP	0.51	15.18	0.26	2.41
GDP^2	–0.0025	–14.05	–0.0012	–2.32
ρ			0.95	28.64
DW	0.16		1.11	
R^2	0.77		0.96	
Turning point	102		107	

ative coefficient for GDP squared. We present two different estimates. In the first version the parameters are estimated using ordinary least squares (OLS), while in the second version the parameters are estimated under the assumption of first-order serial correlation (AR1).

According to the results in Table 15.3, environmental performance deteriorates when income increases, but at a decreasing rate, irrespective of estimation method. Thus we can conclude that economic growth has had a detrimental effect on environmental performance during the early stages of development in Sweden. Furthermore, the results also imply that at a certain point of development, in terms of income, environmental performance starts to improve. Thus, the results are in accordance with the EKC hypothesis. According to the results the turning point (TP) is at an income of approximately 100 000 SEK/capita ($13 000).

A similar analysis can be done for each industrial sector, using a panel-data approach. To do this we specify a regression equation in which environmental performance is a function of GDP per capita and GDP per capita squared, allowing a sector specific dependence. The regression equation is specified as

$$\begin{aligned} D(k,t) &= \alpha_0 + \left(\alpha_1 + \sum_{j=2}^{8} \alpha_{1j}\, Z_j\right)\mathrm{GDP}_t + \\ &\quad + \left(\alpha_2 + \sum_{j=2}^{8} \alpha_{2j}\, Z_j\right)\mathrm{GDP}_t^2 + \varepsilon_{kt}, \\ &\quad k = 1, \ldots, 8, \quad t = 1913, \ldots, 1990, \end{aligned}$$

where $D(k, t)$ is the environmental performance indicator for sector $k$in period t , Z_j is a variable that takes the value one if an observation belongs to sector j, and zero otherwise. That is, the parameters α_{1j} and α_{2j} reflect how the relation for sector $j = 2, \ldots, 8$ between environmental performance and GDP differs from the same relation for sector 1. The remainder ε_{kt} contains the part of $D(k, t)$ that cannot be explained by GDP and GDP squared.

Given estimates of the parameters we can calculate the turning points, $\overline{\text{GDP}_k}$, in each sector by solving for GDP_t in the following equation:

$$\frac{\text{d}\, D(k,t)}{\text{d GDP}_t} = \alpha_1 + \alpha_{1k} + 2(\alpha_2 + \alpha_{2k})\, \text{GDP}_t = 0,$$

which yields

$$\overline{\text{GDP}_k} = \frac{-(\alpha_1 + \alpha_{1k})}{2(\alpha_2 + \alpha_{2k})}.$$

The estimation results, as well as the resulting turning points are presented in Table 15.4.

The first thing to notice is that all of the parameters are highly significant and that they have signs that support the EKC hypothesis. Furthermore, all sector-specific effects are significantly different from zero, which implies that there is a significantly different environmental performance/income relationship between sector 1 and all other sectors. One conclusion then would be that the EKC differs across sectors. If we turn to the calculated turning points we see that the turning point for sector 1, the mining and metal industry, is substantially higher than all other sectors. According to the results environmental performance starts improving at an income level of SEK 96 000 ($13 000). We can also see that sectors 2 and 4, the stone, clay and glass industry, and the paper and printing industry, have relatively high turning points. Sectors 1, 2 and 4 are characterized as capital- and energy-intensive industries, which may explain the result since there are difficulties in substituting away from energy in these industries. Thus it may be inferred that countries that have a relatively large capital- and energy-intensive manufacturing sector will have an EKC with higher turning points than less capital/energy-intensive countries.

To conclude: we have found that environmental performance in Sweden shows a clear pattern over time in the sense that environmental performance deteriorated from 1913 to the beginning of the 1970s. Furthermore we have found a clear relationship between environmental performance and income, measured by GDP per capita. However, this relationship

Table 15.4. Environmental performance/income relation, 1913–1990. Panel data estimation

	Estimate	t-ratio	Turning point	
C	–1.47	–11.90	G1	96.7
GDP	0.14	33.66	G2	68.0
GDP^2	–0.00074	–27.35	G3	42.5
GDP G_2	–0.067	–16.23	G4	70.0
GDP G_3	–0.10	–25.10	G5	44.1
GDP G_4	–0.07	–16.53	G6	41.3
GDP G_5	–0.10	–24.53	G7	44.4
GDP G_6	–0.10	–25.32	G8	56.7
GDP G_7	–0.10	–24.42		
GDP G_8	–0.09	–20.76		
GDP^2 G_2	0.00036	11.49		
GDP^2 G_3	0.00055	17.55		
GDP^2 G_4	0.00041	13.03		
GDP^2 G_5	0.00053	16.91		
GDP^2 G_6	0.00055	17.37		
GDP^2 G_7	0.00053	16.79		
GDP^2 G_8	0.00047	14.89		
R^2	0.80			

seems to depend on industrial structure since the results also indicate that environmental performance starts to improve at higher income levels for industries that are capital- and energy-intensive, than for industries that are not.

5. CONCLUDING REMARKS

In this study we have investigated how environmental performance in the Swedish manufacturing industries has evolved in a historical perspective, and how this is related to economic development in Sweden. The questions considered here are closely related to the discussion about the possibility of an Environmental Kuznets Curve (EKC). To do this we developed an environmental quantity indicator using a directional distance function approach. The data set used is unique in the sense that we have a long time series, 1913–1990, consisting of good as well as bad outputs for eight different manufacturing industries.

The results from the analysis support the EKC hypothesis, but they also show that the turning point, i.e. the income level for which environmental performance starts to improve, differs across sectors, or industries. Energy/capital-intensive industries have a relatively high turning point, indicating that the shape of the EKC depends not only on income, but also on industrial structure.

Since the sectors 1, 4 and 8, the worst in environmental performance, were the sectors that experienced the highest output growth during the period, it is clear that the environment had a very low value until the late 1960s. It also indicates that the weight given to the emissions in the distance function are higher than its historical social value.

Deteriorating environmental performance until 1974 is compatible with qualitative arguments. The Swedish Environmental Protection Agency was formed in 1967 along with an environmental protection legislation based on concessions introduced the same year. This may be seen as a collectivization of environmental demand. It is in addition likely that the combination of the 1973 OPEC I crisis and the ambitious nuclear program contributed to the decrease in emissions. However, also changing environmental preferences are likely to have played an important role, since SO_2, which can be avoided at lower costs than CO_2, shows a considerably steeper decline as compared to the more directly fuel related CO_2. Also worth noticing is that these changes coincide with what has been labeled the ICT revolution. According to Crafts (2002), ICT had a higher total factor productivity (TFP) impact than the steam engines of the industrial revolution and an impact that matched electricity during the so-called second industrial revolution in the early twentieth century. In contrast, Gordon (2000) reported much higher TFP growth rates during the period 1895–1975, which he associated with the second industrial revolution's General Purpose Technology, as compared to the era of ICT. In all cases, the shifts in General Purpose Technologies may have affected the EKC. It does, however, remain a future task for research to disentangle the effects on environmental performance that can be traced to ICT, changing environmental preferences, the collectivization of environmental demand, and changing fuel prices.

ACKNOWLEDGEMENTS

The authors acknowledge valuable comments from the participants at the Karl-Gustaf Löfgren Symposium on Environmental Economics, Ulvön, June 16–19, 2003. We also acknowledge financial support from Riksbankens Jubileumsfond (The Research Foundation of the Bank of Sweden).

NOTES

1. For a survey of the empirical literature in this area, see Stern (1998).
2. Luenberger (1992) introduced this type of distance function.
3. See Balk et al. (2004, p. 153).
4. The bad-output quantity *index* was discussed by Färe and Grosskopf (2004, pp. 57–58).
5. The proof is similar to the one in Färe and Grosskopf (2004, p. 91).
6. In practice, we use the mean of the data as our direction. We then mean-deflate the data and the direction yielding a normalized direction vector of ones.
7. The electric, gas and water utilities sector was dropped from the samples due to data reliability issues.

REFERENCES

Balk, B.M., R. Färe and S. Grosskopf (2004), 'The theory of economic price and quantity indicators', *Economic Theory*, 23, 149–164.

Bimonte, S. (2002), 'Information access, income distribution, and the environmental Kuznets curve', *Ecological Economics*, 31, 145–156.

Chung, Y.H., R. Färe and S. Grosskopf (1997), 'Productivity and undesirable outputs: A directional distance function approach', *Journal of Environmental Management*, 51, 229–240.

Crafts, N. (2002), 'The Solow productivity paradox in historical perspective', Discussion Paper No. 3142, Centre for Economic Policy Research.

Färe, R. and S. Grosskopf (2004), *New Directions: Efficiency and Productivity*, Boston/Dordrecht/London: Kluwer Academic Publishers.

Gordon, R.J. (2000), 'Interpreting the one big wave in U.S. long-term productivity growth', in B. van Ark, S.K. Kuipers and G.H. Kuper (eds), *Productivity, Technology and Economic Growth*, Boston/Dordrecht/London: Kluwer Academic Publishers.

Grossman, G.M. and A.B. Krueger (1991), 'Environmental impacts of a North American free trade agreement', Working Paper 3914, National Bureau of Economic Research, Cambridge, MA.

Grossman, G. and A.B. Krueger (1995), 'Economic growth and the environment', *Quarterly Journal of Economics*, 110, 353–377.

Gunnarsson, G. and T. Lindh (1997), 'Swedish employment in the 1950s – Filling the lacuna', Working Article, Department of Economics, Uppsala University.

Jungendfelt, K.G. (1959), 'Lönernas andel av nationalinkomsten', Mimeo, Nationalekonomiska Institutionen, Uppsala Universitet.

Kindbom, K., K. Sjöberg and G. Lövblad (1993), 'Beräkning av Ackumulerad Syrabelastning. Delrapport 1. Emissioner av Svavel, Kväve och Alkaliskt Stoft i Sverige 1900–1990 (Estimate of Accumulated Acid Exposure. Report 1. Emissions of Sulphur, Nitrogen and Alkali in Sweden 1900–1990)', IVL, Göteborg.

Kommerskollegium (1918), 'Bränsleförbrukningen åren 1913–1917 vid Industriella Anläggningar', Kommunikationsanstalter samt Allmänna Verk och Inrättningar, Stockholm.

Lindmark, M. and P. Vikström (2002), 'The determinants of structural change: Transformation pressure and structural change in Swedish manufacturing industry 1870–1993', *European Review of Economic History*, 6, 87–110.

Lopez, R. (1994), 'The environment as a factor of production, the effects of economic growth and trade liberalization', *Journal of Environmental Economics and Management*, 27, 163–184.

Luenberger, D.G. (1992), 'New optimality principles for economic efficiency and equilibrium', *Journal of Optimization Theory and Applications*, 75, 221–264.

McConnell, K. (1997), 'Income and the demand for environmental quality', *Environment and Development Economics*, 2, 383–399.

Meadows, D.H., D.L. Meadows, J. Randers and W. Behrens (1972), *The Limits to Growth*, New York: Universe Books.

Meadows, D.H., D.L. Meadows and J. Randers (1992), *Beyond the Limits: Global Collapse or a Sustainable Future*, London: Earthscan.

Schön, L. (1988), *Industri och Hantverk 1800–1980*, Lund.

Selden, T. and D. Song (1995), 'Neoclassical growth, the J curve for abatement, and the inverted U for pollution', *Journal of Environmental Economics and Management*, 29, 162–168.

Shafik, N. and S. Bandyopadhyay (1992), 'Economic growth and environmental quality: Time series and cross-country evidence', Background Paper for World Development Report 1992, World Bank, Washington DC.

Shephard, R.W. (1970), *Theory of Cost and Production Functions*, Princeton, NJ: Princeton University Press.

Shephard, R.W. and R. Färe (1974), 'The law of diminishing returns', *Zeitschrift für Nationalökonomie*, 34, 69–90.

Statistiska Centralbyrån (SCB) (1992), *National Wealth and Stocks of Fixed Assets 1980–1990*, Stockholm: SCB-Förlag

Stern, D. (1998), 'Progress on the environmental Kuznets curve?', *Environment and Development Economics*, 3, 175–198.

Torras, M. and J. Boyce (1998), 'Income, inequality, and pollution: A reassessment of the environmental Kuznets curve', *Ecological Economics*, 25, 147–160.

World Bank (1992), *World Development Report 1992. Development and the Environment*, New York: Oxford University Press.

16. Assessing the Economic Impacts of Large-Scale Environmental Regulations in California

Peter Berck and H. Peter Hess

1. INTRODUCTION

This chapter presents the methodology and results of assessing the impacts of large-scale environmental policies on the California economy. California has an economy approximately the size of France, yet being a state rather than a nation, it has no monetary policy and only limited scope for fiscal policy. As a state, it also does not have well measured trade, workforce, or capital flows. The effect of these factors on estimates of policy cost will be explained below. The chapter proceeds from methodological issues, to runs of the policy model, and finally to a discussion of the impact of openness on costs.

The methodology employed is computable general equilibrium (CGE) modeling. CGE models are designed to capture the fundamental economic relationships between producers, consumers, and government.[1] The models are 'computable' because numeric solutions are found using computers rather than solved for algebraically. They are 'general' in the sense that all markets and all income flows in the economy are accounted for. They reflect 'equilibrium' insofar as prices adjust to equilibrate the demand for and supply of goods, services, and factors of production (labor and capital).

The specific models employed here are modified versions of E-DRAM (Environmental-Dynamic Revenue Analysis Model). E-DRAM was built for the California Environmental Protection Agency's Air Resources Board (ARB) by researchers at the University of California, Berkeley (UCB). E-DRAM evolved from DRAM (Dynamic Revenue Analysis Model), which was developed jointly by the California Department of Finance (DOF) and Berkeley researchers to perform dynamic revenue analyses of proposed legislation as mandated by the California State Senate Bill 1837 in 1994.

The types of regulations considered for pollution control vary considerably. The ubiquitous target is the control of motor vehicle emissions. California was the pioneer in requiring lower emissions from passenger cars. Since there was no reasonable way for California to clean up its air and meet the requirements of the Clean Air Act while using the Federal standards for automobiles, California was (and is) permitted to set more stringent standards than the Federal standards. Success in reducing auto emissions matched with California's continuing nonattainment requires further actions to clean up the air.

The actions to clean up the air are codified in the State Implementation Plan under the Clean Air Act, which is promulgated by CAL EPA/ARB and must be accepted by the US EPA. The major areas for reducing air pollution have been stationary sources, consumer chemicals, automobiles, and now trucks.

Stationary sources, like automobiles before them, have been very tightly regulated. The original means of regulation was to require emissions limits based upon known technologies. In the case of the South Coast Air Basin (LA), such regulations were not stringent enough to clean the air. A cap and trade program, called RECLAIM, was instituted in that air basin for sulfur oxide (SOX) and nitrogen oxide (NOX) in order to reduce pollution beyond what could be accomplished with known technologies at reasonable cost. Each year, fewer permits are issued, which controls the output from the larger stationary sources at a predetermined level.

Automobiles, as was already mentioned, are already tightly controlled. Future controls include a mandate for zero emissions vehicles, though as of this writing it is not clear whether that mandate will continue in the face of nearly no emission hybrids, which are currently commercially viable.

Uncontrolled until recently, trucks, buses, construction equipment and other diesel equipment are now a major remaining source of pollution, particularly of less than 10 micron particulates. Further controls on this category of polluters are under consideration. There are many consumer products (like spray paint, hairspray, etc.) that are now falling under regulation, and further regulation is in store for this category of goods.

Taken together, these categories of goods account for much of the economic costs of air pollution control.

The California legislature has gone further, at least in its studies, than conventional pollution control, to an examination of strategies to reduce greenhouse gasses. Potential fuel saving or fuel substitution scenarios which we have evaluated for the legislature go much further in changing the makeup of output than previous regulations.

In California, air pollution control is a potentially large constraint on economic activity. The research reported in this chapter was done in the course of providing studies for the State Implementation Plan for the Clean Air Act and for a series of petroleum sparing potential scenarios.

This chapter will consider three policy options, a tax option, a collection of policies aimed at pollution, and a collection of policies aimed at attaining fuel efficiency. They will be compared in the conclusion.

The next section is a nontechnical description of E-DRAM. Section 3 outlines modifications made to E-DRAM for this project. Section 4 presents baseline solutions to the model for the years 1999 and 2020. Section 5 evaluates various policy scenarios in 1999 and 2020. Section 6 offers concluding remarks.

2. A DESCRIPTION OF THE E-DRAM MODEL

E-DRAM describes the relationship among California producers, California households, California governments, and the rest of the world. Rather than tracking each individual producer, household, or government agency in the economy, however, E-DRAM combines similar agents into single sectors. Constructing a cogent sectoring scheme, the first step of model construction, is discussed immediately below; this discussion is followed by a description of the key agents in the economy: producers and consumers.

For the E-DRAM model, the California economy has been divided into 93 distinct sectors: 29 industrial sectors, 2 factor sectors (labor and capital), 9 consumer good sectors, 9 household sectors, 1 investment sector, 45 government sectors, and 1 sector representing the rest of the world. These aggregates generally represent the major industrial and commercial sectors of the California economy, though a few are tailored to capture sectors of particular regulatory interest. For instance, production of internal combustion engines and consumer chemicals are each delineated as distinct sectors.[2]

Data for the industrial sectors originate from the US Department of Commerce's Bureau of Economic Analysis (BEA), and is based on the Census of Business – a detailed survey of US companies conducted every five years.[3] The survey contains information about intermediate purchases, factor (labor, capital, land and entrepreneurship) payments, and taxes. Although quite extensive, the survey only allows inference about groups of firms at the national level. The conversion of national data to updated California data is accomplished using a combination of state level employment data and estimates from DOF's econometric modeling.

Like firms, households are also aggregated. California households are divided into categories based upon their income. There are seven such categories in the model, each one corresponding to a California Personal Income Tax marginal tax rate (0, 1, 2, 4, 6, 8, and 9.3 per cent). Household income data come from the California Franchise Tax Board Personal Income Tax 'sanitized' sample. Data on consumption by income class is derived from national survey data.

Firms are assumed to maximize profits. Households make two types of decisions: they decide to buy goods and services; they also decide to sell labor and capital services. They are assumed to maximize utility. Household demand functions are estimated from the US Bureau of Labor Statistics' Consumer Expenditure Survey data. Labor supply is taken from published literature.

In addition to the household and firm decisions described, firms have an investment function that depends upon their aftertax rate of return and households have migration functions dependent, inter alia, on their after tax real wage.

Governments are represented in great detail. The California government is assumed to have a balanced budget. Increased taxes fund education according to state law (Proposition 98) and the remaining funds are allocated in proportion to historic levels. Deductibility of state from federal income taxes is also accounted for.

The model calculates the prices (relative to a base of one) which clear all of the markets.

Figure 16.1 shows the flows in the model. For instance, households pay money (dotted line) for goods and services (solid line) and supply factors – labor and capital – (solid line) and receive income (dotted line).

3. REGIONAL AND NATIONAL MODEL DIFFERENCES

Regional, or sub-national, CGE models are very similar in design to national and international models, but exhibit major differences in several key assumptions. The seven most important differences between national and regional CGE models are discussed below.

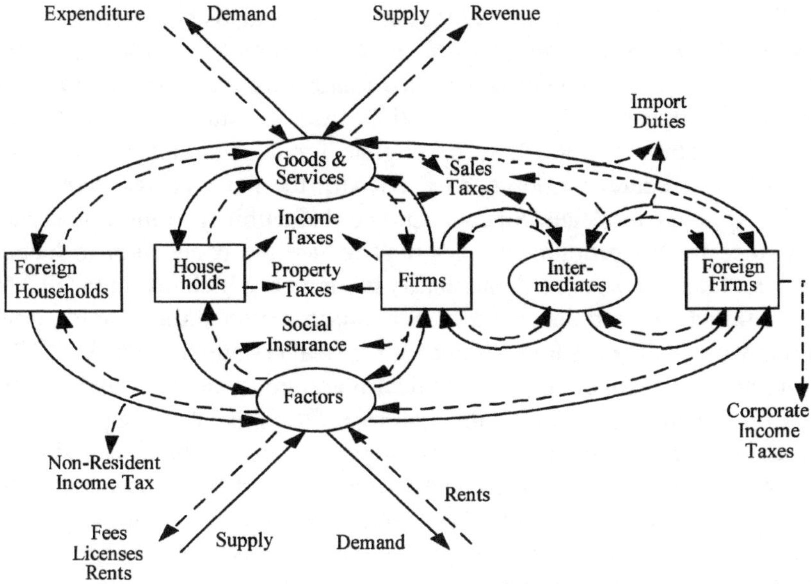

Figure 16.1. The complete circular-flow diagram

The first, and maybe most important, difference is that regional CGE models do not require that regional savings equal regional investment. When Californians save more than California investors want to use, excess savings flow out of the state. When the converse is true, savings flow into the state. Rational economic agents would not accept less interest on their savings from California investors if higher interest rates were available in other states or countries. Conversely, rational investors in California would not pay higher interest for the use of Californian savings if other states or countries offered lower rates.

The second difference is that regional economies trade a larger share of their output. Therefore, trade is more important in regional models. Note that interstate trade is part of the Rest of the World for California but ignored in national considerations of trade.

The third difference is that regional economies face larger and more volatile migration flows than nations. Regional and international migration to California is a major factor in the State's economy.

The fourth difference between national and regional CGEs is that regional economies have no control over monetary policy. The Federal Reserve is responsible for monetary policy and is a national institution.

The fifth difference is that in regional models taxes are interdependent through deductibility. Some local taxes are deductible from incomes subject to California personal income taxes and bank and corporation taxes. Some local and state taxes are deductible from incomes subject to federal personal income tax and may be eligible for deduction from corporate incomes for federal purposes. In E-DRAM, the personal tax deductibility is explicitly modeled. Since corporate deductibility is more uncertain and since the apportionment rules may reduce the connection to federal corporate taxes, corporate deductibility has not been included in E-DRAM.

Sixth, while good data for a CGE are hard to find at the national level, in many cases they are nonexistent for regional economies. The E-DRAM uses published economic and statistical literature to simulate much of the data important to our model. In some cases, such as labor supply, a wide variety of results is presented in the literature. This problem is addressed in three ways: (1) values are chosen so as to avoid the extremes, (2) the model is tested to determine the degree to which results are dependent upon our assumptions (this process is called 'sensitivity analysis'), and (3) the use of published literature, especially of national results, has been minimized.

Seventh, the California CGE differs from a national CGE in that California faces a balanced-budget requirement. Even if this is ignored in the short run, bond markets tend to reflect this fact. When California issued bonds to cover short-term deficit spending in the early 1990s, bond ratings forced up the cost of borrowing. Ultimately, California would face unreasonable borrowing costs should it decide to maintain this level of borrowing.

4. FUTURE MODELS AND THE PETROLEUM SECTOR

For examining petroleum dependency issues in particular, the E-DRAM built for ARB as described in Berck and Hess (February 2000) is enhanced in three ways. First, Petroleum sector data is modified. Second, the 1998/1999 base year model is extrapolated out to 2020 and 2050 based on state population, personal income, and industry-specific forecasts. Third, parameters to adjust for technological change in the form of increased fuel efficiency and fuel displacement are incorporated into the model.

E-DRAM's original industrial accounts are national accounts scaled to the state level using California employment data. These accounts have been reconciled with more California-specific petroleum sector figures, originally sourced from US Energy Information Administration data.

Estimates for 2020 and 2050 were obtained by first determining the overall demand for finished products. This was estimated from the CEC projections of baseline fuel demands (CEC, 2001). Fuel use was projected to grow at rates between 1.6 per cent for gasoline and 3.4 per cent for jet fuel. In line with recent experience, California refinery capacity is assumed to increase at one-half per cent per year until 2020 and then not at all. Lack of additional refinery capacity is a consequence of environmental restrictions, including regulation under the Clean Air and Clean Water Acts. CEC estimates of the price of crude oil for 2020/bbl were $22.50, only slightly higher than today. Nonenergy related items were increased at an average annual growth rate of 2.84 per cent for the years 2000 to 2020; an average annual growth rate of 2.58 per cent was assumed for 2020 to 2050.

DOF projections suggest a California population growth rate of 1.36 per cent annually. Compounding this rate delivered scale factors for re-basing employment data. Based on these growth factors, a model was constructed for 2020. Since population growth is slower than output growth, the model assumes a modest degree of labor-augmenting technical progress. Table 16.1 displays some of the salient characteristics of the projections incorporated in the 2020 based model and allows comparison with the 1999 based model.

5. THREE TYPES OF POLICIES

With these preliminaries behind us, three possible environmental policies will be described and evaluated. The first policy is simply a tax on fuel. While a tax is the answer most prescribed by economists to compensate for an externality, it does not perform in the context of an open economy nearly as well as other possible measures. The actual measures chosen to reduce pollution in California are standards for both mobile and stationary sources. The next experiment is a package of such measures, scaled to the same magnitude as the tax. The measures are broadly representative of the additional measures California is now considering to meet its obligations under the Clean Air Act. The final experiment comes from a study of fuel saving policies and is far larger in its costs than either of the two previous measures.

Table 16.1. Model data for 1999 and 2020

	1999 Model	2020 Model
CA output ($ billion)	1378.0905	3078.0223
CA personal income ($ billion)	892.4894	2009.5373
Labor demand (millions)	14.0483	18.6605
Energy Minerals		
Output ($ billion)	5.8789	6.2086
Jobs (millions)	0.0178	0.0182
Imports ($ billion)	17.5404	36.0105
Exports ($ billion)	0.4375	1.0965
Petroleum Refining		
Output ($ billion)	24.8156	39.3048
Jobs (millions)	0.0220	0.0292
Imports ($ billion)	2.8058	15.6834
Exports ($ billion)	6.4746	11.9979

5.1. Taxes

From the point of view of a state, the ideal tax on the petroleum industry is a sales tax on refinery product independent of origin. Such a tax does not disadvantage California refineries relative to out of state refineries and discourages use and refining, both polluting activities. California law makes it easier to levy a tax that is tied to an environmental purpose than to levy a general tax increase. It is doubtful that a tax that also fell upon out of state refiners could be justified under this tied theory by appealing to the environmental benefit of discouraging refining. To achieve the favored legislative treatment the tax would also need to be dedicated to an environmental purpose such as cleaning up refineries or brown fields. Here we consider the simple sales tax on petroleum, levied on all sales to California entities by the petroleum refining sector. The tax falls upon jet fuel (J4), diesel and, of course, gasoline. Since the E-DRAM production technology is Leontief in intermediate goods, the model response is to consume less of the goods that are petroleum intensive. In this case, the possibility of fuel switching seems quite low, so the only avenue available to respond to high price is conservation. The model, however, fixes the technologies available and the higher prices do not call forth more high fuel-efficiency cars, trucks, and jets. In the consumer sector, the elasticity of demand is

−0.2, which accords well with published studies, although those studies also do not have a time period long enough for vehicle fleets to change.

The experimental tax is set at $500 million and is levied as a sales tax upon first the energy minerals sector and then the petroleum sector. The California demand for these sectors is 23 billion and 21 billion dollars respectively. The required sales tax rates are 2.2 and 2.4 per cent respectively. California imports approximately three-quarters of its energy minerals, largely oil and gas. On the other hand, it is a net exporter of refined products. In these experiments, the revenues from the tax are spent in the same way as other general fund revenues. The results are in Table 16.2. The tax on energy minerals decreases personal income by 970 million dollars while the tax on the refined product reduces personal income by the somewhat smaller 860 million dollars. The mechanism by which personal income is reduced is first by diverting income from people to the government, where it is spent, and second by making California products more expensive, reducing both external and internal demand. The reduction in demand in turn lowers real labor incomes and drives people out of the California labor market (either by being nonparticipants or by migration). The demand for labor decreases by 5000 and 8000 for the two taxes. The taxes on petroleum and on energy minerals have nearly the same effect on petroleum supply and demand. In theory, the tax on energy minerals should have been superior since taxing petroleum allows the import of refined products and discourages export, but the model results are simply very close.

Adding a rebate of $500 million to the bank and corporation taxes brings personal income back above the base level. This is a clear double dividend effect. However, the increased level of economic activity brings with it additional pollution and that too returns to above the baseline level. In this model pollution is more sensitive to the level of economic activity than to the price of the necessary input.

The inability of the model to produce a substantial decrease in pollution when a tax is applied is a direct result of a low elasticity of demand for the refined product. The following simulations all have regulations that force changes in the technology, presumably changes that consumers and firms would not make without much more drastic price changes.

5.2. SIP Pre-Studies

In preparing the State Implementation plan under the Clean Air Act, CAL ARB examined a large number of pollution control scenarios. These differ from the fuel-saving scenarios discussed later, in targeting sectors of the

Table 16.2. Pollution tax

	Today	Tax on ENMIN	Tax plus B&C	Tax on PETRO	Tax plus B&C
Pers. income	891.7924	890.8225	892.1676	890.9243	892.27
Labor demand	14.04438	14.03724	14.04233	14.03626	14.04135
ENMIN demand	22.98002	22.82141	22.82423	22.91646	22.91939
ENMIN supply	5.880738	5.766593	5.768016	5.853002	5.854437
PETRO demand	21.14617	21.08048	21.06924	21.01005	20.999
PETRO supply	24.81637	24.57412	24.56372	24.66112	24.65092
NOX tons per day	3071.29	3067.38	3071.977	3069.795	3074.395

Notes: Pers. income is personal income, ENMIN is the energy minerals sector, PETRO is the petroleum refining sector. All figures are for California only.
Source: Computed.

economy beyond transportation and also in not having tangible fuel saving benefits. The scenario is evaluated here for the year 1999, and the 2020 results were very similar. The total cost of the control measures was scaled to be $500 million, which is somewhat less than the packages of measures currently under consideration. The policies consist of requiring that transport vehicles, consumer chemicals (like hairspray), and some other manufactured and service products be made in a more expensive and less polluting fashion. The additional expense is modeled as an increase in the purchases of intermediate goods by the sectors that produce these outputs. ARB estimates that the benefits to consumers from the measures would be more than twice the costs. The model does not account for these benefits of the measures, cleaner air, and as a result shows that people would emigrate from California. One way to include the benefits is simply to assume that the measures benefits would outweigh the costs in the migration decision, and therefore a second scenario was run in which migration was constrained to zero. In that case the losses in personal income were less. However, workers still have less disposable income and respond with lower labor force participation rates. Table 16.3 provides a short form of the results. These exercises show that the costs to the state of pollution control are greater than the static costs, but are still less than the benefits.

Table 16.3. Pre-SIP studies

FUB99I	Today	SIP	No migration
CA output ($ billion)	1377.413813	1376.4573	1376.6695
Change CA output		–0.956513	–0.744352
CA personal income ($ billion)	891.792411	890.94384	891.09303
Change CA pers. inc.		–0.848567	–0.699381
Labor demand (millions)	14.044381	14.038663	14.040936

5.3. Reduce Petroleum Dependence Strategies

Below we analyse one of four alternate strategies for reducing California's petroleum dependence that were developed for the Legislature. The scenario chosen for analysis has the largest cost-benefit ratio. Each scenario is built around two elements: (1) reduced gasoline demand from improved light-duty vehicle fuel economy, and (2) diesel fuel displacement from gas-to-liquid (GTL) or Fischer Tropsch diesel fuels. The scenarios were constructed to try to 'bound' the possible impacts to the California economy. Scenario 1 combines off-the-shelf fuel efficiency improvements in light-duty vehicles with a 33 per cent blend of FTD in diesel fuel to meet ARB's future ULSD specification. Scenario 2 is like Scenario 1, but includes more fuel saving technology. Conversely, Scenarios 3 and 4 incorporate more aggressive and therefore more costly fuel efficiency or displacement options. Scenario 2 is presented in detail below.

Each scenario is modeled and coded as some combination of increased transportation costs and altered – generally decreased – fuel costs. The rationale is that more efficient transportation is costlier to produce, but saves fuel.

The CEC estimates that residential use accounts for roughly 90 per cent of gasoline consumption in the state. Hence, 90 per cent of projected increases in engine costs are apportioned to household and 10 per cent are apportioned to industries. Likewise, 90 per cent of projected fuel savings are apportioned to households and 10 per cent are apportioned to industries.

Table 16.4. Estimated economic inputs for Scenario 2: ACEE-Advanced fuel economy improvements

Changes in Consumer Expenditures	**Million 2002 $**	**Changes in Sector Revenue**	**Million 2002 $**
	2020		**2020**
Cost		Benefit	
Household (inc. vehicle cost)	4197	Vehicle Mfg. (inc. vehicle revenue)	4197
Household (inc. PZEV cost)	501	Vehicle Mfg. (inc. PZEV revenue)	501
Commercial (inc. GTL-diesel cost)	125	Foreign GTL Producer (inc. revenue)	125
Total Cost	4824	Total Benefits	4824
Benefits		Cost	
Household (dec. gasoline expenditure)	9284	Refiners (decrease in revenue)	7246
		California Excise Tax (dec. revenue)	1019
		Federal Excise Tax (dec. revenue)	1019
Total Benefits	9284	Total Costs	9284

5.4. ACEE-Advanced Fuel Economy Improvements

Scenario 2 incorporates fuel economy technologies in light-duty vehicles. In this case, technology costs and benefits were determined from ACEEE analysis for advanced fuel economy improvements. It was assumed that these improvements would be implemented in all new light-duty passenger cars and trucks starting in 2008.

Table 16.4 shows our estimates of the economic inputs for modeling.

Scenario 2 is implemented in the following manner.

The cost of consumer transportation (CTRNS) increases by 90 per cent of projected consumer cost. These additional costs are inserted such that the new, higher amount of consumer transportation spending is expressed as the appropriate multiple of old spending.

The cost of industrial engines increases by 10 per cent of the projected consumer cost, plus the commercial costs. These additional costs are inserted such that the new, higher amount of industrial spending on engines is expressed as the appropriate multiple of old spending.

Similarly, 90 per cent of the projected savings from increased fuel efficiency accrue to consumers. These savings are inserted such that the new, lower amount of consumer fuel spending is expressed as the appropriate fraction of old spending.

Ten per cent of the projected savings from increased fuel efficiency accrue to industry. These savings are inserted such that the new, lower amount of industrial spending on fuel is expressed as the appropriate multiple of old spending.

Table 16.5 compares selected results for the base model and Scenario 2 runs of E-DRAM. Results show that Scenario 2 slightly reduces state output (by 0.26 per cent in 2020) while leaving state personal income essentially unchanged. Real personal income remains constant while output falls because of increased consumer purchasing power due to improved fuel efficiency. Results indicate that the price of consumer fuel – interpreted as the price of vehicle miles traveled – is roughly 9 per cent lower in Scenario 2 than in base.

Increased fuel efficiency reduces the demand for refined petroleum products. E-DRAM predicts petroleum sector output being 12 per cent lower in 2020 under Scenario 2 vs. base. Decreased petroleum sector output adversely affects upstream crude oil suppliers. The model predicts energy and mining sector output being 7 per cent lower in 2020 under Scenario 2 than base.

Money freed from fuel expenditure is spent in other sectors. Scenario 2 raises both food and apparel sector output by 6–7 per cent over base.

5.5. Sensitivity Analysis

The fuel saving scenario was subjected to several sensitivity analyses. Making the demand for fuel more elastic decreases the fuel savings because fuel saving is equivalent to decreasing the price of miles driven. Making the supply curve of the rest of the world of refined

Table 16.5. Fuel saving technology

	Base model	Scenario 2
CA output ($ billion)	3078.0223	3070.0183
CA personal income ($ billion)	2009.5373	2010.4295
Labor demand (millions)	18.6605	18.7119
ENMIN		
Output ($ billion)	6.2086	5.7836
% Change output	0.08	–6.84
Imports ($ billion)	36.0105	32.6693
% Change imports	0.07	–9.28
Exports ($ billion)	1.0965	1.1419
% Change exports	–0.07	4.15
Petro		
Output ($ billion)	39.3048	34.7300
% Change output	0.07	–11.64
Imports ($ billion)	15.6834	15.3455
% Change imports	0.01	–2.15
Exports ($ billion)	11.9979	12.2159
% Change exports	–0.02	1.82

and crude product less elastic (2 to 0.1) shifts more of the burden of the decreased demand to the California energy sector and lowers state output. Conversely, if the decrease in demand were taken up in its entirety by decreased imports, all fuel saving scenarios would lead to much higher California output and income. The rationing of rights to use clean air in California is a reason to believe that California refineries are earning above market returns – more California competition is precluded. However, the same regulatory scheme increases the cost of operating locally and militates for the opposite conclusion. At present, the California refinery capital stock includes at least one economically marginal large refinery and on balance it is likely that a decrease in output would be taken up partially locally and partially from imported product. As far as the California welfare is concerned, this split is not known and crucial. The final sensitivity experiment was to increase the price of crude petroleum – it is held at its current value in the experiments, since forecasts for large increases have so far been false. With 20 per cent higher crude prices, fuel saving results in about $20 billion more in income and output.

6. CONCLUSIONS

Prediction is always a sobering exercise, making apparent a very limited knowledge of future possibilities. Besides the usual problem of estimating workforce and output for twenty years hence, future CGEs require a host of details, including the technology (here pessimistically assumed to be constant at today's level for the use of intermediate goods), tastes (people are implicitly still assumed to want today's vehicle mix and SUV's), and trade relations. The last of these is particularly troubling for the petroleum saving strategies. The building of the model assumes that nearly all of California's energy will be imported at prices as favorable as today. It seems that if the whole world were modeled as growing as in the 2020 scenarios, the energy sector would require considerable nonoil output to meet the predicted demand at the predicted price. Generating the 2020 scenario and then asking how it would change with changed policy assumes a lot. It assumes that a 2020 economy can be achieved that looks a lot like a scaled version of a 2000 economy.

Taxes fare very poorly as an instrument for pollution control in this model. Low elasticity of demand for petroleum means that they have little deadweight loss, but also little effect. When a more distorting tax is rebated (Bank and Corporation Taxes, in this model) to keep a balanced budget, there is indeed a double dividend and income rises. However, there is also a double whammy, and pollution increases with income. A large income elasticity and small price elasticity make this result a certainty. This is a new reason why taxes do not work.

The pre-SIP study experiments are all about changing technology to be less polluting. These experiments introduce new (and less efficient from a money perspective) technologies. Most of these measures are not energy saving, and some are energy using, so a tax on petroleum will not call most of them into use. Indeed pollution has such large effects on health and crops that these measures are believed to have benefits in excess of twice their costs. The economy-wide costs are only slightly larger than the direct costs, particularly if one believes that people will remain in California with cleaner air.

Taken in sum, the result of these simulations is that pollution and energy control is possible at acceptable economic cost, even if unilaterally undertaken by California. The surprise in these simulations is how ineffective taxes are at controlling pollution or energy use. Put differently, the simulations show how much people are willing to pay to continue with larger vehicles.

NOTES

1. The explanation which follows is closely adapted from 'Dynamic Revenue Analysis for California' (Berck et al., Summer 1996), available at www.dof.ca.gov/HTML/FS_DATA/dyna-rev/dynrev.htm; chapters cited in sections of this report refer to chapters of that document.
2. The alcohol, tobacco, and horse racing sector, distinct in DRAM, has been folded into the foods sector in the latest version of E-DRAM.
3. The survey is conducted in years ending in 2 and 7 and data is released after processing. E-DRAM uses data from the 1997 release, which contains processed 1992 survey data.

17. Voluntary Road Pricing

Lars Hultkrantz

1. INTRODUCTION

'Traffic becomes more difficult each day in the streets of the capital', observed Louis Figuier, the author of *Merveilles de la Science*, describing Paris in the 1880s, adding 'the traffic of vehicles at the intersection of boulevard Montmartre and rue Montmartre, vulgarly called the Crossroad of run-over-pedestrians [...] reaches more than 100 000 per day'.[1] The streets of Paris were overcrowed already at the beginning of the nineteenth century, but as the number of horses increased fivefold from 1819 to 1891 the problems became out of hand.[2] But it could become even worse. After the first automobile show in Paris in 1898, motor vehicles began to try to make their way through the narrow streets of the city. The result was an incredible congestion, a lot of dust making it hard to breathe, and even more accidents, raising the annual number of fatalities in the city from around 80 in the 1880s to a peak of 300 in the 1930s (Barles and Guillerme 2003).

The main solutions to problems such as these, as they spread with urbanisation and industrial development all over the world, have relied on engineering. Huge infrastructural investments have been made to expand the capacity of the traffic networks. Vehicles have become much more safe and clean. Advanced technical systems for traffic control have been developed. However, this has also promoted further traffic growth. The decoupling of traffic-related problems and GDP growth has not yet happened (Kågeson 1997, Ch. 18). Congestion remains a major issue. At the beginning of the twenty-first century, the average speed of traffic in the central business districts of some large European cities is no higher than at the end of the nineteenth century. Macadam and asphalt reduced dust, but urban populations still suffer from exposure to unhealthy particles from diesel engines, tires, etc. Noise, nitrification, terresterial ozone, carbon dioxide and several other things hurt local and global environments. The death toll from traffic remains intolerably high.

To economists, this is a case of 'tragedy of the open access' due to insufficient rationing, and the profession has long since argued that the most efficient instrument to influence the decisions of numerous car drivers would be price. By road user charges internalising the negative externalities of driving, motorists can be given incentives to adapt behaviour in accordance with the social good. Since the seminal contributions by Pigou (1920), Knight (1924), Walters (1961), and Vickrey (1963) economists have tried to convey this 'obvious' insight to policy makers and the general public.

Few have listened, though. So far, only Singapore, London (February 2003), and now, possibly, Stockholm have decided to levy charges on cars with the main purpose of alleviating urban congestion. Road and bridge tolls are sometimes used for funding purposes, but charges mainly aimed at affecting driving behaviour have mostly failed to receive public support. Traffic control has therefore remained in the engineering realm.

The reasons for the resistance to the use of economic incentives in this field are plentifold. First, congestion charges can be regressive as the poor are priced off the road (Richardson 1974, Glazer and Niskanen 2000).[3] Therefore, the median voter may find herself a prospective loser from a suggested road-pricing scheme, at least if redistribution of the toll revenues is ignored. Also, citizens appear to find willingness-to-pay to be the least fair of many allocation mechanisms, including queuing (Oberholzer-Gee and Weck-Hannemann 2002). Second, many drivers oppose the loss of a kind of usufructuary right, i.e., the right to move their vehicle in the streets for free (Jakobsson et al. 2000). Third, various institutional obstacles, such as the need for horizontal and vertical cooperation of local and central government, can make it difficult to design credible and effective compensation schemes for redistribution of the social gains. The specific institutional circumstances of Singapore, which is both a city and a country, made such issues more simple to resolve than in other places.

However, these difficulties are much related to the coercive nature of the suggested road pricing schemes. These are framed as tolls, i.e. mandatory payments required from all drivers entering a city or an urban zone. In this chapter, we will discuss voluntary schemes that are embedded within a broader set of services offered to motorists, allowing drivers to choose charges or premiums that depend on driving behaviour.

2. ROAD PRICING AND SUBSIDIES

Internalisation of the external cost of transport is at the top of the European transport policy agenda. For road transport, the European Commission has given support to a broad policy of km-taxes on heavy haulage, congestion charges, and extended differentiation of traffic insurance rates. Hitherto, the internalisation debate has focused on (rough) internalisation by driven distance. To handle the externality in speed choice, most countries instead rely on a combination of regulations (speed limits), enforcements (fines) and insurance schemes (deductions and bonus/malus). A common problem in the implementation of all these instruments is the limited possibility to observe actual behaviour.

In many instances, economic incentives in the form of sticks (charges/fines) are preferred to carrots (subsidies). The Polluter Pays Principle gives an ethical argument for that choice. In the transport context motorists are polluters, in contrast to victims such as residents or walkers suffering from pollution, noise, accidents, etc. However, transport-related externalities are to a large extent reciprocal, making it difficult to sort sinners from saints at heaven's gate (through which presumably walking only is allowed).

Another motive for choosing charges instead of subsidies is that a programme based on charges can be expected to be more effective and efficient than a compensation programme (Baumol and Oates 1988, Ch. 14). Whilst a charge or a subsidy may be equivalent as means of promoting the technical changes by a firm toward cleaner technologies there is a significant difference when it comes to the effects on changes in consumption. Charges induce further reduction of pollution by reducing consumption of 'dirty goods', while subsidies may give rise to changes in the opposite direction. In the road pricing context, as observed by Hau (1994), even if a usage-based compensation scheme would affect motorists' driving behaviour in a desired direction, it would also induce them to drive more. This argument in favour of charges instead of subsidies is further strengthened by the observation that subsidies have to be financed, and therefore are burdened by the marginal cost of public funds, while public revenues from road-user charges, on the contrary, can be used to reduce other taxes.

However, we submit that compensation to drivers who voluntary accept charges that are more differentiated than regular taxes or charges on traffic may be a very useful means for influencing car driving behaviour. In voluntary programmes that encourage social responsible ('safe', 'green', or whatever) driving, it is possible to implement pricing schemes that more closely reflect the variation of the social marginal cost of different ways of driving than can be made with regular (more uniform) taxes and charges. The case against subsidies is less clear when subsidies are used for awarding enrolment to such more differentiated charging schemes. This is so for several reasons.

First, while road pricing more or less by assumption is Kaldor–Hicks efficient, it seldom fulfils the Pareto criterion. The task of compensating the heterogenous group of losers is overwhelming. This category includes motorists who pay the road toll (if their individual assessment of the value of time saved, and the reduction of the variation in travel time, is lower than the toll), previous motorists that change mode or reduce their travel, and passengers by public transportation modes if their comfort is lowered when some motorists switch mode.

Compensation schemes therefore as a rule are designed so as to target broad categories, such as commuters in mass transit, not the single individual. In both London and Stockholm, enhanced bus services are provided as a part of the road pricing bundle. That will be enough compensation for some, but probably not for everyone. Also, many may suspect that the compensation given is temporary, while the road toll will last, or that other public spending will be cut.

Charges based on participation in voluntary programmes can be expected to have less of a problem in this respect. Compensation is given on an individual basis and anyone who wants can stay out of the programme. Of course, third parties can still be harmed and subsidies have to be funded in some way, so some distributional issues may remain. Also, issues concerning legality and integrity are less likely to arise in implementation of non-coercive programmes.

A second reason for subsidies arises in cases when the countervailing effects of a subsidy on pollution/congestion/safety from increased consumption are desirable. This can be so, for instance, if substitution from car to public transit evoked by a congestion charge would increase congestion in the public mode.

In particular, Glazer and Niskanen (2000) observe that a policy involving a toll on car travel only will unambiguously hurt the users of the public transportation system, when both modes are subject to congestion and there is no redistribution of toll revenues. They conclude that this can make it difficult to get political support for congestion charges in cities with well-developed mass-transit systems, at least in absence of a credible compensatory scheme, as both users of cars and of public transportation will oppose it; car drivers because they are charged, users of public transportation because the will suffer from increased congestion.

However, motorists who want to avoid a road toll can change mode or time of departure. In a recent survey in Stockholm (Bång et al. 2003), 37 per cent of car commuters responded that they will leave home earlier or later if a road toll is levied between 7.00 am and 9.30 am. Assuming that there is no congestion at off-peak time, such adaptation will not increase congestion on the slow mode. As shown by Armelius (2005), it is possible to design road-pricing schemes that enhance substitution from peak to off-peak car travel and thus reduce or completely avoid effects on public transportation. That, however, requires that a toll on peak travel is combined with a subsidy to off-peak car travel. This can be done in an integrated road and parking pricing scheme, as described below, by reduced parking charges to motorists arriving during off-peak times.

Third, car driving is subject to multiple taxes and charges. These include petrol taxes, vehicle taxes, and insurance premiums. Therefore, the net effect on car use of a subsidy hinges on whether it is combined with changes of taxes or charges that also affect car use. A voluntary programme that seen in isolation implies a net subsidy, can in a broader context be a usage-based differentiation of a tax or charge that allows lower payments for drivers who behave in a certain manner. Whether 'dirty' consumption is promoted or deterred depends on this broader context.

For instance, a mandatory traffic liability insurance can be combined with a 'voluntary' programme that awards good driving behaviour by reducing the insurance premium. Although a subsidy is given to anyone who complies with the programme, the insurance as a whole is not subsidizing car use.

Another example would be a city with a cordon-based road toll that offers motorists an option to be charged in a more differentiated way according to the actual position of the car and/or the time of the driving. Such an option would only attract car users that benefit from it, so it has to involve a differential 'subsidy' to the regular toll. However, in evaluating the net effect of the programme on car use one would have to consider whether the net subsidy was funded by an increase of the level of the cordon toll.

Another possibility is to integrate congestion and parking charges. The road tolling system in Stockholm will be based on automatic vehicle identification with road-side microwave transmitters and on-board transponders. Similar systems are already in use for parking control in garages and public parking areas. It is therefore possible to design an integrated system for automatic payment of both road toll and parking duties (Ny Teknik 2003). With such a system, the car users can be separated into, for instance, peak and off-peak arrivals, which makes it possible to differentiate both the road toll and the parking charges.

Fourth, intelligent transport system (ITS) devices for improving the functioning of the traffic system often involve electronic equipment for mobile communication and data processing that is installed in the cars. Such on-board units may provide more efficient means for monitoring and charging driving than traditional methods (such as police surveillance, Eurovignettes, etc.). However, the consent and cooperation of the driver will be needed, as they easily can be obstructed. A voluntary system based on a combination of subsidies and charges is likely to be more easy to implement than a system based on charges only, combined with mandatory use of on-board units.

Finally, as is well known in the organisation literature, real humans' responses to carrots and sticks differ from the reactions of the *economic man*. Recent research in experimental economics has shown that many individuals choose strategies in social interaction that are based on 'similar responses', i.e. by rewarding friendly acts and punishing hostile behaviour (Rabin 1993). Therefore, it could be conjectured that car drivers that were rewarded for 'good driving' would feel a stronger responsibility for compliance to the rules of the programme than car drivers who received fines punishing 'bad driving'.

The scope for offering bundles of services and charges that depend on individual choices and behaviour is now rapidly widening due to the progress of information and communication technologies. We will now briefly review some insurance policies that already are offered to car owners; experimental research on how economic incentives can be used to increase car drivers' compliance to speed limits; and ideas on how congestion charges can be embedded within an information system for motorists, giving real-time route navigation advices and making reservations and payments for parking and public transit.

3. PAY-AS-YOU-DRIVE CAR INSURANCE

Car insurance premiums depend on features of the car and driver, such as type of car driven and security, job, marital status and even habits like smoking. The inclusion of driver characteristics suggests that insurance companies indeed consider driver behaviour to be an important determinant of accident risk. However, car usage is normally taken into account only as crude differentiation according to mileage, often within broad intervals. Hence, the insurance cost of a marginal kilometre will often be zero. Nor are insurance payments affected by where, when, or how fast a car is driven. Car insurance premiums therefore do a poor job in internalizing the marginal external costs of traffic accidents due to driving and driving behaviour.

Lack of differentiation of insurance schemes gives rise to moral hazard and adverse selection. The former is mitigated by excess and no claims bonuses, i.e. by reductions of the effective loss coverage. Adverse selection is reduced by legal obligations for insurance of liability to other persons, but probably curbs demand for insurance above that. Young drivers, motor cyclists, and drivers that have been previously involved in an accident are some categories that may be especially hurt by the inability of current insurance policies to take into account the real individual variation in risk. Their payments are based on the high average risk of their category, although individuals with a safe driving behaviour may have a considerably lower risk.

The effect of a move towards a differentiation of insurance payments that better reflects the variation in risk would therefore be twofold. One is to reduce adverse selection and thereby increase the demand for extended insurance coverage by low-risk drivers. Another is to reduce moral hazard and therefore the probability that accidents will occur as well as the cost of the inflicted damages.

A few insurance companies have launched insurance policies that use on-board units to monitor driving, though. In the United States, the insurance corporation Progressive has developed a policy called ‘Autograph’. Customers choosing this policy get special tracking equipment installed in their vehicles. It uses global positioning satellites to constantly record the car’s location, direction and speed. At the end of the month the device calls in and tells the company’s computer where it has been, and the customer is charged accordingly.

Based on an exclusive agreement with the Progressive corporation, the insurance group Norwich Union, in cooperation with IBM and Orange, offers a similar ‘pay-as-you-drive’ policy in the United Kingdom. The scheme uses a combination of GPS tracking and wireless communication to track where, when, and how often a vehicle is used. Detailed journey data are used to calculate insurance premiums based on vehicle use. The system also allows drivers to send and receive messages about insurance, routes and traffic problems via their mobile phones.

According to the website of Norwich, customers choosing this insurance 'will benefit from individual premiums based on how often, when and where they actually used their cars. Motorists would receive a fairer deal as this initiative provides them with the opportunity to really be in the driving seat when it comes to controlling their premiums'. The 'pay-as-you-drive' policy is provided as an option, along traditional schemes. It is thus a voluntary scheme.

So far, these insurance schemes are still being offered on a limited scale and just by these two companies. At present insurance is charged by the mile, but the on-board monitoring uses GPS and maps so the insurances group also know about among others overspeeding.

4. INTELLIGENT SPEED ADAPTATION

The possibility of enhancing safety through a subsidy to safe drivers was mentioned by Boyer and Dionne (1983) but never explored because 'it is usually either very difficult or extremely costly to observe self-protecting activities of a particular individual'. This has now changed. Intelligent speed adaptation (ISA) represents a range of technologies used to help keep drivers from exceeding speed limits. Some systems are based on short-distance microwave conveyance from roadside beacons, others are based on GPS positioning.

A large-scale field trial funded by the Swedish National Road Administration between 1999 and 2002, involving around 10 000 drivers in several urban areas and using different technologies, indicated that significant reductions of speed violations could be brought about with an ISA device (Vägverket 2002). A display in the vehicle shows the going speed limit and an annoying acoustic signal alerts the driver if she goes faster than that. By comparing speed during months when the device was switched on to speed during the first months when it was dark and silent, it was found to reduce averge speed by 7 km/h. According to the National Road Administration's evaluation (Vägverket 2002), the accident risk of drivers with this equipment was thereby reduced by 20 per cent. However, surveys to test drivers revealed that few would like to have it installed in their cars. Only one third of the drivers would buy this equipment at any (positive) price and the average willingness to pay was below 40 Euros, as a one-time payment.

Two recent experimental studies (Hultkrantz and Lindberg 2003, Nilsson and Thomas 2004) have investigated the effects of real economic incentives on the use of ISA. Such incentives could be provided by reductions in insurance premiums, or by differentiated vehicle taxes, such as a km tax. In the first study, 114 private car owners who still had the equipment installed were invited to participate in an economic experiment for two months (September and October 2002). They were informed that they would receive a monthly initial bonus with a reduction for each minute they drove faster than the speed limit. They were randomly assigned to a high or low initial bonus group (250 SEK/month or 500 SEK/month). Each group was further divided into thre sub-samples; with no, low, or high charges for speeding. The three-tier charge in the low charges group were 0.1, 0.25, and 1.00 SEK/minute for speed offences at 0–10 per cent, 11–20 per cent, and above 20 per cent of the speed limits. The charges were doubled in the high charges group. The experiment was designed so everyone would at least have a payment of 75 SEK each month. The result showed that participants who were charged (low or high charge) reduced their severe violations (i.e., more than 10 per cent above speed limit) significantly more than the two reference groups of car drivers who were offered just the lump-sum bonus, i.e. with no charge; the former had an average reduction of 64 per cent while the latter only had a reduction of 15 per cent.

These results were obtained within a strongly selected group of mainly middle-aged male drivers.The recruitment to the first vehicle trial had among others failed to attract young drivers. Nilsson and Thomas (2003) therefore performed a recruitment experiment targeting a randomly selected sample of 636 young drivers (under 29) in the same town. All drivers were offered a free installation of ISA equipment, but one subsample was promised a fixed annual remuneration at approximately 200 Euros, irrespective of speeding behaviour, while a control group was given nothing. The results confirmed that young drivers are reluctant to install such equipment, but that money helps a lot, raising yes-responses from 2 to 10 per cent (as a percentage of letters sent out).

A similar study (Forslund 2004) has explored the willingness of young motor cycle drivers to accept a similar device. Insurance premiums to young motor bikers are very high. Annual premiums in Sweden for a 23-year-old driver with a four-year-old driver's licence range between a third and a half of the price of a new Yamaha R1. In a stated preference survey to intercepted young drivers, Forslund found that close to 50 per cent would consider installing ISA equipment if this were combined with a significant reduction in the insurance payments.

5. THE DRIVER'S LITTLE HELPER

Road pricing has so far built on the notion of the driver as a rational consumer, reacting on price information conveyed directly to her. However, driving is to a large extent driven by habits, changing only slowly over time. Also, the driver must not be disturbed while driving by cognitive demanding information, such as complex road price information, as that can inflict upon safety. Therefore, road pricing schemes are as a rule simple cordon or zonal tolls, with possibly a two-tier structure to affect peak/off-peak driving. They are also fixed for some time, at least a few months, and are communicated to drivers by announcements in newspapers, and so on.

This limits the scope for using road pricing as an instrument for short-term traffic control. The so-called HOT ('high occupancy/toll') lanes at some freeways in southern Californa and in the Houston area in the US provide an exception. For these lanes, prices are adjusted frequently ('dynamic pricing') to ensure a minimum speed in the lane for which a charge is required. The toll is announced on a message sign prior to the point where the driver has to choose which lane to enter.

Congestion is indeed very dynamic. There is often a large regular variation over time in the demand for road space, especially by commuters, and more or less stochastic fluctuations occur due to accidents, road work, etc. Furthermore, even very small disturbances can be magnified and cause considerable traffic perturbations through complex interactions among motorists. By a simple fixed road-pricing scheme one can hope to reduce overall traffic demand, which will reduce traffic in noncongested areas as well, and will not eliminate severe traffic disturbances that are due to short-term variation or unpredicted events.

Road pricing based on cordon tolls therefore has a service-quality problem: you may not get what you pay for. Toll payers may find themselves at one time in the middle of a jam, another time driving in streets with traffic that is far below the free-speed capacity limit. Similar problems are pervasive, for similar reasons, in parking. Parking fees are not adjusted to clear the market in the short term. As a consequence, car drivers often have to cruise for a long time to find an empty parking lot, even though there is a price-rationing system. When cruising for parking congests both parkers and through traffic, the benefits from pricing are substantially reduced (Anderson and de Palma 2004).

New information and communication technologies seem to be ready to offer a way out of such dilemmas, though. On-board units with GPS positioning and mobile communication, similar to the ones used for 'pay-as-you-drive' insurance and for ISA, can be used to give guidance to the driver, based on complex real-time information and customised to the individual preferences. Information sources that can provide data have been developed by traffic authorities in many metropolitan areas in recent years. They use sophisticated systems for monitoring traffic flows, increasingly combing static sensors with GPS-based floating-car information, and make short-term forecasts. This is used for direct traffic control, for example by traffic lights, and to give warnings and recommendations to drivers over the radio, road-side displays or the Internet.

A 'smart' on-board micro-processor unit that receives such information by mobile communication can utilise it in more precise ways. As the position of the individual car is known to the system, it can filter out infomation that is of relevance only to drivers at a specific place and time. Also, the on-board unit can be adapted to the specific preferences of the individual driver by menu choice-based pre-programming. Furthermore, the driver can be reached, wherever she is, over the mobile phone. Therefore suggestions and recommmendations on time of departure, route choice, and so on, can be given at a convenient time, for instance before leaving home or work, and not just en route.

As shown by the insurance and ISA applications, such devices can also be used as instruments for road pricing. In fact, similar devices are used in the German km-tax system and in road-pricing trials in some European cities within the EU-funded PROGRESS project. The focus of interest in these cases, as well as in the pay-as-you-drive insurance, is on the possibility to charge according to the distance driven.

However, the current technology can achieve much more than that. A 'smart' on-board unit does not have the informational processing constraints of the human mind. It can be loaded with much more, and more detailed, information about the traffic system than the driver. Based on real-time information and on pre-selected choices (such as 'I want to get home as quickly as possible' or 'I want to park as cheaply as possible, within a ten minutes walk to my office'), the device can give advice (for example, 'wait another quarter of an hour', 'choose the northern route', 'park at garage B'). Such recommendations and suggestions can be given in ways that are simple to understand and adapt to, minimizing the risk of distracting the driver's attention. An on-board unit and the driver can communicate within the car by different means (a display, voice control, and so on) or outside the car over the mobile handset of the driver. Given the driver's acceptance of a proposed action, the unit could book and pay road tolls, parking charges, and tickets for public transportation.

The detailed information processed by a 'smart' unit could contain not just 'ordinary' traffic information on disturbances, average projected speed in various parts of the road network, and so on, but also current price information. As an on-board unit lacks the cognitive restraints of a human driver, this would allow complex and frequently adjusted prices for the use of both roads and parking space. It would therefore make possible 'dynamic pricing' schemes like the ones used for the 'HOT lanes' (or for air and rail tickets bought over the Internet) for increasing the utilisation of capacity of the road and/or parking infrastructure.

There is currently no such system in operation. However, a study by the Swedish National Road and Transport Research Institute (Hultkrantz et al. 2003) on a possible implementation in Stockholm ('Smartic') shows that most components needed in an information and payment system of this sort are already in place. Real-time information on current speeds by different routes, parking vacancies, delays in public transit, and so on, is available over the Internet (www.trafiken.nu). Individual profiles can be choosen for selected information. Also, parking can often be paid for by mobile phone, and prototypes have been developed for systems for reservations in advance for parking space, much as flight seats or hotel rooms.

However, all these systems are not yet integrated. Nor are they readily accessible in vehicles. The information systems are maintained by national and local public authorities, parking by public and private parking lot operators, on-board technology is sold by car dealers and telecom operators, and so on. To build a complete, fully integrated system, it is necessary to get cooperation among several public and private actors.

Also, congestion and speeding are public bads that will be excessively provided even if drivers have complete information about the current traffic. Hence, charges are needed, but as is evidenced in the ISA applications, few motorists will deliberately buy devices that make that possible without subsidies. As the 'smart' unit is an impure public good that provides both public and private services, the willingness to accept such a device will depend on both the monetary remuneration offered, on the quality of the private services that are provided (such as reservation in advance of a parking space), and on how closely they are bundled to the provision of the public services.

6. CONCLUSION

The problems already encountered in Paris in the nineteenth century remain basically unsolved. Transport appears worldwide to be the sector of the economy where particularly strong policies will be needed in order to reach sustainable growth. The problem is that technical fixes are not enough, so behaviour has to change. However, as can be seen for example from the resistance to gas taxes in the United States and to road pricing almost everywhere, the reforms of taxes and charges needed to induce such changes in behaviour are often blocked by political opposition.

In this chapter we have paid attention to the scope for using emerging technologies, in particular mobile communication and GPS positioning, to charge traffic in ways that reflect the substantial variation of the social marginal cost of car driving under different circumstances. By combining such charges with subsidies, or with valuable informational services, it may be possible to enrol a substantial share of motorists to voluntarily accept such differentiated incentives.

In the words of Olson (1965, p. 51), the large group of motorists is a 'latent' group that has a latent power or capacity for collective action that can be realised or 'mobilised' only with the aid of 'selective incentives'. These 'selective incentives' can be either negative or positive, in that they can either coerce by punishing those who fail to bear an allocated share of the cost of the group action, or they can be positive inducements offered to those who act in the group interest. The new information and communication technologies have thus advanced new possibilities to assemble a mix of positive and negative selective incentives for reconciling the decisions by numerous individual motorists to the common interest of themselves and society as a whole.

NOTES

1. Figuier cited from Barles and Guillerme (2003).
2. From 16 000 in 1819 to 78 851 in 1891 (Martin 1894, cited in Barles and Guillerme 2003).

3. However, in cities with a well-developed mass transit, like many European cities, this is reversed (Armelius 2004, Ch. 4), or more precisely, the middle class is losing, while individuals at both tails of the income distribution will find themselves better off.

REFERENCES

Anderson, S.P. and A. de Palma (2004), 'The economics of pricing parking', *Journal of Urban Economics*, 55, 1–20.

Armelius, H. (2004), 'Distributional side effects of tax policies: An analysis of tax avoidance and congestion tolls', Economic Studies 84, Department of Economics, Uppsala University.

Armelius, H. (2005), 'An integrated approach to urban road pricing', *Journal of Transport Economics and Policy*, 39(1), in press.

Bång, K. et al. (2003), 'Förstudie för utvärdering av näringslivseffekter av miljöavgifter i Stockholm', Department of Infrastructure, The Swedish Royal Institute of Technology.

Barles, S. and A. Guillerme (2003), 'Traffic congestion: Problems and solutions in Paris, 1830–1939', Paper presented at the First International Conference on the History of Transport, Traffic and Mobility, Eindhoven, The Netherlands, 6–9 November, 2003.

Baumol, W.J. and W.E. Oates (1988), *The Theory of Environmental Policy*, Cambridge: Cambridge University Press.

Boyer, M. and G. Dionne (1983), 'Sécurité routière: Efficacité, subvention et réglementation', Publication #3030, Université de Montréal.

Forslund, E. (2004), 'Efterfrågan på säkerhetshöjande utrustning på motorcykel', Master Thesis in Economics, Örebro University.

Glazer, A. and E. Niskanen (2000), 'Which consumers benefit from congestion tolls?', *Journal of Transport Economics and Policy*, 34, 43–54.

Hau, T.D. (1994), 'A conceptual framework for pricing congestion and road damage', in B. Johansson and L.-G. Mattsson (eds), *Road Pricing: Theory, Empirical Assessment and Policy*, Dordrecht: Kluwer Academic Publishers.

Hultkrantz, L. and G. Lindberg (2003), 'Intelligent economic speed adaptation', Paper presented at the 10th Internation Conference on Travel Behaviour Research, Lucerne, 10–15 August 2003.

Hultkrantz, L., G. Lindberg and J.-E. Nilsson (2003), 'Stockholm–Mälardalen traffic information concept, SMARTIC', PDF file available at www.vti.se/tek.

Jakobsson, C., S. Fujii and T. Gärling (2000), 'Determinants of private car users' acceptance of road pricing', *Transport Policy*, 7, 153–158.

Kågeson, P. (1997), 'Growth versus the environment – is there a trade-off?', Dissertation, Department of Environmental and Energy Systems Studies, Lund University.

Knight, F.H. (1924), 'Some fallacies in the interpretation of social cost', *Quarterly Journal of Economics*, 38, 582–606.

Ny Teknik (2003), 'Mikrovågsläsare hetast för Stockholms biltullar', *Ny Teknik*, 14 October 2003.

Oberholzer-Gee, F. and H. Weck-Hannemann (2002), 'Pricing road use: Politico-economic and fairness considerations', *Transportation Research D*, 7, 357–371.

Olson, M. (1965), *The Logic of Collective Action. Public Goods and the Theory of Groups*, Harvard, MA: Harvard University Press.

Pigou, A.C. (1920), *The Economics of Welfare*, Macmillan.

Rabin, M. (1993), 'Incorporating fairness into game theory and economics', *American Economic Review*, 83, 1281–1302.

Richardson, H.W. (1974), 'A note on the distributional effects of road pricing', *Journal of Transport Economics and Policy*, 8, 82–85.

Thomas, F. and J.-E. Nilsson (2003), 'Willingness-to-accept safety-enhancing devices in cars: A field experiment to induce drivers to use an impure public good', Unpublished paper available at www.du.se/~jen.

Vägverket, 2002, 'Resultat av ISA-försöket', Unpublished report available at www.isa.vv.se.

Vickrey, W.S. (1963), 'Pricing in urban and suburban transport', *American Economic Review*, 53, 251–261.

Walters, A.A. (1961), 'The theory and measurement of private and social cost of highway congestion', *Econometrica*, 29, 676–699.

Index